The Volunteer Subject
by Robert Rosenthal and Ralph L. Rosnow

Innovations in Client-Centered Therapy
by David A. Wexler and Laura North Rice

The Rorschach: A Comprehensive System, in two volumes
by John E. Exner, Jr.

Theory and Practice in Behavior Therapy
by Aubrey J. Yates

Principles of Psychotherapy
by Irving B. Weiner

Psychoactive Drugs and Social Judgment: Theory and Research
edited by Kenneth Hammond and C. R. B. Joyce

Clinical Methods in Psychology
edited by Irving B. Weiner

Human Resources for Troubled Children
by Werner I. Halpern and Stanley Kissel

Hyperactivity
by Dorothea M. Ross and Sheila A. Ross

Heroin Addiction: Theory, Research and Treatment
by Jerome J. Platt and Christina Labate

Children's Rights and the Mental Health Profession
edited by Gerald P. Koocher

The Role of the Father in Child Development
edited by Michael E. Lamb

Handbook of Behavioral Assessment
edited by Anthony R. Ciminero, Karen S. Calhoun, and Henry E. Adams

Counseling and Psychotherapy: A Behavioral Approach
by E. Lakin Phillips

Dimensions of Personality

edited by Harvey London and John E. Exner, Jr.

The Mental Health Industry: A Cultural Phenomenon
by Peter A. Magaro, Robert Gripp, David McDowell, and Ivan W. Miller III

Nonverbal Communication: The State of the Art
by Robert G. Harper, Arthur N. Wiens, and Joseph D. Matarazzo

Alcoholism and Treatment
by David J. Armor, J. Michael Polich, and Harriet B. Stambul

A Biodevelopmental Approach to Clinical Child Psychology: Cognitive Controls and Cognitive Control Theory
by Sebastiano Santostefano

Handbook of Infant Development
edited by Joy D. Osofsky

Understanding the Rape Victim: A Synthesis of Research Findings
by Sedelle Katz and Mary Ann Mazur

Childhood Pathology and Later Adjustment: The Question of Prediction
by Loretta K. Cass and Carolyn B. Thomas

Intelligent Testing with the WISC-R
by Alan S. Kaufman

Adaptation in Schizophrenia: The Theory of Segmental Set
by David Shakow

Psychotherapy: An Eclectic Approach
by Sol L. Garfield

TREATING THE ALCOHOLIC

TREATING THE ALCOHOLIC

A DEVELOPMENTAL MODEL OF RECOVERY

STEPHANIE BROWN
Stanford Alcohol Clinic
Stanford University

With the editorial assistance of Jill Mellick

A WILEY-INTERSCIENCE PUBLICATION

JOHN WILEY & SONS

New York · Chichester · Brisbane · Toronto · Singapore

Library of Congress Cataloging in Publication Data:

Brown, Stephanie, 1944–
  Treating the alcoholic.

  (Wiley series on personality processes)
  "A Wiley-Interscience publication."
  Bibliography: p.
  Includes index.
  1. Alcoholism—Treatment. 2. Psychotherapist and
patient. 3. Alcoholics Anonymous. I. Mellick, Jill.
II. Title. III. Series. [DNLM: 1. Alcoholism—therapy.
WM 274 B879t]

RC565.B76   1985   616.86′1   85-3172
ISBN 0-471-81736-8

Printed in the United States of America

10 9 8 7 6 5 4

For Bob and Makenzie

Series Preface

This series of books is addressed to behavioral scientists interested in the nature of human personality. Its scope should prove pertinent to personality theorists and researchers as well as to clinicians concerned with applying an understanding of personality processes to the amelioration of emotional difficulties in living. To this end, the series provides a scholarly integration of theoretical formulations, empirical data, and practical recommendations.

Six major aspects of studying and learning about human personality can be designated: personality theory, personality structure and dynamics, personality development, personality assessment, personality change, and personality adjustment. In exploring these aspects of personality, the books in the series discuss a number of distinct but related subject areas: the nature and implications of various theories of personality; personality characteristics that account for consistencies and variations in human behavior; the emergence of personality processes in children and adolescents; the use of interviewing and testing procedures to evaluate individual differences in personality; efforts to modify personality styles through psychotherapy, counseling, behavior therapy, and other methods of influence; and patterns of abnormal personality functioning that impair individual competence.

IRVING B. WEINER

University of Denver
Denver, Colorado

Preface

This is a book about alcoholism. It is a book about drinking, about recovery, and about treatment—specifically a new model of treatment that combines Alcoholics Anonymous (AA) and psychotherapy. It is a book that merges theory and practice from diverse schools of psychology with the concrete experience of AA members.

Several key problems are addressed. First, problems in communication and understanding between alcoholics and their helpers contribute to animosity and a defensive separatism. AA members and professional helpers are often pitted competitively against one another, limiting treatment options for alcoholics who may require a variety of treatment resources. Second, traditional theories are inadequate in explaining alcoholism and providing the basis for a comprehensive theory of treatment.

In this book, I side with the alcoholic—the alcoholic who is still drinking and the alcoholic who is sober. I am sympathetic to the alcoholic who mistrusts professional helpers and therefore believes that those who have not experienced alcoholism firsthand cannot understand or help the alcoholic. Although I am sympathetic, I also believe that the alcoholic badly *needs* the professional.

This book is a challenge to professional helpers and nonalcoholics from all disciplines to reexamine their own beliefs, values, and theories about alcohol and alcoholism. We lack both confidence and belief in our present knowledge and treatment of alcoholism. We also have severe breakdowns in communication and understanding between professionals and alcoholics.

If you are suffering from alcoholism, it is likely that your alcoholism will *not* be diagnosed by physicians, psychologists, or other helping professionals. If your alcoholism is diagnosed, the chances are good that you will receive an inappropriate referral for treatment. You may be told to "cut down" on your drinking, or you may be sent to a psychiatrist to determine what the real problem is. If you are abstinent and recovering from alcoholism and need professional help for other life problems, the chances are good that you will be too afraid of the professionals to seek the treatment you require. Of course, there are many exceptions, but it is a bleak picture.

This book addresses the overwhelming problems of diagnosis and treatment. These problems start at the level of helpers' basic values and beliefs and are then compounded by lack of training and professional education. We must examine conflicts in values and beliefs as well as difficulties in traditional theoretical approaches to treatment. It is impossible to address the problems in diagnosis and treatment without examining all levels.

The book is first a report of a study of people who stopped drinking and what happened to them when they stopped. From this experiential base, I developed a model of alcoholism that served as the theoretical and applied base of a new outpatient clinic designed to offer treatment to fit the changing needs of the alcoholic over time, from drinking through ongoing recovery.

This book evolved from my belief in the necessity and potential for a positive, synergistic partnership between the domains of AA and professional helpers. However, there is a severe ethical and moral problem that interferes with the realization of such a partnership. There is an unstated belief within the culture and its professional community that its trained helpers—physicians, psychologists, psychiatric social workers, ministers—know how to diagnose and treat alcoholism. Yet recovering alcoholics report strong feelings of betrayal and fear of these so-called trained helpers. It is the belief of these recovering individuals that they were *not* helped and, in fact, they were even delayed or derailed by these helpers. The original research for this book is based on the experiences of 80 sober (nondrinking) members of Alcoholics Anonymous who reported their experiences in sobriety in an effort to improve knowledge about alcoholism and thereby narrow the gap in communication and understanding between the professional helping community and alcoholics, both drinking and sober. The research emerged initially from my own experiences with this "gap." I had long heard animosity expressed by some recovering alcoholics toward doctors, psychologists, and all professionals outside of AA for their lack of understanding. I had heard animosity expressed by some professionals toward AA and its members for their lack of understanding. Many believe this division is the natural expression of a basic contradiction and incompatibility between AA and traditional forms of therapy. I had worked as a psychotherapist with sober alcoholics who were frightened of combining therapy and AA because they believe that the two conflicted or that they would be forced to give up their AA beliefs; yet they felt a strong need for psychotherapeutic help in addition to AA.

The impetus for the original study was also based on my belief that theories of alcoholism were inadequate and even damaging to successful intervention and long-range treatment of alcoholism. Theories about alcoholism had focused only on the drinking alcoholic, stopping with abstinence, insanity, or death. Developing alcoholism had been outlined as a progressive illness (Jellinek, 1960) with identified symptoms, but, beyond drinking, nothing was defined. As a result, abstinence was viewed as an end point on a downward spiral of progressive alcoholism. Abstinence was, therefore, implied to be a static state, yet it seemed to me that abstinence is, in fact, a middle or beginning point within a larger process. Recovery, or abstinence, must be considered as much a part of alcoholism as drinking.

The purpose of the original research was, therefore, twofold: first, to improve understanding between alcoholics and professional helpers, based on increased understanding of what happens to people who stop drinking, thereby improving the psychotherapeutic treatment of alcoholics, and second, to define a new process model of alcoholism that includes recovery.

The resulting process model of alcoholism and its application to the treatment of alcoholics, both drinking and sober, includes using AA, not as an adjunct to psychotherapy, but as the primary partner. Psychotherapy is a third partner, equal in principle, but, at most times in the developing progression of drinking and recovery, a secondary adjunct to AA.

Certainly, schools of psychotherapy that value the preeminence of the dyadic psychotherapeutic bond will find the notion of a triadic therapeutic relationship, with the therapist equal and at many times secondary to AA, unacceptable. But this book is not designed to make alcoholics better fit traditional strategies of psychotherapy. It is designed to illuminate for professionals what happens to alcoholics in drinking and recovery and how they, the professionals, must alter *their* theories and practice to better fit the changing needs of the alcoholic. Consequently, this book will be of limited value to the therapist who is not willing to reexamine theoretical positions and especially to accept a fluid and changing role in the therapeutic relationship; it will also be of limited use to the professional who is unwilling to reexamine basic values. For it is differences in values and beliefs that contribute to and perpetuate the continuing difficulties between AA and non-AA approaches.

Do not expect discussions of various theoretical approaches to alcoholism—disease versus moral versus learning models. Do not expect an examination of AA as an entity. Rather, expect to explore ways to integrate experience, application, and theory—a new conceptual framework combining behavioral, cognitive, dynamic, and spiritual principles.

This book evolved over a period of more than 10 years. It began with my recognition of the animosity and mistrust that existed between AA individuals and professionals. In working with recovering alcoholics in psychotherapy, I could see the tremendous potential benefit for these individuals if they could overcome their fear of professionals. Clearly, there was a need for partnership but no base for it. The persistent mutual mistrust led me to speculate that problems with psychotherapy of the alcoholic might be related to the lack of an adequate theory about alcoholism. There are numerous theories about the development of alcoholism and much controversy. But all of these theories focus only on the drinking alcoholic. There is no model of alcoholism that includes recovery.

Through working with abstinent alcoholics who were members of AA, I could see that abstinence did, indeed, involve many changes. Abstinence also required the careful integration of psychotherapy with AA. There was, however, no theory of recovery in alcoholism and no theory to determine the guidelines for partnership.

Chapter 2 marks the beginning of the resolution of these problems. The experiences of abstinent AA members provided the basis for defining a *process* of recovery that includes stages. The development of the model pointed out the incompleteness of previous theories and, therefore, the lack of a model to determine therapeutic intervention and therapeutic partnership in a rational way.

The model defines a process of recovery that is multileveled and multidimensional. It demands the integration of several theories and therapeutic interventions.

The next step after defining the model was its application. The Stanford Alcohol Clinic was founded in the fall of 1977 with the expanded model of alcoholism as a philosophical and practical foundation. Chapters 4 through 8 describe the stages of drinking and recovery and the therapeutic task required in each, based on the integration of theory and practice used by the clinic.

Chapter 9 addresses the issue of partnership between AA and psychotherapy. It outlines how to use the continuum to determine treatment focus and modality, including partnership with AA. Finally, it offers a translation of the 12 steps of AA into psychological terminology. Appendix A practically defines what the application involves in a clinical setting.

Our clinical experience demonstrated the need for further theoretical integration. It was now clear that the model followed a developmental progression and that the development encompassed a wide spectrum of issues. From the research project with AA members and the clinical application of the new model, it was clear that the theory had to include behavioral, cognitive, and affective elements.

The reported experiences of AA members emphasized the critical importance of a new identity as an alcoholic and the ways in which that identity serves as the core of the developmental process of recovery. Cognitive theory provided a base for understanding recovery as a process of new knowledge construction, including the progressive development and integration of behavioral, cognitive, and affective elements. Chapter 3 provides a theory of integration for these elements within a developmental framework. The purpose of this chapter is to provide a rational method of determining treatment, task, and modality, or a *combination* of tasks and modalities at any given time.

After this work, however, there still existed an apparent incompatability between therapy and AA. That incompatability centers around the issue of control. With that recognition, it became startlingly clear: This is a book about individuals who have accepted loss of control.

Of primary importance in the book, providing the foundation for all that follows is the last clearly stated piece of the formulation. The development of the model, its subsequent application to treatment, and its theoretical grounding in developmental theory are all based on an acceptance of loss of control. It is acceptance of loss of control that provides the first step for understanding the developmental process of recovery.

Chapter 1 outlines various theories of alcoholism and pinpoints the central feature of this one: loss of control. Which means that the concept of control and the controversy over controlled drinking had to be addressed at the beginning. This critical issue sets the foundation for everything that follows. The model of alcoholism and the theoretical formulation of therapeutic treatment based on development rest on an acceptance of loss of control, which is based on conversion. Chapter 1 provides a conceptual framework that places conversion and what happens to people in AA out of the realm of magic and craft and into the realm of theory. With this foundation, the process of recovery begins.

Loss of control is the central feature of recovery for AA members. It is the core thread in new identity formation, and it is central to the philosophy of treatment. The concept of loss of control clarified differences in psychotherapy and treatment approach as well as differences in individuals who use AA and those who do not.

It is a central purpose of this book to state clearly that for the person who has accepted that he or she is alcoholic, there is no such thing as controlled drinking. It is the purpose of this book to outline why the notions of control and controlled drinking are so frightening to alcoholics, and why debate about the possibility of controlled drinking does indeed retard progress for many.

This book begins with an acceptance of loss of control, and on that foundation a new developmental process of recovery begins.

STEPHANIE BROWN

Stanford, California
February 1985

Acknowledgments

The task of writing the acknowledgments seems as formidable as that of writing the book. I have had so much help and support in many varied and complex ways for many years—help and support that have enabled me to first think about the questions I am raising and then proceed to answer them, or, much more often and more accurately, unearth new complexities and confirm the lack of answers.

The book is about development—a developmental process of recovery from alcoholism. Like its subject, the book is also a product of long years of development; thus my thanks go back a long way.

First, I express deep gratitude to the members of Alcoholics Anonymous who participated in the original research that resulted in the developmental model of alcoholism recovery. These individuals gladly participated with the expressed hope by many that sharing their experiences would result in improved communication between professionals and alcoholics, both drinking and recovering, and, thereby, improved treatment.

Next, I wish to thank Drs. Irvin Yalom and Thomas Gonda for providing the opportunity for alcoholism research and support for an alcohol clinic at Stanford.

Deep gratitude goes to Thomas and Katherine Pike, mentors both, and backers in every way. They too, supported the idea of an alcohol clinic and have provided ongoing emotional, professional, and financial support for its development.

Deep thanks and appreciation go to all our "patients." They reaffirm over and over the old proverb that the "child is father to the man." I learn from them continually. Many of these individuals are also members of the AA–Al-Anon community. They have illuminated and shaped the guidelines for partnership and cooperation so central to this book.

Thanks go to the staff of the alcohol clinic. Each therapist, staff member, psychology intern, and psychiatric resident has brought an attitude of openness and willingness to break new ground in understanding alcoholism and to form the bridge combining AA and psychotherapy. It is a difficult task requiring constant reflection, examination, and challenge of one's deepest professional and personal beliefs. I thank the staff for their dedication and for the support of their shared belief in the importance of what we're all doing.

We have been constantly reinforced by similar support from the non-AA professional community. Our colleagues have sent referrals and provided clinical supervision for trainees, thus underscoring the significance of partnership and their interest in bridging disciplines.

The AA-alcohol world, including individual members of AA and Al-Anon, treatment centers, the National Council on Alcoholism and Alcoholism Council information and referral services, and employee assistance personnel have also been supportive. This is a wide and critically important network that has also expressed a continuing interest in the bridging of disciplines and supported the importance of our work. Many granting institutions and individual donors have supported the clinical, training, and research development of the Stanford Alcohol Clinic over the past eight years. Thanks to NIAAA, Thomas and Katherine Pike, Ms. Mary Pike, the Fluor Foundation, the Kaiser Family Foundation, the J.M. Foundation, the Rudolph Driscoll Trust Fund, and many individual donors for their grants and gifts. We could not have survived without them, or without the expert counsel of many individuals who have served as advisors and volunteers.

Several individuals deserve special mention. Dr. Susan Beletsis has worked with me since the clinic's second year, offering invaluable support as a superb clinician, supervisor of training, and enthusiastic collaborator in theory development and clinical application. She provided an invaluable critical review of the manuscript.

In the same category of involvement and ongoing support is Dr. William Fry. I am indebted to him for his long-standing wise counsel and support.

I have been exceptionally fortunate in having superb secretarial collaboration. My deepest thanks to Ms. Bea Mitchell for her outstanding typing, good humor, and ready availability, and to Ms. Diana Kennedy for her superb administrative skill in managing the day-to-day operations of the clinic.

Thanks and appreciation also go to Dr. Jill Mellick for her help from start to finish in the organizational development of the book.

Special thanks to Drs. Vicki Johnson and Bob Matano for their personal encouragement. Finally, my deepest thanks go to my husband, Bob, for his critical review of the manuscript and to Bob and our daughter, Makenzie, for their unwaivering support.

S.B.

Contents

TREATING THE ALCOHOLIC

PART ONE

Model Building

Chapter 1

Central Challenges
to Alcoholism Treatment

TRADITIONAL PSYCHOTHERAPY AND THE ALCOHOLIC

The alcoholic has long been defined as a notoriously difficult patient by all treatment providers, but few understand why (Kurtines, 1978). For years, failure to successfully treat the diagnosed drinking alcoholic has been attributed to the patient, who appeared to remain willfully isolated in an entrenched, defensive system of denial and rationalization (Woodward and Duffy, 1965; Knox, 1969). These individuals are likely to be labeled "unmotivated" (Koumans, 1969) and perhaps unsuited to treatment because of their unwillingness to adapt to the therapist's model of treatment. Many therapists expect their alcoholic patients to stop drinking and forfeit their main defenses to demonstrate their motivation and capacity to form a traditional treatment alliance. Because many alcoholics are not able to meet such conditions at the time they seek treatment, a climate of animosity and mistrust has developed between both helpers and those needing help. More recently, Zimberg (1982) suggested that there exists a therapeutic nihilism regarding alcoholism. There is strong prejudice against alcoholics and a belief that alcoholism can't be treated.

Animosity also has developed between professional helpers and sober alcoholics. The latter recall negative, unhelpful experiences with therapists when they were drinking (Brown, 1977) and are reluctant to trust the therapist or the therapy process now that they are sober (Zinberg and Bean, 1981). Many of these individuals state specifically their fear that therapy will interfere with Alcoholics Anonymous (AA), their newfound base for abstinence and security.

Thus, drinking and nondrinking alcoholics fear psychotherapy: For the drinking alcoholic, therapy might come too soon between the patient and the bottle; for the sober alcoholic, therapy was a potential wedge between the patient and AA. Understandably, therapists respond to these feelings with defensiveness.

Recently, however, therapists have acknowledged their part in perpetuating these difficulties (Vaillant, 1982; Hellman, 1981; Goby, Filstead, and Rossi, 1974; Janz, 1971; and Reineke, 1969) and have identified the main origin of these problems as lack of knowledge—about alcoholism, about the needs of the

3

alcoholic, and about the tasks of therapy. Moore (1965), Knox (1969), Canter (1969), and Krueger (1982) also have examined the failures of both therapists and patients, focusing on transference and counter transference phenomena.

Psychotherapy has an important place in the treatment of alcoholics, but this role is neither properly understood nor properly used. Hill and Blane (1967) provide an overview evaluation of psychotherapy with alcoholics. There are many problems with psychotherapy that alcoholics have identified (Brown, 1977).

PSYCHOTHERAPY: ITS USE AND USEFULNESS

According to AA members, conventional psychotherapeutic treatment has been most used, and least useful for, the drinking alcoholic and most useful and least used by the abstinent alcoholic. Seventy-seven percent of the AA participants in our research study (see Chapter 2) had experienced some form of psychotherapy before abstinence, yet 30% believed their experiences to be of no help. By contrast, 45% had been in psychotherapy after abstinence, and only 3% described this experience as no help. Only 16% believed therapy before abstinence was very helpful compared with 64% who had therapy after abstinence. Those who had never been in therapy, more than one-half, considered it *after* abstinence. Almost two-thirds would have chosen some form of psychotherapy if they had sought help in addition to AA.

Yet AA research participants saw psychotherapists as being relatively unaware of and incompetent to handle alcohol issues. They criticized therapists for their failure to identify and label alcohol as *the* major problem. Murphy (1980), Zimberg (1982), and Bissell (1982) found that failure to diagnose and mismanagement by the therapist were the primary sources of hostility. One respondent described a collusion of denial between herself and her psychiatrist:

> Therapy allowed me the illusion of doing something about myself while continuing to drink. I had expressed concern about my drinking to several therapists, who, as I, chose not to recognize it as a problem.

Participants overwhelmingly agreed that, for the active alcoholic, drinking must be labeled as the primary problem, and it must stop before therapy can proceed to other issues with any success. The common dynamic view that alcoholism is a symptom of another more primary problem (Bissell, 1982) maintains this idea. Bean (1981) and Vaillant (1981) are outspoken in their descriptions of professional counter transference, denial, and collusion.

When asked whether or not and how therapy could be helpful to abstinent alcoholics, respondents further underscored the issue of mistrust. About one-third believed psychotherapy can offer specific help with emotional and psychological issues other than alcohol. Several emphasized their similarity with nonalcoholics, noting that their underlying problems are just like everyone else's, and they should be treated similarly in therapy. Many also suggested partnership between therapy and AA, seeing both as valuable; these were individuals who currently used both AA and psychotherapy and reported favorable past experiences.

The need for therapists to change themselves before focusing on how therapy could be helpful to abstinent alcoholics, was emphasized by a number of respondents. They believed therapists must improve their understanding of alcoholism and of the AA program. Still others criticized therapists not only for their ignorance but for their attitude of omnipotence. Murphy (1980) and Krueger (1982) suggest that these criticisms are valid. The research participants also stressed the importance of equality; a few even stated that only an alcoholic can understand and treat another alcoholic. This group tended to fear therapy as an intrusion and a threat to AA and adamantly disavowed any need for help outside of AA. A number of theorists have recognized the need for psychotherapeutic modifications in working with alcoholics (Blane, 1977; Blum and Blum, 1967; Silber, 1974: Scott, 1961; and Strecker, 1951).

What can we make of this large number of disappointing experiences and equal number who see positive potential in psychotherapy? We need to more clearly define the role and task of therapy. But first, we will briefly examine the most important models of alcoholism treatment.

MODELS OF ALCOHOLISM

It is the rare major text on alcoholism that does not include a review of the most important and controversial models of alcoholism. Part of the continuing difficulty in understanding and treating alcoholism is the acknowledged complexity of cause and treatment. Although critics of a particular model abound, few would fault the necessity for a multimodal and multidisciplinary approach to understanding cause and treatment. Kissin (1977) typifies the introductory review. He summarizes six models, considering their primary differences and potential conflicts, the first of which is the medical model.

The *Medical Model* is based on the disease concept and therefore designates the physician as the primary therapist. Kissin emphasizes that the medical model tends to stress biological mechanisms with little attention paid to psychological and social problems. He also notes that adherence to the medical model places great emphasis on the use of tranquilizers and medications such as disulfiram (Antabuse) (Kissin, p. 33).

Kissin next defines the *Behavior Modification Model*, which emphasizes conditioning principles, both in understanding the development of alcoholism and its treatment. The latter includes behavior modification therapy, aversive conditioning, and positive reinforcement behavior modification.

The *Psychological Model* includes aspects of the "alcoholic personality," but places its emphasis on subconscious conflict. Kissin suggests important modifications to traditional psychoanalytic theory including concepts such as social psychiatry. He emphasizes the importance of the alcoholic's immaturity, inadequacies of personal and social relatedness, and an unwillingness to face reality.

Kissin defines the significance of social forces resulting in psychological dependence as the key to the *Social Model*. He includes socioeconomic status, ethnicity, subcultural mores, and elements of family interaction. He suggests that the importance of peer approval helps explain the success of AA and its incorporation into treatment systems.

Kissin next elaborates on the *Alcoholics Anonymous Model* from the point of understanding why it works and for what population it is best suited. He recognizes that AA is not a formal model, but includes it because it is one of the major treatment systems. (Kissen, p. 40).

Finally, in the *Multivariant Model*, Kissin emphasizes the validity of all the other models and the need to more carefully fit the model and the treatment to the individual.

Schuckit and Haglund (1977) provide another framework for viewing models of alcoholism. They break their classification into psychological and sociocultural theories and biological factors. Within the psychological framework are included the tension-reduction, reinforcement, transactional, psychodynamic, and personality theories. Sociocultural aspects include understanding similarities and differences among cultural groups and subgroups. Under biological factors, they include abnormalities of body function and genetic factors.

CURRENT THEORIES OF ALCOHOLISM AND THE ISSUE OF CONTROL

Despite their range and complexities, these past models of alcoholism all suffer from several serious inadequacies. They focus on the drinking alcoholic, ignoring abstinence and recovery. They view alcoholism as static, rather than progressive; this is reinforced by their view of alcoholism as a symptom or result of other problems, such as lack of will or emotional disturbance, rather than a disorder or illness with a developmental course of its own. The thought that loss of control is a permanent condition of alcoholism is a possibility that is either accepted, ignored, or rejected. This controversy about control is at the core of misunderstanding about the development of alcoholism, treatment goals, and recovery.

Progressive Stage Theory

In defining a progressive, addictive medical disease by stages, Jellinek (1952 and 1960) dramatically altered conventional theoretic approaches to alcoholism.

He described a downward spiral of identifiable symptoms and behavior distinguishing certain stages: The purely symptomatic stage, which includes, prealcoholic and prodromal phases, differentiated by the development of tolerance; and the addictive stages (including a crucial and finally a chronic phase), marked by physical dependency and loss of control. Jellinek worked within a medical framework, classifying alcoholism as a disease with more than 40 specific symptoms. Jellinek emphasized the importance of the issue of control: The link in the progression from symptomatic to addictive drinking, according to him, is the onset of loss of control.

Although Jellinek's theory remains controversial among professionals (Khantzian, 1980) and between professionals and alcoholics, it nevertheless had a profound impact on theory and treatment by defining a progression of alcoholism and by bringing it into the realm of medicine.

The Interpersonal Approach

Using interpersonal theory, Bacon (1973) elaborated on Jellinek's model. He extended previous identified stages to include symptoms of increasing social difficulties and emotional disturbances. Like Jellinek, Bacon focused on loss of control, but stressed its social context. Instead of viewing loss of control as a simple turning point, Bacon suggested that it can be viewed developmentally through time according to learning theory. He developed a progression of symptoms, associating the increased use of alcohol with progressively severe social isolation and feelings of low selfworth.

The AA Approach

AA members have long recognized the progression leading to and reflecting loss of control as they tell "what it was like" (AA World Services, 1955). The traditional story or "drunkalogue" abounds with reports of broken homes, lost jobs, lying, stealing, hospitalizations, drunk driving arrests, accidents, and blackouts; events which increase in degree but continue to be denied or rationalized. The individual suffers tremendous shame and remorse but cannot connect the glass in hand to the later drunken state.

As the alcoholic becomes progressively worse, with unacceptable behavior more visible and isolation and loneliness more total, the sole friendly companion remains the bottle. AA members report "hitting bottom" when they feel alone, totally hopeless, and defeated in what many describe as a battle to control their drinking. Feelings of worthlessness, self-disgust, and self-hatred prevail. The downward spiral includes not only loss of control but loss of relationship, position, health, and self-respect. It is a cycle characterized by failure and eventual despair. The increasing losses and social isolation elaborated by Bacon and by members of AA confirm Jellinek's emphasis on the loss of control.

There is virtually no disagreement among theorists as to the importance of this concept. But until recently, there has been much less general knowledge and almost no theoretic formulation or agreement about what happens after abstinence.

Theories of Abstinence

AA, its history and its mechanisms of change, has been described by numerous authors (Kurtz, 1982; Blumberg, 1977; Thune, 1977; Clinebell, 1963; Holmes, 1970; and Maxwell, 1962 and 1984). Only a few theorists (Tiebout, 1944; Merriman, 1959; Blane, 1977; Vaillant and Milofsky, 1982), however, have recognized the importance of examining abstinence as a part of the total process of alcoholism. This recognition also is explicit in the standard AA story as related by the AA member who tells "what it was like when she or he was drinking," "what happened," and "what it is like now" that she or he is abstinent (*AA World Services,* 1955.) Implicit in each of these is the recognition of movement and change, as opposed to a static view of abstinence.

Bacon too speculated about the experience of recovery, describing it as a "mirror process" that reflects the reverse image of alcohol addiction. Although he noted the existence of new language and labels, he did not integrate these new elements into his mirror hypothesis. However, he did stress the critical importance of recovery, noting that "this is also a progressive phenomenon" (1973, p. 24). Bacon's developmental approach to alcoholism and recovery holds within it the foundation for a new comprehensive model of alcoholism. By understanding what happens to people who stop drinking, it becomes possible to construct a multidimensional model that includes recovery, focuses on process, and emphasizes the established significance of loss of control.

The AA View of Recovery: From Outside and Inside

The experience of AA members shows again and again human differences and the complexity of change. AA members are not simply "recovered." They emphasize the ongoing progressive nature of abstinence by using the term "recovering." A professional who uses the term "ex-alcoholic" reveals immediately his or her lack of understanding of both the complexity and the process (Bissell, 1982). The term "ex-alcoholic" implies a static state, which recovering alcoholics know does not exist.

AA terminology and custom add further complexity such as stages in recovery. The celebration of "birthdays," for example, serves as an important marker and suggests a developmental process. Newcomers, often in their first year, are referred to as "babies" or "pigeons," emphasizing their novice stature. Later they become "sponsors" to other newcomers as they mature and assume the role of teacher. The distinction AA members make between staying "dry" and remaining "sober" is another example. "Dry" refers to the state of abstinence; the individual is either drinking ("wet") or not drinking ("dry"), and "sober" encompasses the quality of that state. At any given time, an individual may be only dry or both dry and sober. An individual cannot be sober, however, without being dry. Thus, the term dry represents a continuing focus on alcohol or abstinence from alcohol, whereas "sobriety" encompasses the content and quality of other changes and concerns. Such important distinctions suggest a multidimensional recovery process and the need for a theory that encompasses this complexity.

A number of writers, researchers, and AA observers have recognized the importance of abstinence and the existence of a process of recovery. Rubington (1980) refers to a "career of recovery," Wiseman (1981) writes of "sober comportment" and stages of sobriety, and Mulford (1977) emphasizes the dynamic nature of the recovery process. Blane (1977) and Zimberg (1982) recognize stages in psychotherapy that correspond to stages in recovery.

For dynamic theory, the most important and definitive work on recovery is Bean's (1975a&b.). Her clear emphasis on the importance of process, coupled with Jellinek's and Bacon's work, laid the foundation for my research and subsequent model of alcoholism recovery. In two singularly important monographs, Bean examined various facets of AA, describing what happens to people who stop drinking from a psychiatric point of view. She emphasizes the importance of process, developing a progression of recovery based on changes in defensive structure, self-esteem, and role:

> It seems helpful to make distinctions about the therapeutic power of AA's methods for different people and for one person at different times in his recovery from alcoholic drinking. That is, to conceive of recovery as a process rather than a steady state, with different needs and problems at different phases. (1975a, p. 10)

Bean describes in detail the AA program, offering a model of the psychodynamics of recovery and good explanations for the difficulties psychotherapists experience in working with alcoholics. Throughout, she accents the value of AA, emphasizing the importance of support and the gratification of dependency needs:

> We have delineated how AA's great strength lies in meeting the alcoholic on his own turf and basically allowing him to stay there, giving him a safer expression of his regressive, self-destructive, and frightened qualities without requiring promises of future good behavior, insight, or alliance with healthy maturity. It is a stroke of genius or rather a work of art. (1975a, p. 57)

Bean takes a major step in defining recovery as a process. She describes the simultaneous development of mature defenses, improved self-esteem, and object relations. However, she does not explain what happens to people; how they change or the therapeutic strategies most useful at different times. In a later work, Bean (1981) describes the failure of therapists to understand the alcoholic's experiences, meaning, and psychology. She suggests how psychotherapists can be most useful to alcoholics by linking the alcoholic's subjective experiences with the way he or she presents clinically. In chapters 6 and 7, I develop further the "comprehensive theory" of recovery that Bean advocated and follow her lead in emphasizing the importance of the subjective experience of the individual after alcoholism begins.

PROBLEMS WITH INTEGRATING PSYCHOTHERAPY AND AA

Although much has been written about the positive benefits of AA (Fox, 1957; Leach, 1973; Beckman, 1980; Ripley and Jackson, 1959; Trice, 1970) and few, if any, would fault the success of AA (Bebbington, 1976), there is still a major gulf between professionals and AA members. Furthermore, many, while praising the benefits of AA, also point out deficiencies (Kalb and Propper, 1976; Bean, 1975b; Tournier, 1979) or criticize the organization and its methods. Leach and Norris (1977) summarized the range of criticisms of AA and AA members. Often, these criticisms reflect professional misunderstanding of what happens in AA, or an expectation or wish that something else should happen. Beckman (1980) acknowledges the problems of professionals and their criticisms of AA. She suggests that clinicians have trouble reconciling their assumptions about the nature of alcoholism and psychotherapy with their assumptions about AA, and they contribute to the continuing mistrust and animosity between alcoholics and their professional helpers. In fact, many of the so-called negative aspects of AA are actually positive and can be integrated into a multidimensional theory using AA and psychotherapy as cooperative partners.

A major criticism of AA is its unscientific bias. Critics (Kalb and Propper, 1976) point to AA's refusal to open its membership to critical examination and to controlled studies as evidence of its antiintellectual nature. AA has now undertaken studies of its membership (1970) and has been studied in detail by observers since its beginning (Bailey and Leach, 1965; Bales, 1944; Streesman, 1962; Tiebout, 1944; Thune, 1977; and Maxwell, 1984). Some observers (Tournier, 1979) have their criticisms validated; their frame of reference reflects certain intellectual values that do not recognize the critical positive function of methods or beliefs that appear to be regressive, inhibiting, or unsophisticated.

Recently, Thune (1977) answered these criticisms with an analysis of the very unscientific nature of AA. He suggests that AA cannot be understood from an analytic, positivist model. He suggests that a phenomenologic, subjective perspective is required to understand the meaning of alcoholism, the self, and the world. He suggests that AA is not a science and by implication cannot be evaluated as such because its meaning only exists in a particularist, personalized form within a person's life history. His analysis also may help to explain why an acceptance of conversion is so neglected in understanding recovery.

Augmenting the controversy is the disagreement about the conversion experience as a necessary foundation for a developmental theory of recovery. Because AA does not provide a conceptual framework in which to explain conversion theoretically, AA is seen only as a craft, and therefore, outside the realm of science. As such, the experiences of AA members and the process of recovery in AA cannot be incorporated within traditional theories.

Another primary criticism of AA is its continuing focus on alcohol, (Chavetz and Demone, 1969) so fundamental and predominant at the observable level of an AA meeting. Observers express concern that this focus may prevent development of other aspects of the member's life (Bean, 1975b).

Many observers tend to see the continuing preoccupation with alcohol as restrictive, limiting, and defensive, rather than as the foundation of a new developmental progression. In fact, the emphasis on alcohol serves a critical function; it establishes the foundation and the structure for subsequent change and development. The acceptance of loss of control and the identity as an alcoholic form the core of the continuum of recovery.

In the beginning of recovery, the focus on alcohol is essential as is an emphasis on behavioral change in early sobriety. This is at the heart of staying dry. With a base of abstinence established, individuals look at cause as they begin to reconstruct their stories, uncovering *how* they became alcoholic. At the same time, however, they eschew efforts to understand *why*. Paradoxically, members know that a focus on cause holds within it a belief that drinking can be controlled and maintained, once the cause is determined. Yet they also know that if they do not understand the kinds of thinking and behaviors that perpetuated drinking, they will return to it. Causes are thus defined very broadly: attitudes, character defects, and beliefs. Elimination of the causes is inherent in the 12 steps (AA, 1952), which will be closely examined later in this text.

The focus in an AA meeting is indeed on alcohol. Members know that being "dry" is clearly behavioral and absolutely essential to progress. But being "sober" requires more than behavioral change. If members want to improve the quality of their lives, they must actively engage in vigorous self-exploration. There are even AA meetings designed to facilitate this process through close attention to the 12 steps.

Fanaticism, cultism, and intolerance of other methods are other criticisms of AA (Cain, 1963; Bean, 1975b). This fanaticism is another example of paradox. Zeal is a necessary ingredient for many to sustain early abstinence. Members have experienced a conversion and require intense focus and concentration of behavior and attention to maintain the conversion. The fear of falling into old beliefs and patterns is countered by the fanaticism. Zeal is maintained beyond early recovery by the legitimate fear that non-AA individuals (including and especially professional helpers) do *not* understand the importance of establishing an identity as alcoholic and continuing to focus on alcohol. AA members do not usually trust professionals to properly take into account or guard their sobriety. It is extremely difficult for a member of AA to have to explain and convince a family physician, minister, or therapist of the continuing need for AA and a continuing focus on alcohol. Outsiders simply do not understand the function of this focus and may, therefore, unwittingly interfere, communicating the conflicting value that continued dependency on AA is a sacrifice of independence (Gerard, Saenger, and Wile, 1962). AA members with some length of sobriety would suggest to the skeptic that independence is gained by acknowledging dependence. Often this paradox is lost to the professional who continues to devalue growth and development as long as it occurs within the context of a dependent stance, such as AA membership or a belief in a higher power. Bean (1975b) and Lovald and Neuwirth (1968) typify critics who are concerned about the cost of continuing the "alcoholic role." Bean notes that many members of AA might be able to terminate the alcoholic role but there is no mechanism to do so.

Yet the alcoholic role is more than a "role." It is a new identity that forms the core of new behaviors, attitudes, and beliefs. Whereas many AA members do reduce the frequency of their attendance at AA and even stop going entirely, they do not relinquish the identity. Understanding the key significance of this identity is at the heart of this book.

In summary, differences such as these discussed contribute to serious and continuing misunderstanding, mutual hostility, and lack of trust. The understanding and integration of the surface structure of AA and the underlying mechanisms of change requires suspension of single-dimension theory and observation, and particularly, examination of conflicts in value. Bean correctly suggests that educated individuals have trouble accepting the inspirational focus of AA. Yet, as we shall see, the suspension of intellectual explanation is essential at certain phases of recovery; it is precisely the intellectual's wish to be able to explain what is happening or to attribute cause that impedes progressive movement into recovery.

PARADOX AND CONTROL

How can an observer accurately describe what happens in AA, but view as negative what members of AA would consider positive? This contradiction brings us to the significance of paradox and the issue of control.

Until recently, few theorists adequately considered the importance of paradox to behavior and psychological change. Systems and communications theorists have drawn more attention to paradox and the nature of change. Understanding AA and the complex process of recovery requires an acceptance of the central role of paradox and, for most, a relinquishment of key intellectual values (Thune, 1977; Mack, 1981).

AA members have an intuitive appreciation of paradox as they describe in their stories how they had to lose in order to win; they had to admit defeat and then surrender in order to win. It is defeat at their efforts to control their drinking. It is this very notion, the essential step in moving into recovery, that is foreign or distasteful to most individuals who value control.

The Concept of Control

There is probably no concept more significant to understanding problems in the theory and practice of treating alcoholism than the concept of control (Marlatt, 1983: Armor et al., 1978; Pendery et al., 1982; Miller, in press; and Royce, 1981). Differences in belief and values held about the concept of control maintain problems in knowledge and communication and keep many recovering alcoholics frightened of professionals. As we have seen already, the complaints from the AA respondents in the study about the ignorance of professionals centered on two main areas: first, the therapist's failure to identify and label alcoholism as the major problem; second, a belief system shared by both patient and therapist, based on control. Both patient and therapist believe that individuals should be able to control their drinking, and that they will be able to if only they can find the proper answer or the right approach.

Therapists and patients with this belief in control may identify alcoholism as the problem, but reject abstinence as the solution. They spend months and years trying different methods of controlled drinking while searching for the underlying problem. Neither can acknowledge that lack of control is the paramount problem and a permanent one, and that the imposition of control is not a desirable solution. Therapists and patients who share this belief system equate abstinence with an admission of weakness and failure. Both strive to demonstrate that the patient can quit any time, cut down, or switch to "softer stuff"; proof that abstinence is temporarily possible through will. If the patient can stop any time, the logic goes, there's no problem with control and no need to ever stop, certainly not for good. Only alcoholics must quit altogether because alcoholics have lost control.

In this lies the popularity of the "problem drinker" diagnosis. It is a problem that can be solved without change in basic behavior or belief system. Use of the term problem drinker underscores the belief that control is a virtue and possible for all but the weakest willed. In a relationship in which both partners share this belief in control, therapist and patient will undermine permanent abstinence, spending long hours chalking up the signs of improved self-management. Mack (1981) states this dilemma clearly. "It is a far more useful step therapeutically for the alcoholic to acknowledge his powerlessness than to have it demonstrated that he still retains an element of control" (p. 133). Mack adds that an emphasis by the therapist on the dimension of control creates more guilt and deepens the sense of failure. In such a situation, the patient who wishes to give up his faulty belief in control must either see himself as a failure in relation to the therapist or must give up treatment to achieve and maintain abstinence. In other words, successful abstinence equals therapeutic failure.

It now becomes more understandable that recovering alcoholics believe that only another acknowledged alcoholic can understand them. The person maintaining abstinence has acknowledged a lack of control and is not striving to regain it. A helper who has not also experienced a similar internal struggle with an acceptance of loss of control may focus the treatment on the exact opposite, still holding onto the basic belief that self-control is the ideal goal. The patient's move toward abstinence destroys the alliance built on denial of alcoholism and a belief in control.

Sometimes therapists recognize that abstinence must be the goal, but still believe that self-control is the ideal. The patient senses the judgment of weakness. To now acknowledge a lack of control is to lower self-esteem in relation to the therapist. Once again, unless the basic values of control are examined, patients may have to leave treatment to accept abstinence; they cannot accept that they are so different from and inferior to the therapist in matters of self-control.

Several other reasons why therapists do not diagnose alcoholism also center on control: control by the therapist, not the patient. First, many therapists believe that to label a patient alcoholic is an awful thing to do (Mack, 1981; and DiCicco et al., 1978)—such a label must be avoided at all costs because a diagnosis of alcoholism is an acknowledgment of a shameful and embarrassing failure. It also means that a person must stop drinking. No one wants to pronounce that sentence on anyone else. Furthermore, many therapists do not know the limits of their responsibility. Many believe that if they diagnose alcoholism, they also must be able to make the individual stop drinking. But they do not know how to do that and neither does the patient. Why not? Because both believe in the myth of self-control. The doctor tells the patient to cut down, and the patient agrees to do so. Neither can acknowledge that this is not possible precisely because it is the core problem. If control is based on will, then both should know how to limit drinking.

This circular faulty logic leads to deepening denial and frustration. The therapist knows that the treatment for alcoholism is abstinence but doesn't know how to facilitate it for the patient so doesn't make the diagnosis. The therapist does not appreciate that diagnosis and referral are the limits of therapeutic responsibility. The therapist cannot make the patient stop drinking or do it for the patient. The therapist's inability to recognize his or her own helplessness and limits of responsibility results in a defensive, omnipotent attitude toward the patient and a corresponding refusal to act for fear the patient will not cooperate.

The patient, indeed, may not stop drinking, but that does not reduce or eliminate the therapist's responsibility to make the diagnosis. In a negative alliance, based on a belief in self-control, the therapist says the patient has failed at self-control by making the diagnosis of alcoholism, and the patient says the therapist has failed by refusing to stop drinking.

These and other problems in treatment of the alcoholic stem from the deepest underlying belief systems of both patient and therapist (Knox, 1969, 1971). First a belief in self-control runs absolutely counter to a comfortable acceptance of abstinence. Second, a belief in total responsibility by the therapist for making the patient change leads to a therapeutic relationship based on the struggle for control. In such a misalliance, the partners are unequal and the treatment centers on a fluctuating struggle for dominance. When success of the treatment, as defined by the therapist, is based on abstinence, the patient has the power to make the therapist fail.

As long as the therapist maintains a belief system based on the idea of self-control and the belief in the responsibility and power to make the alcoholic change, treatment for alcoholism will remain problematic. With that belief system, treatment must center on denial of alcoholism to maintain the myth of self-control, or, if diagnosed, treatment centers on getting the patient to stop.

So what is the place for psychotherapy in the treatment of alcoholism? There is no relevant place unless the therapist can alter basic beliefs. Therapists must recognize loss of control for the alcoholic and must accept their own total lack of control in being able to make the patient change. Therapists who recognize their own limits can then begin to help the alcoholic accept the diagnosis of alcoholism, the lack of control that goes with it, and the abstinence required. The therapist can then help the patient learn how to stay abstinent.

Theories of Control

Several key theorists have offered conceptual frameworks based on the concept of control to explain what happens to the alcoholic who stops drinking. The best known and most comprehensive examination of what happens to alcoholics who recover was provided by Harry Tiebout, M.D. in the 1940s (1949). Tiebout saw the successful turn from drinking to abstinence as a conversion phenomenon that he defined as a "psychological event in which there is a major change in personality manifestation" (p. 48). In other words, he saw that a conversion experience that results in the creation of a positive attitude toward reality follows an act of surrender.

Surrender is the moment of accepting reality on the unconscious level (Tiebout, 1949). The individual knows the deepest truth, regardless of wishes or explanations to the contrary. Defenses used in the service of denying that reality (denial and rationalization, defiance and grandiosity) no longer work. According to Tiebout, when true unconscious surrender has occurred, the acceptance of reality means that the individual can work in it and with it. Reality is loss of control—powerlessness over alcohol (Mack, 1981, p. 146). The individual who has accepted the reality of loss of control can proceed to live with that reality, beginning the process of recovery. Paradoxically, the state of surrender is positive and creative as Kaiser (1955) suggests. Rather than an abnegation of responsibility, the admission of powerlessness is the first step in the assumption of responsibility.

The difference between compliance, that temporary submission to abstinence with an unconscious intention to return to drinking, and surrender (Tiebout, 1953) is seen in the transitory and fluctuating experiences with abstinence that so many patients demonstrate. It is also this distinction that creates so many difficulties between patient and therapist. Compliance is an act of will undertaken with conscious control. The reality of loss of control is accepted consciously but not unconsciously. The individual accepts for the moment and temporarily alters behavior. But it is, at best, a superficial yielding. The individual believes unconsciously that he or she will drink again.

Two important characteristics of the alcoholic, suggests Tiebout, hinder the process of surrender and result instead in compliance. These characteristics are defiance and grandiosity. These qualities serve the alcoholic well in denying the reality of loss of control. As Tiebout (1953) explained "grandiosity claims there is nothing it cannot master and control, though the facts demonstrate the opposite" (p. 52). Thus the conscious mind denies or rejects what the unconscious mind perceives. The individual may respond to the conscious demands of reality with a compliant abstinence, but as soon as the unconscious elements of defiance and grandiosity surface, the individual is drinking again.

Tiebout defines the characteristics of defiance and grandiosity as the key qualities that make the patient resist recognition of the reality of loss of control. He defines defiance as "that quality which permits the individual who has it to snap his fingers in the face of reality and live on unperturbed" (p. 51). He continues:

> Defiance is a trustworthy shield against the truth and all its pressures. Defiance masquerades as a real and reliable source of inner strength and self-confidence since it says, in essence, 'nothing can happen to me because I can and do defy it.' For people who meet reality on this basis, life is always a battle. . . . (p. 51)

That battle is fought with the aid of grandiosity. The individual engages in a life and death struggle to prove that the truth isn't so. Grandiosity and defiance are often centered on the battle of control, specifically, "I can control my drinking." The defensive belief that the individual can control the drinking supports an otherwise depressed and deflated ego. Relinquishment of defiance and grandiosity accompany surrender.

Tiebout's concepts of hitting bottom and surrender have a counterpart in systems theory. Gregory Bateson (1971) outlines a theory of the logic of alcoholism in cybernetic terms. At the heart of Bateson's theory is a recognition of the importance of defeat. According to Bateson:

> The first two steps of AA are as follows:
>
> 1. We admitted we were powerless over alcohol and that our lives had become unmanageable.
>
> 2. We came to believe that a power greater than ourselves could restore us to sanity (AA, 1939).
>
> Implicit in the combination of these two steps is an extraordinary and, I believe, correct idea: The experience of defeat not only serves to convince the alcoholic that a change is necessary; it is the first spiritual experience. The myth of self-power is thereby broken by the demonstration of greater power. (Bateson, p. 3)

Bateson suggests that the first step is not a surrender but a change in epistemology, a change in how to know about the personality in the world. Bateson then outlines an epistemology of cybernetics to explain the paradoxical and vicious cycle of alcoholic drinking. He defines alcoholic pride as an important component. This is a pride based not on success but rather on an obsessive acceptance of a challenge to repudiate the proposition "I cannot." This pride places alcoholism outside the self with the individual engaged in resisting it or controlling it.

The corollary to Tiebout's concept of conversion is Bateson's discussion of symmetric and complementary relationships. He suggests that the individual locked in alcoholic pride also is locked in a symmetric relationship with others in the world. The symmetric pattern is primarily a competitive one. The alcoholic locked in a symmetric struggle must prove repeatedly that the bottle cannot kill him, and that he can control his drinking.

Bateson suggests that the religious conversion experienced by the AA member reflects a dramatic shift from the symmetric habit or epistemology, to "an almost purely complementary view of his relationship to others and to the universe or god" (p. 11). He asserts that the symmetric pride of the alcoholic is a picture of the state of mind of the alcoholic battling with the bottle. This battle is embedded within an epistemology of self-control. However, after hitting bottom, the symmetric epistemology shifts to a complementary one. Central to the complementary epistemology is a sense of being part of something larger than self: the theology of AA emphasizes the importance of a belief in a power greater than the self. This shift from symmetric pride to a complementary relationship describes the internal change necessary to sustaining abstinence and underscores the success of AA.

Bateson emphasizes the central significance of the systemic, part-to-whole relationship:

The single purpose of AA is directed outward and is aimed at a noncompetitive relationship to the larger world. The variable to be maximized is a complementary one and is of the nature of "service" rather than dominance. (p. 16)

He demonstrates the critical function of a belief in a higher power to facilitate and maintain a shift in personal epistemology. Central to this shift is relinquishment of a belief in self-control.

A third theoretical formulation further illustrates the concept of control. Watzlawick et al. (1974) are interested in the notion of paradox as a central feature of change. They also describe first and second order changes. First order involves changes that occur within a consistent and logical framework with no change in underlying premise; second order change requires a leap and a shift in underlying premise. They exhort therapists to understand and facilitate second order change; a change that corresponds to Tiebout's conversion phenomenon and Bateson's shift from symmetric to complementary. According to Watzlawick et al. (1974) and Levenberg (1981), the target of change must be the attempted solution. The attempted solution of the alcoholic is the repeated efforts at control, that is, how to control drinking without giving it up.

The move from drinking to abstinence requires a fundamental change in the central premise of control. The individual shifts from a belief in self-control to a recognition of loss of control. This has profound implications for therapeutic strategy.

All three theories of change clarify the problems therapists have with their alcoholic patients, both drinking and sober. First, the therapist may be identified consciously or unconsciously with the grandiosity and defiance of the patient and, therefore, side with the belief in self-control (Tiebout, 1949). Second, the therapist may be symmetrically oriented toward others and the world and, therefore, be incapable of imagining or helping the patient shift to an acceptance of loss of control and a complementary relationship with the world (Bateson, 1971). Third, the therapist, because of his or her logical framework, may impede the patient's shift to a second order level of change (Watzlawick et al., 1974).

"Controlled Drinking"

It now should be obvious that the current intense controversy that exists between adherents to abstinence and those who believe in the possibility of controlled drinking may be understood and explained according to the three theoretical positions outlined above.

From Tiebout's position, the belief in control is linked to the traits of defiance and grandiosity. It is the belief in control and the striving for control that keeps the individual so resistant to surrender. To repeat: The belief in the possibility of controlled drinking is antithetical to surrender.

Those who believe in the possibility of control remain within Bateson's symmetric system. Efforts to control drinking are undertaken within the logical framework of a belief in control. The alcoholic who has hit bottom, surrendered, and in essence accepted a new identity as an alcoholic based on the acknowledgment of loss of control has everything to lose by reinstating a belief in control. With that new identity comes the shift to complementarity, which is antithetical to a belief in control. In Watzlawick's terms, the belief in controlled drinking exists within a first order framework. The move to recognition of loss of control that cannot be regained is a second order change.

The issue of conversion provides a crossroads in theory and practice. Critics of abstinence and AA (Kalb and Propper, 1976) and adherents of controlled drinking as a treatment goal for alcoholics separate AA from the plane of valid, scientific inquiry. AA is variously described as religious, folklore, or craft (Kalb and Propper, 1976). In fact, Kalb and Propper called for the end of the craft versus science debate. They suggested that AA craft technology is incompatible with science and should not be compared or viewed on the same plane. Thune's (1977) phenomenologic and existential framework lifts AA out of the pejorative realm of craft.

Professionals who continue to believe in control remain on the same theoretical plane. The belief in loss of control requires a transformation and the subsequent development of a new belief system. This theory rests on acceptance of loss of control and immediately moves past arguments about its feasibility.

Controversy about the concepts of controlled drinking for the alcoholic versus loss of control may relate to the fact that there has been no theory of recovery. Individuals who have remained abstinent and who belong to AA have not been studied for the purpose of theory development or expansion. Thus, the theory and practice have supported the belief that recovery ends with abstinence, or that recovery might include moderation in drinking levels for people who have lost control. Bateson and Tiebout provide a theoretic base for the phenomenon of conversion that removes it from the realm of craft or folklore. Conversion marks the beginning point of the developmental process of recovery, rather than an end point.

This expansion in a developmental continuum illustrates why the issue of control is so threatening to the alcoholic. To the recovering alcoholic member of AA, a belief in the possibility of controlled drinking represents a regression to an earlier plane of development. It represents the erosion or rejection of the conversion experience and the loss of the transformation of belief. Mack (1981), too, states that for the alcoholic in AA, controlled drinking is outside his capabilities (p. 134). The person who believes in control sees it just the opposite. Control is seen as the highest level of development. Loss of control is viewed as a regression rather than the first step of a progression leading to mature and autonomous development.

The gulf that exists between many theorists, therapists, and recovering alcoholics is due in large part to an inability to comprehend alcoholism in developmental terms and to include recovery. It also is due to a failure to accept and understand the concept of conversion as a legitimate theoretical construction that forms the foundation of a developmental process of recovery. Relegating conversion to the status of craft closes the door on theory development and tends to maintain the concept of controlled drinking at the highest level of development rather than the lowest, as it exists for adherents of the loss of control theory.

Individuals in AA who argue against controlled drinking are arguing from a different developmental plane. They already believe in loss of control and have moved beyond it. To speculate again pulls them back. Mack (1981) states that the 12-step program of AA "seeks to enlarge progressively the capacity of the chronic drinker to govern (the impulse to drink) in the absence of alcohol" (p. 134).

The controversy over the possibility of controlled drinking remains extremely problematic. The belief in control cannot be measured. Yet it is that belief that is the chief mechanism of denial for the individual who has lost it. Thus, an emphasis on control coupled with a belief that controlled drinking is the highest level of development, does indeed retard the progression into recovery for many. From this point of view, there is no room for the *possibility* of controlled drinking in the future and, therefore, no valid therapeutic approach that can work toward the resumption of controlled drinking as Khanztian (1981) suggests.

THE PLACE OF AA

Is AA Necessary?

There has been considerable research on the characteristics of people who affiliate with AA (O'Leary et al., 1980; Edwards et al., 1966; and Trice, 1957), and among observers of AA there is general agreement that AA is not for everyone (Tournier, 1979; and Ogborne, 1981). These observers believe that an important goal of research is to determine the most suitable and the least suitable candidates for AA. The latter should not be referred. Bean suggests that AA "allows and prescribes a low level of adjustment and insight and therefore a therapist should not refer patients to it blindly as a method he critically endorses" (Bean, 1975b, p. 11).

The belief that AA is not for everyone contributes to the continuing dissonance. Why and how should a therapist determine that a particular person should not use AA? The belief that AA may not work for all people clearly stems from differing and more traditional beliefs about the nature of addiction, the process of recovery, and the nature of treatment. The observer with an intellectual bias interprets the surface dynamics of AA as regressive, ritualistic, rigid, authoritarian, and perhaps superficial (Bean, 1975b), and, therefore, a less ideal choice than psychotherapy. These interpretations do not reflect the complexity of the AA program (Hellman, 1981; and Alibrandi, 1982), particularly the critical importance of paradox and the necessity for the suspension of an intellectual bias. Hellman (1981) suggests that devaluing of AA by professionals is a serious problem. These negative judgments and interpretations are ultimately communicated to patients. What patient can successfully make use of AA when his or her therapist is uncertain of its value, condescending, or critical?

The position that AA is for some and not others widens the gap between professionals and AA members. Patients and therapists alike tend to believe that being able to stay sober without the use of AA is superior to using it. Patient and therapist may both believe that AA is not for bright, capable people who can make use of a therapist:

> Dr. M finally sought help at the alcohol clinic after many years of intensive psychotherapy. She was threatened with the loss of her practice and had to seek treatment for alcoholism in order to retain it. Dr. M recognized that she had a problem with alcohol. But she had steadfastly refused to go to AA because she believed that she could not continue her intensive psychotherapy if she was also a member of AA. She believed that belonging to AA meant she was not bright enough or healthy enough to control the problem through intensive analysis. She believed that people who go to AA are less intellectually competent and require much gratification for their dependency. She was sure that she would no longer be a "good psychotherapy patient" if she went to AA.

Mr. T provides another example. He joined a therapy group for individuals concerned about their drinking (Brown and Yalom, 1977) and 10 years later reported on that experience:

> I managed to stay sober during that entire two and a half years of therapy. I did not want to go to AA and felt I didn't need to. I was superior. I could stay sober without it. But at the end of treatment, I had not internalized the means of staying sober. In fact I had never learned. I had no concept of personal responsibility either. My abstinence was fragile but I didn't know it. I felt assured and very safe. I found my way back to drinking through wine tasting. It fit with my superior upper-class view of myself.

> I finally stopped again two years ago and have been going to AA regularly. Now I can see that I never altered my belief in self-control, which was maintained by my arrogance. Why didn't you push AA attendance more rigorously?

The sense that staying sober on one's own strength, or via the therapeutic relationship is superior to membership in AA may stem from the belief that AA membership requires acceptance of a sick role with the corresponding privileges of dependency and relinquishment of autonomy and self-determination (Bean, 1975b).

Certainly, gratification of dependency needs is inherent in the structure of the AA program (24-hour help available, frequent meetings), but built on that gratification is the simultaneous development of responsibility and movement toward autonomy with high levels of emotional development and adaptation possible within the framework of the AA principles. Psychotherapeutic help may be necessary for some and certainly is desirable for most, but only if the therapist can appreciate the positive, ongoing value of AA and the importance of an integrated triadic therapeutic approach.

I recommend a referral to AA for anyone who is concerned about drinking and absolutely for all who wish to stop. Not everyone will accept the referral. The difficulties that individuals have in accepting a referral or in attending AA and belonging become part of the therapeutic process. Resistance to AA or difficulties in belonging will be addressed as a therapeutic issue throughout this book.

Is there recovery for people who do not go to AA? Yes, according to studies of spontaneous recovery (Waldorf and Biernacki, 1979; Lemere, 1953; Kendall and Stanton, 1966) as summarized by Zinberg & Bean (1981) and Orford and Edwards (1977). However, this book is not about people who remain abstinent and do not go to AA. Individuals who are not members of AA were not part of the research project. Few would question the validity of recovery from alcoholism without the use of AA. An AA member sums up his concept of the key to his recovery:

> I could not have maintained a comfortable sobriety without having had a spiritual awakening and the resultant radical shift in my beliefs and my entire being in the world.

Although he attributed great importance to the fellowship of AA, it is the spiritual conversion that held the key to his comfortable abstinence.

Gianetti (1981) and Boscarino (1980) examined differences between AA members and nonmembers. From our clinical work, we have seen that the critical difference lies in the experience of conversion and subsequent beliefs. Individuals who remain on the same belief track may have experienced hitting bottom and surrender, but have not developed the concept of a higher power, which sustains such surrender. Some individuals who remain on the same belief track still believe in control and experience their abstinence as an achievement of will. They may hope to drink like normal people again and, thus, hold onto the promise of remaining a drinker. Others may develop reliance on an external authority such as Mr. T illustrated. Psychotherapy offered him the identification and attachment to sustain his abstinence; it did not provide him the modeling he also required. As he described, he did not develop the belief in loss of control nor a concept of personal responsibility.

Unless the process of psychotherapy is *directed* at the issues of transition and early recovery that focus on loss of control and the new identity as an alcoholic, which emphasizes the conversion experience and new beliefs (see Chapters 5 and 6), traditional group and individual work is likely to skip the critical behavioral and learning focus necessary to these stages. Thus, individuals may stay sober via the transfer of authority to an external figure or group, but they fail to internalize the behaviors and cognitions that would help them maintain abstinence on a day-to-day basis.

Other individuals may rely on conditioning or aversion therapy (Wiens and Menustik, 1983; and Miller and Hester, 1980) to remove the compulsion to drink and, therefore, ensure abstinence. Whereas many individuals do remain abstinent, our experience with these patients indicates that they also fail to develop a sense of personal responsibility. Many are fearful that the aversive conditioning may "wear off" and they will find themselves helpless to ward off an impulse to drink. The developmental perspective explicated in Chapters 2 and 3 illustrates why new learning must occur if individuals are to remain abstinent.

The recovering alcoholic in AA, for the most part, has adapted a belief in a power greater than self and thereby relinquished the belief in self-control. A therapist who has not experienced a similar struggle with control and an acceptance of loss of control is a severe threat to the alcoholic.

Professionals and AA: A Partnership

Controversy over the primacy of treatment rather than the notion of partnership has characterized the alcohol field for more than 50 years (Zinberg and Bean, 1981). A major purpose of this book is to improve knowledge and communication between professionals and alcoholics based on integrating psychotherapy and AA. The idea for a partnership is not new. In fact, it originated with AA. Bill W, one of the founders of AA always advocated the cooperation of AA with various other disciplines. In fact, he repeatedly emphasized the debt that AA has to the medical profession for its discoveries in psychiatry and biochemistry (Bill W., 1958, p. 10). He also emphasized his personal debt to his own physician, William Silkworth, M.D., for declaring Bill hopeless; medicine could not help him. Bill had to turn elsewhere, and AA was born.

In a series of talks to the medical profession, Bill W. emphasized that AA is a "synthesis of principles and attitudes which came to us from medicine and religion."

We alcoholics have simply streamlined those forces, adapting them to our special use in a society where they can work effectively. Our contribution was but the missing link in a chain of recovery which is now so significant and of such promise for the future. (1958, p. 5)

Bill described the case of Mr. R who sought psychotherapeutic treatment for his alcoholism from Carl Jung. It was through Jung that the bridge between medicine and religion, or what members of AA refer to as spirituality began:

> Mr. Rs depression deepened. He asked "Is there no exception; is this really the end of the line for me?"
>
> Well, replied the doctor, there are some exceptions, a very few. Here and there, once in a while, alcoholics have had what are called vital spiritual experiences. They appear to be in the nature of huge emotional displacements and rearrangements. Ideas, emotions, and attitudes which were once the guiding forces of these men are suddenly cast to one side, and a completely new set of conceptions and motives begin to dominate them. In fact, I have been trying to produce some such emotional rearrangement within you. With many types of neurotics, the methods which I employ are successful, but I have never been successful with an alcoholic of your description.
>
> But, protested the patient, I'm a religious man and I still have faith. To this Dr. Jung replied, ordinary religious faith isn't enough. What I'm talking about is a "transforming experience," a conversion experience if you like. I can only recommend that you place yourself in the religious atmosphere of your own choice, that you recognize your personal hopelessness, and that you cast yourself upon whatever God you think there is. The lightning of the transforming experience of conversion may then strike you. This you must try—it is your only way out (1958, p. 6–7)

As Bill W. related his own progression of recovery he emphasized the spiritual, noting the profound influence of William James on the formulation of the principles of AA, specifically the concept of conversion:

> Conversion does alter motivation, and does semi-automatically enable a person to be and to do the formerly impossible. Significant it was that marked conversion experiences came mostly to individuals who knew complete defeat in a controlling area of life. The book certainly showed variety. But whether these experiences were bright or dim, cataclismic or gradual, theological or intellectual in bearing, such conversions did have a common denominator—they did change utterly defeated people. (1958, p. 10)

Although Bill W. emphasized AA's debt to medicine and religion, he acknowledged difficulties in establishing a cooperative attitude:

> It used to be the fashion among some of us in AA to decry psychiatry, even medical aid of any description, save that barely needed for sobering up. We pointed to the failures of psychiatry and of religion. We were apt to thump our chest and exclaim, "Look at us. We can do it, but they can't!" It is therefore with great relief that I can report this to be a vanishing attitude. Thoughtful AA members

everywhere realize that psychiatrists and physicians helped to bring our society into being in the first place and have held up our hands ever since. (1958, p. 16)

Bill W. concluded his talk by again emphasizing the need for a spirit of cooperation:

> We clearly see that by pooling our resources we can do together what could never be accomplished in separation, or in shortsighted criticism and competition. (1958, p. 17)

Bill W. determined that the hostile, competitive attitudes were diminishing.

Certainly, the American Medical Association has taken a firm position on identifying alcoholism as a disease and supporting AA. The Committee on Alcoholism and Drug Dependence of the American Medical Association defines alcoholism as

> an illness characterized by preoccupation with alcohol and loss of control over its consumption. Alcoholism is regarded as a type of drug dependence of pathological extent and pattern, which ordinarily interferes seriously with the patient's total health and his adaptation to his environment. (AMA, 1973)

AA's view of alcoholism is similar:

> Alcoholism, in AA's opinion, is a progressive illness, spiritual and emotional (or mental), as well as physical. The alcoholics we know seemed to have lost the power to control their drinking. (AA as a Resource for the Medical Profession, 1982)

The importance of partnership has been a key element of the American Medical Association and government health agencies. In support of AA, William Mayer, M.D., suggests the following:

> AA by and large works better than anything we have been able to devise with all our science and all our money and all our efforts.
>
> If you are ignoring the utilization of AA groups—interaction with them, referral to them—then you are ignoring a critical, crucial part of the important kinds of care people with this disorder deserve and must have.
>
> AA has shown the way and presented us with a model of long-term care that is really not care. It is participatory self-management. It is an assertion of the autonomy of the individual. Instead of his thinking of himself as a victim, a helpless person,. . . AA gives a person the kind of sense of self-worth and along with it the kind of humility and reality testing that are absolutely essential in the management of alcohol problems.

In further support for the importance of partnership, a physician states the following:

> The recognition and management of alcoholism, one of the most untreated, treatable illnesses, is well within the scope of any physician who is willing to test his diagnostic acumen on a wide spread, multiple system disease which masquerades in many disguises. Paraphrasing Osler's remark, one may say that "to know alcoholism is to know all medicine."

> The physician who works closely with Alcoholics Anonymous in his community is in a key position to provide leadership, education, and support in an area which will pay great dividends in the quality of care and rates of recovery of those still suffering alcoholics. (*AA as a Resource for the Medical Profession*, 1982)

The official position of both AA and medicine has clearly been one of cooperation and partnership, and guidelines have been provided by some (Fox, 1973; and Rosen, 1981). Mack (1981), too, offers the hope of collaboration between AA and psychoanalysts. Partnership does exist in certain quarters, especially in the alcoholism treatment hospital where medical intervention and AA participation go hand in hand (Aharan, 1970). But the alcohol treatment clinic or hospital is isolated from the rest of medicine and the other helping professions. It may even be viewed with skepticism by physicians and helping professionals. Unfortunately, the knowledge and experience of an effective working partnership are not communicated in medical or professional schools or in practice (Pokorny et al., 1978; Rosenberg, 1982; Khantzian, 1980). Thus, the majority of treatment professionals are undereducated and even ignorant about alcoholism and its treatment. As Bissell (1982) notes, therapists need special training but don't know it. Zinberg and Bean (1981) summarize the lack of training and subsequent problems of diagnosis for physicians.

The preponderance of mistrust, tension, and hostility (Leach and Norris, 1977; Dancey, 1968) is an unhappy reality that must be acknowledged before the partnership that both desire can be effectively realized. The challenge for professionals is how to acknowledge their own lack of control and that of their patients and proceed with the task of recovery that follows this surrender of control by both. A successful alliance between alcoholics and therapists requires a multiplicity of roles for therapists, predicated not on a static condition in which abstinence is perceived as the single goal and an end point in treatment but on a new theoretical model that views alcoholism as a process.

Chapter 2

A Dynamic Model
of Alcoholism Recovery

RESEARCH FOUNDATIONS FOR A NEW MODEL

The AA Exploratory Study

Before this study, research had always focused on the drinking alcoholic. Since then, others (Blane, 1977; and Wiseman, 1981) have developed the concept of stages in recovery.

Could the process of recovery be classified into stages similar to those already identified by Jellinek and others for the drinking alcoholic? To see whether or not the process models of Jellinek and Bacon might extend into abstinence and to test the validity of Bacon's notion that recovery would be a mirror process to that of developing addiction, I designed a study that would examine the experience of recovery from the point of view of 80 (40 men and 40 women) abstinent alcoholics in AA; their personal experiences, relationships with others, personal and interpersonal adjustments, and major changes. The only criterion for inclusion was self-declared AA membership. Demographic characteristics of the sample are presented in Appendix B.

Participants were divided according to length of abstinence, that is, the time since the last drink. This, therefore, represented total length of continuous sobriety. Appendix C presents a breakdown by sex, age, and length of sobriety.

As part of a more extensive testing program, the participants answered an open-ended questionnaire (Appendix D), which included extensive questioning on a variety of personal experiences during abstinence; occupational adjustments, major life events, perceived turning points in achieving and maintaining abstinence, problems, conflicts, disorders and symptoms, important people and the nature of their influence, and experiences with psychotherapy and AA. The questionnaire was designed to determine what the basic views and issues are in recovery. Two exploratory questions formed the basis for the questionnaire:

1. What are the key issues and/or events (intrapsychic, interpersonal, problems of adjustment) with which the abstinent alcoholic must contend?

27

2. Is a continuum based on length of sobriety helpful in understanding and differentiating these key issues?

Results

Among the most interesting results was a paradox: There is a decrease in emphasis on alcohol with the passage of time, yet it remains an important underlying, ever-present issue. Participants explained this by stating that maintenance of sobriety is the least and most of their concerns: Change and growth are only possible when founded on abstinence; thus alcohol remains a prominent concern.

Recovery seemed to involve three major components: alcohol; concerns such as occupational adjustments, major life changes, the emergence of depression, suicidal feelings, and other disorders and symptoms with which they had to cope; and a third that involved a change in attitude toward and consequent interpretation of self and others. This third component encompasses the belief in a higher power that AA members refer to as spiritual in nature.

The whole concept of recovery as simply a mirror image of the downward progression also was shown to be inaccurate. Although the experience of abstinence might involve some reversal of previous failures and losses, such reversals do not necessarily or automatically occur! Abstinence involves the addition of *new* experiences, making "recovery" more than a mirror image or reversal, a critical conceptual point also emphasized by Wiseman (1981). It involves a network of continuing experiences, reinforcing and building on one another. Most important, abstinence is now seen as a midpoint, or even a beginning point, on an expanded continuum of alcoholism, not an end in itself. Rather than the last phase, ending in insanity, death, or abstinence, drinking is now the first phase of a broader continuum that includes recovery.

Problems with both Jellinek's and Bacon's theories were immediately apparent. The overlap and concurrent experience of these three components demonstrated that a one-dimensional construction such as the mirror model was inadequate to portray the depth and complexity of recovery. The process of change occurs along several dimensions and therefore requires a construction that can include several lines of simultaneous movement. Recently developed, more sophisticated diagnostic criteria (NCA, 1972; and Operation CORK, 1982) list at least five tracks of developing alcoholism, operating simultaneously. Diagnosis can be made along any single dimension or combination. CORK guidelines list family, social, employment, physical, and behavioral categories, for example. Within these tracks, it is also possible to distinguish between early, middle, and late symptoms as well.

With such complexity, can we monitor an individual's movement? Critical to the success of any team effort in alcoholic recovery is the ability to define the stage of the disease and the recovery and to determine movement among stages.

It is only through such fine tuning of movement that a specific treatment or combination of treatments can be determined appropriately and altered as the needs of the individual dictate. But before examining movement and defining the dynamic model of alcoholism, several key issues that underlie the new model require elaboration.

KEY ISSUES IN THE NEW MODEL

The Long-Time Perspective

There is always widespread cultural pressure for quick results. The employer wants his key manager back to work and functioning at capacity quickly; government funding agencies expect evaluation statistics on the success of treatment at six or 12-month intervals. Eighteen months is the usual limit to which such outcome statistics can be extended. And patients themselves expect instant, permanent cure. There is great reluctance to undertake treatment that demands patient participation in the process and major changes in values, beliefs, and way of living. Many individuals avoid AA and intensive psychotherapy because they know that they must be actively involved. AA members indicated they appreciate the value of a long-time perspective. Only from this vantage can patients and therapists appreciate the complexities of movement and continuing change. However, many acknowledge that they would not have undertaken the recovery process had they realized initially the time commitment involved. This commitment is not for days or months but for years—many years.

Individualization of Treatment

Research participants demonstrated that the course of treatment before and after abstinence is individualized. Subjects outlined a variety of key people and critical interventions or "turning points" that, in combination, led them to the point of surrender (see Appendix G). They also elaborated a variety of key people and critical interventions necessary to sustaining abstinence (Appendix G). Whereas many of these elements occur within the general principles outlined in AA, the interpretation is an individual one. Always, the acceptance of loss of control and the decision to abstain were very personal; dictated by circumstances, events, and interventions that the individual could not have predicted.

What it took and how much it took to move the individual toward abstinence was unquantifiable. As many individuals in AA recount, the point of surrender follows a personal recognition of "being sick and tired of being sick and tired" (Brown, 1977). This recognition may have been facilitated by psychotherapy. More frequently, psychotherapy has played a minor role, or even has inhibited movement toward abstinence.

A new model would have to permit the course of treatment and its pace and direction to be determined by the individual patient and not by the therapist, contrary to other theoretic and practical models that had expected the patient to adopt a particular style or belief system in order to begin treatment (Knox, 1982). A new model would have to acknowledge the importance of individualized treatment and use of different treatments separately and together, according to the phase of recovery (Kinney and Montgomery, 1979). It would have to offer an integrated treatment concept, using various resources including AA, physicians, psychotherapists, and other helping professionals. To accept such a model would require changes in the therapist's definition of psychotherapy, the expectations of patient and therapist, and the roles assigned to each.

A Developmental Framework

A new model would have to take into account that recovery seemed to be a developmental process that was not a mirror image of the development of alcohol addiction as Glatt (1958) suggests. What is lost in drinking is not automatically gained in abstinence. The broken marriage is not necessarily repaired, the lost job not automatically reinstated.

The points of surrender and beginning of abstinence signal the beginning of a new building process based on acceptance of loss of control. The progression of abstinence is best conceived as a developmental one because of the stage-specific tasks identified by respondents. Development is ordered, based on a progressive building process (see Chapter 3). Respondents described the course of their recovery comparing the critical tasks at the beginning of abstinence with their assessment of the key tasks required of their present stage. Through their comparative judgment, it was possible to define general tasks and general categories of time.

THE DYNAMIC MODEL OF ALCOHOLISM RECOVERY

An Overview of the Dynamics

At least three major components of alcoholism recovery operate simultaneously: the alcohol component that reflects the major focus on alcohol, environmental interactions including the interplay between the individual and factors beside alcohol, and interpretation of self and others, or the frame of reference through which the individual interprets self in relation to others and the world. Time is a key issue in the model's development. Another key issue is the necessity to allow for individual paths to recovery and therefore individualized treatment. The model includes four major stages based on the passage of time.

The four stages are:

1. Drinking
2. Transition
3. Early recovery
4. Ongoing recovery

Within these key stages three components operate simultaneously:

1. The alcohol axis
2. Environmental interactions
3. Interpretation of self and others

The relative importance and patterns of interactions of these components, coupled with the stage of recovery, define the task of therapy. The interaction between these components is complex and constantly dynamic. Each component operates in each stage of alcoholism recovery but operates differently. For example, the alcohol focus before abstinence is a dominant, negative focus that results in cognitive and emotional constriction and increasing interpersonal isolation. After abstinence, the focus on alcohol continues, but becomes a positive one that generates new development and expansion in cognitive and emotional frame.

Figure 2-1 illustrates the interaction between components and the progression

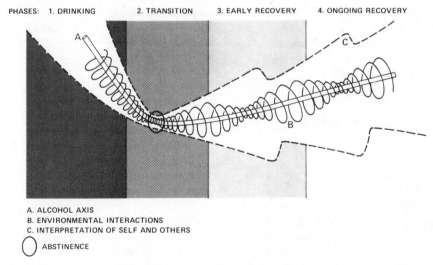

PHASES: 1. DRINKING   2. TRANSITION   3. EARLY RECOVERY   4. ONGOING RECOVERY

A. ALCOHOL AXIS
B. ENVIRONMENTAL INTERACTIONS
C. INTERPRETATION OF SELF AND OTHERS

ABSTINENCE

Figure 2-1. Dynamic model of alcoholism recovery.

of the stages. The alcohol component is characterized by change in the kind of focus but not in the focus itself; the other two components—environmental interactions and interpretation of self and others—each change in content and process depending on its interaction with the other two components.

The relative dominance of the alcohol focus at any given time is what dictates the focus of intervention and treatment. In the drinking, transition, and early recovery stages, alcohol is dominant. With movement through recovery and the passage of time, the primacy of the alcohol focus recedes. The individual does not require a continuing focus, that is, attention on alcohol to remain abstinent. Thus, ongoing recovery reflects much more activity in the other two components.

Alcohol: The Central Organizing Principle

Most noticeable about this new model of alcoholism is the role alcohol plays both before and after abstinence. Alcoholism provides the continuing, central organizing role in an individual's experience. Before abstinence, there is a decreasing interest in other issues and increasing focus on alcohol. Much of the individual's energy goes into maintaining a belief in control. During the drinking stage, the individual undergoes a narrowing of experience with increasing emotional and cognitive constriction and interpersonal isolation. Alcohol is the overwhelming focus, although the predominant organizing role of alcohol in fact reflects an increasing loss of control in all aspects of life.

Abstinence begins with a similar intense focus on alcohol. That focus now serves to support a new identification as an alcoholic and new belief in loss of control. In the shift from drinking to abstinence, the alcohol is the only continuous focus. As Bateson and Tiebout describe (1971, 1949, and 1953) the individual experiences a dramatic disruption in beliefs about the self in direct relation to alcohol. The person now believes "I cannot control my drinking" and "I am an alcoholic."

STAGES OF RECOVERY

The Drinking Stage

Many writers have described the process of developing alcoholism (O'Neill, 1955; London, 1981). Increasing isolation, constriction, and a narrowing of the individual's world to an overwhelming focus on alcohol and the struggle for control: these are the patterns that characterize AA members' description of their move toward abstinence. The individual struggles to conquer or master alcoholism by force or sheer will. As Bateson described, the individual is pitted in an internal battle to overcome and control what is seen as an external de-mon—the bottle (1971). With the belief that control is possible, there is no room for acceptance of error or defeat. Increasingly determined to control drinking, the individual attacks again and again only to be controlled by the bottle.

Acceptance of failure and loss of control mark the point of abstinence. In addition, a wide range of influential turning points and events indicate that the turning point from drinking to abstinence is the result of the multiple impact of many experiences and interventions, none of which may necessarily stand out in isolation. Individuals describe a combination of internal and external events that have led them toward this point of self-loathing and hatred; coupled with constant fear, these characterize the internal progression. Individuals in AA often describe this turning point as a sudden recognition of being "sick and tired of being sick and tired." External events such as an unhappy, nagging, or con-frontive spouse, a divorce, loss of job, or publicly humiliating experiences con-tribute to or underscore the internal despair.

Central to the turning point is the concept of "hitting bottom" or "surren-der." In Bateson's schema, it is the collapse of the logical framework that sup-ported a belief in control. For Tiebout, it signals the point of conversion. The turning point is characterized by a sense of defeat and an inability to try any longer or any harder to control one's drinking. The combination, or "fit" of turning points is unique to each individual as the following examples illustrate.

> I finally got ready. I reached a point of terrible self-loathing and despair. This time I couldn't reason or excuse my way out of it. I knew it was me—all alone—who was doing this to myself and no one else.

> It's funny. I didn't know it was coming and I couldn't have predicted it. The night before was nothing special. But I woke up that Friday morning and I knew that it was over. I had had my last drink. That's all I knew but it was crystal clear. Then I had to learn how to stay sober.

These examples emphasize an internal recognition or point of despair. The next series illustrates a combination of external and internal events.

> I was so disgusted with myself and so tired of covering up. Plus, my friends had all told me of their concern.

> I was arrested for drunk driving. I was a well-bred, upper-class lady sitting in the drunk tank. The humiliation was more than I could bear. I knew I was an alcoholic that night.

> I don't know why these events were so significant *this time*. I'd done all these things before. But on this occasion the truth sunk in. It was as if I could suddenly *see* myself. First, I arrived at a board meeting drunk. Second, I had a black-out at the same meeting and failed to follow through on a major assignment. Third, I

felt so tired of the charade. There I was, trying to look and act like an executive while falling out of my chair.

The Transition Stage

The transitional period is characterized behaviorally by a shift from drinking to not drinking. At the cognitive level, the individual changes from the belief "I am not an alcoholic" to an acceptance of the belief "I am an alcoholic," with the accompanying belief in loss of control.

The transition stage is dominated by the shift in epistemology described by Tiebout and Bateson in Chapter 1. If the individual has truly "hit bottom" and surrendered in Tiebout's schema, there will be an acceptance of loss of control followed by a conversion. Bateson describes this conversion as a shift from a symmetric, competitive relationship with the world to a complementary stance in which the individual sees him or herself as part of a larger whole.

The individual who has not truly surrendered or accepted the belief in loss of control may periodically shift back and forth from drinking to not drinking. The abstinence is not a surrender to loss of control but a temporary compliance. Drinking will be resumed as soon as the individual feels strong enough to control it again. This individual has not shifted epistemology or experienced a lasting second order change.

AA members' experience reinforced the significance of a transition period. In the research sample, an average of 20 months elapsed between initial contact and acknowledged membership in AA, and another eight months passed before the average respondent achieved abstinence. This finding suggests that the move from drinking to abstinence, and the corresponding change in identity from nonalcoholic to alcoholic, is a fluid process. It also suggests that recovery may actually begin during drinking as the individual unconsciously begins the process of fluctuating behavior and identifications in preparation for the stable shift that lies ahead (see Appendix E).

The transition phase is a move away from isolation as described by AA members. Members describe themselves as infants, building a bridge to abstinence by trading dependency on the bottle for dependence on other objects. Members rely on frequent AA meetings as a place of safety and actively substitute reading, speaking, and other substances (coffee, honey, orange juice) for drinking. The focus on alcohol and absorption in AA aids identification as an alcoholic, produces feelings of belonging and security, and provides explanations for past incomprehensible behavior. This focus on alcohol is essential to ensure that the behavioral and cognitive components of change will occur and solidify. Without a constant focus on alcohol, the individual may be lured back into a belief in control and the cycle starts again.

Early Recovery Stage

With the passage of time, the individual begins to incorporate the second component, that is, interactions with others and the environment without the presence of alcohol. The abstinent individual continues with or returns to family and work, beginning some major adjustments. These changes also are affected by the incorporation of the third component, interpretation of self and others. With the acceptance of loss of control and a new identity as an alcoholic, the individual's world view unconsciously expands and changes. The same experiences no longer have the same meanings. New attitudes and values dictate new directions and a different way of evaluating oneself and one's experiences. New ways of integrating and new terminology are required to reflect these changes. In the drinking phase, individuals emphasize control; they see the world as an unconquerable mountain, yet they hold to the belief that somehow conquest is possible. In the early abstinence phase, they accept that the mountain can't be licked; they now begin to take their direction from the mountain, moving backwards, forwards, and sideways, steadily gaining ground. By changing the style of their approach and their course, a wide range of new experiences occurs.

This movement into abstinence is a new journey, both exciting and frightening, sustained by feelings of identification and belonging. To embark requires hope, faith, and support from others. Members explore new territory and describe themselves as toddlers looking with new eyes on a world they could not see before, or one that could be seen and interpreted only in order to support a belief in control. Early abstinence is also a period of active dependency. Members maintain a solid tie with AA, venturing into the environment and returning for support, staying close to the alcohol focus.

This need for support was emphasized by research participants. In the transition and early abstinence phases, their active dependency involves a receptive posture, which includes receiving advice and answers from others. Members also noted the importance of meetings, which provide a place to go, inanimate objects such as literature to read, and tasks to be performed such as cleaning or making coffee. This active dependency may involve constant activity as well. Some individuals literally "drink in" abstinence in AA in the same way they used to consume alcohol.

The value of objects and tasks illustrates an important way the structure of AA accommodates individuals with intense dependency conflicts: Affiliation does not demand interpersonal involvement, yet members can participate and be dependent while remaining interpersonally isolated for as long as necessary. In this way AA provides a supportive framework in which dependencies can be gratified, with members regulating their pace and involvement. AA members noted a startling change in their sources of support before and after abstinence. Before abstinence, members relied on family, although this reliance was often negative and based on hostile dependency by all and a shared denial of alcoholism. The respondents did value the confrontation of their partners when it led to their abstinence.

However, in abstinence, members did not continue to see family members as their key source of support. In abstinence, that base and the feeling of dependency shifts to AA and to individuals within the organization. Members noted that it was easier to place themselves in a dependent position among others who have been in the same difficulties. Of course this has ramifications for the psychotherapeutic relationship. AA members often report the same mistrust of a dependent relationship with a therapist who is not also recovering.

The organization of AA (its structure and the program) and its many members provide a base for a more tolerable, dependent position. The varied experiences and the large number of helpers give the new member many models for identification and the safety of spreading dependency needs among many listeners. The individual must ultimately assume responsibility because these members are not as personally invested in that person's sobriety or drinking as family members and perhaps therapists are likely to be. AA is seen as a source of stability, hope, and security and a classroom of life as the following individual points out:

> I view AA meetings as a form of drinking party in which I am weaned from the association of an intoxicant with undefensive, noncompetitive, open, friendly, responsive behavior. In this sense, it is a sort of training session in which the attitudes and behavior which I should cultivate at all times are reinforced to the extent that I don't revert to a more secure defensive position as a result of a few minor setbacks or rebuffs. Also, it helps me to view matters from others' point of view. I also find that meetings are intellectually stimulating.

To absorb new experiences, sights, and sounds and to learn new ways of relating requires an openness and innocence possible only in an environment of certainty and safety. Individuals repeatedly stress the importance of AA for this security. There is no push or time limit, no goals or ends to achieve. Members can move and grow at their own pace, responding to their internal needs. It is a time of positive self-indulgence; in learning to recognize their needs and to care for themselves, members are reassured of their ability to do so and later freed to move outward.

Ongoing Recovery Stage

As time passes, members report the increasing importance of interdependent, sharing relationships and internal, self-reliance as a source of support. These are both helped by strong identification with and internalization of AA principles. Interpersonal relationships and environmental concerns become more important as the individual begins to integrate internal needs with external demands. The individual expands awareness and receptivity not only to the mountain, but to the surrounding environment, climate, and other climbers.

Though important at all points in AA membership, a growing interest and integration of a spiritual factor is reported at this stage. Some describe this as a reliance on a "higher power," continuing steadily from the point of initial abstinence. For others, a spiritual focus emerges later, expressed again as a belief in a higher power or in the form of existential questions or beliefs. Whatever its form, the result is a move away from a self-centered view of the world to one which places the individual in relation to a larger universe. It is an emergence of a self in relation to others.

Only when the base of abstinence is firm with new behaviors and cognitions solidified can development of spirituality or "complementarity" as Bateson described occur. Much of the process of ongoing recovery is the development and fine tuning of the self in relation to a larger whole. During this time, growing self-acceptance, enhanced by the positive experience and achievement of sobriety contributes to an adaptive spiral, moving the individual in a forward momentum similiar to that described for the downward progression. The three components of movement are now integrated, with the total flow neither steady nor linear; rather, recovery is the interactive flow of a network of experiences, new ideas, and new behaviors, reinforcing, reshaping, and building on one another on the base of a new belief system about the self in relation to alcohol and to the world.

MAJOR COMPONENTS OF THE MODEL

The Alcohol Axis

Movement into abstinence and the transition phase is based on identification as an alcoholic with a corresponding recognition of loss of control. This represents a reversal of key beliefs about the self. This reversal and the emphasis on alcohol represents the continuing link in the developmental continuum. The focus on alcohol is primary in the drinking phase and primary in the early phases of recovery. The focus on alcohol reflects the level of epistemology defined by Bateson and Tiebout. The alcohol axis in the drinking phase represents a belief in control and the identity as a nonalcoholic. The alcohol axis in recovery represents the belief in loss of control and the new identity as an alcoholic. The alcohol axis serves as the pivotal organizer of the process of recovery, as illustrated in Figure 2-2. Figure 2-3 illustrates the lines of movement.

If we consider the alcohol focus in drinking and abstinence to be the organizing principle in an individual's life, it is possible to understand the dramatic

PHASES: 1. DRINKING   2. TRANSITION   3. EARLY RECOVERY   4. ONGOING RECOVERY

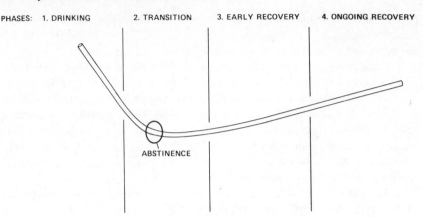

ABSTINENCE

Figure 2-2.   The alcohol axis: The central organizing principle.

and all-encompassing change that is required when the individual moves from drinking to abstinence. In drinking, the individual's interactions with environment and the view of self and others are filtered through and reflected by a belief in the ability to control one's drinking and the belief that "I am not an alcoholic." In abstinence, the reversal of these beliefs ultimately requires new interactions with the environment and new interpretations of self and others through the new focus on loss of control and being alcoholic. The new beliefs are a radical departure from the old.

As such, newly abstinent individuals resemble infants developmentally. They are extremely dependent, often unable to remain abstinent or even care for themselves initially without strong external supports such as a hospital, residential

PHASES: 1. DRINKING   2. TRANSITION   3. EARLY RECOVERY   4. ONGOING RECOVERY

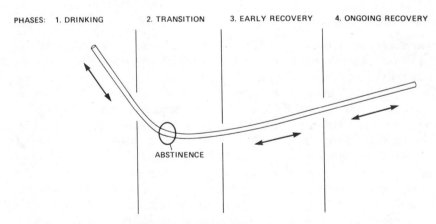

ABSTINENCE

Figure 2-3.   The alcohol axis: Movement.

recovery home, or twice-daily AA meetings. They know they must remain abstinent but they do not know how to do that behaviorally. They know only behaviors that accompany drinking. Khantzian (1982) supports this view, suggesting that alcoholics are deficient or underdeveloped in their capacity to care for themselves.

So, like infants, they require a safe and secure environment and great support. Soon, as they move from the transitional phase into early abstinence, they will come to resemble toddlers, learning new behaviors and ways of thinking about themselves as a result of listening to and imitating others and exploring the environment. As with toddlers, the exploration into the world is tempered by frequent returns for contact and "refueling" (Mahler et al., 1975) with "mother"—in this case the AA meeting and/or AA sponsor.

A look at an AA meeting or close examination of an AA member in the first year of sobriety will reflect this emphasis on dependency. The individual is seeped in learning AA language and behavior, perhaps unquestioningly so. If the observer does not understand the significance of this dependency period to establishing the base for long-term autonomous development, the appraisal of this dependency emphasis is likely to be negative (as with Bean).

Ongoing recovery incorporates developmental tasks of adolescence and adulthood. The peer culture that is so important in AA carries an adolescent flavor for those in their early months and years of abstinence. AA members form lasting friendships with peers who "come in together" and often report fondly that they "have grown up together." The adolescent tasks (Blos, 1962) of identification and individuation are predominant issues in early and ongoing recovery. Individuals move into the world away from AA gingerly at first and then solidly, taking their increasingly comfortable identification as alcoholics and their new behaviors and beliefs with them.

As with normal development, there is no end. AA remains a concrete and more than ever, a symbolic home base to which members return regularly or periodically throughout their abstinent lives. AA—and later the principles of AA—is the "homebase" from which individuation occurs. That individuation can only proceed on a firm base of early development in which the identification as an alcoholic and the new behaviors accompanying that identification are firmly rooted.

Those who skip the early developmental stages have no foundation for continuing abstinence and frequently flounder, returning to alcohol. As Figure 2-4 shows, some individuals may move in a line from drinking to abstinence, continuing through the phases of recovery with uninterrupted sobriety; others may fluctuate between drinking and abstinence, a process characterized by alternating self-identifications, what Bean describes as "fits and starts." For example, in a fit of remorse, some people swear off alcohol, proclaim a loss of control, and try on the label "alcoholic." At an unconscious level they maintain a belief in control (Tiebout, 1953). When they feel better, a sense of power returns. Then they change their minds, reassert a belief in their ability to control their drinking, and reject the alcoholic label. They move from abstinence back to drinking.

Individuals may remain in this transition period, fluctuating in identity and behavior, for varying lengths of time. As is clear from Figure 2-4 and the emphasis on the alcohol axis, fixation on the drinking side results in a very narrow obsessional emphasis on alcohol and control. Individuals are rigorously identifying as nonalcoholics and defending their ability to control. On the abstinence side, they acknowledge a lack of control, identify as an alcoholic and then learn what that identity means, both concretely and abstractly. A singular emphasis on the alcohol axis is critically important during this transitional phase to stabilize the new identity and to initiate practical education on how to maintain abstinence. The stress on alcohol is, most importantly, the core of a new foundation of belief.

In this phase any emphasis on the value of control by patient or doctor actually impedes progress and solidification of a new identity as an alcoholic. To move through the transitional phase, individuals must accept a lack of control and the new identity as alcoholic. In a value system that still emphasizes control, these are perceived as failure.

After identifying as alcoholics, people learn concretely that:

1. "It's the first drink that gets me drunk."
2. They must refrain from drinking "a day at a time."
3. They accomplish abstinence today by "keeping the plug in the jug."

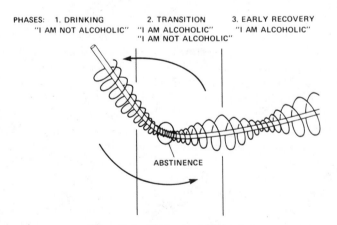

PHASES: 1. DRINKING   2. TRANSITION   3. EARLY RECOVERY
"I AM NOT ALCOHOLIC"   "I AM ALCOHOLIC"   "I AM ALCOHOLIC"
"I AM NOT ALCOHOLIC"

ABSTINENCE

Figure 2-4. Fluctuating self-identity.

They learn to make concrete behavioral adjustments to support their sobriety: they are taught to reach for the telephone instead of the drink, to substitute an AA meeting for a bar, and to read about alcoholism and other alcoholics to foster their identification.

On the symbolic level, the alcohol axis represents a source of safety and, paradoxically, a tool of control. In the transition phase, individuals concretely hang onto the alcohol axis, reminding themselves repeatedly that they are alcoholic, attending many meetings, and actively keeping themselves away from alcohol. This emphasis on alcohol and staying dry is often what predominates and is observable at the AA meeting as Bean reported. Individuals learn that they have the final choice and therefore bear the ultimate responsibility for taking a drink or not taking a drink. A strong alcoholic identity reminds individuals of that choice and of their ability to be in control of their abstinence. Paradoxically, individuals achieve control by acknowledging their lack of it.

As with the transition phase, early abstinence requires a continuing focus on alcohol and on similarities betwen alcoholics in order to cement identification. Part of this identification involves learning new behaviors, attitudes, vocabulary, and expectations about themselves. It involves above all a focus on alcohol. In early abstinence, new learning is achieved by listening to others and by actively mirroring the behavior of older members. Identification fosters the development of basic trust (Erickson, 1963) and a sense of security and belonging, all of which are necessary before environmental interaction and deeper interpretations of self and others can begin.

Identification, based on the recognition and acceptance of shared experiences, is the central focus. This emphasis on establishing similarities is accented in AA meetings through the sharing of the AA story or "drunkalogue" and the discussion of the 12 steps.

Many individuals initially shy away from attending AA because they do not want to acknowledge their similarities. Identification as an alcoholic remains distasteful. Others experience a deeper fear that the identification must be total. Joining AA brings up fears of engulfment and loss of self, rather than presenting a possible path toward autonomy.

In fact, AA members reveal an ongoing interaction between identification and differentiation. One such individual reflects his need for identification with others and his search for an individual identity through establishing differences, finding a compatibility, and interplay between the two as he reflects on his view of AA:

Each individual seems to have an attitude toward the program. Some are hardline, some middle of the road, and some very liberal. I tend to attend middle of the road or liberal groups. I like groups that are mixed as to age, sex, and background.

These seem to strengthen my tolerance of others and reinforce my feelings that I can only gauge my growth by me.

This interplay—between identification and differentiation, dependency and autonomy—and the search for a balance reappears in a variety of forms. The developmental movement from dependency toward autonomy is portrayed paradoxically. Members indicate a need for independent action and a chance to stand on their own which becomes possible after a committed involvement with AA and other people. The interaction between dependence and independence and the focus on alcohol and other issues continues indefinitely. Instead of disappearing, the focus on alcohol serves as an anchor, a continuing source of identity that is a symbolic link to the new idea of being part of a larger whole. Independence is possible only in the context of this linkage.

Structure, too, is inherent to the alcohol focus, both concretely and symbolically. Through different types of groups, and through the broad structure of the organization of AA, there is room for individual movement and variation as the following quote suggests:

In the beginning I deliberately chose speaker meetings to avoid being called on at discussion groups because of fear. Now I want to participate and don't currently like the large social meetings (200 people).

This man indicates awareness of specific change within himself and seeks a group whose structure will accommodate and strengthen this change. Khantzian's (1982) psychodynamic viewpoint underscores the importance of structure.

The dual importance of a continuing alcohol identification and a structure that can accommodate change is further accented as members describe the ways AA helps them. They stress the importance of security and consistency to identification and to development of basic trust:

Gives me a feeling of belonging, acceptance, and having an extended family, always available—any place; feeling of security if I need help to stay sober.

Created an environment where I am accepted, through being able to accept others. Allows me to participate in the human race—without being the island I had become.

I know I'm not alone. I can count on it to be there. It's enabled me to see myself through others. It saved my ass and has given me the keys to a life I didn't think I could have. It helps me (subtly now) to not take that drink.

Within this formal, well-defined structure that provides safety and certainty, there exists a looser body of knowledge, experiences, and principles (the program) that people can continually apply, reinterpret, and redefine to fit their growth and changing needs. Some members liken AA to early family: It provides the base from which the sense of individuality can grow and then return.

> AA is the physical embodiment of what I consider to be an outstanding philosophy of life. It is like a home and family in that it is a place where you can be completely yourself, where you are encouraged, accepted, and loved and where you can learn strong and healthy values and manners of dealing with life.

This woman illustrates the paradox in which autonomy is facilitated by first accepting dependence.

Members also illustrate how their membership in AA promotes movement away from isolation toward an acceptance of their common humanity. Being alcoholic is a symbolic reminder of that humanity—the link to others—by being part of a larger whole.

> I feel loved and loving, forgiven and forgiving. I feel good and at the same time, myself, the alcoholic. I am seldom out of touch with my own humanity, like it or not. Someone always understands intuitively where "I am."

> Talking with and listening to other alcoholics takes away my feeling of being special, different. It also focuses the problem totally on me, where the answers are. It has permitted me to see love in action and to kindle my hunger for freedom from me.

AA and its focus on alcohol helps its members build their own resourcefulness via mutual support and sharing and by developing a belief in a higher philosophy of living, encompassed in the 12 steps. Within these steps is an acceptance of dependence on a higher power, which provides the foundation for movement toward autonomy.

Members describe cycles of movement from extreme dependency to greater independence. They also provide a link between dependency and autonomy, pointing out the realistic limits of what they can expect to receive in AA. They emphasize that they must do certain things for themselves, as illustrated in the following examples: "AA is not medical—it doesn't solve things for you—it shows you how to live and face your problems"; "It doesn't pay my rent, help me put my pants on in the morning, or make my decisions for me."

Movement on the alcohol axis from identification to emerging autonomy is shown by changes in the kinds of support required in the early versus later days of abstinence. As noted earlier, in the beginning, support is direct and predominately external, such as advice, teaching, and learning. This same support system broadens to include emotional sharing with an increasing balance between external and internal supports. Bean was concerned that individuals do not give up the alcoholic role. The identity as alcoholic and the shared acceptance of the responsibility to "carry the message" continually emphasize the individual sense of self as a part of a larger whole. Relinquishment of the alcoholic identity and accompanying role carries the threat of a return of old beliefs and attitudes emphasizing control and the centrality of self.

This basic need for support does not disappear or even diminish. Its character changes instead, shifting from a recipient tone emphasizing extreme dependency with a need for concrete advice and answers to one of mutual sharing and equality. These changes parallel a move away from total dependence in the beginning towards greater autonomy. An AA individual illustrates the kinds of support required at first with that necessary in ongoing recovery:

> *Help needed at first:* I went to two meetings a day many days for months. I got support at home that gave me freedom to go outside to get help.

> *Help needed now:* I need very little direct help now as I claim the right to stay well and I know my needs.

Environmental Interaction

When individuals can identify concretely and symbolically with the safe, consistent concrete structure of AA, they also can begin to move away from a constant alcohol focus (alcohol axis). Focus on alcohol decreases as attention to and awareness of other concerns and interests increases (Figure 2-5). They retain the symbolic alcohol identification and move away from the central axis into wider environmental interactions, integrating other issues and concerns thus adding a new level and direction of movement. The progression now includes simultaneous horizontal movement on the alcohol axis with circular movement into the spiral (Figure 2-6). New concerns may represent the emergence of other

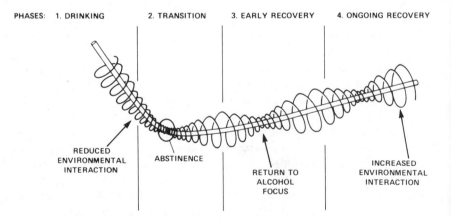

Figure 2-5.   Environmental interactions.

PHASES: 1. DRINKING   2. TRANSITION   3. EARLY RECOVERY   4. ONGOING RECOVERY

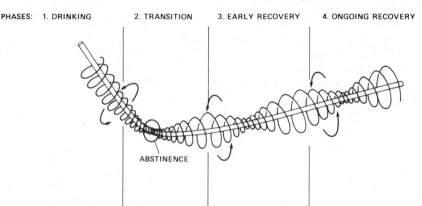

ABSTINENCE

Figure 2-6. Environmental interactions: Movement.

issues covered by alcohol or they may be the result of directed movement and exploration facilitated by the solid base of abstinence.

This is a period of experimentation, corresponding developmentally with the move away from intense dependency toward independence. A beginning shift from external support to internal control regulates movement. Individuals learn to monitor the degree of external control they require and to know when they need to return to an alcohol focus by their levels of anxiety, desires to drink, and comfort in the world away from AA.

AA members categorize the regulator of their movement as the distinction between being "dry" and being "sober":

It has been easy to be abstinent—not so easy maintaining an even emotional balance. I have been forced to deal with a lot of painful areas and conflicts, so my life has become easier and much more difficult at the same time.

No problem with booze, but great extremes from manic to depressive. Great problems with anger and violent moods.

Staying dry has been very easy; the attempt to achieve sobriety—growing, achieving emotional maturity, achieving serenity, etc., is fairly difficult.

Giving up alcohol was easy; working the steps and taking care of my living problems was something; I think being dry and having poor quality sobriety isn't worth a shit.

Recognition of problems besides alcohol emerges. Members expect changes with abstinence. They convey an underlying positive attitude and pride in their ability to accept and adjust to change and a willingness to actively seek change themselves. This willingness to seek change reflects a more active involvement in their own destiny, a major shift from the passive series of losses and failures characterizing the downward drinking spiral.

Many different kinds of changes encompass the experiences of sobriety and the movement along the spiral of environmental interaction. Occupational adjustments, including job changes and shifts in work attitudes and habits, are a frequent result of and an equally important factor in maintaining sobriety:

> Changing old habits like long lunches; changing friends.

> Learn to slow down and not work everybody to death just because I felt so good.

> Bartending, my major source of income, was obviously out of the question.

The following description portrays the depth and degree of change required in attitudinal and concrete terms:

> I took a job in a small factory when I came on the program. I had never worked under heavy supervision before—in the six years before I had never worked for a straight salary—I had a lot of personal freedom. I really had to learn how to handle an eight-hour day job. Standing at a bench. No matter how fast I worked I still had to stay there eight hours a day. I had to learn how to slow down—how to work two hours at a time; how to stay there when it was driving me up the wall. How to go when I didn't want to. I did it and became comfortable on the job. I had always been a loner—I couldn't take supervision because it meant criticism. I learned to handle that.

Although this example emphasizes the individual, the environment is also important. One individual noted that his selling occupation did not necessitate drinking only because of the mystique and importance of his company. He meant that drinking is generally an expected occupational requirement. He could afford not to drink because he did not have to sell himself along with his company's product. A lack of structure in the occupational environment became a bonus for the drinker and a potential handicap for the person trying to abstain. As one member notes, "I did not want to return to a job with so much driving and free time."

The importance of a structure that provides a set of simple rules and expectations for behavior is repeatedly stressed as it was in relation to AA. Members do not feel confident of their ability to remain abstinent solely on their own internal initiative. Thus, they may need to alter their occupational environment to provide additional structure that will reinforce their identification and support their abstinence.

Examination of specific problems and conflicts provides a detailed picture of the kinds of issues concerning people during abstinence. Over time, the only change in the kinds of problems people face is a decrease in concern with alcohol. Otherwise, people are concerned with emotional problems characterized, for example, as guilt, anxiety, and jealousy. Spiritual changes, such as learning to "let go" (reflecting the third step of the 12 steps), and interpersonal problems including marital difficulties or involvement with sober people are other examples of the kinds of problems that emerge. The following examples illustrate these changes more specifically and indicate a move in the continuum from a more narrow focus to a wider expansion of interest and concern. These examples also illustrate the move away from alcohol, isolation toward more involvement with others, and the beginning of spiritual exploration.

At first: learning basic coping skills; learning to do things sober; learning to deal with depression and mood swings.
Now: dealing with anxiety—relationships with other people and high-stress situations; mood swings and very heavy conflicts with male–female relationships. More emphasis on spiritual growth; feel a real need to grow spiritually—maintain contact with my higher power.

First: fear above all
Now: accepting things as they come and working through something instead of against it.

First: thirst (colloquial for craving a drink), tranquilizers, guilt, fear of loneliness, closeness, women, image.
Now: first time in my life am starting to become "one of the guys"; also enjoy time with myself, still stuck with procrastination, coupled with impatience; also image and reality gap.

First: tolerance, keeping things "just for today" (like not being able to sleep because of worry about tomorrow); expectations of others.
Now: letting go of old ideas of happiness and performance expectations—to really feel for another human being and show it. Let go of the feeling a man will "make me happy."

How does the individual AA member experience focus on alcohol and initial interaction with the environment? In the transition phase and very early abstinence, the recovering alcoholic restricts social life to AA meetings. In later abstinence, people prepare for first evenings out—at a restaurant with spouse and old friends, for example. In the past, such an event automatically symbolized alcohol; without question a fine restaurant equaled fine wine. Relying on their education about alcoholism and their identities as alcoholics, individuals now determine several possible courses of action. With a solid identity they construct a plan of action: They can go to dinner, enjoy the company of old friends, and give new symbolic meaning to the social experience of eating out. They learn to dissociate fine wine from fine cuisine by reminding themselves they are alcoholic: One drink will destroy the pleasure they are now receiving.

Even with a solid alcoholic identity, such a comfortable adjustment may be far down the road. Behavioral patterns and old associations stimulating a craving for alcohol may still be too strong. Individuals may not trust their own ability to say no. They may suspect that the environment of the restaurant and old friends will generate a desire to drink. The environmental pull toward alcohol can dilute the knowledge they have gained about alcoholism and shatter their alcoholic identities. They may suddenly even decide they are not alcoholic—one drink won't hurt: "I can now control my drinking." Such a choice sends these individuals back to the drinking side of the spiral with an emphasis on control.

Aware of their danger, they see several choices that emphasize the behaviors of abstinence and strengthen the cognitive identification. They can cancel the dinner and go to an AA meeting instead (a concrete behavioral return to the alcohol axis), they can telephone an AA friend just before dinner to gain support for their abstinent stance (strengthen their behavioral plan and the identity as an alcoholic), or they can take an AA pamphlet in their wallet and refer to it in a moment of temptation or anxiety. In this case, they carry a concrete object representation of the alcohol axis along with them. Or, on this first venture out, they may choose AA dinner companions instead of old friends, thus actively ensuring ongoing external support and the continuing identification on the alcohol axis.

Behavioral, cognitive, and object representations of the alcohol identification are absolutely necessary during this period. Individuals fear they will lose their new identities if they stray too far or too long from a concrete AA alcohol focus. The new identity and new behaviors are not internalized. Individuals need constant external behavioral, cognitive, and object reminders that provide external support.

With successful experiences on the environmental axis, individuals begin to move more freely, developing a pattern of living that incorporates a steady and wide-ranging flow of movement on and around the central alcohol axis.

Interpretation of Self and Others

The alcohol focus emphasizes staying dry behaviorally and is characterized by extreme dependency on external sources of support in the early phase of recovery. As the new identity and the foundation of abstinence become more secure, other changes occur. There is a decreasing content focus on alcohol, although the behavioral focus continues and there is an increase in attention and awareness to other concerns and interests. Much attention to alcohol may be occurring outside of AA meetings with members beginning to pay close attention to the 12 steps.

This shift is characterized in the model by increasing involvement with, value of, and interpretation of self and others. This component reflects Bateson's

PHASES: 1. DRINKING   2. TRANSITION   3. EARLY RECOVERY   4. ONGOING RECOVERY

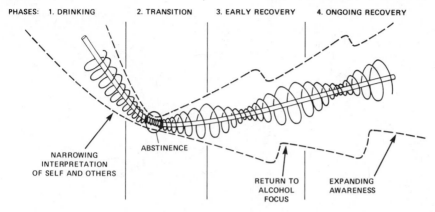

Figure 2-7.   Interpretation of self and others.

change in epistemology, from a view of self at the center to a view of self as part of a larger whole. Individuals are engaged in self-exploration through the 12 steps and are beginning to incorporate a belief in a higher power (Figure 2-7).

Movement in the model is now multidimensional, regulated according to the need for an active behavioral, cognitive or symbolic identification on the alcohol axis (Figure 2-8). As an alcoholic identity and the behaviors consistent with that identity are internalized, the alcohol axis becomes increasingly abstract, serving as an underlying secure foundation and the base of identification from which individuals venture out. Concrete behavioral and cognitive focus moves from a constant emphasis on alcohol and attendance at AA meetings to involvement in many other life concerns with movement out into the spiral and thus into the world outside of AA meetings.

Changes such as occupational adjustments, emotional difficulties, the learning of new behaviors, and spiritual and interpersonal exploration emerge. The process slowly begins to change from passive identification to more active involvement in the beginnings of separation and a move toward self-awareness and autonomy. The environmental spiral broadens as members are now able to relinquish an alcohol focus (dry), increase autonomy, and direct their attention to sobriety—the state and quality of their lives (Maxwell, 1984).

Movement along the continuum is now characterized by continuing interaction between the alcohol axis and the other two components (Figure 2-9). In addition to the major problems and conflicts, respondents accent a wide variety of concrete life changes and adjustment in their life view. The tendency of most members to use words such as "learning," or words with a cast of action such as "move," "stop," or "question," adds further evidence that recovery involves expansion in frame of reference, acquisition of new attitudes, behaviors, and

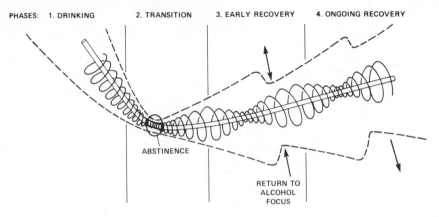

PHASES: 1. DRINKING   2. TRANSITION   3. EARLY RECOVERY   4. ONGOING RECOVERY

ABSTINENCE

RETURN TO
ALCOHOL
FOCUS

Figure 2-8.   Interpretation of self and others: Movement.

beliefs, as well as active participation. This expansion is illustrated by four examples that show changes in attitude and value, and two examples that show the move from passive to active stance and the assertion of autonomy.

To be less structured in my thinking as well as my actions. To keep my mouth shut. To stop dealing in absolutes and to stop insisting on knowing everything.

Accepting change as a value rather than as something to be feared. Coming to question old values and people. Seeing myself as a very different person than I thought.

Learning to live with someone instead of despite someone else; learning to become tolerant and loving—not perfectly by any means but to try because even though it's hell a lot of times the rewards are great.

I had to change my attitude toward: 1. the necessity of alcohol to get along in sophisticated society, 2. the need for any type of crutch, 3. life in general—I came to realize that each of us creates our own opportunities and sets our own limitations.

I have learned to be able to do things that are right for me rather than having to depend on other people to make me feel that my existence is worthwhile.

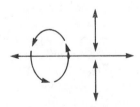

Figure 2-9.   The three axes: Integrated movement.

My problem is finances. I have always kept myself in debt so I have to do without. The biggest was leaving my family. I couldn't stay sober there. Learning to get off my ass and do it. Oh, and one of the first biggies—shutting my mouth.

A merger in the two lines of the continuum is reflected in the following example as the individual describes the necessity of altering his environment to protect his sobriety:

Reduce work load and targets to attainable levels—thus eliminating stress threatening my sobriety.

Another person illustrates the emergence of internal exploration and the importance of attitudinal change:

I've become more confident of my resources and knowledgeable about my limitations. Looking at my life and who I am is a major event.

The experience of other disorders and symptoms appears to be a common and important aspect of recovery (see Appendices F and G) varying in degree from severe disturbance to lighter forms of discomfort, often recognized as normal or natural aspects of living. A number of other researchers who have studied abstinence since this research was completed agree (Blane, 1977; Kurtines, 1978; Massman, 1979; Rubington, 1980; Wiseman, 1981; and Khantzian, 1980). Respondents indicated a high degree of awareness about themselves and the difficulties they were experiencing, reflecting a good deal of self-examination. Their ability to recognize and label their experiences represents advances in coping skills and in many cases, increased knowledge and ability to deal actively with their problems.

Depression (Weisman and Myers, 1980) is a common experience during all periods of abstinence, but is most frequent, severe, and frightening during the first year. Two-thirds of the sample experienced depression within the first year and many within the first days and weeks of abstinence suggesting that a honeymoon or "pink cloud" phase (a period of high spirits and high denial) is not as widespread as commonly believed or at least should not be presumed certain. Depression lasted for months or longer for almost one-third of the group, with several suffering severe depressions for more than a year. One-third reported feeling suicidal since becoming abstinent; strong evidence of the severity of depression.

Although members report needing a good deal of support during these times, the high percentage of respondents reporting depression suggests that it may be a necessary part of recovery. A vast majority of respondents report that their depressions occur in cycles and grow shorter and less intense with the passage of time. Surviving the first severe depression without drinking is a tremendously important achievement, raising self-esteem and providing individuals with a greater sense of their own strength and ability to cope.

Speculation about the possible causes for depression emphasizes the variety of changes occurring and differences in individual adjustment. Depression may be a characteristic, life-long problem involving manic depressive features for some. It also may be the first feeling to emerge after the deadening effects of alcohol. Depression may occur as a result of facing inadequacies, doubts, self and/or other destructive behavior, losses, guilt, shame, and emptiness, concerns noted already by members as important areas for exploration. Anxiety and feelings of hopelessness about really changing and/or fear of changing also may cause depression, as will the mourning for the loss of alcohol and the drinking way of life which Bean emphasizes.

Recognition of depression suggests a time of vulnerability and constriction with lowered defenses, corresponding to the data reported by women but not by men. Perhaps the latter can acknowledge initial depression more freely in retrospect. It also is possible that the "pink cloud" that men experience more than women in the first year is a reflection of denial of depression because they require a longer period for effective identification.

Two-thirds of the sample also reported the incidence of other disorders and symptoms. Not well defined by a specific time frame, these are nevertheless pervasive, and probably cover more severe depression. Depression and other symptoms are related to the alcohol focus; they serve to displace strong feelings about the alcohol and what the alcohol covered. Depression or other symptoms such as phobia or anxiety may also be a substitute for the alcohol or the response to loss.

The frequency of other disorders and symptoms and depression illustrates the intensity of emotion previously covered with alcohol and now emerging with abstinence. Examples of those experiencing anxiety include:

> Anxiety, fear, murderous rage, hatred, and anger; compulsion to drink; the insanity of being ashamed of my illness; harshly judgmental and critical of self. It seems to me now that my symptoms went farther back than my alcoholic drinking—fear of flying, riding in cars with others as drivers, and being buried alive, etc.

> Anxiety; scared I will die if I don't know what is going to happen. Indigestion; uptight situations. Overeating; afraid I won't get my share; have to fill my spiritual void. Fears of abandonment; people near me leave and I react like a baby.

Others experience phobias:

> Don't like elevators now (don't like to feel restrained); phobias; fear of being alone, heights, flying, elevators, crowds were all very much with me throughout my life until I was about three to four years sober; they have eased lately.

Still others overeat:

> I've been overeating compulsively since leaving Overeaters Anonymous; I just said screw it—I'm primarily AA and I can't handle both programs.

People who have experienced suicidal feelings or attempted suicide illustrate a depth of despair and in several cases an existential crisis emerging after abstinence. Such a crisis is noted to be an important element on the drinking spiral toward abstinence, known as "hitting bottom" along with the concept of "surrender." For some people such a downward spiral toward despair is repeated with abstinence:

> Shotgun suicide gestures at least twice because I felt unliked, unaccepted, unloved, useless, a failure, dead.

> Upon accepting my condition, I became aware that my life was in my hands, and I went through a period of appraisal if it was worth it.

> Suicide is just another way to run away. As time passes, I want to run away less from life.

> I was about two years sober and it seemed like it was just too hard and my whole world around me was falling apart (divorce, unhappy job, no action in the program, no God).

> Sometimes, if anxiety or depression is very severe, it seems that the ultimate escape—death—will provide relief, even though intellectually this is not so; also think of it when overwhelmed with feelings of futility—like what's the use? Nothing gets better anyway.

Other disorders and symptoms may represent expanded awareness and greater emotionality as a result of abstinence. They may be evidence of stress resulting from a movement away from the alcohol axis with increasing involvement in other life concerns.

With ongoing interaction and expansion of the continuum, it becomes clear that abstinence is more than a mirror image or reversal of the process of addiction. Sobriety entails new experiences, attitudes, and concerns for many. New and old issues in the environment are reexamined and reinterpreted from the new frame of reference. Much of the territory is unfamiliar, and in this sense, the process is not a "recovery" at all. Consciousness is broadened and a new language is acquired. People's experience of themselves and their world is different—more complex, sensitive and aware than ever before.

A sense of themselves as distinct individuals with particular needs and feelings is emerging. It is accented by daily cognitive and behavioral reminders that they are alcoholic and, therefore, always must give their abstinence the highest priority. The alcohol focus serves as the anchor and core of their new identity. They learn to focus on themselves positively by learning what they need to do to maintain sobriety. Nothing takes higher precedence.

When the steps necessary to maintaining abstinence are firm and beginning to be internalized, they venture out to establish new relationships and interactions with others in their lives, but always with the central confirming resolution that regardless of who I am with or where I am, I am an alcoholic and that means I do not drink. This identity provides a necessary sense of separateness and community at the same time and a structure from which to organize and interpret one's life.

Implications of the Model

This introduction to the phases of alcoholism recovery and the complex dynamics of the components describes a process of movement and change. It is a description of what happens to people when they stop drinking, reported by members of AA in their own terminology. It is a description of stages of recovery loosely defined from the reported experiences.

It is clear that the developmental model of alcoholism is not in itself equal to "treatment." It also is clear that no one mode of treatment is sufficient to deal with the constantly changing complexities of the process of recovery. It is not a report of the outcome of "treatment." The experiences of recovery may have included treatment for some—medical detoxification, inpatient alcohol program, psychotherapy before or after abstinence—but that treatment is a part of the process.

Because of the multiple components and changing needs over time that members described, a continuum emphasizing one dominant treatment mode is bound to fail at some point along the process. How then do we translate the experiences of sobriety and the dynamic model of alcoholism into a model of psychotherapeutic intervention and treatment? How can psychotherapists make use of the model to determine the most appropriate treatment at any given time? And how can a therapist use the model to change therapeutic emphasis with the speed and flexibility required by the patient? The dynamic model of alcoholism outlines the complex components that comprise the task or simultaneous tasks of recovery at any given time. The interpretation of these tasks in psychotherapeutic terms offers a first step in developing a successful partnership between AA and psychotherapy. It is to a theory of the integration of treatments that we next turn.

Chapter 3

Theoretical Perspectives

At its core, the alcoholism recovery process is one of construction and reconstruction of a person's fundamental identity and resultant view of the world. The proposed dynamic model of alcoholism is, therefore, primarily a developmental model of knowledge construction and reconstruction.

"Learning"—a developmental process—is accomplished through behavioral change, cognitive reorganization and restructuring, and object substitution and replacement. It involves parallel, simultaneous, and/or reciprocal interactions between behavioral, cognitive, and affective components. Likewise, the model encompasses behavioral, cognitive, and dynamic therapeutic treatment modes.

The research demonstrated that the disease of alcoholism demands an interactive, dynamic therapeutic approach, involving behavioral, cognitive, and dynamic therapies, singly and in combination throughout the course of treatment. It is the ability to correctly determine the task of therapy at any given period and tailor the approach to meet the specific needs of the patient that is most critical and most difficult in working with alcoholics.

What are the developmental tasks of the drinking, transition, early recovery, and ongoing recovery phases? What are the primary therapeutic treatments appropriate to each? What is the theoretical rationale for choosing and/or combining particular treatments?

Many theorists such as Mahler (1975) and Erickson (1963) have emphasized the importance of a developmental point of view. However, Piaget (1954) emphasizes both development and the process of knowledge construction. His theories, as interpreted by Greenspan (1979), are used here to describe an analogous developmental process in recovery.

THE DEVELOPMENTAL NATURE OF RECOVERY: A PIAGETIAN VIEW

Phase Development

In its broadest sense, active alcoholism is a primary behavior disorder—the act of taking a drink and the inability to stop—maintained and denied at the same time by a thinking disorder. The individual uses language and cognition to deny behavior. Thoughts, feelings, and behaviors mutually interact and vary; this process matches Mahoney's (1977) concept of reciprocal determinism. The loss of control that is diagnostic of alcoholism is a behavioral phenomenon exemplified by the act of taking a drink. The individual who is losing behavioral control must resort to a rearrangement of the cognitive schema to begin to explain uncontrolled impulses and behavior. The individual begins to build a defense centered on two key premises: denial of loss of control (behavioral) and the maintenance of an identity (cognitive) as a nonalcoholic.

The drinking alcoholic is, therefore, characterized by a belief structure that requires increasingly massive restriction of incoming information to be maintained. According to Piaget's concept of constructive structuralism, mental structures develop by taking in new sets of variables. Through processes of assimilation and accommodation, these structures evolve to new ones that become self-regulating at a new, higher, or expanded level of equilibrium. The drinking alcoholic can neither assimilate nor accommodate information about the realities of drinking behavior. Craik (1943) explains this well in describing a form of adaptation. He suggests that individuals narrow and distort the environment until their conduct fits it, rather than altering their behavior and expanding their knowledge to cope with the larger, real environment. As alcoholism progresses, it becomes more and more difficult to integrate behaviors into the existing belief structure. To preserve its integrity, the system must disregard information that is contrary to its basic assumptions. The reality—in this case, out of control drinking behavior—cannot be incorporated into the existing cognitive structure without an adaptation of that structure (Greenspan, p. 67). As a result, the continuing need for denial results in a massive reduction in individual consciousness.

The AA concept of hitting bottom defines an end point in that constrictive process. The structure can no longer accommodate the denial or distorted explanations of reality. The deepest beliefs—"I am not an alcoholic" and "I can control my drinking"—are challenged and a transformation occurs. The individual suddenly shifts beliefs and enters a process of new construction of a new structure of personal identity (Guidano and Liotti, 1983) in which behaviors, cognitions, and affects are congruent.

The turning point—what AA calls hitting bottom—may be likened to what Piaget calls the "grasp of consciousness." It appears as a sudden insight, but, in fact, may have been preceded by a gradual tacit process of new knowledge construction. In the transition phase, the individual succeeds in defining explicitly and incorporating an alternate vision of the self into the personal identity, thus making it a new point of reference and continuing comparison. The core of this alternate vision is the new identity as an alcoholic. The new structure is based on two beliefs: "I am an alcoholic" and "I cannot control my drinking." In this sequence, the shift in cognition precedes behavioral change. Individuals suddenly see that their drinking is out of control. Behavior change, from drinking to abstinence, hopefully (but not necessarily) follows.

For others, the sequence is reversed. They maintain their belief in control, but alter their behavior, changing from drinking to abstinence. For some, this, going on the wagon, is a temporary maneuver designed to regain control with a return to drinking anticipated. For others, the shift in behavior paves the way for the succeeding change in belief. Thus, there are individuals who try AA and abstinence and then slowly change their beliefs and their identities. The personal identity, "I am an alcoholic," is congruent with the behavior of abstinence.

Transition and early recovery phases must be viewed as primitive developmental levels; the transformation involves a total reorganization of actions, cognitions, and affects. The new beliefs—"I am an alcoholic" and "I cannot control my drinking"—outline the new behavior that will be congruent with these beliefs: abstinence. But very often, the individual does not know how to stay abstinent even though the new cognitions are now undeniable.

Piaget's framework and his theory that the roots of knowledge lie in behavior (Lewis, 1977) help us recognize this early developmental level and the need for emphasis on new behaviors that can reinforce and shape the new beliefs. If we think of the newly abstinent individual in early developmental terms, we can see that this individual is at a correspondingly primitive level of cognitive and affective development. Transition and early recovery, therefore, may be likened to infancy and early development. The emphasis in AA on action teaches, in a concrete way, the behaviors necessary to maintain abstinence. These behaviors build new action patterns that form new cognitive schema, which then order behaviors. However, some individuals are so defenseless at the point of transition that they can do nothing but alter basic, rote behaviors. Cognitive abilities are damaged or as yet nonfunctional. These individuals often require a sheltered and very structured program of early recovery that is protective and nurturing and that provides concrete instructions for new behavior.

The range and level of cognitive and affective equilibrium during transition is as restricted as those at the end of the drinking phase. The cognitive and affective structures based on the new epistemology are too new and undeveloped to integrate environmental stimuli; particularly if that stimuli is unsympathetic to the new belief structure and accompanying behaviors and, instead, emphasizes the old belief structure.

In transitional and early recovery phases, affect may be diffuse and overwhelming, absent, or contained. Acquisition of new behaviors and a new language to explain past and present emotions and behavior offers early protection against the fear of new and unknown affect. The primary emphasis on behavior and cognitive changes at this period is an essential protection. The emergence of affect, without a new concrete behavior plan and subsequently a new language to explain that affect, results in a return to drinking to achieve external control over internal feelings and impulses that are out of control.

The newly recovering person is at a primitive level of behavioral, cognitive, and affective development that corresponds to the new primitive structure; this requires a concrete and titrated therapeutic approach. The defenses and secondary process abstract reasoning that supported denial of alcoholism will not fit the new structure. The individual who appeared to operate at a higher cognitive and affective level during drinking now appears to have lost those abilities or regressed. The pull of the transition and early recovery phases is often toward a return to old defenses, most easily activated by picking up a drink. The ability to tolerate primitive emotions and an infantile need for dependency are critical components of these periods.

Many individuals react to this primitive state by activating defenses other than drinking (Bean, 1975a; Wallace, 1978). Denial of all other difficulties and denial of affect are common. The individual is free to concentrate solely on behavior. Reaction formation is a common defensive pattern. Individuals feel elated at the discovery that their alcoholism is transforming what was the worst possible identity into one of strength and freedom. Those who cannot make use of this mechanism are most likely to suffer severe depression in early recovery.

The process of recovery is one of new construction of self-knowledge that holds within it new behaviors, new language, and new affect that will be progressively synthesized and integrated into more mature cognitive and affective structures with greater ego flexibility and a higher equilibrium level. As the behaviors become solidified and internalized with the new cognitive structure, greater control is gained, but only within the new epistemology of loss of control. Instead of immediately substituting a new action for an impulse to drink—going to a meeting, making a call—the individual can now use language to exert control and think about the impulse and what triggered it. The individual begins to integrate the beginnings of affective understanding and expression with dynamic exploration and development.

In the beginning of this process, the new structure is bounded tightly by reminders of alcoholism, such as the predominance of the alcohol focus, attending many AA meetings, new AA friends, and discussions about alcohol, all serving to provide safety for primitive structures and functioning as the roots for cognitive and affective restructuring. The narrow structure provides the actions and language for reinforcement and guidelines that structure the new identity.

The beginning of expansion away from this concrete alcohol focus heralds progression and development. With new action patterns and cognitive controls in place, the individual can continue the developmental building process by expanding the range and depth of cognitive and affective equilibrium.

Ongoing recovery is characterized by the progressive development of higher order equilibrium states with greater ego flexibility. The maturing process of knowledge construction assimilates and accommodates new information into an existing structure centered on the beliefs—"I am an alcoholic" and "I cannot control my drinking."

Language Development

Piaget stresses the importance of the development of language as the mediator between emotional and cognitive development (Lewis, 1977). Several dynamic theorists provide additional weight to the fundamental importance of language in both facilitating and ordering the development of the new structure of abstinence.

Santostefano (1980) and Lewis (1977) consider the acquisition of language to be a critical developmental step, following the earlier and more primitive development of behavior and action patterns. Lewis suggests that inner language structures are derived from the earliest sensory motor schemas. In other words, action and behavior patterns form the foundation for language.

The acquisition of language is seen by all as a higher level of development. Language permits individuals to express behavior in more delayed, planned, indirect, and organized terms (Santostefano, 1980). The acquisition of a language of recovery is a critical factor in the developmental process. Without the development of a language that corresponds to the new behaviors of abstinence, the progression of recovery is stalled and maintained at the most primitive behavioral level. Thus, one sees individuals who are newly sober simply "going through the motions." They follow instructions for altering their behavior, but they can make no sense of these changes cognitively. As one newly abstinent individual stated, "All I know is behaviors—I am an acting thing."

The language of recovery provides an intermediary control between the impulse to drink and the act of doing so. As these theorists all point out, the early behavioral patterns (in this case drinking) are not erased but remain potentially active. If the higher level of language that corresponds to the new behaviors of abstinence is not developed, conscious behavioral control remains the only mediator between the impulse to drink and the act of doing so.

In the progression of recovery, behavioral action is a necessary first step in the developmental continuum, especially when the individual is dominated by the act of drinking or a predominance of impulses in the transition and early recovery phases. The emphasis is initially on action with a corresponding acquisition of new language. The developmental progression moves from more direct, less delayed behavioral expression of impulses to more indirect, delayed behavioral and ultimately cognitive expression.

Why is a new language so important in the transition and early recovery phases? According to Lewis (1977), "words have a concretizing effect as they provide labels, shape, and control over affects and fantasies." Lewis suggests that the more a child's cognition develops, as reflected in language procedures, the easier it is to understand feelings and make connections. Language enhances mastery and allows greater energy for cognitive growth. Conversely, cognitive leaps, which are reflected in language development, promote the mastery of emotions that is necessary for healthy growth and adaptation.

This reciprocal process is illustrated by the individual's progression in AA. At first, the emphasis is entirely behavioral. The individual will not comprehend the language, or may reject it, finding it corny or even superficial. The clichés that emphasize behavior may be viewed with disdain. As the individual progresses in abstinence, the language of AA and the steps take on new meaning and deeper significance. The language of control learned earlier with the behavioral emphasis now provides the base for further language and cognitive expansion.

New members hear from older members that the meaning of "the program," the 12 steps, will change over time. It is not unusual to hear an AA member's story change with the passage of time. Not only are events reinterpreted, but the language to describe them and the meanings attributed to them have changed and matured.

Key Development Concepts

Several developmental concepts—assimilation, accommodation, equilibration, and ego flexibility—can be used to describe the process of development and construction in alcoholism.

> Stated most simply, the equilibrium process is the process of bringing assimilation and accommodation into balanced coordination. (Flavell, 1963, p. 239)

> Assimilation is the taking in aspect of intelligence by which appropriate cognitive stimuli are drawn into or incorporated within a structure and accommodation is the change of a structure itself, which enables it to process a given stimulus. (Greenspan, p. 65)

The concept of ego flexibility as an indicator of the ego's ability to experience a broad range of thoughts, wishes, and feelings relates a flexible ego to a higher order equilibrium state (Greenspan, p. 67). The existing laws of transformation can deal with most cognitive events; a flexible ego deals with a variety of stimulus inputs within the existing structural organization. "Existing regulations and defenses are both flexible and stable enough to protect the ego's basic functions without resorting to accommodations that compromise the range of events dealt with (e.g. an ego constriction characterized by massive denial)" (Greenspan, p. 68).

The advanced drinking phase reflects the predominance of defensive operations and the resultant narrow, inflexible ego. Massive denial is necessary to preserve the now unstable and very narrow equilibrium.

The beginning process of recovery, with the congruent identity and behaviors of abstinence, represents a new structure with its own developmental processes of assimilation and accommodation. The phases of transition, early recovery, and ongoing recovery correspond developmentally to the progressive development of intelligence and internal intellectual structures. Psychoanalytic theorists offer a parallel concept of progressive development and synthesis of affective elements. (Greenspan, p. 71)

The importance of the developmental emphasis in the model of recovery is underscored by Piaget's idea that assimilations are possible only to the extent that they occur in the context of age-appropriate capacities and lead to a new accommodation only when they are close enough to age-appropriate capacities to tax the system and force it to alter itself. The process of recovery may be viewed as a progressive interplay between assimilation and accommodation organizing the development of a new, mature structure.

> Piaget's is a specific model of development that describes the alteration of the internal structure through action on the external environment; through this experience, a new internal structure is formed. Once the structure is formed, the organism is able to tie together different dimensions of the system. (Greenspan, p. 70)

This is a similar process to insight in psychoanalysis:

> Once the patient integrates an insight that enables him to synthesize a number of dimensions, there is a spreading of range of internal experience available to him and a generalization of conceptual base of the insight to other areas of his life. (Greenspan, p. 70)

It is the integration of Piagetian and dynamic concepts that forms the analogy for the ongoing dynamic process of recovery. That process involves the development of a new structure of the self, based on the new identity as an alcoholic. Within that new structure increasingly mature and complex behavioral cognitive and affective development occurs. This rudimentary explanation sets the stage for understanding the phase-specific developmental tasks of recovery (Table 3-1).

THE DEVELOPMENTAL TASKS OF RECOVERY

The Drinking Phase

The primary focus of advanced alcoholism is on alcohol. Most of the individual's energy and attention go into the maintenance of denial in order to preserve

TABLE 3-1. Phase-Specific Developmental Tasks of Recovery

Phase	Component	Epistemological frame	Therapeutic strategy
Drinking	Alcohol axis	1. I can control my drinking. 2. I am not an alcoholic.	*Cognitive:* Breakdown of belief system and denial. *Behavioral and dynamic:* to facilitate an epistemological shift. Object attachment is to alcohol.
Transition	Alcohol axis	1. I cannot control my drinking. 2. I am an alcoholic.	*Behavioral:* Emphasis on action, learning, new behaviors. *Cognitive:* Emphasis on identification with AA stories, learning new language of recovery. Object attachment to books, phone, AA meetings.
Early recovery	1. Alcohol axis a. Environment (b. Self–other)	1. I cannot control my drinking. 2. I am an alcoholic.	*Behavioral:* Same as transition. *Cognitive:* Same as transition. *Object attachment:* Same as transition. Also to sponsor, principles, and higher power. *Dynamic:* Emergence of affect, self-exploration through 12 steps, work with therapist.
Ongoing recovery	Alcohol Environment Self–other	1. I cannot control my drinking. 2. I am an alcoholic.	*Behavioral:* In place. Person practices behaviors of abstinence. Activates behavioral emphasis if necessary. Attends AA. *Cognitive:* In place. Person practices cognitions and language of abstinence. Activates cognitive emphasis by attending AA. Reading and talking with other alcoholics. Construction of new personal identity as alcoholic and reconstruction of past. *Dynamic:* Integration of affect with behaviors and identity as alcoholic. Uncovering, insight, self-exploration through 12 steps, work with therapist. *Object attachment:* To AA principles, book, meetings, higher power.

the two basic beliefs: "I am not alcoholic" and "I can control my drinking." The mature process of knowledge construction, characterized by a balance between assimilation and accommodation, ego flexibility, and equilibrium is severely hampered by the emphasis on denial. To maintain denial of alcoholism individuals must become selective in what they register. Only information that is considered to be in keeping with the structured self-image is retained and incorporated.

Guidano and Liotti (1983) describe a circular process of perception and cognition that maintains denial and, therefore, the closed system of personal identity. They suggest the selection of data maintains the perceived personal identity and that there is a strong tendency toward reconfirming that identity even with evidence to the contrary. Individuals engage in repeated attempts to control their drinking, such as switching drinks, applying new rules, or attributing the problem to something else. Even with repeated failure at solutions, individuals are unable to eliminate their attempts.

The problem is defined in a way that is coherent with the individual's subjective representation of reality. Typically, the drinking alcoholic will first deny that there is any drinking difficulty and then explain it as the logical reasonable consequence of another problem; for example, "I wouldn't drink so much if it weren't for my wife." Soon the individual must construct and invent a reality that externalizes the problem and thus provides the logical rationale for drinking. This process of construction becomes the thinking disorder that maintains and explains alcoholic drinking.

Denial, a primitive defense, requires the systematic exclusion or distortion of environmental data, resulting in a narrow range of what can be assimilated. Drinking individuals who may be capable of more mature cognitive organization in other arenas in which denial is not threatened, or, who operated at a high cognitive level of development before becoming alcoholic, now appear anchored at a level of primitive cognitive development corresponding to the preoperational phase outlined by Piaget. This level of thinking is concrete (Erwin, 1981).

The drinking phase is characterized by the predominance of the behavior, or action mode, that is, the repeated act of drinking; the most primitive phase in Piaget's developmental schema (Piaget, 1954). The action is supported by an equally primitive level of cognitive operation that is characterized by denial. It is the analysis of these very behaviors and cognitions that is the target for change; analysis that centers on the breakdown of denial. That breakdown is targeted at the core of the individual's personal identity as a nonalcoholic. As Guidano and Liotti (1983) explain, such a breakdown can be achieved by building a relationship that respects the patient's personal identity as long as possible and does not confirm the basic pathogenic assumptions.

The therapist must know that the central problem is the loss of control and not be sidetracked or fooled by the patient's alternate constructions. The therapist then helps the patient break down the structure of beliefs that maintains the false personal identity. It is false because the patient knows at a deep level that loss of control of drinking is the problem. The breakdown of denial involves making this tacit knowledge explicit.

The closed system of the drinking alcoholic is maintained by the interaction between behaviors and cognition. The repeated behavior of drinking with loss of control creates continuing dissonance and threat to the personal identity. Breakdown of both the cognitions and the behavior is essential. A purely behavioral approach focuses either on gaining control to align the behavior with the belief in control, or behavioral abstinence is felt as dysphoric; it is not necessary because the individual does not perceive him or herself as an alcoholic.

Unless the core belief about being alcoholic is altered, behavioral attempts at abstinence will be undermined by the concomitant thinking disorder. As Mahoney (1977) notes, an individual cannot achieve an insight outside of the framework of the current cognitive structure. The individual who still believes in control cannot also see him or herself as an alcoholic. The system stays closed. Core beliefs are maintained despite evidence to the contrary.

The Transition Phase

The major and often sole focus of the transitional phase is on alcohol. The transitional phase signals the start of a new developmental structure, based on the new identity. It is a primitive developmental level and, therefore, centers on action to build the new structure of self-knowledge.

The emphasis on alcohol provides the concrete directions for new behaviors that support and define the new identity. The corresponding development of a new language that dictates behavioral action offers the beginnings of cognitive control. Typically, in the transitional phase, the individual is too confused or frightened to integrate the new language and cognitions. Simple behavioral imitation may be all that is possible.

The transitional phase is characterized by the shift in the core personal identity. The individual moves from a belief in control to acceptance of loss of control and to the corresponding acceptance of being alcoholic. For interpreting the world, individuals with this new identity will develop a new "ordering schema" through the ongoing process of knowledge construction and the development of cognitive controls with an emphasis on action during the transitional and early recovery phases.

It is through the actions and behaviors of abstinence that new self-knowledge can be constructed and uncovered. Cognitive and affective development proceed from this action base and from the acquisition of a new language that begins concurrently.

According to Piaget (Greenspan, p. 32), the new structure encompasses new sets of variables and evolves into a new structure that becomes self-regulating or closed on a new level. The new structure operates at a very narrow and primitive equilibrium, unable to integrate environmental input that does not directly support the new alcoholic identity (Piaget, 1970).

The acquisition of knowledge is not passive, especially at the sensory motor and prelinguistic levels of cognitive adaptation and intellectual development according to Piaget (Greenspan, p. 58). To know the object, the subject must act on it and therefore transform it. A new structure is constructed as the result of interactions between the subject and the object; in this case, between the individual and the new objects and environment of abstinence, such as AA meetings, literature, and the experiences of other AA members.

In the transitional phase, the individual remains anchored to patterns of organizing reality typical of primitive thinking. Therefore, the new level and method of learning must be consistent with that primitive pattern. Imitation and identification form the behavioral and cognitive modes of learning.

According to Guidano and Liotti (1983) imitation is the behavioral side of modeling and identification the cognitive. The latter is possible only with the acquisition of new rules and beliefs. With identification, the individual actively (although perhaps unconsciously) selects aspects of the model's attitude to imitate and reconstructs these data on the basis of the cognitive structure the person already possesses.

The new identity and beliefs constitute the core of a new cognitive structure. The focus on alcohol structures the selection of information that now will constitute the new structure. A focus away from alcohol runs the risk of interfering with the new building process, particularly if the focus is incompatible with the new identity. In the transitional phase, individuals imitate the behaviors of abstinent AA members and begin to selectively identify with the attitudes and beliefs of those individuals.

Whereas identification is predominantly a cognitive process, it also has a component of object attachment. As individuals shift their object and behavioral attachment away from alcohol, a concrete emotional and representational attachment develops to AA and to the individuals within it, and this becomes the basis for identification. Individuals shift a behavioral attachment from drinking alcohol to attendance at AA meetings, reading, and supportive telephone calls. They also shift an object attachment to the identification of the attitudes and beliefs of abstinence. For some, older AA members become the ego ideals around which the attachment and identification can occur. For others, the writings become the object of identification. The Big Book presents many "stories" with which new and old members can identify.

The choice of therapeutic treatment or combinations of treatments at any point along the continuum is determined by the level of development of the new structure. Because the new structure is so primitive, the need for an action focus to develop the sensory motor and prelinguistic aspects of self-knowledge is primary. The action focus, that is, the behaviors of abstinence, becomes the base on which subsequent knowledge construction or reconstruction occurs.

The development of new knowledge is accomplished through an assimilation and accommodation that produces alterations in the new structure. The anxiety that accompanies the shift from assimilation to accommodation is often experienced as a fear of drinking or a return to the old belief that drinking can be controlled. That anxiety dictates the need for a behavioral focus to strengthen the new action base of knowledge before integrating new learning.

Gradually, from the point of transition, the individual begins to construct a new behavioral cognitive and affective structure with ongoing assimilation and accommodation and an ever widening range of equilibrium. A return to the alcohol focus and the behaviors of abstinence is solidifying when incompatible environmental input is threatening to the new structure. The process of assimilation involves "taking in" from the environment new information that supports the new identity or reinterpreting old information from the point of view of the new identity. With the processes of new construction and reconstruction of the personal identity, the individual can proceed toward reorganizing his or her attitudes toward reality. The "taking in" also involves uncovering what was formerly denied or covered by the use of alcohol.

The distinction between imitation and identification emphasizes the need for a combined behavioral–cognitive approach. Successful movement into the transitional phase and the subsequent development of a new equilibrium requires congruence between behavior and cognition, between imitation and identification.

The individual imitates the behaviors of abstinence and reinforces the behavior with a congruent identity. (I am alcoholic and, therefore, I do not drink. I take the actions (I behave) that reinforce my identity as an alcoholic.) In AA, the individual hears the concrete behavioral message: "Don't take the first drink, stay away from slippery places, and go to 90 meetings in 90 days." The individual also hears the cognitive corollary: Remember, "I am alcoholic and it's the first drink that gets me drunk." Individuals who struggle with abstinence may be in conflict with behavior and cognition. The individual may accept the identity as an alcoholic but be unable to perform the actions to sustain abstinence.

Higher level defensive operations or an intellectual focus can often interfere with the development of a behavioral base of abstinence. Individuals often believe ironically that behavior can be changed without altering behavior. That is, the individual should be able to stop drinking without changing behavior, substituting new behavior, or altering environment. Armchair psychotherapy often contributes to this intellectual interference. It is seductive to believe that one can think about a problem and solve it intellectually. The individual may be able to accept the reality of loss of control from the armchair but cannot alter the actions to support that insight. The therapist must understand the behaviors necessary to abstinence in order to facilitate movement.

Alternatively, the individual may abstain, but not believe he or she is alcoholic. Without the very primitive solidification of new behavior, a return to drinking will be imminent.

In the transition and early recovery phases a constant attention to the alcohol focus dictates the way in which new and old information will be perceived and integrated into the new personal identity.

The Early Recovery Phase

The period of early recovery is a more stable continuation of the transitional phase. The emphasis remains on solidifying behaviorally and cognitively the new identity as an alcoholic with the corresponding belief in loss of control. The focus remains primarily on alcohol with beginning movement into the environment. That movement away from the alcohol focus starts the process of interaction and reciprocal construction.

According to Piaget (Greenspan, p. 77), the external experience interacts with and provides the impetus for the further differentiation of the existing structure. The new cognitive scheme reflects and repeats the action patterns that generated it. Action and cognition now reciprocally codetermine subsequent development. The individual is engaged in selective attention and perception toward the task of developing the new schema of being alcoholic.

A new logical structure is developing. Individuals begin to construct a "story" that attacks their former logic and behavior and reinforces the new. That story is the AA drunkalogue in which individuals tell "what it was like, what happened, and what it is like now."

The continuing focus on alcohol allows for the firm development of the base of behavioral and cognitive knowledge. Often in the early movement away from an alcohol focus, the individual is faced with the threat of old action and cognitive patterns. Individuals intuitively recognize this threat as they chuckle together about the lure of alcoholic thinking or old ideas. In an AA meeting, one can hear many references to the danger of old cognitive patterns. For example, individuals share the difficulties they have remembering that they are alcoholic and refusing a drink at the Christmas office party. The permanence of the old patterns is not disturbed initially. Instead of "going for a drink" after an AA meeting, members go for coffee. It is a substitute rather than an immediate shift in pattern.

In early recovery, a continuing repetition of the new behavioral and cognitive patterns serves as an essential anchor for maintaining the stability of the new identity. The individual is continually reinforcing new knowledge by emphasizing that the new identity is correct and the old incorrect. Integration of new behaviors and language contributes to this reinforcement.

With new action patterns and cognitive schema firm, the processes of assimilation and accommodation—movement into the spiral and the expansion of that spiral—can proceed without disrupting the new schema. These need to be securely in place so they may order new perceptions and construction.

At some point in early recovery (typically during the first year), an affective component emerges. At the transitional phase, the individual is characterized by an absence of or narrow range of affect. Often individuals do not know that they have feelings because their feelings were covered or neutralized by alcohol. An absence of feeling is a common characteristic of early sobriety.

For others, feeling is present but reduced. Often individuals may continue with feelings of despair, depression, and hopelessness that accompanied their drinking, or they may feel elation due to abstinence. Regardless of the feelings, individuals are instructed to emphasize behavior and not to act on feelings.

As affect emerges, it will be integrated with the new behaviors and cognitive schema of abstinence. The affect will now codetermine the subsequent processes of assimilation and accommodation and the progressive development of the new personal identity.

The period of early recovery may be characterized by high denial and therefore a continuing narrow equilibrium. Existing defenses, as Bean (1975a) describes are primitive and neither stable nor flexible. An individual cannot recognize certain feelings as his or her own because the emotional range congruent with his or her self-image is limited.

According to Piaget (Greenspan, p. 69), in early cognitive development, the child cannot hold two dimensions. For example, the child can see only length. The ability to hold two dimensions comes with advances in cognitive development. In early sobriety, the individual can grasp only the cognitive focus on alcohol and being alcoholic. If that attention is shifted, the individual may lose the footing, "forget" that he or she is alcoholic. A young child must deny new feelings or external events that do not fit the picture of self (Greenspan, p. 71). At this stage the new picture of self is primitive and often undifferentiated, and much denial may be necessary.

As affects emerge and the individual begins interacting with the environment, the stability of the ego and internal object relations are altered. Initially, the individual must move to the alcohol focus to deal with the threat. This means that the individual attends more AA meetings and increases cognitive attention to being alcoholic. In cognitive and dynamic terms, this represents a regression before a new leap in assimilation or accommodation or a move to a new affective development level.

The rhythmic mechanism of the rituals of AA provides the behavior and cognitive ordering that members return to periodically as a part of the momentum of development. Object attachment remains to the behaviors of abstinence, substitutes for alcohol and now through identification with members of AA. In early recovery, individuals often choose a sponsor or actively engage in selecting various members of AA with whom to identify. Behaviors, cognitions, affects, and attachments now order the ongoing construction and reconstruction process.

With the introduction of affect, the process of dynamic exploration and understanding also begins. Members begin to tackle self-exploration through the 12 steps. A move from purely supportive treatment to a more dynamic, insight-oriented psychotherapy now may be a beneficial addition. Before early recovery, insight psychotherapy may be useful to facilitate behavioral and cognitive solidification. However, insight that displaces the primary behavioral cognitive focus, or interferes with the new base of knowledge construction, may create high levels of anxiety and confusion that dictate a return to old thinking and behavior patterns, that is, drinking. The primary therapeutic emphasis in early recovery remains behavioral and cognitive. Individuals are altering action patterns and developing a new cognitive schema for ordering and interpreting the world. With this solid base, integration of dynamic exploration is possible.

The Ongoing Recovery Phase

Ongoing recovery is characterized by the continuous interaction of three component axes: alcohol, environment, and self and other. The behaviors of abstinence have become more routine and even may feel natural or syntonic for some. The new cognitions and the development of a new language are well rooted and integrated with the identity as an alcoholic. As a result of a continuing active attention to behaviors and cognitions—attendance at meetings and reading, for example—the individual now focuses on self-exploration through the 12 steps and perhaps with a therapist.

The identity is firmly rooted in the beliefs "I am alcoholic and I cannot control my drinking." Through the developmental processes of knowledge construction and reconstruction, the individual has defined a more comprehensive, complex story and often a corresponding intricate understanding of "what it is like now." Development in all modes—behavioral, cognitive, affective, and attachment—is more mature. As Piaget outlined, many individuals in ongoing recovery now resemble adolescents in their development.

Ongoing recovery is a process of progressively more adequate equilibrium states, marked by greater mobility, field of application, permanence, and stability. The constructive process develops from interactions between the organism and environment and the action of the organism on the environment in a reciprocal ongoing process. Communication is an essential element of this process (Rappaport, 1951).

In ongoing recovery, the continuing communication provided by the structure and content of the AA meeting provides just such stimulus to mature development. Interactions within the environment of AA and outside of AA provide a continuing external experience that interacts with and provides the impetus for further differentiation of the existing structure. In both analytic and Piagetian schemes (Greenspan, p. 82), through feedback from the environment, the child gets a beginning sense of his or her own boundaries. Soon, through continuing feedback, the child begins the first imitative movements that provide the base for internalization and structure formation.

In Piaget's terms, ongoing recovery can be primarily characterized according to the concepts of ego flexibility and equilibrium. Ego flexibility is an "indicator of the ego's ability to experience a broad range of thoughts, wishes, and feelings without pathological defensive operations . . ." (Greenspan, p. 67). A flexible ego is related to a higher order equilibrium state that can assimilate new information without major accommodations. According to Piaget, a flexible ego can deal with a variety of inputs (affect, human interaction) within its existing structural organization. Existing defenses are both flexible and stable so that the individual doesn't have to resort to accommodations that compromise the range of events dealt with (Greenspan, p. 68).

Such stable development, characterized in the model by an expanded continuum, is rarely operative until well into ongoing recovery. The early years of ongoing recovery are characterized much more by a stable core of behaviors and identification, with wide fluctuations in assimilation, accommodation, ego flexibility, and equilibrium.

After the period of early recovery with its emphasis on identification, affect emerges and becomes a routine aspect of ongoing construction and integration. The emergence and integration of affect characterize ongoing recovery and now combine with behaviors and cognitions to alter and determine the new developing structure.

Wide fluctuations in the continuum are not uncommon as individuals struggle with new affect and new insight resulting from self-exploration through the 12 steps and perhaps more uncovering work with a psychotherapist.

Movement of the continuum encompasses three continuing interactive levels: the alcohol focus, interactions with the environment, and changes in the structure, affecting interpretation of self and other.

In ongoing recovery, the stability of the ego and internal object relations will, for the most part, not be altered dramatically by changes in feelings. This new stability is very different from early recovery, a time when a sudden change in feeling state is interpreted as a severe threat and, therefore, activates the behavioral and cognitive return to an alcohol focus.

From the point of transition and the acquisition of a new epistemology, "transformations now account for change within the system that constitutes the structure, thus permitting a process of movement which yet remains within the boundaries of the system." It becomes self-regulating, with input processed by the structure which then becomes part of it (Greenspan, p. 75).

The long-term maintenance of abstinence (behavioral) and the corresponding development of a new structure (cognitive and dynamic) result in internalization of behavior. The initial rhythmic behavior patterns become the primary building blocks of a new internal structure that is progressively more self-regulating. Ongoing recovery may be broadly characterized as a process of increasing internalization and self-regulation with concrete behavioral and cognitive supports much less frequently required to maintain stability.

With the early developmental levels of behavior and cognitions more firmly rooted, the individual demonstrates the capacity for higher level development and integration in all modes. The development of a new language moves the individual from an action basis of control of drives and impulses (if you have an urge to drink, go to a meeting) to control through language. Individuals remind themselves they are alcoholic, emphasizing the behavioral correlates, "I tell myself I am alcoholic and don't pick up a drink." But now they also examine the source of anxiety generated in the present. Through the fourth step, moral inventory and later a continuing daily inventory, they engage in a process of uncovering self-analysis. By understanding, accepting, and changing what are called in AA "character defects" they become much more aware and, thereby, continue to build and alter the personal identity.

As Bean noted, the individual also has progressed into higher order defense mechanisms that correspond to the higher level of development in other areas. The more mature behavioral, cognitive, and defensive structures permit deeper self-exploration and the continuing integration of more complex and conflictual affect.

The level and degree of comfort versus anxiety and the depth of self- and interpersonal exploration determine the continuing nature and focus of ongoing recovery. Individuals often follow a routine with integrated behavioral, cognitive, and dynamic components continuously operative.

In summary, alcoholism may be viewed analagously to a largely Piagetian development process with specific developmental and therapeutic tasks appropriate at each stage. Within the broad concept of development, the critical process of recovery is one of knowledge construction and reconstruction.

Alcoholism is primarily a behavioral and cognitive disorder maintained by a faulty core belief. Altering that belief—shifting identity from nonalcoholic to alcoholic—involves a major transformation in identity and, thus, heralds the beginning of a new developmental process and structure of the self. Recovery involves integrating new behavioral, cognitive, and affective elements into the new personal identity as an alcoholic.

This complicated process becomes comprehensible and workable when viewed analogously to several schools of behavior and developmental theory. The necessity for integrating behavioral, cognitive, and dynamic theories underscores the multifaceted process of alcoholism and recovery. It emphasizes that human beings cannot be understood in one-dimensional terms and that a singular therapeutic approach is certain to be inadequate at some point along the developmental continuum.

With this grounding of the dynamic model in developmental theory defining the developmental task of each stage of recovery and the most appropriate therapeutic strategy, we now can examine each stage of alcoholism and integrate theory and practice.

PART TWO

Clinical Applications

Chapter 4

Drinking

THE TURN TOWARD ALCOHOL

Developing alcoholism is characterized by changes in drinking behavior and changes in thinking. The individual is characterized by an increasing need for alcohol and a corresponding increase in the denial of that need. This behavioral and cognitive emphasis is characterized in the model as an increasing focus on alcohol and a narrowing of other interests, relationships, and activities. The process of developing alcoholism requires the exclusion of any incoming information that might challenge the behavior of drinking or the accompanying denial and rationalization.

The individual is therefore enclosed by a view of the self and world based on a belief in self-control. This belief colors all incoming information and interpretation of the environment, self, and others. It requires an emphasis on the defensive maneuvers of denial and rationalization, which results in an increasing distortion of the external environment and interpretation of self and others. The progression of drinking is not an expansion of self-knowledge, characterized by the processes of assimilation and accommodation, but rather a narrowing, restrictive process. Incoming information from the environment and knowledge about the self must be construed and constructed in a way that supports the denial of loss of control.

The primary focus is on alcohol, the drinking behavior, and the primary cognitive focus is on denial of that behavior. The structure is narrow, rigid, and inflexible, a closed thinking system as Rokeach described (1960). The individual becomes increasingly isolated, unable to integrate new information, and dominated by both a behavioral and a cognitive focus on alcohol in an ever narrowing, constrictive progression.

Patterns of Development

A number of theorists have developed categories of alcoholism and different patterns of development (Royce, 1981). There is general agreement today that alcoholism is probably better defined as alcoholisms with varying signs, symptoms, and developmental patterns.

One of the best known patterns is the typology developed by Jellinek (1960) distinguishing alpha, beta, and gamma alcoholics according to drinking style. In AA there is recognition of both different styles and different developmental patterns (AA, 1955). Some members of AA describe themselves as "daily drinkers," whereas others followed a "periodic" pattern, drinking alcoholically in time-limited binges, without a compulsion to drink in between.

Some drinkers describe the pace of their developing alcoholism as slow, but others move from nonalcoholic "social drinking" into alcoholism quite rapidly. Research on women alcoholics (Gomberg, 1976; 1977) highlights their more frequent tendency toward rapid, "telescoped," development, moving from non-problematic drinking into advanced alcoholism within a period of months, seeming to bypass the identified early and middle developmental stages (Jellinek, 1960).

Alcoholics in AA provide another variable in relating their experiences. Some describe an "invisible line," the point at which they moved from social drinking into alcoholism. But other AA members never crossed such a line. They describe themselves as "always alcoholic," "alcoholic from the start," or "alcoholic before I ever took a drink." These individuals have never experienced what others call social drinking, that is, the ability to stop drinking once started or to experience the pleasures of one or two drinks with no wish or need for more. These individuals who were always alcoholic began their drinking alcoholically; they were dominated from their first drink by a compulsion to drink with no sense of internal control that would signal the need or wish to stop.

The children of alcoholics often fit this latter pattern. Although the combination of factors, genetic, environmental, and psychological, involved in the transmission of alcoholism is not yet well understood, it is well documented that alcoholism runs in families (Goodwin and Guze, 1974; Goodwin, 1971; Goodwin et al., 1973; Schuckit et al., 1972).

In our work with the adult children of alcoholics, we have traced a constant theme, regardless of present or past drinking behavior. These individuals all fear that they are alcoholic by nature, suggesting, "It's in my genes," "It's in my skin," "I'm afraid I'm just like my father," or it is inevitable that they will "turn into" alcoholics (Cermak and Brown, 1982; Brown and Beletsis, in press) unless they exercise a constant self-control and vigilance over their own out of control impulses.

Many children of alcoholics become alcoholics readily, following the dominant family pattern. Others do not; they concentrate instead on disidentifying, on not being like the alcoholic. Still, for both, the focus on alcohol is a predominant aspect of their lives. For these individuals, the focus on alcohol develops early, as they struggle to make sense of parental drinking behavior and distorted thinking patterns. For this group, there is no invisible line and no discernible "turn toward alcohol," a point that can be defined for others.

Although preoccupation with alcohol and addiction may develop slowly, it is still possible to recognize the beginning of an addiction before the addicted person is medically diagnosable (Operation CORK, 1982). A major characteristic of any addiction is the individual's behavioral and cognitive preoccupation with a substance and an overwhelming compulsion to have it. Early recognition requires examination of the individual's daily structure and habitual thinking processes, that is, examination of these cognitive and behavioral patterns.

With alcoholism, both the preoccupation with not being alcoholic and a focus on alcohol grow, eventually encompassing the individual's life. Two factors, the availability of alcohol and the opportunity to drink, become the only main criteria for personal decision making. Relationships and activities not related to alcohol, such as church activities and association with nondrinking friends, are replaced by drinking activities and drinking friends.

Subtle though it may be, the individual's life becomes gradually dominated by alcohol. This change in style of life may be characterized as a turn toward alcohol; alcohol begins to serve as the organizing principle in life. This turn is the point at which the individual ceases to choose alcohol freely and begins to need it. The need for alcohol becomes the central focus (most often unconscious) and, in effect, the organizer of the individual's behavior and thinking. The need to include more and more alcohol in one's life without disturbing the central belief in self-control becomes the dominant and incompatible focus of daily life.

> I loved the way drinking made me feel—warm, sexy, funny. I always felt out of it—frumpy and unattactive. With alcohol I could soar—feel sexual and be sexual. It was my freedom from my troubled adolescence. As soon as I discovered it, I looked for situations in which I could drink. I began to date older men and to run with a drinking crowd. My old friends seemed boring and stodgy to me.

> The world is divided into two kinds of people: drinkers and nondrinkers. I am a drinker and these are the people I seek.

> As I look back, I realize that alcohol was playing an increasingly prominent role in my life though I couldn't see any problems. My wife and I grew comfortable with our nightly cocktail, which became two and then three. We joined a wine-tasting social group and often built our weekend entertainment around tailgate parties or Sunday brunches. I became noted for my gin fizzes. Our lives slowly involved a lot of alcohol everyday, but not in a way that seemed problematic to us or anyone else. We gave up cycling together and reading in the evenings but it seemed like a good trade-off. We were on the way up and felt we belonged to an active, attractive social group.

The Secret Partner: Family Adaptations

Alcohol becomes the organizing principle for the family as well as the alcoholic. Faced with the threat of the reality of alcoholism, family members must fit into the denial pattern. The adult child of an alcoholic explains the guiding principles of her family:

1. There is no alcoholism in this family.
2. Don't tell anyone.

Because of the central importance of alcohol and the equal significance of denial, the presence of alcohol, that is, the reality of the drinking behavior, often functions as an additional family member. Alcohol is somewhat like an in-law who had always lived with the family or who has moved in to stay. The alcohol is special to the alcoholic, like a secret partner. It is an intruder to the rest of the family members who must make major adaptations in their personal relationships within the family and outside it. They also must make continuing adaptations in their perceptions, often developing the same distorted thinking necessary to maintain what is now the family's denial (Brown and Beletsis, in press). As a result, the "turn toward alcohol" may be characterized from the point of view of the individual alcoholic or the family as a whole. Chapter 8 examines the family in detail.

Each family has a different way of including this new secret family member in the family structure. An alcoholic mother illustrates her adaptation as she made the turn toward alcohol:

> I had four children and was very active in daytime school affairs. It was no problem. I had a standing policy; I volunteer in the morning and I "take" in the car pool. I could never "clean up" or "pick up" because I couldn't predict what shape I would be in when it came time to pick up.

This kind of adaptation to alcohol eventually extends to the other family members as alcohol becomes the dominating force around which rules and rituals are constructed and enacted.

> The best time to ask my mother for extra money is at four o'clock in the afternoon. She is most relaxed then and most likely to say yes. I never ask her for anything in the morning. She's too grouchy. But it has to be pretty close to four. If I wait till Dad comes home, she is often upset, or they're arguing. Yes, four o'clock is best.

> I should know better! You have to call home before 11 a.m. or my parents forget what we talked about. I really slipped up this time. I forgot my parents' anniversary and had to call late that day. My parents were drunk and I got a letter a few days later chastizing me for forgetting to call.

Describing alcohol as a secret partner often enables the patient to see how alcohol was the primary bond in the establishment of a relationship. The "alcoholic marriage" is a prime example:

> My husband and I found each other through alcohol. We met in a single's bar, dated over Bloody Marys, champagne, white wine, and candlelight, and built our

marriage around the cocktail hour. It's a special time for us. We both attribute "clear thinking" to alcohol. Everything looks better with a drink.

The therapist must discover the family's accounting system, the ways in which family members explain the drinking to make it acceptable, in order to help the individuals unravel their own denial.

My sister was passed out in the study, with cigarettes and beer cans everywhere . . . none of us, not me, her friends, or my parents, believed she had an alcohol problem. We were overreacting to say she was alcoholic because she only drank beer.

As alcohol settles in firmly as the organizing principle for the individual and the family, an illusion of free choice enables the individual and others to retain a belief in self-control. As long as the individual can explain increased drinking in a reasonable, sensible manner, he or she does not have to deal with the reality of need and loss of control. Maintaining the belief in free choice produces what AA calls "alcoholic thinking," a way of explaining away increasing drinking through rationalization and denial.

Alcoholic thinking is a curiously illogical way of explaining one's behavior. It involves distorting cause and effect and logical sequencing in order to build a defense of one's drinking. Examination of the three major dimensions of the alcoholism model shows the predominance of this thinking disorder for the drinking alcoholic.

The Alcohol Axis

The alcohol axis represents the individual's focus on alcohol, behaviorally and cognitively. It reflects the degree to which alcohol dominates and directs the daily life of the individual and that person's interpretation of that dominance. With the progressive development of alcoholism, the alcohol axis becomes the dominating force and organizing principle, illustrated in the model by a narrowing of the continuum to a primary focus on alcohol.

Drinking alcoholics live within a behavioral and cognitive trap. Alcohol is becoming the organizing principle of their lives, determining daily activities, choice of job, and friends. But that organizing principle must be denied. Paradoxically, in order to keep alcohol as the organizing principle in their lives, they must see themselves as nonalcoholic. If they are to preserve the belief that they are nonalcoholic, they also must believe in their ability to control their drinking. The drinking alcoholic fervently holds onto two beliefs:

1. I am not alcoholic.
2. I can control my drinking.

Alcoholics rationalize these beliefs with a personal accounting system that keeps their drinking behavior within their own definition of "normal."

> I know I'm not alcoholic because I'm able to refuse alcohol. If you're alcoholic, you can't refuse it. I refuse drinks. I save space in case I might want another later on in the evening, so it's a way of keeping tabs on myself.

I am not alcoholic, because I don't drink before noon. The individual begins to construct an explanation that will dissolve the incompatibility between drinking behavior and beliefs about the self.

In some cases, individuals can recognize alcohol as an important part of their lives and explain it, while not fully accepting its organizing function.

> Sure, I drink some at sporting events! But that's because beer goes with football and I love football. It's got nothing to do with needing it or having to have it.

> Wine is a part of sophisticated social life. I enjoy wine tours with friends, gourmet cooking parties where I taste several varieties, and dessert parties where we sample sweet wines. It's not the wine itself that's important. It's a lot of fun and a good way to be with friends.

Of course not all individuals who drink are alcoholic (the majority are not), nor are those who enjoy beer with football or wine tasting necessarily alcoholic either. The distinction lies in the degree to which alcohol is the dominant organizing principle in a person's life because it has to be. That is, the point at which individuals must design their lives to fit that need. They may deny that alcohol in any way organizes their behavior and thinking as the above examples illustrate. Or, if they acknowledge its importance, they must explain it as secondary to a higher ordering principle (the importance of football).

It is very difficult for the individual and those close to that person to recognize the difference and pinpoint the distortion in thinking.

Interactions with the Environment

To keep alcohol as the organizing principle and to preserve the nonalcoholic belief, alcoholics must construct and interpret environmental interactions in ways that fit and maintain their belief systems. Environmental interactions involve intrapersonal and interpersonal factors that must be interpreted in relation to the primary focus on alcohol. These may involve the individual's interactions with others or the person's relationship with and interpretation of internal or external events.

> My stomach would hurt like crazy every morning after I'd had my two vodkas and orange juice for breakfast. I told myself it was the orange juice that was upsetting my stomach and decided that I better take the vodka straight in the future.

This kind of thinking often seduces not only the drinker but the drinker's companions.

> I was too drunk to walk back to the motel so my buddies helped me into the car so I could drive back.

Alcohol can even be construed as a means of coping better with the environment:

> I can't stand valium. I don't want to become one of those valium addicts. So I just keep to my beers at lunch and bourbon at night. No more. Not at work. They calm me down so I can function better.
>
> Sometimes I just decide to escape the pain, you know? Rheumatoid arthritis is a hell of a thing to live with; there's pain all the time. A few drinks in the afternoon help the pain—at least, I don't care as much about it—and I can get some things done. If I didn't do that, I'd sit around and cry and feel sorry for myself. I can't see anything criminal in wanting a bit of relief from pain, can you?

And if coping with the environment becomes impossible because of alcohol, alcoholism can be used as a way of helping to deal with the failure it produced:

> With the agoraphobia, I'm stuck at home all the time and even though I've got a lot of things to do, it's still hard. So I have a few drinks at lunch because afternoon's the hardest. The kids understand. They know Mom just enjoys her lunchtime drinks. So even though the phobia's gotten worse, I don't mind as much now. I'm finding ways to live with it, to keep cool.

This woman identified her major problem as phobias, so any misuse of alcohol was rationalized as a solution to her major difficulty.

Interpretation of Self and Others

Interpretation of self and others is the third axis, encompassing the individual's view of the self and world. The drinking alcoholic is dominated by the false belief in self-control and a behavioral and cognitive focus on alcohol that must be denied. The individual's ability to process incoming information is severely restricted to the degree that such information interferes with the drinker's belief in self-control and denial of alcoholism. Thus, the interpretation of self and others is very narrow and influenced by the predominant focus on alcohol.

Just as alcoholics begin to alter the physical environment to fit the organizing principle of alcohol and their identification as nonalcoholic, so they also alter their social environment. They unconsciously evaluate and interpret family members' actions and friends' responses on the basis of two things: first, "Do they permit me to continue to drink," and second, "Do they support my conviction that I'm not alcoholic?" Family cooperation—either passive or active—in the denial and rationalization become imperative:

> You see, my husband doesn't give me a lot of space. He's always there . . . hovering. It's really hard to feel like an individual when you've got someone hanging over your shoulder all the time, you know? Now, when I'm alone and can sit down with a couple of drinks, I can get back my feeling of individuality. The drinks just help me get back that sense of space. I don't want our marriage to break up . . . I really love Bert, but in order to keep up, I have to be able to get away in a way I choose.

> My husband never questioned my drinks before dinner or even when I lingered at the table with a glass of wine. He didn't understand why I wanted a drink after dinner and suggested to me that I might be developing a problem. So I started sneaking after that and he was relieved to see that I could control myself so easily.

Drinking alcoholics not only save themselves from themselves, they also use their drinking to "save" their friends and family from themselves, from their darker side. By doing this they reinterpret, in effect, their relationships with others without ever discussing their feelings or perceptions with those people:

> Look, I get these really big swings in mood. One day I'm high as a kite. The next, I'm in the pits. It's hell on the kids, on Betty. I feel terrible about it. I spend money like crazy when I'm high and it beats hell out of the budget. The alcohol just gets me in a place where I can control all of that. It helps the swings and it makes me better to live with. I don't go out and spend as much money. It's cheaper, it works, and it's more considerate.

Drinking alcoholics often seduce others into the same kind of thinking in order to elicit their support. The woman in the following example clearly sees alcohol as the solution to her marital difficulties. The lure is appealing because the alcohol accomplishes the stated objective, at least in the beginning:

> He gets so angry. So angry! He used to hit me when I answered back. So I decided not to answer back anymore and that's helped. He hardly ever hits me anymore. But sometimes I get real angry and think I'm going to answer back and then there will be a big scene and upset my youngest kid. So I just go have a scotch and that calms me down and it all blows over. I love him and it's just not worth breaking up the family over it.

In summary alcohol is an organizing principle in the alcoholic's life. In the process of developing alcoholism, alcohol becomes more and more important.

Much of the person's daily routine—job, family, and friends—will be designed and/or interpreted according to the need for alcohol.

Yet, what is most dominant in the individual's life, alcohol, must be vigorously denied. In the Piagetian framework, the drinking alcoholic is characterized by a narrow equilibrium: Not much information can be taken in either through assimilation or accommodation. The ego is inflexible because the individual is dominated by the defense structure of rationalization and denial. These defensive processes result in greater and greater restriction, behaviorally, cognitively, and affectively. We now turn to the question of therapeutic intervention and appropriate choice or combination of therapeutic treatments.

BEHAVIORAL CONSIDERATIONS

What is a behavioral intervention or a therapeutic modality that emphasizes behavior? The answers to these questions are not straightforward or obvious. In fact, it is through the inappropriate use of behavioral intervention that much of serious therapeutic error occurs. What is a behavioral intervention, when is it called for, and when is it inappropriate?

Active alcoholism is a behavioral problem. The individual has lost control of drinking. But, it is not just a behavioral problem that can be solved by prescribing new behaviors. Active alcoholism is also a thinking disorder. A cognitive, defensive structure of denial and rationalization is firmly rooted in order to maintain the behaviors of drinking and simultaneously deny the loss of control of that behavior. Mahoney's (1977) concept of reciprocal determinism is important in guiding therapeutic strategy: cognitions influence behavior, which influence cognitions, which influence behavior. The failure by the therapist to comprehend the dual nature of the alcoholism, its behavioral and cognitive components, will likely result in efforts by the therapist and patient to change the behavior without confronting or altering the thinking.

Such a singular behavioral focus might include the direct suggestion to the patient to stop drinking or a homework assignment to chart drinking behavior. These behavioral suggestions may be quite useful in clarifying behavior patterns for both the patient and the therapist. Usually, however, the patient has already tried these suggestions and numerous others in an effort to gain control. The patient has switched from hard liquor to wine, has stopped drinking before noon, or only stops at the bar two nights a week instead of five.

Unless the patient has acknowledged the loss of control and has expressed a wish to stop drinking, a singular behavioral focus is likely to occur within a cognitive framework still based on a belief in control. It is therefore behavioral prescription designed to gain control that is problematic, whereas examination of the reality of drinking behavior as a method leading toward recognition of loss of control can be useful.

Pitfalls of an Isolated Behavioral Focus

A singular emphasis on behavioral change is the logical prescription for the patient and the therapist who believe in the feasibility of control. The logical treatment is to focus on changing behavior to fit the belief in self-control. Thus, therapist and patient engage in behavioral plans that will hopefully lead to confirmation of the beliefs: "I am not alcoholic" and "I can control my drinking."

Individuals must deny failures in behavioral control because such failure would require challenging their basic belief in control. The individual who starts on a program to learn to control drinking behavior must believe he or she has been successful. Such an emphasis requires increasing denial and distortion.

Another pitfall of a singular behavioral approach occurs with the individual who is concerned about drinking and wants to cut down or stop, but does not believe that he or she is alcoholic. Patient and therapist may design a behavioral plan that the patient follows temporarily. Soon, the patient feels better and begins to question whether or not abstinence is necessary. If the person is not alcoholic, then it's OK to drink. The individual expects not to have trouble behaviorally after this temporary abstinence.

There are exceptions. Some alcoholic individuals, when told by a physician to stop drinking for their health, do so. They may remain totally abstinent and never believe that they have lost control of their drinking or accept the identity as alcoholic.

Other individuals stop drinking almost spontaneously, seemingly with no directive (Lemere, 1953; Kendall and Stanton, 1966; Waldorf and Biernacki, 1979). They too, alter behavior but do not see themselves as alcoholic. It is impossible to know how many individuals do stop in this way because usually they are not in AA, or in treatment for their drinking. We know only about those who believe they can stop drinking at anytime, but do not try, or those who have repeatedly tried to stop and have been unsuccessful.

Behavioral Interventions

Suggestions from the therapist to alter behavior in order to maintain abstinence are not likely to be heeded if they precede the acceptance of loss of control and the expressed desire of the patient to stop drinking. There are considerations, however, that involve the therapist's focus on the reality of the patient's drinking behavior that can be useful in helping the patient break denial.

Early recognition of alcoholism, recognizing it before it has produced severe medical complications, requires two things from the therapist: a high index of suspicion and a willing ability to pursue the topic of alcohol with the patient. Regardless of the presenting complaint, any therapist should approach an initial interview with a patient with the idea of *ruling out* alcoholism; the therapist needs to presume the presence of alcoholism until proven otherwise. The therapist sets out to prove otherwise by investigating alcohol consumption.

Investigating Alcohol Consumption

Investigating drinking behavior involves a straightforward and perhaps aggressive approach toward information gathering, as outlined in detail by Whitfield (1982). The therapist recognizes that facts about drinking behavior are likely to be distorted, particularly if the individual does have a problem with alcohol. Yet the therapist can still get a sense about the organizing function of alcohol regardless of the validity of the "facts." The patient who is seriously concerned and willing to examine drinking behavior directly may be able to honestly answer the 20 questions (Seliger, 1946) or the Michigan Alcoholism Screening Test (M.A.S.T.; Selzer, 1971). Individuals who are still invested in denial can easily distort the answers in a way that confirms the absence of a problem with alcohol.

The therapist asks directly and in detail about drinking behavior, listening for the warning signs (see 20 questions) and following through to determine the extent of the turn toward alcohol and to determine whether or not alcohol is already the organizing principle in the patient's life.

CLIENT: I have a few drinks before dinner and wine with my meal.

THERAPIST: On a regular basis?

CLIENT: Everyday.

THERAPIST: Sounds like alcohol is an important part of your daily routine.

CLIENT: Yes, but it's not a problem. I never drink during the day and never after dinner.

(The therapist hears the client's accounting system and makes note of it.)

THERAPIST: You may not consider your drinking a problem for you now, but it's still a good idea to recognize its importance to you because that can lead to trouble.

The therapist may or may not have the patient's willing participation in this examination process. The patient who is already concerned about alcohol consumption may yield information when guided by the therapist to focus on alcohol. This sincere and gentle interest by the therapist can lend legitimacy to the patient's concern. However, the patient may resist, hoping, often unconsciously, that the therapist will support denial and shift the focus away from alcohol.

I first saw a psychiatrist many years ago. The doctor asked me about my drinking and informed me I was not alcoholic because he believed what I told him: "I have one or two social drinks a day." I was grateful to that psychiatrist for diagnosing me as nonalcoholic and continued to see him regularly for several years. I was diagnosed as depressed and began a long course of antidepressants, lithium, and sleeping pills to regulate my shifting moods. I was elated to find my problem was depression because I could continue therapy without interrupting or altering my drinking.

Using a Behavioral History

The above "story" told by a young member of AA, illustrates how a therapist can use behavioral criteria to determine a turn toward alcohol. This account is retrospectively repeated from the point of view of someone who has acknowledged his loss of control of drinking and his alcoholism. This individual most likely would have denied the reality of his behavioral turn toward alcohol if questioned about it early in his drinking years. It is therefore the difficult task of the therapist to elicit a behavioral history that identifies the turn from a patient who is invested in denying it.

In an early intervention, the therapist could have identified the patient as "at risk" because of his father's alcoholism. The therapist then suspects automatically that behavioral problems, such as work absence and angry outbursts, may be a direct consequence of alcohol or drug use. The therapist suspects that the behavioral problem can be directly tied to alcohol. Unless the alcohol use is given primacy, the turn toward alcohol consumption cannot be recognized. When alcohol use is identified as secondary, it is viewed as a symptom. Both patient and therapist believe it will go away once the primary problem is solved.

It may have been impossible to determine whether or not this individual was an alcoholic at early intervention. Still, it was possible to label his drinking as a problem for him and the cause of his other difficulties.

Developing a Drinking History

Sometimes a drinking history can elicit warning signals. Any family history of alcoholism, in father, mother, or siblings, is critical and should be followed up carefully (Whitfield, 1982). Not only does a family history of alcoholism increase the risk in offspring; it also indicates that other presenting problems such as depression, anxiety, or insomnia, might be related to a family problem of alcohol. For example, the patient may not be concerned about drinking but may be depressed about a spouse's drinking or about continuing problems with an incapacitated alcoholic mother.

A thorough investigation includes gathering the facts about the drinking behavior of the patient and of people close to the patient. It requires focusing on alcohol and using the same strategies of eroding denial and perceptions to shift the patient's beliefs:

Paula was depressed, anxious, and missing time from work. She consulted a therapist for help with these problems, which she attributed to her failure to be a good wife for her husband. She felt guilty about working and concerned about abandoning him each morning when she left for work. If she were more available to him, he would not stay out at the bar and might come home for dinner. The therapist picked up the clue about a drinking problem and suggested that might have something to do with her problem.

THERAPIST: I wonder if your husband's drinking is a serious problem for you. Your depression and anxiety may be related to your fears about your husband and his unpredictability.

PAULA: Oh no! That's not the problem. My husband is definitely not an alcoholic. If I could just be more supportive and take better care of him, he would change his behavior.

Several years later, her husband sought treatment for his alcoholism. Paula was upset by his acceptance of the label alcoholic and again sought help for herself to deal with it:

> If I accept my husband as an alcoholic I will have to reconstruct my entire life and give new meaning to everything. I feel overwhelmed by what it would mean to give up my denial.

> For Paula to give up denial she had to acknowledge that her father also had been an alcoholic, a fact that she had carefully concealed all her life.

The therapist uses the reported behavior of drinking to challenge or restructure the patient's construction of her problems. The therapist's intervention involves clarifying her husband's behavioral problem with alcohol. After the main problem is properly identified, patient and therapist can both shift to the cognitive level, focusing on the meaning of her husband's drinking and the behaviors that she is engaged in that maintain the problems for her.

In the drinking phase, behavior is the primary problem: The individual has lost control of the desire and ability to stop the behavior of drinking once started. Yet a strict behavioral approach (plans to stop or charting consumption, for example) focusing only on the behavior of drinking is rarely adequate to promote long-term abstinence because what is most problematic and perhaps obvious to others is most vehemently denied by the drinker.

The denial of alcoholism is a cognitive phenomenon, which I have referred to as a thinking disorder. Unless the process of denial is unraveled so that the individual can accept the reality of loss of control, behavioral attempts will necessarily be temporary, stopgap measures, designed to gain control with a return to drinking anticipated.

In the drinking phase, the breakdown of denial is often best accomplished by repeated presentations of the actuality of drinking behavior and its consequences, thereby repeatedly emphasizing the cause and effect linkage between drinking and the results of drinking. Once the reality of the behavior is clarified, the distorted logic that maintains it as reasonable can be examined. It is toward the clarification of the thinking disorder that we now turn our attention.

COGNITIVE CONSIDERATIONS

I have repeatedly emphasized the importance of a combined behavioral–cognitive focus in working with the drinking alcoholic. The importance of denial as a part of alcoholism is now widely recognized (Bean, 1981; Paredes, 1974; Tamerin and Neuman, 1974; Vaillant, 1976). Alcohol addiction involves the individual's thinking, that is, the belief system in addition to behaviors. Thus, the task of the therapist working with a drinking alcoholic centers on challenging faulty logic and belief systems and eroding denial of the behavioral problems maintained by these beliefs.

Cognitive interventions are, therefore, crucial in this phase; they are needed to undermine the watertight logic of the alcoholic thinking. As noted earlier, behavioral interventions, such as making lists of drinking behavior, are useful, but only when clients already have recognized that they have a problem with alcohol and are willing to examine it. This is not usually the case; more often, at early intervention, clients are either denying their behavior or explaining it through rationalizations.

Cognitive interventions during this stage involve examination of the meaning and functions of drinking and questioning the logic of control. This examination of meaning and function teaches clients how to think about their drinking in new ways (Krueger, 1982; Krystal, 1982). Clients who can begin to think about what it means to be alcoholic or what purpose drinking serves, may then be better able to observe their behavior honestly or explore issues that underpin their belief systems and their drinking.

The logic and belief system involves a tightly woven structure that includes several major components. The "accounting system" is the individualized standard of acceptability into which the person's drinking behavior must fit. Supporting the accounting system is the illusion of free choice, the belief in self-control that the individual must maintain. Underlying these beliefs is the deeper question of what it means to be alcoholic. What is it that must be protected against? What meaning and what function require the continuing dominance of the accounting system and the illusion of free choice? What meaning or function produces the thinking disturbance called alcoholic thinking?

These reciprocally interactive components comprise a severely restrictive and seemingly impermeable cognitive disorder constructed in the service of maintaining a belief in self-control.

The Accounting System

Regardless of the time of the turn toward alcohol, most alcoholics begin with a sense of what is "reasonable and appropriate drinking," and most people can specify what constitutes to them "problem drinking": "having a drink before noon," "four drinks before dinner instead of three," "hard liquor but not wine or beer." To maintain this idea of reasonable and appropriate drinking, the individual already must have an inner accounting system. The accounting system can sustain an individual for many years, even into treatment and certainly long past the time when others have relinquished their denial. Speaking in a group about denial, one patient recalls his logic:

> I was detoxed several times but always saw myself as much less "sick" than anyone else. One time I left the detox center with a young lady. I told her she was too young to be an alcoholic and she told me the same thing. We decided to have a drink together. We missed dinner and couldn't have sex because we were too drunk. Two days later I looked at this woman and thought, "My God, she is an alcoholic!"

When the need for alcohol exceeds the level the individual has determined is reasonable and appropriate, rationalization becomes necessary:

> I never used to drink before five. The work day was sacred and I had to be clear headed. But as my promotions came along, I found the need to socialize with my colleagues and clients over lunch to be extremely important to my success. I had always eaten lunch in the company cafeteria but this just didn't cut it anymore. Cocktails and wines are a necessary part of business lunches—how could I refuse?

Rationalization permits individuals to engage in behavior, such as drinking at noon, that is unacceptable within their own belief system and accounting system. Eventually alcoholics alter their accounting to explain the continuing violation of the accounting system and to reduce the guilt and fear produced by this violation.

In the case of a male executive, who came to believe that executives on the way up drink at lunch, this belief enhanced his self-esteem. He thought about potential promotions accomplished over martinis and the pride his family would feel at his advancements. Problems began to occur: he couldn't stay awake in the afternoon, much less be clearheaded. However, he denied the problem itself or came up with another explanation. For example, his afternoon sleepiness was not due to his drinks at noon but to his lack of sleep the previous night. He developed insomnia, and that became the major problem and naturally the explanation for his daytime fatigue. Drinking was now an inherent part of his daily life and altered his belief system about what constitutes success. He therefore could not pinpoint alcohol as a problem.

These two patterns, rationalization and denial of difficulties related to drinking, characterize the organization of the drinking individual's life, behavioral and cognitive. The ability to decode the patient's elaborate structure of logic (Bean, 1981) rests on two premises: the therapist's ability to recognize, or at least suspect, a drinking problem, and the therapist's ability to challenge the logic that supports it. The therapist must approach the rationalization of drinking as a thinking disorder and set about to unscramble the beliefs that maintain it.

Because therapists (just like their patients and everyone else) have an accounting procedure, they must be perfectly clear about their own beliefs about what constitutes alcoholism. Rarely are therapists consciously aware of what these beliefs are. Of course, the therapist's own drinking behavior affects and even determines those beliefs. Thus, the therapist who has three drinks every evening, but not more, believes that four drinks per evening may constitute a problem with alcohol.

If therapists suspect a drinking problem, they must then pursue information from the patient to support or rule out that suspicion. Therapists look for the logic that supports the person's belief in not having a problem. They know that reasons for drinking or the consequences of patients' drinking will be explained in a way that identifies the problem as something else and eliminates a causal connection to alcohol.

For example, a patient explains that he is drinking because of job pressures and that the alcohol helps him cope. He has been confronted about his irritability on the job and explains it as a natural reaction to an unpleasant working environment. The therapist gathers the facts and restates the patient's explanation.

> You see that your main problem is an unfair boss and difficult working conditions. You endure the situation by drinking every evening to relax and close your mind to your troubles. You believe your irritability is due only to the job situation.

After this restatement, the therapist suggests that the patient sees alcohol as a solution to a problem outside of himself that, for whatever reasons, cannot be solved in any direct way (such as dealing with the boss directly). The patient sees no solution and will not be responsive to suggestions from the therapist about solving the problem. Maintaining the problem is necessary to explain continuing drinking.

If the patient can recognize the use of alcohol as a solution, the therapist can proceed to break down the logic, ultimately suggesting to the patient that drinking is the problem and not the solution and a problem that must be examined independent of life circumstances. Such a confrontation may or may not be successful. It may take a number of repetitions to shift the patient from externalizing the source of his problems. The therapist may suggest that the patient is really quite frightened that the problem is inside or that the problem is him and he must look outside to protect himself.

The patient eventually must come to see that: first, the problem is mine, and second, that problem is alcohol. The therapist ultimately will suggest to the patient that reasoning is serving to maintain denial. The therapist says clearly that the patient's drinking is the problem and that job difficulties may well be a consequence of drinking instead of the cause, or in addition. The therapist suggests that the patient's irritability is probably due to withdrawal and a craving for more alcohol, which the patient is denying. The therapist cannot pursue the breakdown of the logic of rationalization if the therapist believes, along with the patient, that the job is really the problem.

Many therapists are able to recognize a drinking problem, but they are reluctant to give it primacy, and therefore cannot attack the rationalization and denial directly. One therapist, for example, knew her patient was drinking too much but did not know how to approach this in the therapy.

It's clear my patient has a drinking problem, but it's secondary to her marital difficulties and anxieties.

When therapists believe alcoholism is secondary, they are unable to unscramble the rationalizations or help the patient see that marital difficulties and anxieties are now (if not originally) a consequence of drinking.

It is, therefore, the major task of the therapist in breaking down the accounting system to repeatedly label alcoholism as the *cause* of other difficulties. The alcoholic cannot link the glass in hand to later difficulties and needs repeated help in making the connection.

The Illusion of Free Choice

As the individual takes the turn toward alcohol, denial and rationalization are required to preserve the illusion of free choice. This illusion is needed to preserve the two core beliefs: "I am not alcoholic" and "I can control my drinking."

ALISON: Drinking is my secret weapon. It's my private territory. I carefully guard and use it as a retreat. I guess I'm confusing drinking with the "thing" that is my independence. But when I choose alcohol, I feel in control and I can defy others. My drinking is not out of control because I am choosing to do it.

THERAPIST: That belief in your choice is really central to your concept of yourself and your freedom. What would it mean to you if you thought you really are not choosing?

Weeks later:

ALISON: I have the choice about whether or not I take a drink. But once I do, I get boxed in and alcohol gets the control. I feel very split inside. Sometimes I see overwhelming evidence that I am alcoholic, but I quickly lose track of it.

Once I really knew I was alcoholic, I saw that I did not have a choice. I got so depressed, I retreated into drinking as a consolation.

Maintaining the illusion of free choice temporarily allays fears about what it means to have to drink.

TONY: I am "playing" with my drinking. I drink some and then stop to test my flexibility and my ability to make choices. I want to be sure that the drinking and the choice belong to me and not me to it.

THERAPIST: You are exercising your will to prove to yourself that you have control. You must be very frightened about what would happen if you stopped testing. If you are testing, you must have some evidence that the choice is not yours.

The fear of being out of control without alcohol is so great that many people hold onto the illusion of free choice by actually maintaining that alcohol provides control:

> I never drink to be nonfunctional! To not drink is to lose control. I drink to loosen up, be sexual, be functional. No one wants you around if you're depressed and can't function.

> I am terrified of sobriety. Drinking helps me with all of my out of control feelings.

Preserving the illusion of free choice also protects individuals from recognizing what they believe to be their lack of will power and the personal inadequacies implied with such lack. A belief in will power in turn reinforces belief that control is possible and suggests that they will be able to drink once they achieve control. This keeps patients who have actually admitted that their free choice is an illusion from progressing toward recovery; rather than acknowledging lack of control and moving into abstinence, they focus on trying to gain it. The following patient, for example, focuses great energy on the matter of self-control and choice:

> I've been experimenting with will power because my mother says I ought to have it. I tried not drinking during the day and it felt like punishment. To choose to drink is to take care of myself. I feel better, more relaxed, and steadier when I drink.

As she pursues her exploration, she reports a dream:

> My mother said to a friend,"Never mind Sally. She's drunk all the time."

She recalled that as a child her mother refused to deal with her if she cried. She had to be in control. Her fears of being out of control without alcohol kept her from joining AA.

> You have to have control before you can ask for help. Remaining isolated, she continued to focus on will power until she can one day get control.

> I know I have to change from "having to have a drink" to "wanting to have a drink." I know I'm out of control now, but I should be able to change my inside feelings. When I can "want" a drink rather than "having to have it," I will get the sense of choice I don't have now. Only when I have a sense of choice will I be able to feel like not having a drink.

Using the term "problem drinking" further supports the illusion of free choice. Although the term targets alcohol as a problem, it still includes an inherent belief in control. People with a drinking problem either work on controlling the problem or do nothing, believing only that they might have the potential to be alcoholic. Such logic denies the lack of control, admission of which is central to acknowledging alcoholism and changing behavior. Problem drinkers can spend years being "problem drinkers," because they see no need to change. Although the term is misleading, it can help individuals and their families take the first step toward recognizing alcoholism. However, it is important to distinguish early with patients the difference between "problem drinking" and "problems resulting from drinking." Patients must see that alcohol causes these problems:

> As long as I thought of myself as a problem drinker, I didn't have to do anything about it. I always assumed my problem was temporary and I would regain control. It wasn't until I recognized that drinking was causing the trouble that I saw I would have to change.

The Meaning of Being "Alcoholic"

Recognizing the importance of the experience of "being alcoholic" is a recent and extremely significant trend in clinical (Murphy, 1980; Bean, 1981; McCartney, 1981) and theoretical research (Thune, 1977).

Underlying the meaning of being alcoholic is the belief system that provides structure to an individual's view of the world, his actions in it, and his definition of self. Being alcoholic often includes within its meaning the worst fears a person can hold and therefore ward off. Because of the stigma still attached to alcoholism and the widely held view that alcoholism is a moral problem, many people consciously fear such a label because of the negative stigma. The therapist questions what is so frightening about the label and hears the implication of failure at control and failure at successfully achieving social acceptance and equality. Being alcoholic is, therefore, an interpersonal competitive failure:

> To be an alcoholic is an erosion of my masculinity. Men can hold their booze.

> If I'm alcoholic I can no longer belong to my swinging social group. If I can't drink, I can't keep up, and there is no place for me.

Being alcoholic is also an intrapersonal failure; evidence of the individual's worst fears about herself:

> Pamela had stopped drinking and was attending AA, but kept insisting she was not an "alcoholic." She had caught herself in time. Though anxious, she was able to think about what it would mean to her to be alcoholic and periodically returned to this question. The people whom she had labeled alcoholic throughout her life all had one feature in common: physical violence. She could not tolerate an identification that would automatically make her a violent person too.

The direct question by the therapist, "What would it mean to be an alcoholic," often elicits the particular fears and core meaning around which denial has been constructed, such as:

> To be "alcoholic" is to be out of control.
> To be "an alcoholic" is to have failed.
> To be "an alcoholic" is to be just like my father.
> If I am "an alcoholic," I will have to reinterpret my whole life.
> An alcoholic can never drink again.
> Alcoholics have to join AA.

Finding out what is so awful or fearful about being alcoholic helps to break down the patient's logic and denial.

The Functions of Drinking

Isolating the functions of drinking (Krystal, 1982) yields important information about intervention. Asking the question, "For what purpose," elicits the functions of drinking and allows the therapist to point out the important function of alcohol as a solution to the individual. By thinking about function, the therapist suggests that drinking is not isolated and unrelated to the person's interactions and self-view. This is an important first step because the individual often believes that drinking has nothing to do with anything; it just is:

I just drink. It's something you do. Everybody does it. No reason.

By suggesting that drinking serves a function, whatever it is, the therapist includes alcohol in a cause and effect linkage. The individual who has not needed to explain drinking behavior must now do so. At first, the function of drinking depends on blaming others; someone or something else is at fault:

I drink because of my difficult boss.
I drink "at" my wife.

When people are better able to recognize problems with alcohol, they can think about function in a more self-serving way: "What does it do or get for me?" Thinking about the real functions or usefulness of drinking (beyond the rationalizations) is, when approached carefully, nonjudgmental and both practical and effective in eroding denial.

The question to ask in therapy is not "Why do you drink?" This leads to excuses. The question is, "What is the meaning/purpose/function of your drinking?"

Harold insisted on using the initial sessions of his therapy to figure out why he drinks, believing if he knew why, it would solve his problems. But, after exhausting the reasons—to unwind, to get back at my boss—he could think of only one major reason: "Because I like to and it's my privilege." It's not related to anything.

The patient who recognizes that drinking serves a function can begin to see its importance and ultimately to question its value. When the patient can see that drinking serves a purpose, the drinking behavior makes more sense logically. The patient can then more readily accept that alcohol is a solution and therefore quite important and quite functional. After this recognition, the therapist helps the patient determine whether or not the solution has, in fact, now become the problem.

When Harold shifted perspective just slightly and thought about what it means to drink, he charted new territory:

Drinking permits me to take time off. It allows me to make a quick transition in my set of mind and attention. A bourbon facilitates a certain kind of attention too. I can justify spending time with people because drinking with them will promote intimacy. Following this line of reasoning permitted Harold to see how his own rationalizations covered the important meaning and function that alcohol had for him. He always dismissed his drinking, but now began to see it as an important factor regulating his daily routine.

Often individuals are so seriously impaired that even when they do not deny that alcoholism is the major problem, they value the "positive" functions of drinking more than the negative. Unraveling the rationalizations and logic of such a situation often uncovers serious disturbances:

> Pete recognized two distinct personalities distinguished by drinking: "When I'm sober, I feel relaxed and ambitious—no need to challenge the system and other people. But when I'm drinking, all people are enemies." Pete maintained that his main problem was an uncontrollable split personality. He convinced himself he didn't have a problem with alcohol because he "looked good": he was successful, a college graduate, a professional businessman. However he recognized a "drinking personality" and did not deny his behavior when that personality was in charge. But this was not he. It was "that other fellow."

> Peter had no access to his internal life and could make no sense initially of the therapist's question about the function and meaning of alcohol. While functional and controlled in his business role, he was virtually out of control at any other time. "When I'm sober, I can't control my spending or anything else. I have to watch TV to control my moods. I can feel myself at the edge and I need to have a plan if I feel the urge to drink. I don't have a methodology, rules I can follow to control myself." Most important, Pete could not tolerate talking therapy or learning to think about himself and his drinking. "I don't have any questions or answers, no meanings, just behaviors. Drinking is the only time I feel control."

> Pete's references to a plan and a method underscore his own recognition of his behavior problem. Pete believed he had no insights, that he was just an acting thing. Talking in therapy made him more anxious and he had to drink immediately after his sessions. Pete had a history of serious crime and several suicide attempts. Even with a plan—attendance at AA every day for example—he could not maintain abstinence without external controls. He required extensive, repeated hospitalizations and ultimately a sheltered living arrangement.

Understanding the function of alcohol may help both patient and therapist clarify its importance and therefore the potential difficulties in relinquishment. Understanding the necessary function also helps both patient and therapist design a treatment plan that addresses this function directly.

If alcohol provides the illusion of control for a person who is just "an acting thing," a very sheltered environment with constant external control may be necessary. If alcohol maintains a problematic marital relationship, examination and restructuring of that marriage may be a necessary component of abstinence.

Understanding the function allows both therapist and patient to pinpoint danger ahead and adjust the behavioral plan accordingly.

Alcoholic Thinking

The increasing importance of rationalization and denial leads to the peculiar kind of logic already mentioned and called by recovering alcoholics and their families "alcoholic thinking." It develops in order to permit more and more opportunities for drinking. Ultimately, it encompasses all arenas of life and activities. Alcoholic thinking makes unacceptable behavior acceptable. Its logic permits both rationalization and denial; its logic both explains and denies drinking behavior:

THERAPIST: Do you drink alone?

GLORIA: Well, I'm single, so I do drink alone occasionally, but since I'd much rather drink with other people I'll say, "No."

Gloria both explains and denies her behavior. She actually drinks every day, whether she is with people or not. Unscrambling alcoholic thinking is absolutely necessary to show the patient the illusion of control and to begin to work through the patient's logic system to the beliefs:

> I've decided that it's my habits and behavior that get me into trouble and not the alcohol. I was in three auto accidents while drinking and so I learned I just can't drink and drive. So I gave up driving. I switched to a bicycle, but I had an accident on that too. Now I'm walking. Yeah, I'm trying AA but it's hard to get to meetings without a car.

> Jane referred to this style of logic as her "drinking frame of mind." But it was more for her than a structural logic. It was an attitude and a way of being in the world. She characterized her "drinking frame of mind" as vague and distant, "preparatory to engaging in a private drinking bout." To prepare her retreat or to explain it, she would suddenly find fault with her mate and angrily isolate herself to punish him. She gained privacy and could drink "at him." Her "drinking frame of mind" carried with it a hostile view of the world and a suspicion that others were against her—jealous, angry, etc. In fact, her suspiciousness also reflected her fear of being caught, not so much for the drinking, but for the secret time she had claimed.

Therapists must realize that alcoholic thinking refers not only to rationalization, denial, and frame of mind, but also to character traits that frequently accompany drinking. These include grandiosity, omnipotence, low frustration tolerance, hostility, and paranoia (Blane, 1977; Krueger, 1982). This unrealistic, inflated sense of self often supports a belief in control. The drinking alcoholic often has no sense of limits nor of mutuality and cooperation:

> I always believed I shouldn't have to wait in line in the grocery store. Sometimes I got so angry waiting, I left the cart and walked out.

> Frequently the anger this patient feels on leaving the store fuels a well-rationalized drinking episode. She experiences the need to wait in line—to be just like others— as a serious injury to her sense of self, but more as a perfect excuse to have a drink. With an excuse, she will not have to recognize the uncomfortable craving for alcohol that she experiences a good deal of the time.

Another member of AA recalls just such a setup:

> I had promised my wife I wouldn't drink during the week. And I didn't. That is,
> I didn't pour any cocktails. But I kept a bottle in the garage and spent a lot of
> time working out there in the evenings. If I didn't feel like carrying on this charade
> I would sometimes walk in from a hard day, find something wrong with my wife's
> greeting, criticize her, she would fight back, and I would stomp out and head for
> the bar, full of self-pity for having to live with such an angry, complaining wife.

Unscrambling alcoholic thinking includes the key procedures already noted.
The therapist suspects the presence of an alcohol problem and, therefore, suspects that the patient will have an elaborate logical construction to defend continuing drinking. Unscrambling involves a constant focus on alcohol, its meaning, purpose, and how the drinking and the rationalizations for drinking cover
the most important problem: Alcohol is the primary problem and drinking is out
of control with a life of its own. The feeling of specialness and the impatience
at having to wait in the grocery store might be defined as a narcissistic character
problem. But, in fact, these feelings provide the excuse to drink and thereby
satisfy the deeper problem—the insatiable need to drink. Jane could see that
alcohol functioned to give her the privacy she could not claim for herself. It was
much more difficult for her to see that she also needed the alcohol for its own
sake, independent of any function. The recognition of need and the craving that
signals it are frightening and intolerable. Alcoholic thinking covers this recognition.

A key component in rationalization is the issue of responsibility. Many individuals suffering from alcoholic thinking disturbances, believe that because
they do not intend to get drunk, they are not responsible for what they do while
drinking:

> Sally indignantly informed the policeman that he shouldn't ticket her for nearly
> causing an accident because she didn't do it on purpose. She was enraged and
> humiliated when the policeman laughed and told her that most people don't intend
> to cause accidents or kill people.

> Sally could not understand this logic. She reaffirmed with alcohol: She doesn't
> intend to get drunk, so, therefore, she's not responsible for what she does while
> drinking.

> This reasoning proved devastating to her when she became involved with an al-
> coholic who beat her. Bruised and frightened, she felt she could do nothing. "He
> was drunk. He didn't mean to do it so how can I blame him?" She could neither
> leave him nor protect herself. The lack of a concept of responsibility left her help-
> less with others and herself. This subsequently fed her belief in the necessity for
> an ultimate magical cure. "I need a hospital, a prescription, a pill. They won't let
> me do these things to myself in the hospital. I can lie there and the cloud will pass
> over. I need mama to make it better."

As she thought about her wish for an all caring mother, she realized she felt angry with AA: "I tried them, but they failed to cure me." Sally countered her wish for a passive cure by explaining her choice to drink as positive action: "I get involved with my self-destructiveness. It is an action, a necessary evil in order to survive. My own death will happen so why should I wait around when I can 'take charge of it.' Drinking is a way to survive and speed up my death at the same time."

Sally also related drinking as a way to survive, to control and choose: "When I'm sober, too many options open up. If you have too many choices, it takes more control to select. It's like a dinner menu. I always feel sad after making a selection. I should have chosen something else and the opportunity is gone forever. To choose is to lose all other possibilities. It's a real loss of freedom. How can I pick sobriety? Why should I permit pain when I can kill it?" In thinking about what it means not to drink, Sally recognized she was terrified of becoming disintegrated if she relinquished her choice to drink, which gives her the illusion of control.

Sally refused to go to AA because "it's based on religion and because of the self-righteous attitude of the members." She did recognize her need for support, and she decided to live with a family who would provide a passive, indirect structure: "After all, I can't walk around drunk, I'll have responsibilities to provide me with control." But she feels hopeless: "I begin each day with a wish not to drink and I start drinking at the same time. What's the matter with me that I can't control myself?"

Sally eventually recognized that she could not control her drinking: "It's like Job, set upon me." But instead of making the leap to abstinence, stayed within the framework of her rationalization: "It's a mystery why alcohol is so necessary to me. I have to understand it so I won't be dependent."

As she progressed she began to understand that control would not come magically: "I realize will power is not the solution. I need a 'road map' because I don't know what happens to me or what direction I'm going." Sally said she needed an intervention: "It's obvious I will have to stop drinking and I'll just have to say I will. But I don't know how. It's like learning to do a back dive, you keep flopping till someone tells you to put your head back." Suddenly she became anxious and reverted to her former logic: "But if I eat ice cream long enough, I won't want to anymore. Maybe I'll suddenly run out of a desire to drink. I can't tolerate feeling deprived." Once again, thinking about the matter of choice: "I didn't choose to start drinking or become dependent, these things just happen to me. I wonder if it's a pretense to think I can help myself."

Sally was afraid of trying, of choosing AA and not being able to succeed. Finally, she thought about what it meant to be alcoholic and to go to AA: "It's repugnant to say 'I'm Sally, I'm an alcoholic. I'm a moral misfit, weakling, worse than a criminal or sex offender.' It's disgusting, but I need to say it all the time to integrate myself. I'm Sally, I'm alcoholic. I'm 'it' in my family, the alcoholic, outsider. Screwing up your life in other ways is not an illness, I didn't catch alcoholism. I did it to myself. Going to AA just confirms my mother's opinion of me as a drunk. Refusing to go is the only way I can say she's wrong. I'm a good person."

In addition to thinking about the meaning of being alcoholic, it is also useful to explore the meaning of being sober:

William notes the fear of being without alcohol: "It feels like being enclosed, a door closing and it's hard to get out. I'll lose more than I gain because that door closes my options. You know, if I go to AA, I'll have to finish my project and I'll have to look at my life. Any commitment requires commitment to all else and I'll suddenly be overwhelmed.

Then he thinks about failure: "What would happen if I started drinking again? If I can't do it right, I'm not going to do it at all. There is a right way and a wrong way to broil a steak, and there must be a right and a wrong way in AA. I need a recipe to tell me how to do it. What's so frightening with abstinence? The worse thing is to be taken by surprise and that's what looms with abstinence. And, what's the matter with AA? AA will see me from a stern, authoritarian, judgmental point of view. I've been on bad behavior, a naughty boy who comes to fess up. How can I be an adult and still be out of control and have problems? It must mean I haven't grown up yet."

Alcoholic thinking is the logic of explaining one's drinking behavior and the necessity of drinking in a way that makes it plausible and still maintains the behavior.

The cognitive factors are extremely important in the drinking phase because it is these processes that maintain and explain drinking behavior. Therapeutic intervention must consistently involve a cognitive focus from the therapist's own point of view and ultimately from the patient's as well. Initially, the therapist listens for evidence of a drinking problem and makes note of the person's individual accounting system. How does the individual account for drinking behavior in a way that denies any difficulties? The therapist brings the patient back repeatedly to a focus on alcohol, challenging the illusion of free choice and directing the patient to explore the meaning and the functions of alcohol.

Finally, the therapist must constantly challenge the logic of the patient—the alcoholic thinking—that makes drinking reasonable and secondary to some other primary problem. Cognitive considerations and a cognitive behavioral focus are essential to breaking down the rigid structure of denial that maintains the drinking behavior. Dynamic intervention, or insight-oriented uncovering work, also may be a necessary and useful tool.

Dynamic psychotherapy may be indistinguishable from cognitive therapy in many instances, particularly as the individual considers the meaning and functions of alcohol. I refer to dynamic therapy as the uncovering of unconscious dynamic meaning as opposed to the more conscious cognitive process.

DYNAMIC CONSIDERATIONS

The primary task of the therapist in the drinking phase is to focus on alcohol, erode denial, challenge perceptions, and help the patient shift basic identity and beliefs. These tasks are achieved predominantly through the use of cognitive intervention with deeper uncovering therapy and behavioral intervention used to facilitate the cognitive shifts.

Indications

Dynamic therapy can be very useful with a drinking patient who is seriously motivated to change. Uncovering work can help a patient break through denial or can provide understanding of an unconscious dynamic that is blocking a conscious desire for abstinence.

Many individuals consciously recognize that alcohol is a serious problem, but to identify themselves as alcoholic is tinged with unconscious dynamic meaning; they cannot move from recognition to acceptance and behavior change without giving up deeper defenses:

Harriette wanted to stop drinking but was afraid to try. Suggestions to use AA for help and support were resisted with the explanation that "the people in AA were too groupish and cliquish" and that she would have to "swallow it all" to fit. With careful exploration, she recalled her painful decision at age 14 to join the Catholic church. She adopted the beliefs of the church with zeal and became contemptuous of nonCatholics, including her Protestant mother. Her dogmatic attitude covered tremendous guilt about abandoning her mother and she now reexperienced this conflict in the decision to join AA. When she recognized the similarity, she began to attend AA meetings.

Mike provides another example of the importance of unconscious factors.

Mike called the alcohol clinic requesting an appointment because he realized that both his parents are alcoholic. On his first visit, he related a history that emphasized his own addiction to alcohol, pot, and prescription drugs, though he vehemently denied any problems with his ability to control his drug use.

In a second interview, Mike revised his family portrait, noting that his mother was the alcoholic, hidden and insidious. He had decided that his father was actually not alcoholic, because he never missed work or lost a job due to drinking.

The core significance of alcohol to Mike's identification with his father was immediately apparent. So was the nature of his accounting system, related to his sense of masculinity and the importance of control.

The therapist made a silent note of the shift in Mike's identification of his father from alcoholic to nonalcoholic. Mike was having serious difficulties in his young adult life but was not yet ready or able to identify alcohol as a problem itself or even a contributor to his other difficulties. He was able to seek help only as the child of two alcoholic parents.

In recognizing and labeling both his parents as alcoholic, he became frightened and revised his view at the second meeting. Mike now denied that his father was alcoholic, demonstrating to the therapist the nature of his accounting procedures (alcoholics miss work or lose jobs.)

Alcohol, and the ability to drink in a controlled fashion, were tied to Mike's identification with both parents. He saw his mother as weak and out of control and rejected any evidence that he was like her. Mike emphasized his father's ability to control himself and accented his own similarities with his father.

In Mike's family, alcohol was a key symbol in forming identifications. The ability to drink in a controlled fashion was tied directly to dominant, masculine behavior and formed the core of Mike's accounting procedure and his own denial.

Over the course of many weeks, the therapist helped Mike to see the central significance of alcohol to the family's interaction and selfdefinitions and the importance that Mike attached to control. Eventually the therapist asked what it would mean for Mike to see his father as an alcoholic too. Mike acknowledged that it would make him feel sad, alone, and orphaned. His father would have sold out to alcohol and his mother, going down the tubes right along with her. The therapist then wondered what it would mean for Mike to think of himself as an alcoholic too.

> Devastating. It would be such a total failure. I would be going right down the tubes with both of them.

Mike worked with the therapist for many months to uncover the meaning of alcohol to his identification with his father and his sense of potential loss of that identification should he decide that his father also was an alcoholic.

This shift became possible as Mike deepened his attachment to the therapist. This attachment permitted him to risk the relinquishment of his identification with his father. When Mike was able to identify both parents as alcoholic, he paradoxically relinquished his identification with his father and confirmed it at the same time by beginning to focus on his own drug use.

This process evolved over the course of several years at which time Mike became ready to acknowledge his own alcoholism. The first step was his own recognition that he too could not control his drinking and wished help.

At this point, the therapist shifted to a behavioral focus. The patient now accepted a suggestion to attend AA (he had tried it several times during the course of his therapy but he "just couldn't identify"), and they shifted the focus of his therapy toward alcohol, specifically his own alcoholism and his new behaviors for maintaining abstinence.

This example illustrates a combined cognitive dynamic approach. The therapist listened for the cognitive factors that maintained Mike's denial, his accounting procedure and the significance of control, and helped Mike uncover the deeper unconscious meanings of being alcoholic, which were related to his identification with his father and mother.

Contraindications

The examples above illustrate the use of uncovering psychotherapy in the service of breaking denial of loss of control and facilitating identification as an alcoholic. Unfortunately, dynamic psychotherapy too often may be used unwittingly in the service of maintaining denial. Vaillant (1981) makes a strong case against traditional psychotherapy with the drinking alcoholic. Too often, therapists and patients believe that alcoholism simply is a symptom of a deeper underlying problem, that the alcoholism can be cured by understanding the deeper issue (Hellman, 1981). This belief denies that alcoholism is a problem in its own right and therefore inappropriately shifts the central focus away from alcohol:

> My psychiatrist told me that depression was my problem. We needed to dig deeper to uncover the source of my bad feelings and then the drinking problem would vanish.

Dynamic therapy is also contraindicated when therapists believe in the alcoholic's capacity to control drinking or when therapists get caught in their own accounting system. For example, one therapist reported that his patient drank a six pack of beer every night but did not have a problem with alcohol because "the behavior was ritualized and therefore under control." The therapist was actually deciding for the patient, based on his own rationale, what constituted control. He was, therefore, unable to hear whether or not the patient indeed had a problem with alcohol or whether or not he even had a serious concern he wished to explore.

The choice between cognitive, behavioral, or dynamic therapeutic focus is often ambiguous and even undifferentiated. The therapist needs to bear in mind constantly the primary task—eroding denial of loss of control—of the drinking phase and then determine the best approach or combination of approaches to achieve it.

As in the case of Mike, alcoholism may be far more than a behavioral problem, developing slowly after years of problem free social drinking. For Mike, alcoholism is at the heart of his own personal identify and it is the symbol of his attachment to others. The task of uncovering his own alcoholism is an intricate one, involving confrontation of his own behaviors, cognitive exploration of the meaning and function of alcohol, and uncovering psychotherapy to understand the unconscious deeper significance of alcohol to his identifications and attachments.

Through a combination of familial, social, personal, and environmental factors and therapeutic strategies, many individuals do achieve surrender, the point at which the reality of loss of control is clear and congruent across behavioral, cognitive, and dynamic domains. Some AA members have described this experience as a "moment of truth." According to our theory, it is the beginning point of a dramatically new progression of development that begins with a self-identity as an alcoholic and evolves into a new way of viewing the self and the world from this perspective. Chapter 5 describes the beginning of this development.

Chapter 5

Transition

THE TURN TOWARD ABSTINENCE

We have characterized the process of developing alcoholism as a turn toward alcohol to a point at which alcohol becomes the organizing principle in an individual's life. Accommodations in all aspects of life are required to maintain the centrality of alcohol and deny that centrality at the same time.

The transition phase signals the beginning of cracks in this rigid system of logic, rationalization, and behavior. The disadvantages and problems of drinking begin to outweigh the advantages. The individual suddenly begins to doubt the rationalizations or is presented with stark evidence of the centrality of alcohol that cannot be easily accommodated. If successful, the breakdown of denial, central to the task of therapy with the drinking alcoholic, moves the patient toward a point of despair called by AA members, hitting bottom or surrender. Surrender is characterized by a collapse of the structure of logic and behavior and a sense of defeat (Tiebout, 1949). The fight to maintain the belief system based on self-control has been lost.

The move toward this turning point is characterized by despair, loss, failures, and increasing isolation. The individual's life has narrowed to a predominant focus on alcohol with environmental interactions and interpretation of self and others completely determined by the alcohol filter. What is it that provides the breakthrough, intervention, or interpretation that triggers the turn toward abstinence?

Individuals report (Brown, 1977) a wide range of influential turning points and events, both internal and external, that suggest that the turning point from drinking to abstinence is the result of the multiple impact of many experiences and interventions, none of which necessarily stand out in isolation.

The task of the transition phase is to move toward this point of despair, which, if successful, leads the individual behaviorally from drinking to abstinence. But even when the physical act of drinking has stopped, the psychological and physical problems associated with the addiction and the belief system that maintain the behavior may linger.

There must be a corresponding shift in central identity as well. Such a reversal is made only with great difficulty, because it requires a total revision of the belief system that was the mainstay of the drinking phase.

The eroding of denial and challenging of perceptions and beliefs held in the drinking phase help the individual to shift the two central beliefs from:

1. I am not alcoholic.
2. I can control my drinking.

to:

1. I am an alcoholic.
2. I cannot control my drinking.

For many individuals, the change in belief and core identity precede the change in behavior and both continue smoothly without interruption. The individual moves from drinking into abstinence, shifts identity, and does not move back into drinking.

> I realized I am an alcoholic, that my drinking was out of control, and, therefore, I had to stop. I came to AA and haven't had a drink since.

Most drinking alcoholics do not simply move from being drinking alcoholics one day to abstinent alcoholics the next, although an abrupt change in drinking behavior may suggest this. It is the difficulty of changing the basic identity and beliefs and maintaining the new beliefs, that is as problematic during this phase as the physical addiction to alcohol. The move through the transition phase is most likely characterized by "fits and starts" (Bean, 1975a) with shifts back and forth in belief system, identification, and behavior. For example, many people will begin to superficially identify themselves as alcoholic and acknowledge that they are unable to control their drinking. They will go off for an evening, holding steadily to these two beliefs and manage to get through the evening without drinking alcohol. However, the next day, having achieved this, they will then use their behavior from the night before to prove that they indeed can control their drinking and are therefore not alcoholic.

> At the beginning of the evening, I kept reminding myself: "I am an alcoholic, I am an alcoholic." I cannot control my drinking so when they brought around the drinks, I said no. And it wasn't as bad as I thought, you know? I thought it would be hard to say no, but I felt really good about saying it. I could have had a drink if I'd wanted one, but I didn't. I thought I would have a really bad time. But I found out last night that I really can control my drinking when I feel like it.

What happened here is a classic example of the ambivalence that is present and active in the transition phase as individuals struggle with both external behavior changes and the shift in internal identity. First John uses his new identity as an alcoholic and as someone who is unable to control his drinking to help him maintain his new abstinent behavior. Then, having exhibited that new behavior, he uses the behavior to return to his old belief patterns, completely forgetting that the new behavior was only possible because of the new identity. He now comes to believe instead: "I must not be an alcoholic after all."

The individual may move back and forth many times from drinking to abstinence, each time reasserting with a firm belief "I am not alcoholic, and, therefore, I can drink," or, "I am an alcoholic, and, therefore, I must stop drinking." This shift in pattern is quite different from the individual who feels remorse or guilt after a drinking episode and "goes on the wagon." Swearing off alcohol or going on the wagon occur within the belief system "I am not an alcoholic." The "wagon" is a temporary maneuver designed to give the individual a sense of control. When the abstinence imposed by will is completed, the individual returns to drinking without ever having shifted identity. If anything, the person takes the ability to go on the wagon as a demonstration that he or she has control and is therefore not alcoholic.

The Alcohol Axis

The alcohol axis is the most important of the three components of the model during this phase. This primary focus on alcohol closely resembles the same focus during the drinking phase. Just as environmental interaction and interpretation of self and others were determined by the individual's relationship with alcohol during the drinking phase, so the focus continues to be on alcohol and on its presence or absence during the transition phase. Just as a widowed spouse continues to act as though he or she is married for a long time after the death of a partner and continues to approach life as though the partner would or should be there, so the alcoholic in the transition phase still orients life around the presence or absence of the alcohol.

A new element often enters the picture in this transition phase: the presence and activity of AA in the patient's life. The patient begins to replace the loss and grief associated with stopping drinking with a positive identification with AA meetings, members, and the principles of abstinence (the 12 steps) (AA, 1955). There is a shift in dependency on alcohol to reliance on other people, specifically AA members.

The erosion of denial and the shift in identity occur over time as evidenced by AA members. They reported a significant lapse of time between initial contact with AA and acknowledged membership and abstinence (see Appendix F), which suggests that the process of recovery, though marked by the point of abstinence, begins during drinking.

The transition period is one of fluctuating identification as individuals struggle with the alcoholic label and the meanings attached to it. Much of the resistance to AA and the deep significance of what it means to be alcoholic surface at this time.

A focus on alcohol and being alcoholic is absolutely essential to sustain abstinence and movement into early recovery. Too quick a move away from the focus on alcohol by either therapist or patient can result in a loss of the new identity and a resultant return to old drinking patterns. Often a shift away from an alcohol focus is seen as an antedote to the despair of the recognition of being alcoholic and out of control:

> OK, I know I'm alcoholic and I've stopped drinking. But I'm not going to AA. It just depresses me to hear all those sad old people talk about alcohol. If I've stopped drinking, that's it. Why do I have to think about it?

This patient moved back and forth from drinking to abstinence several times, always asserting that not drinking was all there was to it. A month later after finally going to AA, he thought about his resistance to thinking about alcohol:

> I thought there was nothing to it, and especially that I could do it myself. I did not want help and I certainly wasn't about to stand up and say "I'm Marv, an alcoholic." I didn't understand that I didn't know how to stop drinking. Wanting to stop was fine, but until I really paid attention to being alcoholic I couldn't learn how to stay stopped. That's still a great shock to me.

The therapist may also inadvertently abort continual movement through the transition phase. Often, the therapist cannot tolerate the despair experienced by the patient either and may step in to cut off or delay the recognition of defeat. A therapist seeking consultation presented her dilemma:

> My patient was so depressed and I was so concerned about the possibility of suicide. I listened to the patient agonize over her recognition that she was really alcoholic and I was frightened about what she might do. I wanted to give her some hope before she left my office, so I said, "Maybe things aren't really so bad. Maybe you can control it."

The period of transition is characterized predominantly by education, which provides guidelines to behavioral and cognitive change. The individual tries on the label alcoholic and then follows with actions that reinforce the new beliefs.

> I am alcoholic and that means I don't take the first drink. When I get the urge, I don't just sit on it, I do something else—pick up the phone, read AA literature, or go to a meeting. I have to do something different or I'm just holding on.

Interactions With the Environment

Interactions with the environment are painful and difficult for the patient in transition. Alcohol remains the primary focus around and through which all interactions are determined and interpreted. The drinking alcoholic controls environmental interactions through denial and the shaping of the alcohol filter. The newly abstinent alcoholic is focused primarily on alcohol as well, adjusting to a new identity as an alcoholic and learning new behaviors to maintain abstinence and support that identity. Interactions not related to alcohol run the risk of detracting from this central focus and learning process. Such interactions also may be very threatening to the newly abstinent alcoholic. The recognition of loss of control must be maintained or the identity shifts back to that of non-alcoholic. But that recognition carries with it a sense of vulnerability and helplessness that requires a protective and supportive environment.

> For those first few days and weeks I was terrified I would find myself taking a drink. Not a decision I'd made, just completely out of my control. I couldn't believe I got from day to day and hadn't had a drink. It didn't feel like my choice at all. It felt like a monster hanging over my shoulder.

For the individual who wants to stop, AA or an alcohol treatment hospital provide such a supportive structure. The family and work place may or may not be supportive, depending on their knowledge of alcoholism and the recovery process. Many unfortunate unintentional errors occur during this period due to lack of knowledge on the part of family and therapists in particular.

Pitfalls With Family Members

Family members, unknowingly, may present an obstacle to easy progression into abstinence.

> They told me at the hospital that I needed to join Al-Anon and get involved in a family group so I could learn about alcoholism and how to take care of myself. I'm sick of alcohol and alcoholism! When he was drinking, I covered up and took over for him, now I have to protect him again. I want my husband back now, responsible and protective of me and the kids!

This wife has an expectation that because her husband is not drinking, he should be "OK" and assume his old responsibilities. She does not understand that her husband feels more vulnerable and more dependent without alcohol. Another wife echoes this sentiment.

> My husband is sober and all he does is go to AA. I lost him to the bottle and now I've lost him to those meetings. Nothing has changed.

Pitfalls With Therapists During Drinking

The primary task of the therapist during the transition phase is to facilitate the change in identity and the recognition of loss of control, and to help the patient move from drinking to abstinence. The primary task for the drinking patient is erosion of denial and/or exploration of the resistance to stopping. Both involve exploration of the meanings and functions of alcohol and a confrontation of the realities of drinking.

This exploration is primarily a cognitive and uncovering task, the effectiveness of which is contingent on the positive motivation of the patient. The individual who does not wish to change or who insists on maintaining the illusion of self-control will resist cognitive or dynamic exploration because they each threaten the basic denial of an alcohol problem. Patients who are moving toward abstinence need a therapist who can support that movement and their new identity, with its accompanying admission of loss of control. The greatest danger for the patient moving toward abstinence is a therapist who gets in the way of that movement.

A therapist can block movement in many ways. First, the therapist may really believe in control. The therapist's notion of a successful treatment may be the patient's ability to continue drinking. Loss of control may be an abhorrent concept to this therapist. Second, the therapist may not be able to tolerate the process of surrender, conceptually or practically, equating surrender, that is, accepting the impossibility of control, as a defeat for both patient and therapist. The therapist may fail to see the paradox: By acknowledging lack of control, the patient can gain control by choosing abstinence. The therapist may abort this movement toward surrender by continuing to emphasize the importance of the feasibility of control.

Third, the therapist may not be able to tolerate the depression and despair that accompany the drive toward surrender and abstinence. The therapist may become frightened and offer an antedote, either the false hope of control or perhaps some medication that reduces the patient's discomfort long enough for the patient to reestablish denial.

Fourth, the therapist's difficulties with the issue of control may be played out in work with patients. The therapist may believe that the patient is indeed out of control and therefore requires the therapist to take over. The therapist may then assume a variety of attitudes toward the patient, all based on therapist control. One of the most problematic is the stance of "knowing parental authority." The therapist with this stance expects the patient to relinquish all control and to trust the therapeutic advice and good will. This may be effective with overtly dependent people who acknowledge their need for a strong authority to guide them or give them answers. A clear-cut example from an early recovery group stands out:

Jane remained extremely anxious in the unstructured, here-and-now atmosphere of the recovery group. She repeatedly asked the group to discuss a topic related to alcoholism or sobriety with some structure and direction. When the group repeatedly resisted, she turned to the therapist and invariably pressed for a psychiatric diagnosis. If the therapist could give her a diagnosis, then he also could give her the instructions for a cure.

Such a clear-cut lack of conflict or ambivalence about control and authority figures is rare. More often, the fear of being controlled keeps individuals from forming a therapeutic relationship or joining AA.

Therapists who equate abstinence with success of the therapy and/or their own personal achievement, may establish an attitude of hostile control, blaming the patient for failing to sustain abstinence or for failing to trust the therapist enough, that is, failure to relinquish total control. The therapist may explain this failure by labeling the patient unmotivated or by pointing to personality defects in the patient to explain the patient's inability to give control to the therapist. This inability is described as a fatal flaw.

The question of control is central to the individual tinkering with the notion of a lack of control. It is central to establishing a therapeutic alliance. A newly recovering alcoholic, for example, explored the beliefs about his therapist, as these centered around control:

I've been thinking about the term "transference," asking myself the question, "Who are you for me?" I've decided you're like a brother. I had a dream in which my therapist was wearing a hospital gown. This illustrated to me that you are a patient too—you are an alcoholic and I can therefore trust you.

He later elaborated, noting that because the therapist had "healed himself," the therapist would know the limits of his practice and not assume the attitude of a god. In this case, the therapist's stated self-identity as an alcoholic allowed the patient to establish an equal relationship. In all his previous therapeutic attempts to deal with his alcoholism, he always felt controlled in the role of the helpless patient, to be fixed by the good, all-knowing therapist.

Many patients report unsuccessful and even destructive therapeutic relationships. Some report, on later sober reflection, that their therapy maintained their drinking and they had to leave the therapy and/or the therapist to stop. Most often, maintenance is based on the shared belief by the patient and therapist that the patient is not an alcoholic, and, therefore, the drinking behavior can be controlled. Often, both believe that the drinking is a symptom of other problems that will go away once the other difficulties are solved.

In this sense, the therapy maintains the structure of the belief system, making it impossible for the patient to shift identity. Behavioral change or attempts at abstinence, are tremendously difficult and dysphoric because they should not be necessary within the belief system of control. Attempts at abstinence are therefore a source of diminishing self-esteem.

The therapist who has conflicts with control may unwittingly act out personal conflicts with the alcoholic, becoming in essence the "enabler" or "coalcoholic" partner. The therapist may start with the belief that the patient is out of control and therefore needs the therapist to exert control. This can grow into an intense struggle with patient and therapist proving that each can't control the other.

It is not unusual to hear of therapists drinking with their patients inside and outside the bounds of the therapeutic relationship. And, unfortunately, sexual contact is all too frequently reported as well.

> My therapist and I worked one week on the problem of my drinking. The next, we drank together in the office and then had sex. That therapy was maintaining everything I needed to change.

It is clear that therapists' beliefs, attitudes, and values exert an extremely important influence in psychotherapeutic work with alcoholics. In learning about alcoholism and psychotherapy with alcoholics, therapists must begin at the foundation level of epistemology as outlined by Bateson, examining their own beliefs and personal way of "knowing." At the heart of epistemology is the individual's beliefs about control.

Pitfalls With Therapists After Abstinence

The therapist who has ridden through the shifting identification may interfere on the abstinent side of the transition. Many therapists believe the goal of therapy with the alcoholic is abstinence; once this goal is achieved, the therapy is finished. Therapists may terminate their patients too early, believing their work has been accomplished. Or, therapists, like family members, have other expectations for their patients. They have worked hard at breaking denial and now expect good psychotherapy patients, capable of in-depth analysis and insight without acting out.

The therapist has no appreciation of the developmental nature of recovery and fails to see or accept that the patient is more vulnerable and more dependent than when drinking. The patient may cancel more frequently and suddenly experience extreme anxiety. The ability to stay abstinent from minute to minute and day to day is paramount. The impulses to drink are, for most people, not gone. The patient is thinking about how not to drink and specifically what actions to substitute for the act of drinking. Therapists who do not understand the nature of alcoholism do not understand the critical importance of a behavioral focus at this juncture. The therapist's wish for the patient to open up to deeper insight is thwarted by the patient's need to close down. When denial of alcoholism is broken and loss of control is accepted, denial of all other problems occurs. It is a protection against overwhelming guilt, anxiety, and depression about the painful realities and damage caused by drinking. Many individuals state in early abstinence that alcohol was their only problem, nothing else. Most change their thinking as abstinence progresses, but such recognition in early sobriety may cause so much guilt as to trigger a drinking episode to counter it.

Often, patients who looked competent and insightful while drinking suddenly decompensate, now only capable of concrete cognitions and rote behavior. Such decompensation is understood in AA and by knowledgeable treatment personnel. Individuals are reassured that their feelings and fears are legitimate and urged to think only about being alcoholic and how not to drink. Patients who want to look more closely at other serious problems are encouraged to put these concerns aside until a firm base of abstinence is established.

> My sponsor told me to go to meetings, use the telephone, and put the plug in the jug. And that's all. She said my thinking got me into trouble before and will get me into trouble again if I try to figure all this out. She said the understanding would come later. So I'm just doing what they tell me. Amazing experience for someone who used to have all the answers.

Some therapists have difficulty accepting this reasoning, and the amount of control turned over to a "sponsor." The therapist may not comprehend the early developmental level of the patient's new behavioral and thinking patterns and, therefore, not understand the sponsor's emphasis on behavioral action. The therapist is likely to be much more confrontational with an intellectual uncovering mode and to devalue the singular behavioral emphasis.

The therapist also may feel competitive with the AA sponsor or caught in the bind of contradicting this newly important individual in the patient's life. The therapist may indeed understand the sponsor's suggestion but feel that the patient can combine the behavioral focus with beginning self-examination and profit considerably. The therapist hears the patient's self-effacement, that is, "My thinking got me into trouble before so I can't trust it now," as unnecessary or even harmful and attempts to contradict it.

Bean's (1975a) analysis of the function of low self-esteem in recovery is useful with a problem such as this. It may be extremely important for the patient to accept the sponsor's judgment without question in order to accept a dependent stance and to maintain the new belief in loss of control. It is very tricky for the therapist to either go along with the purely behavioral focus or integrate behavioral, cognitive, and dynamic exploration without challenging the sponsor in such a way that the patient must choose between them.

Many therapists may be uncomfortable with the degree of control relinquished to a sponsor because of their own personal conflicts about dependency. The therapist also may wonder what role he or she can serve if thinking is not to be allowed. Most therapists, unfamiliar with the developmental progression and the AA sponsor–newcomer relationship, find the concept of such relinquishment very negative and regressive. Such a therapist may easily interfere.

At other times, interference is exactly what is called for. AA individuals often change sponsors or involve several individuals in this role. Difficulties arise as in any personal relationship. Because of the frequently close dependent relationship, both individuals may reenact problematic aspects of attachment. In essence, the early parent–child bond may be awakened and a transference relationship developed, which neither is in a position to clarify. The therapist can be extremely helpful in working with the patient on the transferential aspects of the patient–sponsor relationship, whereas the patient may never develop or examine a working transference relationship with the therapist.

Some patients cannot tolerate their dependency feelings and what they perceive to be the unequal status of the therapeutic relationship. Many may terminate in the transition phase (Kanas, 1982), feeling safer with their dependent feelings in AA. Or, instead of increasing their therapy sessions, which would seem logical on the basis of their need, they will decrease them. They feel more dependent and less in control and, therefore, need greater distance from the therapist.

Newly abstinent patients may not be able to tolerate a 50-minute hour as well. Their impulses may be so strong that they need to be acting all the time—running to meetings, making telephone calls, reading, physically working out, and darting from place to place. Sitting in one spot and talking about oneself for 50 minutes may be intolerable.

There is a danger in treating the wish for decreased frequency as a resistance, and there is equal danger in increasing therapeutic sessions during this period. A drastic increase in sessions may suggest to the patient that he or she does not need extra help beyond the therapy hour, and, in fact, that the therapist can provide all the help that is necessary. The therapist who readily increases the frequency of sessions also has difficulty convincing the patient to use AA instead of the therapist.

A newly abstinent individual may continue therapy, but shift from an uncovering mode to one of high denial and extensive control of the hour. That control may be characterized by detailed reporting of the week's events, filling the therapist in on the ways in which choices were made and abstinence maintained. Such reporting fills the hour and ensures that no unwanted or unconscious material can arise or be presented by the therapist. It also has the important effect of reinforcing the new identity and new learning and providing the individual with a sense of control. The patient tells the therapist about the content of AA meetings and the course of a particular day. Hearing himself relate tells him how to think about himself and what to do the next day. Ultimately such repeated reporting is internalized and the individual experiences the choices for abstinence as coming from within.

I know I am an alcoholic and that means I don't drink. But now it really feels like my choice. I know how to stay sober and I don't want to drink.

Interactions with the environment that are not focused on alcohol are risky during the transitional phase. The individual needs to hold onto the alcohol focus behaviorally as a way of controlling impulses that are not yet within the range of cognitive control. The individual who turns attention away from the cognitive and behavioral emphasis on alcohol runs the risk of finding herself drinking.

It seemed like the car was driving me. There I was, heading for the liquor store and I wasn't intending to go there! I bought a bottle and I wasn't intending to drink it. It started when I decided not to go to a meeting that day. I wanted to give myself a break from being alcoholic.

I got so involved in the fun and excitement I forgot I was alcoholic and there I was, drinking again.

Interpretation of Self and Others

With the shift in identity and the change in behavior comes confusion about how to interpret oneself and how to interpret oneself in relation to others. The shift in primary identity involves a dramatic reversal of key beliefs—from being in control to out of control and from being nonalcoholic to alcoholic. Since much of the individual's interpretations of self and world were imbedded in and re-flected through the logic of denial, much of the view of self and the world no longer fits. Both must be reconstructed. But this is a task for long-term recovery. Much of this interpretation will not be questioned during this period if the be-havioral and cognitive focus remains on alcohol.

Nevertheless, it is difficult for many, and questions arise. For example, the patient with a flux in identity may wonder how to relate to others:

When I first joined the order, all of us priests used to really talk with each other, exchange information, give each other spiritual and emotional support. We really felt like a community. Then we each seemed to get busier and busier over the years and spent less time supporting each other in the same way.

Then we decided at least to spend half an hour or so together before dinner each evening just socializing. It never really replaced what we had, but it helped to ease my loneliness.

That cocktail hour is the only time I ever get to feel like part of a community. I don't think I can tolerate the loneliness if I can't be part of the community even for the short time.

Another individual is concerned about her relationship to herself:

I've always spent that hour in the afternoon just being totally alone. Totally. It was the time in the day just for me. Now I don't have that, now that I've stopped drinking, there is no reason to sit down and just relax and be with myself. I feel completely at the mercy of everyone else's demands. I've lost myself.

For most individuals, interpretation of self and others remains unchallenged or even blocked during this period.

The Role and Tasks of Therapy

The task for the patient during the transition phase is to shift identity and change behavior. The patient moves from a belief in control to a recognition of loss of control and acceptance of being alcoholic. The patient then, abruptly or slowly, stops drinking.

The therapist, at this time, has numerous tasks: continuing the erosion of denial, prodding toward despair, tolerating despair, recognizing loss of control, examining the meaning of loss of control and being alcoholic, and educating patients about not drinking.

The person who is still drinking in the transitional phase requires the same major emphasis as the individual still in the drinking phase. However, the focus is likely to center on what is getting in the way of the individual's stopping. The problem may lie in a shifting identity: the individual decides he or she is not alcoholic and therefore doesn't have to stop drinking. Or, the individual requires additional education about behavioral change. The patient is not maintaining abstinence because he or she does not know how to and is not getting advice. Exploration also may include examination of the patient's environment. Are family, friends, and work supportive of abstinence?

The individual who has moved into abstinence requires a different therapeutic strategy. The primary therapeutic treatments are behavioral, cognitive, and educational, all with a singular emphasis on building and securing the patient's identity as an alcoholic and the abstinent behaviors that support it.

There are two phases to the process of surrender. The first involves recognition of defeat, in this case, acknowledgment that drinking is out of control. Many individuals reach this point and go no further. They stay locked in the belief that control is desirable and may bring themselves out of despair by a new scheme or temporary vow of abstinence. A therapist reported the following chain of events in supervision.

My patient came six weeks ago, concerned about his drinking, hoping to get it under control. We spent several meetings looking at that notion—what did control mean and what did it mean to be out of control. We also examined the problems that drinking was causing.

Last week he came to his session, announced that he is an alcoholic because his drinking is clearly out of control. Then he added that he had decided to stop drinking for three months.

The patient had achieved this awareness through a controlled unravelling of his denial. He could tolerate this recognition by now controlling his abstinence. He decided to stop for three months and did not feel despair nor helplessness. The decision was under his control. At the end of three months, he would decide whether or not to continue. Such an outcome is not to be dismissed nor diminished. It is, however, incomplete and formed within a belief system of control. This patient refuses to go to AA because he needs no help; his abstinence is in his control.

The second level of surrender is to ask for help. The individual admits defeat and the need for help. This request for aid cuts into the omnipotence associated with the value of control and functions as an equalizer. That omnipotence is the false belief in the ultimate power of self and self-will which, in Bateson's (1971) schema, places individuals in a symmetrical, competitive relationship to others. Asking for help involves accepting a failure in the power of self.

The shared belief in a higher power, central to the AA philosophy, permits the adoption of a complementary relationship to the world that emphasizes equality. The therapist needs to be receptive to the request for help and sustain the patient's belief in his or her loss of control. The request for help is not to regain control of the drinking, but to acknowledge and confirm its loss. The patient comes to see paradoxically that because drinking is out of control, the only way to gain control is to stop drinking entirely.

BEHAVIORAL CONSIDERATIONS

At a point of transition when the patient is ready to become abstinent, behavioral interventions are most appropriate. These involve substituting new behaviors for the old patterns that maintained and supported drinking.

Behavioral Adjustments

Behavioral interventions include suggesting that a patient substitute an AA meeting for the difficult evening hours or for the time usually spent in a bar and other similar substitutions and changes as well. The individual used to shared conversation during the five o'clock cocktail hour may find it difficult to give up the cocktail because it implies giving up this protected space. Many feel comfortable substituting a soft drink and continuing the ritual hour of sharing. Others find the setting and cues intolerable. Instead of pleasure, the soft drink is a reminder of deprivation. When the environment remains the same and only the substance is changed, there is greater danger of a move back to alcohol; there is a powerful environmental pull toward drinking.

> For some time I drank soda water while my husband continued having his martini. It went OK, although I didn't get the same sense of relaxation and closeness I had while drinking with him. Eventually my husband and I both decided that I had been so good, a drink with him wouldn't hurt. I can see now that I had to get away from that situation completely. It was too hard to only change the drinking and nothing else.

The therapist may need to help the patient make simple but crucial environmental adjustments that seem at first glance unnecessary or to be "carrying things too far." With the above patient for example, the therapist first determines the drinking pattern and sets about to disrupt it directly. She suggested that her patient take a walk with her partner at five o'clock to interfere with the drinking behavior and the environmental cues that signaled and legitimized drinking.

Patients often have a difficult time making environmental adjustments. Many hope that not drinking will be enough, that they won't have to make other changes. Many also are shocked and disturbed to discover that behavioral change involves not only substitution for the act of drinking, but filling in space that was once occupied by drinking or the drinking way of life. Many alcoholics do not have hobbies or interests. If they do, they are probably rusty from disuse. Many individuals have great difficulty taking the initiative to develop a hobby or interest, even when the behavioral base of abstinence is well established.

Drinking was a way of organizing life so that active, personal initiative was unnecessary. The responsibility for filling one's day may now be very problematic. Issues of aggression, competition, dependency, and role in a relationship may all be tied to difficulties with initiative and require psychotherapeutic exploration beyond behavioral prescription.

Therapists often have a difficult time helping the patient make both behavioral and environmental adjustments, hoping that not drinking will be enough or failing to understand the nature of addiction and the need for such concrete simple behavioral approaches.

Most therapists are unlikely to be active enough in behavioral prescription or education about alcoholism, even bypassing these requirements entirely (Krueger, 1982; Silber, 1974; Blane, 1977). They simply fail to recognize that maintenance of abstinence requires new behavior patterns. Maintenance of abstinence also requires new thinking patterns. However, the therapist may think like the patient: The drinking has stopped so let's get on to other things. Similarly, therapists can devalue or underestimate the educational tasks of the transition phase. In consultation, a therapist expressed the following opinion:

I told my patient to take Antabuse, and he is taking Antabuse. That's it for the drinking problem. Now we're working on important issues.

During this phase, patients are upset at the recognition of helplessness and the reality of not knowing how to stay abstinent, and they need a therapist to legitimize the educational task and to provide a variety of suggestions and advice. Pamphlets about alcoholism are excellent educational tools.

Using AA

A stronger educational recommendation is to use AA. AA is many things, but most importantly it is educational. Individuals learn what it means to be alcoholic, how to think about themselves from this new vantage point, and how to stay sober "a day at a time." Feelings of isolation and despair are softened as they identify with the experiences of other members and learn that it is not only OK to ask for help but vitally important to do so. Those with a comfortable sobriety report that they do not believe they are doing it on their own.

If the patient accepts AA, the therapist can turn these two major tasks of the transitional phase, behavioral and educational interventions, over to AA and then concentrate on providing the patient with clarification or suggestions. The therapist monitors the movement of the patient through this phase, listening for signs of positive identification with AA members, a wish for more meetings, a sense of safety and relief, a feeling of belonging, evidence of new learning about oneself as an alcoholic, or concrete suggestions for staying sober.

The individual who forms a positive and active tie with AA may need little active intervention from the therapist other than wholehearted support for strengthening the AA tie.

I really enjoy the meetings. People are friendly, and I feel like I belong.

I heard a fellow chair—sounded like he was reading my mail! I couldn't believe anybody else ever felt like I did. I drank again after I came to AA, but I never really went back out. I liked what I heard and wanted what AA members have. Drinking no longer worked. I was home.

The therapist listens also for reluctance and resistance, characteristic of the transitional phase, which are often expressed in negative feelings about AA.

I don't like the drunkalogues.

AA is too religious. They talk about God.

They are all fanatics!

I don't want to go to meetings all my life.

> I'm not as sick as they are.

> I'm glad those poor people found AA, but it's not for me.

There is a great risk that therapists who really believe in self-control, who don't understand the nature of addiction, who devalue the behavioral changes necessary, or who wish to compete with AA keeping the patient all to themselves, will hear these complaints as legitimate and not interpret them as resistance.

> My patient tried AA but didn't like the references to God. I don't blame him. That would turn me off too. AA isn't for everyone after all.

Another therapist voices the same complaint but provides a more helpful intervention:

> I told my patient that AA is full of all kinds of people with all kinds of religious beliefs. The most important thing they have in common is the knowledge about how to stay sober and the experience of doing so. I told him not to worry about God at this point. Take what fits and leave the rest.

This therapist provides a framework for the patient to accept attendance without sacrificing other long-held beliefs, in this case, religious. The therapist also strongly, though indirectly, supports the value of AA by suggesting to the patient that he can choose the experiences and the people with whom he wishes to identify, thereby attaining a sense of control and autonomy.

The fact that there are many varied experiences in achieving and maintaining abstinence is a powerful reminder of the individual's ultimate autonomy in personally tailoring a program of recovery. For example, some individuals have a sponsor, others do not; some attend large meetings, others prefer small meetings; some become active in 12-step work immediately, but others do not; and some talk a lot in meetings, and others never talk.

The ability to belong to AA and be like other people and maintain one's individuality at the same time is a very important factor in the success of AA and its underlying emphasis on autonomy.

COGNITIVE CONSIDERATIONS

The Turning Point

The turning point (Finlay, 1978) is marked by an essential crack in the system of logic; rationalization and denial no longer successfully explain behavior that is out of control.

Although the combination or "fit" of turning points is unique to each individual, direct external intervention from relatives, friends, or authority figures (therapists, boss) combined with internal feelings of self-disgust or a recognition of readiness comprise the frame for the decision to abstain, as the following examples show.

I was always fighting. I was paranoid, slandering my sister, parents, boyfriend while drunk. I didn't know what was wrong. I felt my whole world was crumbling and thought of suicide.

It seemed like nothing would ever change. Alcohol ruled my life and I knew it, but I could not change. I had years of crazy behavior behind me but nothing could break me out of the patterns. Then one day I spilled a glass of bourbon on the bed. I was devastated, not about spilling the drink, but in having to change the bed! I immediately thought about going to the psych ward as a way of not having to change that bed! That reasoning did it. That was the end for me.

Where these two examples illustrate a turning point characterized by internal recognition and despair, the following three illustrate a turning point characterized by a combination of both external and internal events.

I felt seriously depressed and full of self-loathing. I had begun to realize that I really couldn't drink socially. My husband was locking up the liquor and telling my parents I had a drinking problem. I was pregnant and terribly worried about the baby. Finally my husband called AA and that was it.

Well, there were lots of things pushing me toward the bottom. I released some major reports while operating in a blackout. My wife told me to go live somewhere else and my partners told me to shape up or their new partnership would leave me out. Finally I just got plain tired of trying to cover up and failing.

I had an increasing fear of people and social contact. I was isolating myself more and more, and engaging in great psychological probing with subsequent despair and self-pity. I was making a public ass of myself more and more and doing things untrue to my principles. My friends expressed their disgust and I felt a fear and a hate of life, people, and myself.

The turning point is a point of fear and despair as the individual's carefully constructed logic begins to crumble.

I am in a holding pattern waiting for the butterfly within me to emerge. One day it will happen: I will wake up and won't want to drink again. But I just don't have self-discipline and I don't want to have to try.

This patient then asks whether or not self-discipline is the same as will power and then considers that abstinence may never feel good.

I can think of a friend who wanted a cigarette everyday of her life. How do I get to the point that I am willing to endure the discomforts? I don't think I can stick to it—I like drinking more than I like life and I don't have to face my hopelessness if I keep drinking. To say I need help! What is that in the eyes of others? Will people stick with me if I'm struggling?

This patient remains stuck in this holding pattern for months. Her denial about being alcoholic was broken, but she could not give up the substance because she imagined she would feel desperately helpless and needy. Holding onto alcohol provided its own hell, but still kept her from the despair of feeling terrified and helpless.

I feel like a prisoner of war. To ask for help is to aid the enemy. I must bear up by myself. It's easier to say I'm crazy than to feel so utterly desperate.

She sinks into greater despair:

I am in "earthquake status." The only thing that matters is to keep alive and hang on. Why am I not more concerned about what I'm doing to myself? It doesn't matter if I break a leg; there is no place to go tomorrow.

She then recalls her first love, an activist in college.

We could both work for something we believed in. I wish I could translate this into a belief for myself right now. I have nothing to believe in.

She had hope when she first came to treatment, but now it has disappeared.

When I first came to treatment, I thought it would be the answer. It would be a matter of desensitizing myself to the idea of being alcoholic. It's like patting a dog—you do so till you're not afraid anymore. But that's not how it's working. I just can't get from here to there. I'm just not at the point where I'm willing to change.

In retrospect, individuals often can construct a chain of events that led to a point of "readiness," though this is rarely evident during the process because denial is still too effective. Often, this reasoning pinpoints clearly the meaning and functions of alcohol. A female patient described how she had crumbled rapidly into despair.

I suddenly reached the point where I wanted to do something about my drinking. I suddenly felt I didn't have a lot of time. I had teenage children who needed me and I could only give them what I had to offer with a clear head. With several years of sobriety now, I realize that the anticipation of my children's departure

opened the way for my move toward recovery. Alcohol allowed me to get through
the difficult childhood years and now it was safe to relinquish it.

Another patient illustrates this reconstruction process. She can trace the crack
in her thinking and her attempts to patch the cracks to hold her denial together.

> I knew I was an alcoholic two years before I came to my first AA meeting but I
> spent the next six years proving it wasn't so—that's right, it took four years after
> first trying AA to finally give up.

> Those were awful years because all my energy went into proving to myself and
> others that I wasn't alcoholic. I was a "social" drinker and that is what I proved
> repeatedly. I drank everyday for hours in a bar because it looked more social, but
> I refused to talk to anyone. I told the people who wanted to be "social" to leave
> me alone; I came to drink! One day it all fell apart and I couldn't keep it up any
> longer.

Shift in Identity

The principle task of the transition phase is a shift in central identity from nonalcoholic to alcoholic. This is accompanied by a new recognition of loss of control. A change in identity is not absolutely central to the maintenance of abstinence; it is possible to maintain abstinence through the exercise of will but at a
cost. However, change in identity is central to acceptance of loss of control and
the corresponding long-term shift in perception and interpretation of oneself and
others.

Terry shows the developmental nature of the progression in the change of
identity and acceptance of loss of control. She reports regaining clarity after
emerging from a drinking episode:

> I can step out of my thinking difficulties by not drinking, taking Antabuse, and
> coming for treatment. I wonder whether it is possible to change my life and not
> just seek protection for myself and from myself. I used to think I could just change
> my habits and my difficulty was one of insufficient self-will. But now I see that I
> have a drinking mentality, a mind set which is intolerant of outside demands and
> which signals drinking to avoid them. And I can't control this frame of mind.

After Terry recognized that abstinence is not a matter of will, she began to
examine the meaning and function of drinking to her. She realized that drinking
was bound up with her sense of autonomy and a deep belief in herself as being
bad. She struggled continually with opposing sides of herself: a good girl or bad
girl. As long as drinking was tied to her sense of autonomy, she saw abstinence
as a capitulation to others' control. Being out of control was tied to her sense
of shame and the belief that she was bad and that she must relinquish control of

herself to others—her husband, therapist, Antabuse. She then struggled with the authorities whom she believed controlled her:

> I feel resentful. Not drinking is an ongoing drag. Having to be "treated" is an intrusion in my life. It's one more thing I have to juggle. Besides, I have to hang onto my deviant image and treatment is interfering!

Terry followed this period of struggle with a brief drinking episode, acting out her struggle for control. She then traced the events leading to her binge:

> I was angry and resentful. I felt forced into conventional behavior. So I told myself I could get to my bad self—that deviant person in me—by drinking. I wonder if I can get to that bad side—even keep that bad side—without alcohol. It feels like giving up a whole part of myself if I take Antabuse. I need to shift my thinking to where I can feel that I gain control by taking Antabuse rather than lose it.

This led to a discussion of whether or not she could control her drinking through Antabuse. She talked about going to AA as a way of coming up for air. She recognized her need for an external structure that she would not need to defy and that would enhance her freedom. Terry could not shift from her one belief in the autonomy of her bad drinking self. She therefore could not free herself from the association of abstinence to loss of herself. Ultimately, she made the following shift:

> For the first time, I can separate being alcoholic from the rest of myself and I see I can do something about it. I really feel like an alcoholic for the first time because I can do something about it. I'm thinking about drinking differently. It's simple and practical: If you are alcoholic, you do ABC. I have to shift outside of myself to get clarity.

She reached an important realization:

> I don't have to spend time struggling with being alcoholic. I feel liberated but endangered for the rest of my life. Suddenly, it's OK to be an alcoholic, although I wonder if I'll be perceived as bad. Feels like my secret is out.

In the next few weeks she adjusted to her new identity and clarified its meaning and the meaning of sobriety:

> I woke up depressed and felt as if I had been drinking. I am beginning to brood, isolate, and retreat. I now recognize this as my "territory" of drinking. But . . . I didn't drink. I feel a revulsion to alcohol, like a hobby dropped. And I feel confused and depressed.

Terry recognized that her depression was attached to the deep recognition of herself as an alcoholic. She reported frequent, unpleasant dreams:

> At the end of every dream and every memory is drinking. I have to give myself time to acquire new memories that don't have alcohol attached. I don't have a history of myself yet as a nondrinker or sober person.

She thought further, recognizing that any history of herself always was connected painfully to alcohol. She now realized that she carefully threw away important work as a way of destroying the evidence of her bad self.

> I don't have a past to build from. I denied my past by throwing it away. Drinking put everything inevitably within a pattern of failure so I threw it all away. Now I am not trapped by my old behaviors. I can build a new history of myself.

As her therapy unfolded, she recognized that denying her alcoholism was the central feature of her drinking life. This awareness came after spending time with an alcoholic who was drinking.

> I recognized that it wasn't worth it for me to drink too. I took my Antabuse because I knew I needed extra protection against the impulse to drink. I realized that it is horrible for me to be alcoholic. I always thought I wouldn't have to be an alcoholic if I behaved like I wasn't. And I made sure I wasn't alcoholic by simply saying I wasn't. I can see that the first order of therapy is to work on being alcoholic—all else has to take second place.

Belonging

Central to the process of identification as an alcoholic is the personal meaning attached to that identity (Thune, 1977). For most individuals, that includes a sense of belonging to that class of people who are "alcoholic." These meanings are often tied to the individual's beliefs about and projections onto AA. The ability to identify as alcoholic is often linked directly to the implied belonging:

> If I identify as an alcoholic, if I say I'm one of you, I relegate myself to the down and outers—I'm forever abnormal.

Another patient realized that to belong to any group was to relinquish her specialness. The more she learned about alcoholism and the more she questioned her own denial, the more she pinned herself in a corner:

> I've always considered myself special and unique. I hate to think I'm one of the millions going through the revolving door of denial. But if I acknowledge that I'm alcoholic, I'll just be one of the many recovering alcoholics. I don't want to belong to either group.

In her next session she announced that she is an alcoholic, but with reservations: She saw similarities between herself and other AA members, but she saw many more discrepancies. She simply couldn't identify with the heartberaking stories and desperation expressed by so many:

> I have never felt I was hanging on to sobriety and I don't want to feel that way. To see myself as an alcoholic is to feel desperately needy and I am resisting that identification.

The Meaning of Being Alcoholic

The shift in identity from nonalcoholic to alcoholic is a fluctuating one as the individual tries on the label and assesses its fit. Blocks in this process come from conscious and unconscious meanings attached to the label "alcoholic." A major part of the breakdown of denial and assisting movement through this phase is an uncovering process that reveals and clarifies the implications of the new identity. Exploration about what it means to be alcoholic forms the central core of an uncovering process: The patient examines deeper layers of meaning that constitute the personal identity (Guidano and Liotti's core construct of self referred to in Chapter 3). Examination of what it means to be alcoholic involves uncovering the deepest personal beliefs that structure the individual's self-view, perception of others, and behavior.

During the course of many months this central question formed the core of exploration in therapy for Terry. In the beginning of her work, she recalled the meaning of alcohol to her family. She recognized that when she thought about drinking, particularly after a drinking episode, she thought of her family. She recalled that she received attention from her parents when she drank. At the same time, alcohol separated her from her family. It gave her a sense of distance and distinction, an important sense of being "outside" her family and her childhood home. She described her hatred of her midwestern suburban town, realizing that she got away from it by drinking. Suddenly she recognized alcohol as a liberator, moving her toward a more sophisticated life. Drinking was a way to make sure she would never have to go back home. In this sense, drinking symbolized self-assertiveness and autonomy. But she recognized that drinking also allowed her to have her family because it made her helpless and in need of support.

Issues of power and helplessness became a central focus for understanding the meaning and function of alcohol. Terry reported a dream in which she was not drinking because she got someone else to do it for her. That other person then became helpless. For the next few days Terry felt as if she had been drunk. She realized that she never "defines a situation" (asserts herself) because her taking charge made the other person helpless. She had a deep identity as someone who was helpless. Yet when she drank, she believed she was in a state of mind in which she could take charge. In reality she couldn't. Terry recognized that her drinking helped her not to be assertive while still giving her an illusion of power. Further exploration revealed Terry's sense of helplessness to be an important cover for her deeper sense of herself as a dangerous, aggressive person. Her helplessness served as a protection for others and from her own recognition of her deep anger.

This theme provided direction for her exploring the meaning and functions of alcohol in her young adult life. She labeled drinking as a compensation for and a defense against someone else's setting the rules, thus enabling her to express her resentment of another's dominance. When drinking, she handed over decision making. This "handing over" gave her the illusion that she was in control when she actually felt the power belonged to someone else. She saw that she operated on the deep belief that someone else would dominate. Drinking was a way to get back at the world that dominated. It was a compensation for stress and a reward. Unfortunately, this pampering was also punitive.

She extended the unraveling of her belief structure noting that she had always experienced life as dangerous. Drinking bought time out from that danger and seemed to give her life coherence and pattern. The more Terry understood the important functions of alcohol, the more meaning she could attribute to it. It allowed her to stay aloof, maintaining herself in a state of demoralized passivity. This state bought time so she did not have to be actively bad, that is, aggressive.

Terry was abstinent during this period of analysis of the important meanings of alcohol to her. Months later she drank briefly and later unraveled the decision that led her to drink. That decision was accompanied by feeling fatigued and susceptible to whim and self-indulgence. She now understood and labeled for herself a "drinking rhythm" in which she bought time out. Drinking changed her sense of time; it magnified her senses and perceptions and slowed things down.

As she identified this rhythm, she began to describe and clarify what she labeled a "drinking frame of mind." This included cognitive and emotional aspects that she, at first, defined as a distinct personality. Now she recognized the "frame of mind" as a thinking state, a drinking mentality that carried its own structure and beliefs and dictated and explained drinking behavior.

Drinking Frame of Mind

The drinking frame of mind (drinking mentality or drinking rhythm) is often what AA members call alcoholic thinking or a "dry drunk." Individuals experience the same thinking, behavioral, and affective patterns that characterize drinking. The only difference is the current absence of alcohol. Individuals often feel they have lost their grounded deep sense of surrender and the complementary view of the world that accompanied it. Old thinking, emphasizing self, power, and control, may predominate in all areas of life. Rather than trust the new routine or an intuitive deep commitment to abstinence, individuals may have to turn their full attention to the concrete behaviors of abstinence to counter the pull to drink that might be triggered by this state. This state is a combination of a thinking disorder and an affective state. The drinking state of mind is often tied to the meaning of alcohol. It also may serve as a defense in abstinence, signaling and covering the emergence of deeper issues, not necessarily related to alcohol.

Abstinent for many months, Barbara explored the evolution of an impulse to drink:

> Following a vacation with my husband, I dreamed about drinking. I realized that the vacation required greater physical and emotional closeness with my husband and awakened a need to protect myself and others from what I call my "overintensity." I feel myself pulled into a drinking state of mind in situations which demand continuous contact and no exits. The drinking frame of mind involves emotional detachment and a "foggy, vague" sense of perception.

This frame of mind accomplishes emotional withdrawal and signals a readiness to act out detachment by taking a drink. The perceptive state may be accompanied by affective components of depression, including sleepiness or passivity.

The meaning and function of the drinking mentality differ. Many people feel detached and isolated without alcohol, so the cognitive and affective state of readiness to drink includes an expectation of achieving closeness and attachment via alcohol, rather than distance and separation. Because the meanings and functions of alcohol are so different, it is vital to carefully unravel and understand the idiosyncratic, multiple, and often contradictory meanings for each patient.

After a drinking episode, Barbara, for example, reported a blurry, foggy state, noting that her mental life was linked to her physical, like a taste in the mouth. She had been sober long enough to recognize that her sense of clarity was tied to her sober frame of mind rather than her drinking mentality. In the past, she believed it was the reverse. A few weeks after recognizing this reversal, she experienced herself out of control without having had anything to drink. She felt unfocused and found herself pretending she was drinking, although not actually doing so. She curled up tightly, in an effort to keep things out of her mind, and she feared falling asleep because she would have a bad dream. For the first time, she recognized that what she thought of as drinking behavior was actually a part of her own self. She was acting as if she had been drinking, and was experiencing all the feelings tied to that experience and state of mind. She related these feelings to what was going on in her life, thus deepening her therapy and her reflections about herself. She suddenly realized it was the first anniversary of her last drinking bout, which she was reexperiencing without actively drinking. She also was able to understand at this time the difference between a mood that is her's and the behaviors that accompany drinking, such as hiding and lying. Until now they were interwoven.

During the next few weeks, Barbara explored her discovery that her drinking state of mind is a regular part of herself, a way to deal with a world in which she felt unhappy. She now labeled her state of mind "depressed," a condition similar to "being drunk," in which she felt ultrasensitive and vulnerable and which influenced her orientation and reaction to others. She now felt her state of mind as an immense obstacle, a habit she fell into that was out of control. She expected to feel good when she stopped drinking, but now had to put up with being herself. No longer did she have a sense of two distinct selves, good and bad, directly connected to drinking.

The need for a continuing cognitive focus and well-established new behavioral routines is shown in this example. The cognitive focus allowed Barbara to understand the various functions and meanings of her drinking, and the behavior prevented her from acting on her feelings of disorientation or the pull back to drinking signaled by the drinking frame of mind and legitimized by the distorted logic of this mentality.

The drinking frame of mind, the pull toward alcohol, and the particular way an individual views the world while drinking are often seductive to the abstinent individual. Many people decide consciously to participate in a state of mind achieved by drinking. It is similar to the rationale of the drug culture that mind-altering drugs are a vehicle to a different state of mind, not obtainable without the substance.

Such logic for drinking may be pure rationalization. It also may be an important cornerstone in the individual's deepest beliefs about self.

> I call my drinking a form of research, an illusory sense that I can cross personal boundaries and merge with someone else's state of mind. It also gives me a profound identification with self-destructiveness.

Barbara continued to believe that her drinking provided her with important emotional experiences she could not otherwise achieve. Only when she began to think of her drinking as protecting her from self-discovery could she begin to challenge her logic. Barbara permitted herself one more drinking episode as a form of research, acknowledging that she expected to deepen her experiences by drinking. After this episode she recognized that the ceremony of drinking actually served as a replacement for the deeper emotional experience she hoped to obtain. What she believed was emotional clarity, she now recognized as unfocused.

For months after this experience Barbara remained abstinent and depressed. She watched herself act out, without alcohol, behaviors that used to accompany drinking. She began to see that drinking was a way of being in the world for her that she did anyway without alcohol. Her drinking frame of mind was "out of touch," and "inaccessible."

As Barbara's thinking altered, she soon described a "drinking day." She felt full of anxiety, "fog," and severe headache, the same as when she drank. She then considered that she might be depressed and examined her identification with her father's helplessness. She soon came to see that her drinking was equal to her father's depression.

Later in her sobriety, she continued to experience depression that she now described and labeled as a depressed, vague mood. She said it was just like being drunk because so much of the behavior is automatic and passive. She said that drinking made her convalescent, unable to respond, and now, since she has labeled her depression, she recognizes the same thing.

The drinking frame of mind, or the "dry drunk" as it is called in AA, is an extremely important part of the alcoholic's drinking and recovery. During the drinking phase, it is difficult to isolate the cognitive and affective components from their fusion with the behavioral act of drinking. The same fusion is characteristic of the transitional phase and thereby produces a serious threat to the newly abstinent individual. This person does not yet have the abstinent behaviors in place or the distance from feelings described by Piaget necessary to separate the feeling from the act. A sheltered environment (AA meetings, not being alone) may be necessary to weather the period without drinking.

As behavioral, cognitive, and affective components develop and the act of drinking is separated from the thinking and affect that accompanied it, individuals may begin to explore the deeper meaning of alcohol or uncover other issues or problem areas that were hidden by alcohol.

The drinking frame of mind becomes a signal to the abstinent individual that a conflict is arising. The individual strengthens behaviors of abstinence and may begin fourth step (see Chapter 9), self-examination with therapeutic exploration to uncover the source of the "dry drunk."

Antabuse

Antabuse (Ewing, 1982) is a drug that, when combined with alcohol, produces mild to severely debilitating nausea. For many, the threat of a potentially violent physical reaction serves as a deterrent to drinking, or at least removes the ability to act immediately on the impulse to drink. The individual who wishes to drink must stop the Antabuse and wait up to three days before it is safe to drink.

Such a safety valve of external control can be extremely useful for the individual who wants to stop drinking but cannot resist acting on the impulse. This person has not yet learned new actions to substitute, or is too frightened of being without alcohol to try. Many individuals are prescribed a temporary course of Antabuse on leaving an alcohol treatment center. It is extra support for the transition from the safe inpatient treatment structure to the often unsafe world outside. Even with the extensive education about how not to drink provided in the hospital, behavioral impulses to drink may still carry more weight on exit. The individual is still dominated by action and the behavior is still drinking.

> I spent four weeks in that hospital and felt wonderful. I was sure of myself as an alcoholic and I knew what I would do when I left. I said goodbye, drove away, and stopped at the first bar for a drink. Everything I'd learned couldn't stop me and I was horrified as I watched myself do it.

This patient was rehospitalized and discharged the next time on Antabuse as an additional external structural support. The patient remained on Antabuse for six months while adjusting to membership in AA and solidifying new behaviors so he could make use of them instead of drinking. It took six months before he could actually choose to go to an AA meeting instead of a bar. With Antabuse, he felt the choice was taken away. Obviously he could have stopped his Antabuse at any time. The success of Antabuse rested on his deep desire not to drink and was thus an ally for him in maintaining abstinence. The success also rested on the proper assessment of the treatment staff and the patient that he required major external supports to maintain abstinence long enough to learn the new behavior patterns he could ultimately exercise himself.

An assessment of this ability is necessarily subjective. It rests ultimately on the individual's desire to remain abstinent and the proper knowledge about how to do so. It also includes an assessment of the environment, including the likelihood that family and friends will be supportive of abstinence. Relapses in the transitional phase may often be pinned to an unsupportive environment. For example, the abstinence of the wife and her new intense focus on herself and her alcoholism may be a severe threat to her husband whose own drinking is now more visible. She senses the threat and determines unconsciously that her abstinence is an aggressive act against her husband. She will be responsible for the breakup of their marriage. Even with solid behavioral and educational training on how to stay abstinent, she cannot do so without the safety and constant reinforcement of an inpatient setting.

Through the peer involvement, she may get a sense of security and a belief that she can tolerate the family disruption and even the breakup she envisions. The inpatient structure allows her time to solidify her abstinence and put it first, over her marriage. It is very difficult for some patients to maintain the primary importance of their abstinence when family, work, or personal relationships dictate against it.

The decision to prescribe Antabuse or to hospitalize rests on several factors. First, the individual may require care for detoxification. When this is not necessary the decision must be based on the individual's ability to remain abstinent without the safety of the inpatient structure.

Many individuals can maintain abstinence from hour to hour and day to day with AA meetings or support groups. The addition of outpatient counseling also may provide a safety valve.

Steve was staying abstinent "one day at a time" by attending AA meetings every-day. When he got anxious during the day he drove to the clinic parking lot where he sat until he felt calm. The parking lot reinforced his identification as an alcoholic and his positive identification with the clinic as a source of support for his abstinence. When he lost the desire to act on his urge to drink, he drove away, back to work and to an AA meeting that night. Steve had been on Antabuse early in his treatment. He decided to stop the medication and substituted the parking lot immediately for his sense of external control.

Partial Abstinence: A Form of Denial

Often the logic cracks enough so problems resulting from alcohol can no longer be denied, but the identity does not change. Individuals recognize that they have problems with alcohol, but see the solution as improving their control by regulating their drinking and their abstinence. The continuing belief in control is a rejection of the reality of permanent loss of control and of the need for help.

Often this ambivalence will be reflected in on and off attendance at AA or the on and off use of Antabuse. Tom started therapy to examine his drinking, which was causing considerable trouble for others. He recognized that he needed to stop and believed he could control his stopping. He began using Antabuse as a way of controlling his abstinence. He bypassed a state of despair and a feeling of surrender. He felt instead a sense of conquest: "I have licked this problem and I don't need any help."

He believed that Antabuse was the answer to his lack of control. Antabuse would provide the temporary control that would permit him to continue drinking over the long run. Tom now interchanged his drinking bouts with periods of abstinence, during which time he reinforced his belief that he now had control. He could not see that the only difference from "going on the wagon" was his illusion that he had relinquished control and was not relying on will power: "I can't drink because I'm on Antabuse." In fact, whenever he wanted to drink, he stopped the drug, thereby exerting his will.

Meg illustrates the same emphasis on control. After a long period of sobriety, maintained by Antabuse, she went on a binge and felt depressed and remorseful.

I was very angry and drank openly to declare that my drinking was not a secret as it had been in the past. I'm sick of being the sober good girl.

But in fact, after playing the binge out and expressing her anger, she wanted to return to abstinence.

I don't like to take Antabuse everyday because I shouldn't need to. But I'm taking it now because I don't trust my mental state. I need the external control because I'm locked into a way of thinking in which I have no control. I need Antabuse when I'm angry, depressed, or losing my focus.

Meg is upset, not about her lack of control of alcohol, but about her lack of control over her Antabuse.

I thought I could tell when I needed it and that I could be in charge of my Antabuse.

Meg maintained abstinence with several brief drinking episodes for several years, using Antabuse as her control. She knew she was alcoholic but could not accept relinquishing the source of control. She simply translated the ability to control alcohol into the ability to control her Antabuse. The therapist suggested that Meg needed to hold onto her choice to drink, that she had not given up and therefore continued to control her drinking even though she is primarily abstinent. Finally, the therapist wondered what purpose it served to hold onto this option. Meg pondered:

I don't know how to say no and it's not acceptable to be overwhelmed. Drinking is a way to fail while denying that I have any limits.

Several months later, Meg contemplated her newly achieved sense of herself without alcohol, but revealed her ongoing struggle with control and her shame about being alcoholic.

I have built drinking out of my life so that even if I lived alone I wouldn't drink.

Later she mentioned that she had made a dessert with alcohol to serve to herself and a friend. She realized the contradiction: I had accepted not drinking while with my friends but I would show them that I still had control by consuming a dessert with alcohol in it.

Many authorities believe a course of Antabuse is a good test of a patient's motivation to stop drinking. It can be a dangerous test, because it can be fatal when mixed with alcohol. However it does provide information.

I was on Antabuse for six weeks and it "broke my spirit." I felt worse rather than better with the pressure of wanting to drink and not being able to have it. I also had trouble sleeping. I decided to drink as a way of getting a rest from the Antabuse and the tension of being abstinent. I fully intended to go back on it after my rest but never did.

This patient was upset and more disillusioned about her ability to ever stop drinking. Shortly thereafter she reported a dream:

> I needed a guide to get me to an AA meeting that was one block away. I arrived late, stumbled into the meeting by chance. I felt a feeling of futility but a desire to try. But I felt shut out and excluded.

In interpreting her dream, she said she felt hopeless. She had to reconcile herself to the fact that she would drink herself to death in the corner. The reason: lack of will power.

Giving up Control and The Concept of a Higher Power

Alcoholics who are reaching the bottom are often paranoid and view the world as their enemy. To put their trust in someone else, therapists or clergy for example, is incomprehensible. As one patient said clearly in rejecting a particular treatment program, "I can't turn over control of my life to a doctor I can't trust." The belief that "I can control myself" is often the only antidote to feelings of despair and hopelessness and a fear that no one or nothing "can help me if I can't do it myself."

However, many individuals can relinquish control to the power of the AA group (AA, 1955; Thune, 1977; Kurtz, 1982). They see that others can stay sober, and they allow themselves to hope or even to trust in the experience of others. This is the beginning step. Much of the work of ongoing recovery is the personal interpretation and development of the meaning of this concept. AA members refer to this as the spiritual nature of their program. A major aspect of the 12 steps is relinquishment of control (see Chapter 9).

Central to the philosophy of AA is the concept of a higher power. It is, in most basic form, a belief in a "power greater than myself" whatever form that may take. It is through and to that higher power that control is relinquished. And it is the nature of the belief itself that is for many people the biggest stumbling block to acceptance of surrender and AA.

Observers of AA often think of the organization as religious. Newcomers sense the same emphasis and are often hesitant about the references to God in the 12 steps and the discussions in meetings. Individuals bring all of their past experiences with religion and God to bear in evaluating their ability to join and use AA. As one individual explained:

> I needed to stop drinking and I needed AA desperately to do it. But I was so put-off by what I called the "God business." It meant to me the old man with the white beard who punished, the concept of an angry God I had as a child. I couldn't imagine that I had to believe in that God again in order to stay sober.

Another individual interpreted the concept of a higher power and references to God as a loss of autonomy.

> It all sounded pretty good to me as far as not drinking. But all this talk about God turned me off. It was corny and I feared I would lose my independence. I would have to start talking like all these people and even start thinking like them. It reminded me of cults and I resisted. For a long time, I insisted I would be a member and not believe in God.

She softened her view when she found ready acceptance from others despite her view.

> I realized I could maintain my own views and there were even others who didn't believe in God. Some of these people told me it was fine. I could believe in the group or the door knob if I wanted to. But I did have to believe that it wasn't me who was the power. That was hard. After all, it is me who doesn't take the drink.

> It made more sense when I realized that I got the strength to stay abstinent by trusting in the experience of others. Somehow their success gave me the courage to keep going.

The concept of a higher power is also a great stumbling block because it holds within it the shift from a symmetric to a complementary view of the world, the key alteration in epistemology necessary to sustain abstinence (Bateson, 1971). Yet from the symmetric vantage point, a higher power is seen as a threat to the power of the self and the belief in self-control. Individuals reject a concept of higher power because to believe holds within it the relinquishment of control. This concept of a higher power is often threatening to individuals contemplating abstinence and membership in AA. The transition period is often characterized concretely by a split in identity with a sense of one foot in and one foot out.

Sally shows her shift in identity and also the blocks to her moving freely into abstinence.

> I was impressed with the courage of a woman who said she was an alcoholic because she is facing herself in a way I cannot do. I'm hiding behind a pillow, peering out and wearing a disguise.

> It may not be devastating to be an alcoholic. But I don't understand AA, particularly the steps. I bought the AA Big Book but it doesn't speak to me. It's spiritual. You have to abandon yourself to a higher power and I'll never get to that stage. I have to do it alone.

Mike illustrates a patient who looks good on the outside: He is abstinent and states his wish to continue, yet he has not restructured his identity to include lack of control:

My goal in therapy is to stop Antabuse without having a fear that I'll drink. To do this I must develop "willpower." Otherwise, I can't trust myself. I know I'll be able to rationalize my drinking.

He is correct about everything except the need to develop willpower.

Another patient, analyzing a drinking episode after stopping Antabuse, realizes he is still ambivalent and upset about being alcoholic:

I'm playing with Antabuse. When I take it, I just feel the humiliation of being alcoholic. When I stop it, that feeling goes away.

He continues his analysis:

My struggle for sobriety is an endless task full of recognizing the ways in which I deceive myself and engage in willful combat. A belief in a crash program or simple solution is seductive.

Accepting that I'm alcoholic doesn't seem to help. To stop drinking now seems equal to defeat. And the will to take Antabuse looks the same. The fact that it stops me from drinking just accents my shame.

I'm not into surrender. Drinking is hooked to something valuable that I'm going to lose.

Shift in Object Attachment

The question of whether alcoholism is related to a disturbance in object relations or a disturbance in the development of ego structures is a critical distinction in psychoanalytic theory (Khantzian, 1982). For purposes of this discussion, we will consider both as valid explanations, focusing on the clinical data to understand the function of alcohol for a particular individual.

Much of the work of the transition phase involves a shift in object attachment. In denying their alcoholism many individuals report a fear of the void, the emptiness that will overwhelm them in sobriety. Alcohol fills a void. For many, it is the primary object that provides consistent support, that can be controlled, and that doesn't disappoint. Alcohol is a buddy, the safest companion. Individuals talk to their bottle, and even take it to bed; for many it has become the primary object of an intense dependency. The idea of relinquishing that bottle without replacement is unimaginable. The notion of object replacement is therefore central to the transition phase.

Early in her therapy, Sally borrowed two books on alcoholism from the therapist. She did not mention them and only returned them when the therapist said she needed to loan them to someone else. Sally kept forgetting to bring them back. When she finally did, she expressed great anxiety:

I hate to return them. These books are a "piece of the rock" that ties me to you in this clinic.

The therapist pointed out to her that she is building a "rock" inside her, but Sally emphasized that she is only beginning. At her next session, she began by telling the therapist the contents of her purse:

> Women need purses to carry things. I've got a book of poems from my father and an AA book. The AA books are a comfort to me even if I can't yet go to the meetings.

She then discussed her lack of belonging:

> The people in AA are competent and have control. I'm incompetent and unstable. I belong on my job because I know the rules. The rules in AA are different and I don't know them yet.

INTEGRATING BEHAVIORAL AND COGNITIVE APPROACHES

Maintaining a Balance

The importance of both behavioral and cognitive approaches during the transition phase cannot be overemphasized (McCourt and Glantz, 1980). The integration of these two may be subtle or quite direct. Much depends on the stability of the patient's identity as an alcoholic and the wish to stop drinking. If both are stated, the emphasis on behavioral change may be pronounced, providing action to back up the new identity. Regardless of the length of sobriety, as long as the risk of taking a drink remains critical, the focus must be on providing action substitutes. During the transition phase, this involves learning a new repertoire of behaviors and habit patterns.

> My behavior when I'm anxious is very mechanical, hasty, and without choice. It is that mechanical response, drinking, that gives me my sense of control.

This patient reported heavy consumption of diet soft drinks as a substitute. They gave her a sense of external control that she still required to keep her internal sense of control intact.

Newly abstinent patients in a group for recovering alcoholics illustrate the same emphasis on control (Yalom, 1974). After several weeks of building emotions, the patients experienced the group as out of control. They became frightened, started to arrive late, and to miss sessions. Finally the fear of drinking emerged. The members needed the therapists to exert control over the group because they could not do it themselves. The fear of drinking held within it their panic at the loss of control they experienced in their external environment. They imagined they could control the anxiety within them by drinking. The therapists actively took control, temporarily applying more structure to the group process (Brown and Yalom, 1977). Members talked about their fears and reviewed the structure of their supports to maintain abstinence. That is, they discussed the actions each would take to bolster their abstinence after the difficult anxiety-provoking group. By actively focusing on the action-oriented alcohol focus, each member renewed his or her commitment to abstinence and provided the sense of control and structure that was previously missing in the group.

The periodic or crisis-generated return to an alcohol focus provides valuable information for the therapist about the solidity of the behavioral substitutes already in place that members can act on after the meeting. This reassurance, rather than a regression or resistance, provides the action and therefore the control that permits the individual to move to deeper exploration.

Failure to pay attention to the importance of control can result in an abortive therapy or a return to drinking as illustrated with Mike. Mike was reluctant to commit himself to therapy or to membership in AA. He came and went, always devaluing his therapy and AA as both became more important to him. The therapist helped Mike examine his fear of staying in either setting. Mike recalled feeling repeatedly abandoned by both of his parents and vowing never to rely on anyone.

After this discussion, the therapist clarified directly the ways in which Mike could control his therapy and his involvement with AA. The therapist explained that Mike could cancel his hour, when and how, and what he would be responsible for financially. The therapist made the same clarification with regard to AA, emphasizing that Mike could choose what meetings to attend, when to arrive, and when to leave, and also that he could change meeting, sponsor, and therapist if he wished. Mike's fear of attachment and his denial of his intense dependency needs made him extremely anxious when he sensed that any commitment would be required.

Object Substitution

During this phase, the impulse to drink is still strong for many and requires actual behavioral substitutes. The substitution of objects shores up the new identity as alcoholic and may serve to satisfy the impulse as well.

> I carry an AA pamphlet, a dime, and a candy bar with me wherever I go. As soon as I feel anxious, I read something. Sometimes that's enough. If not, I chew on some candy and call an AA friend.

The concrete work of the transition phase is to teach new behavior patterns and new cognitive controls. The developmental framework explicated in Chapter 3 is in its early phase. The process of new knowledge construction begins with its roots in new behavior. The language of AA and the cognitive emphasis on the process of identification provide the link to higher development away from action as a means of providing control. John demonstrates the progression of behavioral and cognitive development on the foundation of a new identity as an alcoholic.

> I make a call when I have the urge to drink. I remember I'm an alcoholic and can't drink.

With the passage of time and constant repetition, new behaviors and cognitive controls become internalized. After a year of sobriety, John suddenly reflects:

> For the first time, I realize I don't have to act all my feelings out. I rarely have the urge to drink and I have some time now to think about it. Sometimes that's enough and sometimes I have to act, like go to a meeting.

Changing the Environment

The emphasis of the transition phase is on changing identity and behavior. In fact, the most important work of the transition phase is the integration of the new identity and the behaviors that accompany it. The process involves an interactive focus on cognitive understanding and on active prescription of new behaviors. Not only do these new behaviors substitute for the old ones, but they are congruent with the new identity as an alcoholic. Individuals who have come to acknowledge they are alcoholic but refuse to change or do not know how to change behavior experience great difficulties. The incongruency results in anxiety and often depression. They remain in the same environment, with the same drinking friends, and with the same positive cues for drinking, while saying to themselves that they are alcoholic and therefore cannot engage in drinking behavior. The failure to alter behavior or environment leads to a rigid, controlled abstinence because the individual must constantly be on guard against acting out the habitual behavior patterns.

A changed environment, which obviates the drinking cues, provides a sense of safety. Individuals can feel less guarded or wary about what they might act out. This is part of the safety experienced by AA members in the meeting. They know they are safe from picking up a drink in that environment.

The cognitive awareness provides a framework for understanding the meanings and functions of alcohol and the distorted thinking that leads one to take a drink. It does not necessarily hold within it the guidelines for new behavior to fit the new identity. New behaviors must accompany cognitive restructuring in the transition phase. In later phases of sobriety, with new behaviors in place, the cognitive awareness often functions as its own control. It is not enough in the beginning and can lead to the circular logic described.

> I am alcoholic and didn't drink tonight. But because I was able to abstain, I must not be alcoholic and therefore can have a drink.

The cognitive uncovering process and the breakdown of denial involve anxiety, which in turn leads to an impulse to drink. In the drinking and transition phases, therapeutic sessions are often followed by drinking. This is good evidence of the habitual behavioral patterns of drinking and of the function of drinking to cover anxiety and other self-discoveries.

A disruption in the behavior pattern is ultimately necessary. Otherwise, the patient is knowledgeable and insightful but continues to drink. The therapist must begin to integrate the suggestions for behavioral change as a critical accompaniment to greater cognitive awareness. In AA, members hear the combined cognitive–behavioral focus as a recovering alcoholic relates how he stays sober.

> It is just for today. I know I am alcoholic and therefore I do not pick up the first drink. (The identity and the behavior that accompanies it.) I know I can talk myself into drinking so I do not hang around bars, but go to meetings instead.

How an environment with drinking cues produces a drinking state of mind and a sudden fear of the loss of control is illustrated by Barbara:

> I had dinner with an old drinking friend. This occasion triggered an image of a bottle of bourbon still in my pantry. I later woke up dreaming about it and for several days experienced a craving to drink.

Barbara could not interrupt this obsessive thinking process until she went to a meeting and talked about her "dry drunk" at length. On another occasion, she woke up depressed, feeling as if she had been drinking. She responded behaviorally to this mood, staying alone with curtains drawn for most of the day, as she had done when she was actively drinking. She began to brood, moving herself mentally into her "territory" of drinking. She remained isolated for a good part of the day. Finally she stepped back from the inside of her mood and asked:

> Am I going to drink or am I going to AA? (Which action will I take?)

She chose AA and talked about the episode, learning that many others had had the same experience.

The first and foremost resistance may continue to be to the label "alcoholic," based on what it means. A newly abstinent individual reluctantly joined a group for alcoholics in early recovery. She didn't want to drink but also did not want to see herself as an alcoholic. She arrived at the meeting with a copy of her

MMPI (Dahlstrom and Welsh, 1960) protocol in her hand. She reported happily to the group that she scored very high on the psychopathic deviant scale and very low on the McAndrews scale, the alcoholism measure (Dahlstrom and Welsh, 1960). She told the group she much prefers to define herself as a psychopathic deviate than as an alcoholic. Group members were quick to wonder what purpose this served her, suggesting that she was using the test to aid her in her denial. Several weeks of group work uncovered her wish not to be held accountable for her actions and therefore ultimately not to have to change. She had had enough exposure to AA to know that if she defined herself as an alcoholic, she would have to assume responsibility for her drinking.

The label alcoholic also enters significantly into definitions of interpersonal relationships. Many friendships and marriages are based on the mutual support of denial of alcoholism. The shift in identity of one member of the dyad may create an extreme rift in the relationship. A newly self-identified alcoholic reported his dismay at discussing his new found self-knowledge and accompanying behavior (abstinence) with a close friend who had been a frequent drinking companion:

> My relationship with Hal is really deteriorating. There is so much tension and conflict when we meet, mostly about drinking. Hal insists I can't be an alcoholic because if I am an alcoholic then he must be too. But he insists that can't be so. When I say that I am an alcoholic, he says I am being silly and childish. He even said I was being hostile, by refusing to drink with him anymore! It makes me feel very guilty. I don't want to abandon my friends in order to stay sober.

As Paul progressed in recovery, he more carefully examined the important symbolism of alcohol. He and his friend had shared the belief that drinking was part of their masculine, even macho, identity. They enjoyed "men's" drinking lunches that reinforced their sense of power; "hard drinking men are strong."

Paul continued to frequent these lunches, but had trouble continuing to feel positive about himself as an alcoholic. In AA, he thought of himself as a "winner," with high self-esteem and a sense of strength achieved through maintaining abstinence. At lunch, he doubted his AA experience. On several occasions, he felt depressed after lunch, thinking of himself as no longer a man and now unequal to his peers. He stopped going to lunch when he began to entertain ideas of having a controlled drink or two with his friends. Accompanying that idea was a doubt that he was really alcoholic.

First experiences with AA often occur during transition. Reactions and perceptions illustrate the ease or difficulty of changing identity and assuming the label. Many individuals glean a perception of the deep change that will come, a perception linked to the label and the new language spoken in AA. There is often great resistance to the language ("too religious," "too corny") based on the reluctance to identify and an unconscious recognition that the language is linked to deep internal changes in identity. As one ambivalent new member of AA put it:

> If I say I'm alcoholic, I will have to reconstruct the meaning I have given to my whole life.

Another patient, Sally, began to explore the meaning of being alcoholic. She first recognized that "being alcoholic" didn't fit with her sense of herself or the way she thinks about things. If she thinks of herself as an alcoholic, she feels uncertain, and suddenly unknowledgeable about her views of herself and the world.

> If I can't control myself what does that say about me and the world? If I'm alcoholic, I can't trust the way I see or hear things.

As she progressed in her examination, she reported with frustration the incongruity she experienced between the way she thought in her therapy hour and the way she thought outside of it:

> I just can't hold the same frame of mind outside. I can think of myself as an alcoholic when I'm here but I lose it soon after. I've thought about bringing a tape recorder but I haven't gotten to it yet. I did buy a notebook to try to correlate events with my thoughts.

The therapist pointed out to Sally that her difficulties in adjusting to her new way of thinking about herself were not unusual, adding that people attend AA so frequently for that very reason: to reinforce and build on their new way of thinking. Sally began to attend AA more frequently but continued to waiver back and forth in her identity. The ability to shift back and forth was extremely important to her at this stage because the prospects of abstinence, membership in AA, and identifying as an alcoholic were terrifying. She could only move forward slowly, each time retreating back to the safety of her denial and her identification of herself as nonalcoholic.

> At the last meeting, I wanted to tell someone thanks, but I'm not legitimate yet. I just don't quite belong, I feel like an outsider. AA is for people who used to drink, not for those like me who are still drinking. They (the people in AA) know something I don't know. I don't know the concepts, the steps. These people are talking about how their lives have changed. They're not always talking about drinking, but something else, a reformation of character. I would like to have that too.

After this stated wish to belong, she retreated, now seeing the negative side:

I'm not sure I want to become one of them or have my life revolve around them. I want to be "normal" as opposed to an AA person. Normal means not needing a crutch. Don't you get over this?

Sally continued to hope that she could get over her compulsion to drink without any help and that then she would not need to go to AA. Further exploration uncovered her fear of her own tremendous neediness that was at the core of this wish for self-sufficiency.

I am embarrassed to ask for help. If you lean, the other will give way and you will fall down. It is better to stumble than rely on a crutch that breaks. Besides, if I rely on others, I will be too much for them. You know, in the meeting, they talked about giving up control in order to get it, and I didn't understand at all. What does "turning it over mean?"

She was still locked in the structure of her belief system that equated asking for help with failure. The idea of a "reformation of character" was both appealing and terrifying. Because she still relied so heavily on her belief that alcohol was her protection, she could not imagine relinquishing it.

Feeling badly about myself is something I'm used to; it is familiar and friendly. One day of being good and the next one is reserved for drinking. Being good is unfamiliar, stressful and full of new feelings. It is extremely stressful to look at myself and others in a new way. Drinking allows me to put the lid on. After drinking, I feel emotionally "buffeted."

As she shifted back and forth in her identity, she continued to explore the beliefs that accompanied each identity and frame of mind. She now examined her concept of "duty":

As soon as I decide to do something, it becomes a duty. At the last AA meeting, people praised me for having four days of sobriety. That made me fearful and I wanted to start over. Now these people have hopes and expectations for me. I feel responsible for not letting them down.

She translated their acknowledgment of her success into being "one of them" and therefore responsible to and for them. Any let down by her would now cause them great unhappiness. She could not see the faulty logic in her construction. Instead, she reinforced her own customary conclusion, "The only way not to be on duty is to be alone."

As she later reflected on her four sober days, she realized that she was frightened of continuing abstinence.

> I'm afraid of being enclosed. If I join, a door will close behind me and I won't be able to get out. That door closes my options and I'm afraid I will lose more than I gain.

Sally continued to reason her way out of staying sober. Her fear of becoming responsible for others was at the core of her resistance.

> If I go to AA, I become responsible for everybody there. Then I have to explain to them when I don't go. AA is all or nothing. You're either sober or you might as well drink. I practiced this week getting through 15 minutes and then an hour. I did it and then I felt so what? It's like writing the first paragraph of a composition—it's only the first paragraph and not the whole thing. Going to AA and being sober is a burden to me. I'm a "bottom line" person. A drunk who shows up at an AA meeting might as well stay home and drink. You either do it or you don't.

As Sally advanced her reasons for remaining outside AA, she emphasized her important view of herself as an observer.

> I'm an observer, someone who watches but never joins in. In AA I pretend I'm a writer in order to keep my distance. And I don't want that label alcoholic. I don't want others to call me that because it takes away my choices.

Sally illustrates the importance of understanding the very individualized meaning attached to the construct of "being alcoholic." Unraveling of this meaning is often a necessary aspect of psychotherapeutic work all along the continuum, from drinking into abstinence. In the transition stage, it is often the key to uncovering the blocks and resistances to accepting the identity as an alcoholic.

Changing Labels

Labeling and language are extremely important components of the entire process of changing identity and learning new behaviors. Many people oppose the concept of labeling on the grounds that it isolates or stigmatizes and creates unnecessary distinctions between people. But it is the label "alcoholic" that holds within it the deepest meanings attached to one's personal identity, which form the logic that dictates and rationalizes continued drinking.

Assumption of the label dramatically changes the individual's frame of reference, providing new meaning and clarity to past experiences. Huge areas of life, confused, mysterious, denied, or unexplained while drinking now make sense when related to the framework of alcoholism. Harriette illustrates:

> I have identified myself as an alcoholic for some time and have been wondering whether a close friend would have interpreted her experiences differently if she

had labeled herself an alcoholic. I believe that the structure of my experience depends on my subjectivity, and, therefore, by labeling myself an alcoholic, I have altered the meaning of my experiences.

Harriette recognized that she had both constructed and unfolded a belief system about herself as an alcoholic through her work in therapy, which was very useful to her. She found it ironic that she had "made it up" and it was true at the same time. Before acknowledging and coming to believe and think of herself as alcoholic, she focused on what it would mean to be alcoholic, maintaining she was not. After her acceptance, she then restructured her past experiences, giving them meaning on the basis of her new identity.

The label "alcoholic" and the process of identity give new meaning to behavior and deepest personal identity. Individuals who belong to AA learn a new language tied to the acceptance of the identity as an alcoholic and the accompanying acceptance of loss of control. This language gives the structure for reinterpreting the past, guidelines for interpreting the present, and foundations for constructing new beliefs and behaviors. The language of AA, like the language of psychotherapy or business, provides a common frame of reference for communication and shared experiences by which members claim membership in the particular culture. By providing new meaning to past and present behaviors, the language also serves as a structure and therefore a source of control.

As individuals change patterns of behavior, by reading an AA book, going to a meeting, or choosing not to go to a bar, they solidify and connect their behavior with the new language of alcoholism. In the beginning, the behavior dominates. Individuals must substitute an alternative to picking up a drink. They may be unable to make any cognitive links at all, either because they are too cognitively impaired from drinking or because the new language is still foreign. Then, with stable abstinence and stable new behaviors, the new language begins to provide its own form of cognitive control. Impulses are no longer experienced as overwhelming or as a dictate for action. Rather, individuals can firm up their identity by reading and thinking about themselves in the framework of a new terminology.

A patient with months of steady abstinence now asks of herself in the language of her therapy:

What circumstances made me identify with the drinking life?

And answers:

Vagueness, disorientation, the blurring of myself, an anonymous environment, and the often unconscious perception of someone else in control.

An AA member with months of abstinence asks the same question in the language of alcoholism learned in AA:

What is it that leads to my stinking, alcoholic thinking? What makes me think I'm not an alcoholic?

She answers:

I get too tired, too hungry, or too lonely. I insist on my will, not thine, or I get on the pity pot, feeling sorry for myself and what's been done to me. I also recognize that I am not going to enough meetings. I get comfortable and forget who I am— an alcoholic.

The language provides an alternative to action and a sense of control. The explanation for previously mysterious or unacceptable behavior reduces anxiety and may eliminate a need for concrete action. New behaviors already in place validate and back up the cognitive restructuring; each builds on the other to restructure a new personal identity based on new beliefs and behaviors.

The cognitive may replace or precede the behavioral emphasis with accrued, stable abstinence. In transition, acquiring the label "alcoholic" most often implies the behavioral corollary: "If I am an alcoholic, it means I cannot drink." What it does not hold is a prescription for how to accomplish this. Many individuals can make the cognitive shift, but, do not do so because they have no understanding of how they will be able to refrain from drinking. It is a fear of being unable to change the behavior that often retards cognitive awareness.

If I recognize that I am an alcoholic, but cannot stop drinking, I will be so depressed. As long as I think I'm not an alcoholic, I put all my energy into trying to control my drinking. It is better than admitting I am hopeless and really unable to stop.

It is at this juncture that many therapeutic errors occur. The patient and therapist believe that all that is necessary to abstinence is not drinking. That is true. But the language of AA spells out how to accomplish that in terms of action. Abstinence does not magically occur as a result of understanding why one is alcoholic or even what it means to be alcoholic. Abstinence requires action.

Put the plug in the jug, go to meetings, use the phone, and remember, "I am an alcoholic."

This last example summarizes the critical behavioral and cognitive work of the transition stage. The focus remains on alcohol as the individual shifts identity from nonalcoholic to alcoholic and learns the new behaviors that accompany the new identity and are necessary to maintaining abstinence. The other two axes of the continuum, interactions with the environment and interpretation of self and others, are emphasized only to the extent that they affect the dominant alcohol focus.

The shift in identity involves the important process of surrender, the giving up of one's belief in control. After this turning point, the individual embarks on the new developmental track of recovery. It is a time of intense dependency and early development, similar to infancy, as the individual begins to build a new foundation and a new personal identity as an alcoholic. Facilitating and maintaining the shift are the critical tasks of the transition stage.

Chapter 6

Early Recovery

ADJUSTMENTS AND REACTIONS TO EARLY RECOVERY

Early recovery is characterized by a change in identity and a corresponding change in behavior. The continuum remains narrow for much of this period, with the central focus on the alcohol axis. Integration of the other two axes occurs only to the degree that they affect or impinge on the alcohol focus. The work of early recovery centers on confirming the new identity and behaviors represented by the alcohol axis.

The Alcohol Axis

The period of early sobriety involves a change in identity to "I am an alcoholic," and a change in behavior to "I do not drink." The degree of the depth to the change in identity is extremely important to the individual's short- and long-term success in abstinence, though difficult to assess. The degree of depth often distinguishes the transition phase from the early recovery phase.

This period is characterized by intense dependency and need for external supports (Brown, 1977). These supports, inpatient and outpatient treatment, daily AA meetings, sheltered recovery residences, and protective family members, help to ensure continuing abstinence behaviorally, while individuals learn how to think about themselves as alcoholics and what actions to take to stay sober.

This time is also primarily one of intense education and support for new behaviors. Individuals learn a new language that both describes their new identity and behavior and holds within it the prescriptions for new thinking and behaviors. The phrase, "I am an alcoholic" means "I do not take a drink." With the acquisition of new language, it later acquires broader and deeper meaning (encompassed in the program of AA and the 12 steps).

Superficial Yielding

The person who is wavering in identity or moving back and forth in the transition phase may maintain periods of sobriety. The individual tries on the label "alcoholic" and assesses its fit. But doubts linger. The old belief system, based on

148

the notions, "I am not an alcoholic" and "I can control my drinking," remains the core structure, only temporarily covered by superficial yielding to abstinence.

This person may experience the yielding to abstinence as a submission to a real or imagined external authority or as a struggle between two opposing internal personalities. It is not a surrender that includes a deep recognition of the loss of control. Rather, the person experiences the need for abstinence as a temporary holding maneuver, with a return to drinking as a promised conscious or unconscious condition of the abstinence.

Abstinence, rather than a surrender of will, is an exertion of will. Self-esteem is maintained by the continuing belief in control, now exercised to maintain a temporary abstinence. Individuals who have not altered their deepest belief structure cannot feel comfortable with abstinence because it is incongruent with their belief in control. These individuals often resist AA, or, if they attend, feel different from others and quite dysphoric. Hearing the continuing acknowledgment of loss of control is threatening to the structure of their beliefs and their denial. Many weather a temporary course of AA meetings as medicine, eventually determining that it is not for them.

Change in Beliefs

The shift in basic identity and belief about control may be sudden or accomplished slowly during the periods of transition or early sobriety. Many hold onto their belief in control while they try out abstinence, shifting belief only with the passage of time and the proved ability to remain sober. Maintaining the belief in control serves as a defense against the possibility of failure in abstinence. These individuals approach abstinence as an experiment, willing to relinquish their belief in control if it seems workable. Thus, the person who says, "I will give up alcohol for three months, attend AA, and reevaluate at the end of that period," is quite different from the individual who reluctantly yields to abstinence, perhaps due to pressure from spouse or boss. This individual is pitted against those who would control him and he awaits the day when he can drink again.

Those who experience a sudden change in the deepest structure of their belief system often experience a sense of dysphoria or disorientation as if figure and ground have suddenly been reversed. Old bearings and directives for behavior no longer fit. The individual may feel suddenly defenseless and vulnerable, now certain of only two truths: "I am alcoholic" and "I cannot control my drinking." These beliefs must guide and sustain the individual through the often painful period of withdrawal and the first weeks and months of abstinence.

This period may be likened developmentally to infancy, a time of extreme dependency on external supports and a time when knowledge about oneself is formative. It is, for the alcoholic, a time for starting over with a new identity and the new beliefs and behavior that go with it. For many, it is also a time of confusion, as people embark into a territory of unknown meaning, acquired with the label alcoholic. The defensive structure, tied to the belief in control, is shattered. Individuals experience a sudden loss of control and perhaps fear of the unknown territory of abstinence. This fear is often directly tied to conscious or unconscious recognition of their lack of knowledge about how to stay sober.

Surprisingly, perhaps, individuals do not automatically know that they must alter their behavior to fit their new beliefs. Those who attempt abstinence without supports (AA in particular) often believe they change nothing. They just do not drink. There is certainly evidence to suggest that this can be successful for many individuals (Bean, 1981). But, for many others, it is the lack of support and a failure to learn how to stay abstinent that perpetuates a return to drinking, or repeated recycling through the transition phase.

Focus on Alcohol

Similar to the end of the drinking phase and movement through the transition phase, the period of early recovery is characterized by a predominant focus on alcohol. Rather than breaking down denial and shifting identity, the focus is on solidifying the new identity and providing meaning and new behaviors to go with it. It is also a period characterized by minimal insight and maximal action.

Emphasis on Action

Individuals struggle with what it means to be alcoholic in terms of their personal construction of meaning and what is now demanded behaviorally. Often, individuals are faced with a new profound recognition of loss of control and the fears and feelings that accompany it. The loss of control is often experienced as a terrifying fear of drinking.

> I wake up in the morning and I am instantly watchful. I just can't trust myself not to pick up a drink. The only time I feel safe is when I'm in an AA meeting. I am learning to think out loud and remind myself to pick up the telephone instead of a drink. But these are new ideas and new behaviors that don't come naturally. I can't believe I feel so helpless. I really need someone to tell me exactly what to do next or I'm likely to pick up a drink. That is all I know.

The importance of an emphasis on action cannot be overstated. All the insight in the world will not reduce anxiety dealt with in the past by the act of taking a drink and all the actions of a drinking life style. Suddenly, individuals have to deal not only with not taking a drink, but with filling up time previously dedicated to drinking. For many, drinking was a total way of life.

The behaviors and the way of life have become routine and often unconscious, no matter how unpleasant or dysphoric. There is often a ritual character, played out unconsciously as well. The importance of drinking to fill in space and provide definition to a way of life presents the threat of a tremendous void and severe loss (Brown and Yalom, 1977).

The need for behavioral action and concrete substitution is paramount. First, the action counters the sense of void and provides a behavior, something to do, to replace the act of taking a drink. It may temporarily cover the sense of loss of the substance as well, thus forestalling depression. Without a behavioral action substitute, individuals take action to ward off depression by taking a drink. The replacement action, going to a meeting, reading, or running, provides a sense of control, necessary to weather the initial difficult period.

The alcohol focus serves as a reminder that the individual never needs to pick up a drink. If impulses, fears, or depression gets so bad, there is always an action to take and it is action that provides the sense of control. In the beginning, the action is all that is necessary.

On the drinking side of the continuum, the alcohol focus is centered on denial, primarily of loss of control. In early sobriety, the alcohol focus is the source of control. The individual repeats the new identification as an alcoholic and follows the behavioral course that both substantiates and determines that new identification.

For the most part, individuals do not have the ego strength to tolerate the intense depression or too much insight about their drinking and the damage it caused. The emphasis on action provides an alternative to drinking and puts the focus on learning new behaviors. As the new behaviors become solidified, the individual becomes better able to cope with feelings of depression, and insights about him or herself, without taking a drink in response.

It is therefore extremely important to remember that in the hierarchy of intervention, behavioral replacement and action substitutes have first priority. Not until the new actions are in place can deeper exploration occur. Often, the need for action is prompted by influences from the environment.

Interactions With the Environment

The primary task of early sobriety for both patient and therapist is to maintain and strengthen the focus on alcohol. Environmental interactions need to be evaluated and interpreted according to their impact on the alcohol focus.

Confirming Identification

In early sobriety, environmental interaction will be interpreted and experienced according to the degree of congruence with the new identity as an alcoholic and the new behaviors accompanying that identity. The more structured the treatment program, such as a hospital, the more intense will be the alcohol focus with the emphasis on what it means to be alcoholic. The less structured attention given to early sobriety, the more likely it is that individuals will have to deal with an unsympathetic and unknowledgeable environment with the likelihood of nonalcohol focused demands. The person recovering on an outpatient basis, for example, may have family and employer to deal with immediately, and therefore, have less protected space for the acquisition of the new identity and the new behaviors.

The person in a sheltered recovery program has the advantage of an environment that fully supports the new identity as an alcoholic and instructs the individual to maintain the alcohol focus. The individual must learn to interpret environmental interactions through the new filter of the identity as an alcoholic. This new filtering and interpretive process requires very conscious attention and directed behavior. Individuals must learn to think about their interactions and actions. It is only through this constant focus on alcohol that individuals can begin to achieve a sense of choice and a sense of distance from their impulses and, therefore, a sense of control.

In the drinking phase there is no separation of thought and action; behaviors follow the conscious and unconscious desire to drink. In early sobriety, thought and action remain connected. The individual experiences a desire to drink and must have a new behavioral alternative on which to act immediately. Very shortly, the individual inserts a cognitive step between the impulse and behavior. That step is the reminder, "I am an alcoholic." That cognitive step then directs and instructs future action.

Using the Environment Supportively

Several examples illustrate the importance of environmental adjustment.

> Tom was sober for six weeks. He spent four of those in the intense, protected hospital environment. In his two weeks out, he attended AA five times a week and his outpatient early recovery group once a week. Now, he is invited out to dinner and faced for the first time with the old environment, a favorite restaurant and drinking friends.

There are numerous possible outcomes that illustrate the importance of the solid base of the alcohol focus. Tom feels very confident of his ability to remain abstinent without altering anything in his environment. He feels nothing should change and insists to concerned AA friends that he will have no trouble. In the past, Tom's sense of himself as sophisticated and socially prominent was tied to his valued evenings out in gourmet restaurants, with much fine wine and liquors. No one could tell Tom that reentering that environment so soon in his abstinence could stimulate the old meanings and trigger a desire to drink, nor could anyone tell Tom that remaining sober while all his friends drank would be painful by emphasizing his lack of belonging. Tom was anxious to join his friends again and rejected any suggestions for modifying his plan.

Although Tom may indeed have experienced no difficulty and no dysphoria, such an outcome is unlikely. In this case, Tom set out with every good intention of remaining sober. But, the memories of the positive aspects of drinking were strongly awakened. Without second thought Tom reasoned consciously that it would do no harm to have a glass or two of wine, an inherent part of treating himself to a pleasant reunion with old friends.

His friends in AA would call such an outing "slippery," meaning that old drinking environments and companions are dangerous. The old cues are still too powerful, undermining his still new identity and pulling him back to the lure of drinking. He may suddenly question whether or not he is really alcoholic, or simply decide that one drinking occasion won't matter. He'll go back to abstinence and AA tomorrow. On the continuum, one can note backward movement on the alcohol focus, as the individual moves from early recovery back into drinking. With a good base of new learning about himself as an alcoholic and a healthy concern about the danger of the old environment, Tom could have approached the evening quite differently.

He feels less than confident about his ability to participate in his former social environment without any changes. He talks to several AA friends first, hearing a variety of suggestions, and he listens carefully to the experience of others in similar situations. This process of assessing the environment beforehand helps him establish alternate behavioral options that might not be accessible to him unless constructed outside of the threatening situation. He formed several plans:

1. He postpones the event entirely, feeling that the anxiety and risk are too great and unnecessary at this early stage of sobriety.
2. He goes to the restaurant, but chooses AA companions on his first occasion. He therefore brings his new identity and new abstinent behavior with him, ensuring external support of his new identification as an alcoholic within an environment that pulls for his old beliefs and identity as a nonalcoholic.
3. He goes with old friends, but brings an AA pamphlet along, tucked in his wallet to remind him again of his new identity and the abstinent behavior that accompanies it. He also brings several phone numbers of AA friends, whom he can call in the middle of dinner for support.

By considering all these alternative actions, Tom learns how to first be aware of danger and then to actively construct a behavioral plan to ensure protection of his abstinence and, therefore, the continued strengthening of his new identity. Tom takes the advice of friends who stress the importance of behaving in ways that strengthen the new identity and learns to think carefully about how to construct an environment that will be maximally protective of that identity as well.

Environmental adjustments are often necessary within the work environment. Mike was a successful salesman who built his drinking into his occupational structure. He made his calls in the morning and spent his afternoons in his regular bar. In treatment, Mike recognized the potential difficulties of this structure, but made no changes. He returned to work and for several months continued his pattern. He went to the bar but felt unhappy and bored very shortly. He wandered around for a while and he looked for afternoon AA meetings to fill his time. Soon he recognized that the lack of structure, so valued in his drinking days, was now a severe hindrance, causing him anxiety and depression. He requested a transfer out of sales into an office position, thereby creating structure for himself.

Bill offers a different example of the same need for structural change. In his office job, every afternoon at about two o'clock Bill began to feel anxious and claustrophobic, thinking that five o'clock would never come. He began to visualize the drink that awaited him after work and treated his anxiety through this focus on alcohol. After abstinence, he could not tolerate the closeness he felt within the office environment. When he began to think about drinking again, he requested a transfer to sales, thereby reducing his structure in a way that reduced his anxiety and paradoxically provided security.

These examples illustrate the importance of environmental adjustments, determined according to the alcohol focus for each particular individual. Interpretation of self and others, the third axis, follows.

Interpretation of Self and Others

The primary task of early sobriety is the focus on alcohol and beginning environmental integration. Interpretation of self and others follows the emphasis on these first two. The new identity is the beginning step in the new interpretation. Expanded awareness begins through the focus on alcohol and environmental reconstruction and adjustment. These processes lead to the beginning of new awareness and the construction of new meaning about oneself. The reconstruction of the past follows from the prospective of a new identity.

Interpretation of self and others also involves the uncovering of other issues and problems, areas thought to be the terrain of more traditional psychotherapy. At some point in early recovery, the focus on alcohol and being alcoholic suddenly shifts. The individual recognizes other problems or issues that need to be explored. The integration of this component is minimal in early recovery, with most emphasis on developing the behavioral and cognitive framework of abstinence.

There are two predominant patterns in early abstinence with a wide range of variation in between. One is noted in the folklore of AA as the honeymoon period, and the other is depression, sadness, and loss.

The Honeymoon

The honeymoon phase, also called a "pink cloud," is characterized by elation, pleasure, a veneer of high self-esteem, and especially a high denial of other problems. The individual accepts the identity as an alcoholic and interprets it positively.

> I finally learned what was wrong with me. I am an alcoholic! Before, I was a real loser because of my drinking, but now, I am a winner. I am a winner because I am not drinking.

This individual may embrace the AA program wholeheartedly, announce to close friends and minor friends alike his newfound knowledge, and reorganize his life, feeling pride in his ability to recognize the problem and do something about it. A supportive environment—family, work, and friends—is usually a necessary accompaniment as is high denial of other difficulties. The individual denies any problems besides alcohol, and even alcohol is no longer a problem as long as the person remains dry. Whereas this adjustment may seem incredible to an onlooker (and certainly to a therapist), it is useful and productive for a brief period of time (from days to weeks to as long as a year). The denial of all other problems allows the individual to focus on being alcoholic, the most important task of early sobriety. The individual can emphasize learning new behaviors and adjust to the meanings of the label alcoholic.

In the beginning, that may include only behaviors: I am alcoholic and I don't drink. But it may extend to the arena of deepest personal identity. To the extent that this deeper meaning is problematic, it may interfere with the honeymoon experience and a successful abstinence.

Depression, Loss, and Mourning

The other most frequent adjustment is depression, which may include a mourning for the loss of alcohol and/or guilt at the recognition of damage caused by drinking. It is even more complicated. There are (Brown, 1977) distinct differences between men and women in their self-esteem and levels of denial during recovery. I found a strong pattern of high denial and high self-esteem (honeymoon) for men during their first year and a strong tendency toward depression with very low self-esteem for women during their first year. Although this was not readily explainable by the data from the research, clinical investigation subsequently suggests several hypotheses.

For men to accept the label alcoholic and its inherent meaning of eroded masculinity, they must feel a sense of power and control achieved via acceptance of the label. Women, on the other hand, often feel that alcohol has provided an illusion of independent identity, or at least separate private space in their marital, family, personal, and professional relationships, whereas, in fact, it allowed them to stay in a very dependent position.

In approaching sobriety, these women often equate abstinence with an aggressive, hostile move against their husbands and family. Abstinence now equals independence and is frightening. Women often resist the prescription to attend meetings and to take care of themselves first. These directives run counter to putting other people first and signal separation from their loved ones. Many equate the meaning of being alcoholic with eventual divorce—my husband will not tolerate my independence or I will end up leaving him if I become abstinent. These fears are often conscious or close to consciousness before or immediately after abstinence.

In early recovery the focus is on alcohol, confirming and building the new identity as an alcoholic and solidifying the new behaviors that accompany that identity. Interaction of the other axes occurs to the degree that the environment or interpretation of self and others influence the focus on alcohol. The individual needs to be thinking about being alcoholic. Involvement with AA provides the attention to the alcohol axis required during this stage, with its emphasis in the meeting on concrete behavioral and cognitive restructuring. Therapeutic focus and the integration of AA within a working therapeutic alliance require careful attention.

THERAPEUTIC APPROACHES TO AA

The period of early sobriety is a dramatic shift from drinking that is similar to infancy from a developmental perspective. It is characterized by extreme dependency, whether explicit or denied, and a corresponding need for reliance on external structures and support. The patient who appeared to have a higher level defensive organization while drinking is suddenly defenseless. The patient regresses, with primitive defenses emerging. Insight, available within the framework of the identity as a nonalcoholic, is now gone. Instead, the patient feels frightened, helpless, and in great need of directives for action. The incidence of other psychiatric symptoms such as anxiety, depression, suicide, sleep problems, and overeating rises dramatically (Brown, 1977).

As described, the primary emphasis is on action, substituting new behaviors for drinking. These new actions do not come from within the cognitive or decision-making framework of the individual. They must be learned as the behavioral correlates of the new identity as an alcoholic.

The therapeutic task of early recovery becomes a process of reciprocal determinism as described by Mahoney (1977). Action determines the construction of cognition, and cognition, in turn, influences and determines behavior. In addition, the period of early sobriety requires an external structure to form the environment in which this reciprocal process can occur. There are several components to the therapeutic task: developing a structure to support the new identity and working with the cognitive–behavioral process of knowledge construction that occurs within that structure.

This is a critical period for the patient and therapist who have been engaged in psychotherapy during the drinking and transition phases. The emphasis in those phases was on the breakdown of defenses, particularly denial of alcoholism, and the tentative exploration of a new identity with movement into absti-nence. With early sobriety, the task of therapy shifts dramatically. The patient moves from a strong defense, built on the denial of alcoholism, to a strikingly more vulnerable, defenseless position. Instead of breaking down supports and emphasizing the patient's isolation, the focus is on building up supports. The therapist must shift from a confrontive, uncovering stance to one of greater support.

Because of the emphasis on cognitive and behavioral approaches, and the need for external structure, the emphasis is predominantly on new learning with external directives. The work of this period may thus be characterized as pre-dominantly educational and supportive.

The therapist who has been engaged in an intensive individual psychotherapy may find this period difficult or even unmanageable. The rules of the traditional dynamic psychotherapies may not have built within them the shift in therapeutic stance, from listener and challenger to active instructor and supporter. It is ex-tremely uncomfortable and even unacceptable for many therapists to make this shift because it is inconsistent with their identification with a particular school of psychotherapy.

It may be an unworkable shift because the therapist does not understand the process of recovery and the developmental stages. The therapist does not un-derstand the task of learning and the infantile attentional status required by the patient. And, the therapist does not know what to instruct. Rather than shifting to accommodate the patient's sudden need for support and education, the ther-apist may, instead, expect a more insightful patient, now ready for dynamic psychotherapy because the alcohol has been removed. The therapist is shocked and disappointed to find a regressed, overtly dependent or high denying patient instead. The therapist who does not understand the developmental nature of recovery or who cannot accommodate a shift in the structure of the therapy may react in several ways.

First, the therapist may consider medication. The patient is extremely anx-ious, depressed, and may report severe sleeping difficulties. The therapist may consider medication to ease the discomfort of the patient or as an attempt to improve defensive functioning to restore the patient to the previous appearance of improved cognitive function. Although medications may be required for cer-tain individuals, there is great danger for most. With the relief of the early symptoms of abstinence through medication, there is no need to learn behavioral substitutes.

Many physicians and therapists readily prescribe tranquilizers with the belief that the medication will remove the desire and need to drink. Unfortunately, this is not the case. The individual either shifts the addiction from alcohol to pre-scription drugs, or adds the drugs without changing drinking behavior. Absti-nence requires behavioral substitutes and permanent behavioral change.

The therapist who believes that behavioral change follows automatically or instinctively from insights will not understand the need for a predominant educational focus, nor will she or he be prepared to provide the instruction.

Behavioral change does not automatically follow insight or a change in identity. It is separate and connected to the cognitive changes, through the process of reciprocal determinism described earlier. I have outlined the difficulties therapists face in working with newly recovering individuals. Next we turn to the main task of involving AA.

The Main Task: Integrating and Interpreting AA

Often introduced in the drinking or transitional phases, AA becomes a regular important component of early sobriety. For the patient who has been involved in psychotherapy, the addition of AA creates a dramatic shift in the structure and function of the psychotherapeutic relationship. Primarily, it changes from a dyadic partnership to a triadic relationship, with AA frequently becoming the most important partner. It is within the organization and structure of AA that the predominant cognitive and behavioral work of early sobriety is accomplished.

It is the integration of AA, the shift from a dyadic to triadic working relationship and a shift from an insight-oriented or confrontational stance to an educational supportive posture, that characterizes this period. It involves tremendous change for the patient and the therapist.

The therapist may well understand the frequent complaints of family members during this period who feel abandoned by their partners to the now favored relationship with AA: the organization as a whole and the individuals within it (Brown, 1977). Not infrequently, patients terminate good psychotherapeutic relationships during this time. Many sense that the educational task will be best achieved in AA and determine that psychotherapy is unnecessary. With their new supports, this may prove a positive choice for many, because it solves the difficult problem of integrating AA into a workable triadic relationship.

Many newly sober individuals cannot tolerate their intense and extreme feelings of dependence during early sobriety and terminate their individual psychotherapy in response to their discomfort (Kanas, 1982). AA offers a sense of control to these very dependent individuals. They can choose the meetings they attend, when they arrive, when they leave, whether they talk or not, and whether or not they return. Many later report (Brown, 1977) that their abililty to accept AA rested in the sense of equality between all members, regardless of length of sobriety and the freedom to construct an AA program most suitable to their own personal needs. Psychotherapy is often interpreted and frequently constructed as an unequal relationship, and therefore intolerable to the now extremely dependent individual.

The very structure of the psychotherapy relationship may be problematic. The alcoholic who had no trouble with a 50-minute, insight-oriented psychotherapy while drinking, suddenly cannot sit still for 50 minutes, has no insight, and cannot tolerate the anxiety of the one-to-one relationship. Anxiety builds during the hour to such a degree that individuals must leave early. In this period, the inability to sit still, to process information, or to engage in interpersonal exchange may be acute. Suddenly, the overwhelming need for escape, or for an action emphasis takes over. The individual must shift to "do" something: take a walk, drink a coke, or read an AA pamphlet.

Unfortunately, all too often, such a change in the patient's ability to tolerate a traditional psychotherapy hour will be interpreted as a resistance that should be confronted. Indeed it is resistance, but one that should be supported. The individual is tremendously frightened of the intense feelings and the unconscious material that might arise with too much exploration. The sudden need for action is indeed the individual's defense against unacceptable feelings and insights. But it is a defense that should be fostered. Action is the only antedote to the more frightening act of picking up a drink.

Another common adaptation of early sobriety is the decrease in frequency of psychotherapy. Patients who have come weekly, twice weekly, or more often, now want to change to twice or once monthly, or perhaps, on the basis of need. This decrease may represent the patient's wish to shift primary attachment to AA, the organization as a whole or particular individuals within it. It also may represent the patient's wish to exert more control over the therapy. Dependency feelings can be tolerated if the patient structures the frequency.

Individuals may not find it necessary to leave their hour early or reduce their frequency. Instead, they may fill up the minutes with a barage of reporting, mostly about their new AA experiences. Again, the therapist may interpret the style and content as resistance and attempt to redirect the patient to an insight-oriented approach. Worse, the therapist may redirect the focus away from alcohol.

The AA reporting has the important function of reinforcing the new learning, providing the triadic integration necessary for the psychotherapy by bringing AA to the therapist. If the therapist is not an alcoholic and is not familiar with AA, the patient's reporting functions to teach the therapist about abstinence and what is required in terms of cognitive and behavioral change. The patient's reporting functions as a control over internal impulses and the otherwise uncertain direction of the therapeutic hour. It also is reinforcement of the new learning and language.

Criteria for Successful Integration

The successful integration requires an ability by the therapist and the patient to shift predominant focus to AA, to an action emphasis, and to the process of learning how to stay sober. The therapist who understands the developmental nature of recovery may have no difficulty shifting stance, becoming a supportive figure, or shifting to the background while the patient builds an attachment to AA. This therapist understands that the patient may temporarily terminate or continue in a more concrete, psychotherapeutic relationship but that insight-oriented psychotherapy will return when the new cognitive and behavioral components have been established.

The therapist who does not understand the developmental nature of recovery or who does not believe in the therapeutic efficacy of a triadic relationship, may sabotage the educational, supportive work of this period, unknowingly contributing to a failure to progress, or placing the patient in the position of having to choose between AA and therapy. The therapist may believe in the importance of an undiluted intense dyadic bond with the psychotherapeutic process centering on an exploration of the transference. Such a theoretical stance conflicts with the integration of AA, which is likely to replace the therapist as a primary transference figure and a real object of attachment.

Regardless of therapeutic school, many therapists feel threatened by the addition of AA, believing that psychotherapy should be all that is necessary. If a patient needs to add AA, or a support network, then something must be wrong with the psychotherapy. This therapist feels threatened in his or her basic beliefs and competence and also may feel rivalry with AA for the primary attention and attachment of the patient. The therapist who has worked hard helping the patient move from drinking to abstinence may have difficulty hearing the patient attribute gratitude for sobriety to AA and the people within that organization.

The therapist who believes in the power of the undiluted, intense dyadic psychotherapeutic bond may discourage attendance at AA and thereby cut off the opportunity for the cognitive and behavioral learning absolutely essential to this phase of recovery. Many newly recovering alcoholics quit their psychotherapy because they sense the incompatibility and unconsciously recognize the need for a cognitive, behavioral focus. Unfortunately, just as many choose psychotherapy instead of AA, believing psychotherapy takes its place (Kinney and Montgomery, 1979).

Fortunately, many psychotherapists do understand the progression of recovery, or at least recognize the importance of adding AA. Many simply recognize that the task of staying sober during early recovery demands a 24-hour *network* of available services and objects. Knowledgeable psychotherapists do not expect to be able to supply the variety and intensity of necessary supports.

This therapist appreciates the value of a triadic relationship and often spells it out clearly, challenging the patient's hope that psychotherapy should provide all. The therapist suggests strongly that the patient use AA or insists on it in some cases, outlining the behavior and learning tasks that cannot be effectively accomplished in once-a-week psychotherapy. The therapist may teach the patient a good deal about AA, describing the format of meetings, the variety of age, class, and occupational memberships, the notion and function of a sponsor, and the importance of repetition. The education about AA may soften the patient's move toward joining and dissolve the patient's worries about competition or abandonment by the therapist. Instead of feeling threatened or competitive with AA, the therapist makes the therapy a success by enabling the patient to get to AA.

> Julie had an extremely positive working relationship with her individual psychotherapist. She attended AA, but had great difficulty establishing a firm sense of belonging to the organization. She saw AA as a useful support, but hoped to achieve a comfortable abstinence through a stronger reliance on her therapist and her once-a-week psychotherapy. Julie seemed to progress well in abstinence, but punctured it with infrequent drinking episodes. It became clear to the therapist that Julie's reluctance to solidly commit herself to AA was resulting in Julie's failure to learn behavioral alternatives and to choose them even though she also had developed a strong identity as an alcoholic. It became clear that her reliance on her psychotherapy was keeping her from building a reliance on AA. The therapist insisted that Julie attend AA regularly (two to three times a week) in order to continue her psychotherapeutic relationship. Julie was, at first upset, but smiled. She needed the directive to allow herself to attend AA. Only with the insistence of the therapist could she permit herself to fully join. She did so, establishing a continuous sobriety. She shifted her primary allegiance to AA and within her first year, reduced her psychotherapy.

From Dyad to Triad

The therapist and patient who have been engaged in psychotherapy during the drinking and transition phases are now faced with a difficult shift in their relationship. The therapist who was successful in challenging the logic of the drinking phase, helping the patient accept the identity as an alcoholic and the concomitant loss of control, must now accept the addition of a third party, potentially disruptive to the established therapeutic relationship.

In moving through recovery, from the drinking to the abstinent stages, the therapist must shift task, focus, and even theoretical position. It is impossible for the therapist working long-term with an alcoholic to maintain one therapeutic school into which the patient must fit. What is most important and what stays the same in all the phases is the congruence or lack of congruence of belief by those patients and therapists. The therapist who really believes in the value of control may foster an alliance based on maintaining drinking behavior. The patient who wishes to stop and therefore move into the transition and early recovery phases will perceive an incongruence with the therapist. The patient will either shift back to a focus on control, aligning again with the beliefs of the therapist, or disrupt the alliance. The patient may leave psychotherapy to protect his or her abstinence because the recognizable discord in belief is intolerable. Or, the patient may maintain a tenuous relationship with the therapist, forming a stronger bond with AA.

The therapist may believe in control, but accept the choice of abstinence for a particular patient. If the patient senses the stronger belief in control, he or she will feel inadequate and abnormal in relation to the therapist. It is extremely difficult to feel high esteem through acceptance of being alcoholic when the patient suspects that the therapist views the shift as a failure.

The therapist may be allied in belief but lacking knowledge about the concrete, supportive, and educational focus of early recovery. Here is the benefit of a therapist who is also a recovering alcoholic. That therapist has been through these steps of recovery—acknowledgment of being alcoholic, relinquishment of alcohol, and learning the actions to stay sober. The patient can identify with the therapist on the basis of a congruence in belief and the shared experience of changing behavior. Knowledge that the therapist also is recovering may facilitate the patient's attachment and transference to AA.

Shifting Object Attachment and Institutional Transference to AA

One of the most important and potentially difficult changes in the therapeutic alliance is the shift in object attachment. The drinking patient was primarily attached to alcohol. That person requires an immediate object substitute to move through the transitional phase and to relinquish alcohol as a substance and an object of attachment.

Individuals who are unfamiliar with or who have avoided AA may shift their attachment to the therapist during the drinking phase in preparation for abstinence. But that object replacement is shaky and inadequate to the task. The therapist as object is also out of the perceived control of the patient. A replacement must be under the patient's control and available 24 hours a day just like alcohol.

Peter approached abstinence, unconsciously preparing himself to relinquish alcohol through his growing attachment to his therapist and his perception of the therapist's belief in abstinence. Peter became abstinent and suddenly experienced tremendous anxiety. He could not sleep at night and felt overwhelmingly needy and dependent. He called his therapist several times a day requesting directives for action. The therapist was at first, very helpful, but began to recoil, distressed by the intensity of the patient's needs. Rather than suggesting the substitution of action and AA, the therapist first directed the patient to "hold on" with no accompanying action and then became punitive, insisting that the patient adhere to the structure of the therapy, calling only during working hours, or better, waiting until the therapy hour to deal with the discomfort.

The immediate substitution of AA meetings and the concrete object replacements recommended by AA members fulfill these requirements. The basic education of early recovery involves instruction in object replacement accompanied by environmental and behavioral change. But the most immediate and action-oriented task is object substitution, how to deal with the craving for alcohol and the impulse to drink.

In the beginning, individuals may transfer their attachment to the organization of AA as a whole and the object representation of that attachment, to books and foods rather than individuals. Such a beginning shift, from alcohol to objects representative of AA and sobriety, is an extremely important mechanism. Individuals who have relied on alcohol and the perceived control of that attachment cannot transfer their object dependency to one person—therapist, family, or friend—nor should they. Object substitution allows the individual to experience his or her overwhelming cravings and dependency needs without fear of overwhelming a human figure. The sudden fear of the intimate individual psychotherapy hour by the newly recovering alcoholic is often a fear of impulse. The patient feels extremely dependent and out of control. These feelings are tolerable within the institution of AA where the recommendation is to act on them by substitution.

The therapeutic dyad, unless it also accommodates the need for action and substitution, will emphasize not acting on impulse, which creates intolerable anxiety. The patient in early recovery is absolutely unable to refrain from acting in the interest of thinking about himself instead. And action is what is desireable. It is through the act of substituting a new object for alcohol and changing behavior that new learning occurs. It does not occur through thinking alone. Such a process of learning follows directly from Piaget's concepts of knowledge construction. The period of early sobriety may be likened to that of the sensorymotor, with higher cognitive stages in the background or operating in concert.

The new learning occurs and solidifies from an action basis, which is why it is so difficult for sophisticated individuals to focus on action, the earliest form of learning. The cognitive directives—don't get too tired, too hungry, or too lonely, go to meetings, pick up the phone—provide the action substitute and new language. The stories heard in AA provide the new framework for cognitive explanation and restructuring and constructing new knowledge about oneself and a new identity.

Most therapists are unprepared and unknowledgeable in the rudimentary tasks of learning required during this period. Individuals walk into an AA meeting that they have chosen to attend, immediately pick up a donut and a cup of coffee, choose the seat they prefer, listen to a speaker, perhaps participate in a discussion, help clean up, and chat with a new friend after the meeting. Within this frame are behavioral actions, object substitutes, and cognitive learning. What is missing for most in the beginning is reflection, analysis of one's behavior and thought processes. It is often this latter process that is the heart of psychotherapy.

The Twelve Steps

Within the structural organization of AA, the meetings and the ritual format, is the most prominent representation of the new identification, the 12 steps (AA, 1971). It is these steps that outline the common identity as alcoholic, the acceptance of loss of control, and the directives for action and later self-reflection. It is a behavioral, cognitive, and dynamic structure referred to in AA as the "program."

In the beginning days of sobriety, the object substitutes and attachments may be strictly to the meeting with the emphasis entirely on behavioral substitution. As many say in AA, "Bring the body and the mind will follow." Individuals learn the action routine of attending meetings and substituting new objects for alcohol. They may or may not be able to make sense of the steps at this time, or they may challenge all or part of the program. Many newcomers hear the mention of God and step back, not wishing to identify with a religious organization or religious dogma. Older AA members may suggest that the newcomer ignore the steps in the beginning, focusing only on the act of staying sober. The individual will learn how to do this—what actions to take—by coming to meetings, listening to other members tell their experiences, and following the same actions. At the same time, individuals are encouraged to think about themselves in a new way, with a new language, central to the identification as an alcoholic.

The object replacement includes concrete substitution, institutional and conceptual. As individuals progress in abstinence, the new actions become solidified and there is less need for immediate object substitution. Craving diminishes and individuals move from the need to act on concrete object substitutes to action and dependence on conceptual principles instead. The initial intense reliance on external support and behavioral action changes. The identification with principles and behavior becomes internalized and the need for immediate action recedes.

The Place of the Sponsor

We have emphasized the significance of institutional and object attachments during early recovery; however, there is within the framework of AA the possibility of human attachments as well. This person is called the sponsor (Alibrandi, 1982) and represents the closest counterpart to the therapist and certainly the most difficult to integrate in a triadic relationship.

Although all participation in AA is subject to choice, and therefore to the member's control, there is strong encouragement to acquire a sponsor. Sponsors, like therapists, have different theories about their task, though in most general form, they function as advisor, guide, and teacher of the AA program. The sponsor is an AA member with longer sobriety than the newcomer (there are no set rules, though traditions may set guidelines for a particular area or chapter). This person agrees to be available to the newcomer in a more intense and regular manner. The sponsor may be seen as parent, teacher, therapist, mentor, friend, or advisor, depending on the particular individual and the relationship established.

Some sponsors assume a clear parental function, instructing their sponsorees ("babies" or "pigeons," as newcomers are called) directly; do this and don't do that. The most openly dependent and vulnerable newcomers may value such a clear parental authority to guide them in their sobriety.

Other sponsors are far less active, serving as guides, but not decision makers. They report their own experiences as an example and encourage their sponsorees to arrive at their own conclusions. The range of sponsorship is as broad as the number of individuals within AA.

What is most significant is the intensity of the relationship and the frequent tendency of the newcomer to transfer attachment and former patterns of object relationship to this figure. Whereas there is great leeway for this phenomenon in AA (members often have more than one sponsor or may change at will), there are often problems. For example, an individual's difficulties with authority may be played out in this framework.

The focus on alcohol and the integration of AA with the working psychotherapeutic partnership are central to early recovery. Behavioral, cognitive, and dynamic issues are important therapeutic considerations as well.

OTHER THERAPEUTIC CONSIDERATIONS

Behavioral Issues

Environmental Pulls

The change from drinking to abstinence is not accomplished in a vacuum, totally within the bounds of a shift in internal identification. It is related closely to one's environment as the many examples already illustrate. Often, it is the cues from one's environment, the social class, the cocktail party, or the evening glass of wine with a spouse, that exert the strongest pressure to return to drinking. The memories of the positive identification with drinking or the important symbolization of alcohol are seductive in early abstinence. Typically, the pull to return to drinking appears as a defense, or an answer to a problem encountered in sobriety.

The alcohol may appear as a solution to feelings of depression or low self-esteem, as Peter illustrates. His association of drinking and high social class membership had always successfully provided him with the illusion of belonging. The first drink dramatically shifted him out of the depressed feelings he felt as a result of being alcoholic and, therefore, abnormal.

The environmental pull to drink also may be a means of masking major difficulties in relationships. Though perhaps unsatisfactory, drinking does provide a status quo around which family and friends establish rules for their relationships. The 80 surveyed members of AA agreed almost unanimously that the one most common feature of their sobriety was change, in themselves and their behavior and in their relationships. The pull to drink may avert or postpone the examination and process of change required by all those close to the alcoholic. Shirley illustrates:

> I need to test myself in social situations because it's difficult for me to make decisions about the stresses I can tolerate socially and those I cannot. I feel pressure from my husband to be involved in couples tennis, but the others all drink heavily. There is no way I can join the group without drinking, and not joining makes my husband unhappy. I really feel caught in the middle. I must remember that not drinking is more important than anything else, but I have to be conscious of alcohol every minute.

Shirley recognizes early in her sobriety that the changes she needed to make for herself would directly challenge all of the established rules, roles, and relationships within the family. This recognition alone resulted in a severe depression, with only one month of sobriety.

> I have been immobilized with seven straight days of depression. I feel estranged, like I don't fit anywhere, but I know it would be worse if I drank. I can't sleep. A week ago I went out to a meeting for the first time at night. It was hard for my husband to have me go, even though he approves.

The simple action of going out by herself to a meeting symbolized the deepest and most central issue of Shirley's AA involvement and her therapy for the next two years. Drinking kept her inside her family, dependent and serving others. It appeared to her in early sobriety that abstinence would be the reverse. She would abandon her family for the choice of autonomy. Every small step she took toward ensuring her early sobriety left her feeling depressed about her ability to remain married and active in the role of mother.

As Shirley uncovered her beliefs about her marriage, she was able to begin to recognize the kinds of major changes she and those close to her would have to make.

> My sobriety is shaking up my marriage. My family is beginning to recognize the difference with the alcohol gone. I don't know what monster we'll all have to deal with. The monster is me because I'm unpredictable.

> When I drank I was very dependent and it was certain I could not do things on my own. Now my husband and I are having many more arguments, mostly about my wish to do things on my own. I have to be able to leave my husband as the key source of my support. But he is terribly threatened.

As further evidence of this dilemma, Shirley adds that her husband insists he is not alienated by her going to AA.

> He knows it is important and is happy with the changes in me. Yet he treats me as very fragile. He keeps responding in the same way, wanting to protect me.

At the same time Shirley was recognizing her need to separate from her extreme dependence on her husband and family, she also was in need of their support for this move, a paradoxical dilemma.

> I told my kids about my alcoholism at a time of family celebration, when I typically would be drinking wine with them. My son was relieved and had a lot of questions, but my daughter was very annoyed. She said the drinking problem was mine not hers, and she wanted no part of it.

A few weeks later Shirley recognized that she wanted her husband to feel jealous of her AA meetings. Their relationship was improving, both were beginning to talk about feelings, and he was letting go of having to be the strong one.

As Shirley progressed in sobriety, she became more concerned about her relationship with her husband. After several months of sobriety, she considered choosing a sponsor. She recognized that she was carefully choosing a female who had remained married after her sobriety. Shirley could see that she was terribly frightened that she and her husband would grow apart as she progressed in sobriety. She had to constantly resist urges to control him or try to push him into treatment for himself. These concerns merged when she chaired her first AA meeting.

> I agreed to chair finally and realized this meant I had accepted AA and my alcoholism. I immediately experienced a fear that with this acceptance, I would cut myself off from my husband. I wonder how I can be in AA and be with my husband too.

Soon after this meeting she had a dream in which she was pulled in two opposite directions. She realized drinking had always been the symbol of her escape between opposing poles in her family. Integrating her life as wife and mother with her professional desires was also painful. With the passage of time she found a paradoxical resolution.

> I am coming to value the lifelong support AA has to offer. It's funny, I feel less dependent rather than more. I can recognize my potential to stand on my own feet by having committed myself to group membership.

The Dry Drunk

The uncovering process and the emergence of feelings often creates a state of mind and an attitude that AA members refer to as a "dry drunk." For most, it is unpleasant, reminiscent of the thinking and emotional state while drinking. Individuals may use it as a guide, recognizing there is something to be examined within themselves and proceed with self-examination to locate the source. Most tighten up behavior as well, attending meetings to strengthen sober behavior. Barbara illustrates the illumination and useful discovery about her "dry drunks":

> I had the profound discovery that what I've been calling my drinking state of mind is a regular part of myself, a way to deal with the world in which I'm unhappy. This depressed state of mind influences my orientation to my day. It's like being drunk—I'm ultrareceptive and reactive, full of low esteem and feelings of vulnerability, the pawn of others and an unwilling slave to commands coming from outside. This state of mind is an immense obstacle, a habit I fall into which is out of control. I expected redemption when I stopped drinking but now have to learn to put up with being myself. I'm left with who I am and it's pretty bad. I no longer have a sense of good and bad selves that are directly connected to drinking.

After several "dry drunks," Barbara was no longer so surprised. An encounter with a close friend provided new insight and a new behavior:

> I was sobbing after this exchange. I felt drunk, disoriented, and out of control as if everyone else is in charge of me. I went home and wrote a story about it which was very effective in giving me a sense of control. Before I wrote, I had the same feeling I used to associate with drinking as a way to regain the power I had lost to another. Now the writing took its place.

AA members are encouraged to begin writing early in their recovery through the personal, moral inventory of the fourth step, the list of people to whom amends must be made (step 8), and step 10, the continuing daily inventory. The writing provides a sense of control by clarifying internal feelings and beliefs, that is, making them real by externalizing them on paper. It also stimulates the uncovering process by permitting new insights. Finally, it is an action, and therefore a substitute for the act of drinking, as Barbara noted.

Many individuals are not able to write early in their sobriety. Writing is feared as a loss of control. Individuals fear what they will learn about themselves, and stick to the clear behavior guidelines and AA reading material for many months.

> Barbara continued to explore her "dry drunks" however, finding much insight to her nondrinking behavior and view of the world.

> I have a drinking "attitude" that feels out of control, but it doesn't have to do with drinking directly. I've been gaining weight and feeling out of control in many areas. I'm obsessed with getting control. I was in a situation where I gave more information about myself than was appropriate. Suddenly I was embarrassed. I was drinking without drinking. Spontaneous, self-expression equals being out of control.

Later on in her recovery, the dry drunk is no longer frightening nor necessarily considered negative. Rather it is an important marker.

> I feel drugged with emotion, just like a hangover. It is a powerful sense of depression, weighing me down. I feel angry and helpless just like I did when I was drinking. But I always thought it was only because of the drinking. Now I see that anger belongs to me regardless.

A newcomer in sobriety, not yet able to use her moods for insight, illustrated the power of the dry drunk period.

> I had a terrible experience which others tell me is a dry drunk. I felt I was in an altered state, frightened and out of control. I was driving erratically and feeling over elated. This experience was identical to the way I used to feel as I was getting high. I was banging into things and could only slow myself down by heading for a meeting. That stopped the rapid motion.

This is an extremely common experience in early sobriety and initially very frightening. The individual feels a speeding up and perhaps a rising mood. The person feels out of control, but perhaps in a very positive way. It may be the state of mind that was sought and achieved by alcohol in drinking days. The individual may not want to change it or slow it. Of course, without the new behavioral alternatives, the shift in mood may be the primary trigger for a return to alcohol.

Other individuals are frightened by their mood swings and attempt through action, going to meetings, reading, or talking, to stabilize their internal mood. In the beginning, extreme shifts from very depressed to very elated and out of control are frightening and common. Action is the prescribed antedote for both.

Emphasis on Action

The primary intervention of early sobriety is action, the substitute for the act of taking a drink and as a necessary means of learning new behaviors that will eventually feel syntonic and therefore not require (at least most of the time) conscious effort.

In early sobriety, conscious attention to actions broken down in small pieces (pick up the phone, go to a meeting) have highest priority. It is this emphasis on action that provides the earliest source of control, as Barbara illustrates:

> All my energy is going into filling up my time with substitute activities for drinking. I am afraid of feeling and afraid of myself. I have to fill up space in order not to sink so low. I'm terrified of what I will do to myself so I must exert strong control to ward off my own impulses.

With six months of sobriety, Barbara reflected back on her intense need to control and channel her impulses when she was newly abstinent. She recognized that a shift away from a hypervigilant stance in that early period would have resulted in a loss of control (I will not exist) or the intrusion by someone else (I will be swallowed up.)

> All my energy went into one channel—obsessive addiction to something. First it is drinking, then a compulsive need for candy bars in early recovery, and now over involvement in meetings and school. I know this obsessional behavior is a protective screen. If I wasn't addicted to something, I would be so vulnerable.

But now, with six months of sobriety, she continued.

> I suddenly feel more control over my impulses. I know now that I can make a conscious choice before acting. For the first time I can decide whether I want to go to a meeting, whether I need a meeting, or whether I might do something else.

Barbara illustrates the beginning of impulse control achieved through the substitution of new actions, played out obsessively or impulsively and therefore without control. With the passage of time and accrued sobriety, she illustrated the introduction of cognitive processes before action, thus developing a higher order of control. The development of cognitive controls does not come without a preceding change in action (Santostefano, 1980).

"Armchair" sobriety, or sobriety exerted through will, results in tension and anxiety (white-knuckle sobriety), because the syntonic action (taking a drink) is not altered.

> I kept trying to stay sober by thinking about it. It seemed all I had to do is tell myself that I would not drink and that would be enough. But it just didn't work after a while. My mind was telling me I could not drink and my arm was raising the glass. Not until I started moving, doing things instead of drinking and instead of thinking, did I get comfortably sober.

Another patient, Patty, illustrates how action provides learning and control that precedes cognitive understanding and control.

> I have great feelings of turmoil and confusion. I make it worse by sitting at home and trying to reason it through. I cut through it by calling someone immediately or heading for a meeting. By cutting through, I stop a downward spiral of depression and give myself a feeling of control.

Patty elaborated about this emphasis on action at her next meeting.

> I recognized that my emotional awareness often precedes my intellectual understanding and creates many difficulties for me. I can feel my emotions, but I have no logical explanation for them. I sometimes feel tempted to deal with them by

drinking. The ability to intercede on my own behalf by calling someone or going to a meeting until I can understand what I am feeling is vitally important to my sobriety.

Many newly abstinent members of AA attend AA meetings everyday and spend much of the rest of the time on the phone with new AA friends and sponsors. As Joan proceeded in recovery, she focused on her need for control.

When I used to feel "out of control" in any way, I immediately started to look for ways to buy drinking time. Now that I'm sober, this space is filled with anxiety. Instead of constructing an escape to drink, I fill up the space with phone, meetings, reading, or even sleeping.

The Need for Structure

An ongoing group of highly anxious individuals in early recovery illustrate the need for therapist interpretation and intervention as a way of providing structure and control.

The group members spent half of the meeting in an excited discussion of the need for strict punishment and incarceration of criminals. The therapists wondered several times why the members were so animated and why they were focused on criminals outside of the work of the group. Finally the therapists understood when all of their efforts to interpret the discussion as a resistance failed. The discussion was a displacement of the fear of their own impulses and their felt need for external limits and structure. One of the members was newly abstinent and severely depressed. Members were telling the therapists to intervene and do something with this out of control, depressed patient.

Another group of individuals in early sobriety illustrates this issue. The intense anxiety, fears of drinking, and issues of impulse control were the impetus for the therapists to develop specific mechanisms of structure to enable the members to tolerate rapidly escalating anxiety (Yalom, 1974).

After several weeks of building emotions, members came late and missed sessions. The therapist started the next meeting with an agenda on the board, suggesting that the members felt the group was out of control.

Members agreed readily, with several stating their expectation that the therapist should provide more structure and therefore more control. With careful exploration, members revealed their fears that the process of self-exploration and revelation would result in someone taking a drink. They would then be the cause of someone else's return to drinking, an intolerable notion.

The therapists explored the fears of drinking in-depth and the feeling of responsibility for someone else's sobriety. They reviewed with each member the frequency and structure of their external resources of support (i.e., what would they do after the meeting and tonight?). They continued to use the agenda for several weeks until the anxiety diminished.

One newly sober group illustrates still further the need for an active therapist and a defined structure.

> The therapist began the first session of the new recovery group in the same way she had always begun traditional long-term therapy groups, with silence. Members fidgeted and began asking her what was supposed to happen. She described the here-and-now process of the group, but gave no guidelines for action, for what to do next.
>
> Finally, a marketing executive announced his agenda and the manner in which the group would proceed. With anger he told the therapist, "This group needs a leader and if you're not going to take over and run the meeting, I will."
>
> The following week the therapist arrived with her own agenda typed out on a piece of paper which she distributed to the members. She therefore stated her assumption of leadership. This procedure was only necessary for two more weeks after which issues arose from within the group context.

The members were so frightened of their own impulses and those of others they needed to see clear evidence that the therapist was in control. When they had it, they didn't need it anymore.

Many individuals and groups for people in early recovery require a lot of structure for a long period (Hellman, 1981). Members who attend AA are used to the very structured and ritualistic order of AA meetings and often expect the same format in group. With time, many prefer a looser group structure because they appreciate the therapeutic benefits when they can tolerate the anxiety without acting on it.

The need for structure is intense and critical in the beginning days of sobriety. The structure provides the sense of security against out of control impulses and the directives for behavioral action.

> I recognize that I need to keep coming to treatment. I need the structure because I have never been in this state of mind. Before when I stopped drinking, it was time out. I didn't intend to stop or change my behavior. Now I need support and direction.

A member of AA illustrates several of the principles we are describing: the need for action, structure, and external control. He illustrates the importance of the concept of a higher power to provide that control.

> I relied on my wits to get me through life, but I can't rely on my wits to stay sober. My wits got me drunk over and over again. I need the program and I need to rely on God.

Many individuals appreciate rapidly the concrete security provided in an AA meeting ("I know I won't take a drink when I'm sitting there"), but others grasp a greater security that is elusive and difficult to describe, especially in the beginning.

> There is really a paradox about closeness in AA. In meetings, I feel vulnerable within an atmosphere of impersonality and safety. This can't be how life is—to feel close and not threatened without actually being involved closely?

Later she expands:

> I'm recognizing the value of the lifelong support offered in AA. I don't understand it: I feel less dependent rather than more after committing myself to the AA program.

Behavioral issues are critical in their early recovery and must be given priority. However, parallel and linked to the behavioral issues are cognitive concerns that require attention as well.

Cognitive Issues

We have described the period of early sobriety as a time of new learning, behaviorally and cognitively. The latter includes consolidation of the new identity as an alcoholic, reorganization of one's environment to fit the new identity, and the beginning of a reconstruction of meaning about the past and the present from the framework of the new identity. This period is characterized by a number of central issues.

The Meaning of Being Alcoholic

Individuals exert great effort in early sobriety to concretely learn the meaning of their new identity in the present as a directive for behavior (I am alcoholic and therefore don't drink). Problems in the meaning of being alcoholic may begin to emerge as individuals have difficulty making a distinction between their new identification and their old life-style and friends. Bradley illustrates the critical dynamic significance of the label alcoholic in his unconscious attempts to simultaneously hold both identifications—I am an alcoholic and I am not an alcoholic.

> Bradley had been separated from his drinking partner for many months and now decided to move his belongings out of their home. He deliberated over which friends to invite to his moving party: his old drinking friends, including those friends shared with his wife, or his new AA friends. Should he have a keg of beer?

He explored the split in his own identity and his sense of the incompatibility between the two groups. But then he denied it, fantasizing that the two groups would come together and it would be a lovely party.

Finally he examined his difficulty in acknowledging that drinking is a major issue for him in relationship to his wife. He has long denied that she is alcoholic in an effort to smooth the wide breach in their relationship since he joined AA. If he really recognized the split—he is alcoholic and sober and she is alcoholic and drinking—he will experience the deep loss between them. The fantasy of the moving party permitted him to merge incompatible identifications and therefore deny the reality of his loss.

On further examination Bradley realized that he hoped his wife would recognize her alcoholism and join him in AA. Bringing AA people to help him move would expose her to AA indirectly. It would also be a way of protecting his new identity by bringing concrete support with him. AA people would protect him from his impulse to drink. Acting on that impulse to drink would eliminate his need to move.

At another session, Bradley continued exploration of his struggle to hold onto two opposing identifications. He recognized that he holds onto the idea that he can drink as a way of symbolically maintaining his attachment to his wife. He speculates that to give her up and recognize that his marriage is over is a part of step one, acknowledging that he has lost control. He examines the central role of alcohol in their marriage and then its centrality throughout his life.

He suddenly recognizes that the question of whether or not to have a keg of beer at a moving party symbolized the central significance of alcohol in his life and he wanted to deny it. It feels to him like somebody is dying and then there is nobody there.

If you take away alcohol, there will be nothing there.

Other difficulties in early sobriety, such as anxiety, depression, a conscious wish to drink, or a fear of drinking, also relate to the meaning of being alcoholic. Peter, sober eight months, illustrates the manner in which he explores what it means to be an alcoholic and links that to his recent fear of drinking and the power of his environment to change his thinking. Both operate in a powerful reciprocal manner that feels out of his control.

I have been thinking about drinking and afraid I might do it. I've tried to examine it, seeing how it relates to being alcoholic. I know that means I don't belong to my privileged social group. When I'm not drinking, I feel bored, isolated, an outsider. So I start to fantasize that I can achieve a sense of belonging by rejoining the cocktail circuit. When I go to those parties, I cannot resist taking a drink. The pull of that setting is just too great.

Peter then shifts focus, describing his nondrinking wife as boring, dull, and lifeless. He recognized that he was projecting his own meaning and perceptions onto her and began to explore the ways in which alcohol has bolstered his self-image and provided him a sense of group identification.

After several months of painful, teeth-clenching sobriety, Mary expressed her resentment at the hospital staff where she had been in treatment.

> I kept insisting that I was not being heard, that I was not getting the help I needed. The counselor didn't know anything about me. He was just putting me in a box and I was supposed to fit! I wanted help and I didn't want to be alcoholic!

Mary had struggled to maintain several months of abstinence, focusing primarily on her anger at being controlled by others and her wish not to be an alcoholic. She now began to explore in her outpatient therapy what it meant to her to be an alcoholic, and she began to examine her long-standing problems with authority.

The difficulty with the meaning of being alcoholic is further illustrated by Gwen. She read an article on alcoholism in the *Stanford Magazine* (Brown, 1982), stopped drinking that very day, and called the clinic for a consultation. She was breathless and excited about having stopped drinking and adamant that she was not an alcoholic. The therapist asked her why it was so important not to be an alcoholic and she was stunned. When the therapist next asked her what it would mean to accept the label, she burst into tears.

> It would mean I am just like my father, an identification I have avoided and denounced all my life.

Gwen attended AA meetings occasionally but always focused on her difficulty identifying.

> I know I am what *they* call dry and not sober. But I just can't think of myself as an alcoholic.

As individuals progress in early recovery, denial unfolds, often creating a crisis centered on the meaning of being alcoholic. After several months of sobriety, Shirley called the clinic in crisis.

> I hadn't appreciated the extent of my alcoholism and the amount of my denial. I suddenly became terribly concerned about how my children feel about my being alcoholic and the public exposure when I go to AA. I feel so upset; I want to become a recovering alcoholic and not be an alcoholic at all. I hate my husband for getting me here, but when I feel good I thank him. Part of me realizes I want help and part of me does not. Part of me believes it's a disease and part of me does not. It's OK for others to be alcoholic, but not me.

Several months later she recalled these comments and added several others from her deeper understanding.

> When I filled out the clinic questionnaire, I described myself as a problem drinker. That was a euphemism. I was in terrible trouble and needed help desperately.

After six months of sobriety, Shirley deepened her exploration, relating the meaning of being alcoholic to sickness and then autonomy.

> I never said no on the basis of not wanting to do something. I needed to be sick or drunk in order to say yes or no.

For the next several months, much of the focus of Shirley's therapy and her interpretations of the AA program involved learning how to determine what she wanted and to say yes and no from that basis. As Shirley told her therapist, integrating AA through the serenity prayer:

> I need to learn to accept the things I cannot change and to change the things I can.

She spent great energy changing and adjusting her plans in an effort to discover what she really felt and wanted. In the beginning of her sobriety she felt a powerful tug, embracing AA completely and rejecting her family or vice versa. By reminding herself that she is alcoholic and, according to that identification, she is her number one priority, she began to be able to make choices on her own behalf.

Having felt overwhelmed and controlled by others, she now embarked on five years of combined psychiatric therapy and AA, working toward a middle ground in which she would move easily between an interdependent relationship with others and her own independent sense of herself. That independent sense of herself was achieved and is now maintained through her identity as an alcoholic.

> I am alcoholic and I must take care of myself first. I must learn how to make the choices that will enable me to remain sober.

Gwen explored the impact of AA meetings and her resistance to the label. It signaled to her helplessness and dependence, both intolerable.

> After a meeting, I think more deeply about alcohol. I finally got some phone numbers but can't imagine using them. I just can't envision myself landing in the gutter like those other AAs and then needing help.

On further reflection, she added what acceptance of the label would mean:

> I don't want my whole life to revolve around alcohol, 12-step work, and rescuing others. Once I commit myself to acknowledging the truth, or make a commitment,

it is final. My commitment to that truth is unshakeable, irrevocable. To consider myself alcoholic means that my commitment and alcoholism will have to become very important in my life.

Working With Fears of Drinking

In early sobriety, the fear of drinking is a common and important occurrence, serving many functions. Because individuals feel so helpless and uncertain about their new identity and because the nondrinking behaviors feel so foreign, many experience a constant preoccupation with the danger of drinking. In the earliest days and weeks of sobriety, individuals have no sense of internal control and imagine "finding themselves" with a drink in their hand. The fear of drinking is very adaptive during this juncture. The preoccupation keeps the focus on alcohol so the individual must actively choose not to drink and actively engage in constructing an environment that will be protective.

In early sobriety, individuals have very little learning yet about themselves as alcoholics so the focus is predominantly on substitution of new actions to deal with the wide range of feelings and impulses emerging with the absence of alcohol. The fear of drinking is an expression of the individual's deep belief in being out of control. Later on in early sobriety, the fear of drinking is an alarm, to alert the sober individual to signs of danger, old thinking patterns or an old environment suddenly reappearing, which enables the individual to take actions he or she now knows are necessary in order not to act on the impulse.

The fear of drinking is also a symbol, alerting the individual to deeper meanings. In psychotherapy, or the process of working through the steps, the fear of drinking is a defensive operation, alerting patient and therapist to deeper self-revelations about to emerge. It is important to understand the fear of drinking as a concrete expression of one's sense of lack of control to be addressed behaviorally and as a symbol, to be unraveled for it's deeper significance. Peter illustrates:

> My "alcoholic thinking" scares me. It's Christmas and my association of being OK goes along with being able to participate in my old social group and drink like my friends. I am making different choices this year. I will go to an AA meeting instead of a cocktail party. (Peter focuses on his own behavioral change and next examines the meaning of his wish to drink.) I still get moments of discomfort and low esteem in my sobriety and I immediately feel I must be failing. If I have come this far, I shouldn't be feeling bad. I start to think that a drink will restore my self-esteem.

Peter then realized he would soon be celebrating a year of sobriety and examined his fear of drinking in relation to this important milestone.

> I decided that I wanted one clean year and I'm now afraid I will sabotage that success, or after having a year, it won't matter anymore and I'll drink then. I am

beginning to realize that "turning it over" (AA third step) means my whole life and my whole way of thinking. It seems monumental. I see that I must really begin to "work the program" and get into the fourth step (a moral inventory.) I don't think I've been totally honest and I am afraid of the painful task of self-examination that lies ahead if I really want a comfortable sobriety.

Peter now thought about his comments a week earlier and understood the meaning of his fear of drinking expressed at that time.

I feel like I'm on a plateau. I am suddenly into "alcoholic thinking," wanting to drink. I heard someone say at a meeting that you have to change your life style completely. I just hadn't heard this so clearly before. I began to wonder if I really was an alcoholic. To ward off this feeling, I've been dredging up all the bad memories of drinking and pushing away the good, but I still am preoccupied with the wish to drink.

Another patient, sober for ten months, thought about the idea of drinking in relation to his association with the past. He was able to see that he used fantasies about drinking to establish or perpetuate a mood which he then acted on.

I had a good conversation with my ex-wife and suddenly felt pulled back into the past when things were good. Being with her made me want to drink, to relive our old romantic sojourns and to hold onto the mood of the present moment. Suddenly I saw how readily I generated myself into a frame of mind associated with drinking. I thought I could keep my new perspective—that I could slide into the mood and the memories without acting on the impulse to drink. But there I was, telling myself to take a drink and luxuriate in the memories of my drinking past. I got good and scared. I finished my conversation and ran to a meeting.

After this occasion, Chris became very depressed. He had recognized his deep lack of control and the power of his thinking to quickly alter everything he had struggled so hard to learn in the last few months.

I suddenly recognized a deep fear that I will die with a drink in my hand. I am terribly afraid. I know I have the capacity to die an alcoholic death.

The therapist pointed out to Chris that he was locked into a pattern of controlling his abstinence, just as he had tried to control his drinking. The therapist then introduced the topic of a higher power, integrating the concept and the language of AA into the therapy. It was an issue that Chris had discussed, but always tabled. The therapist suggested that Chris had not developed a relationship with a power greater than himself, central to the AA program, and was therefore claiming control, rather than acknowledging the lack of it.

For the first time, Chris understood. Loss of control meant always. How could he rely on himself and his own desire to remain abstinent with the evidence of his ability to deceive himself so clear. The power to stay sober would have to come from outside himself.

Gwen illustrates the fear of drinking as a signal preceding insight.

> I woke up craving a drink and I never wanted to drink in the morning. I woke with a feeling of dread and terror and asked myself, "Why is it getting harder?" Then I settled back and realized I am upset with my husband and family. My new attitudes and behavior are ruffling the feathers in the nest. I'm not having any difficulties deciding now and realizing that I come first. I must put my needs ahead of those of my family and I am very frightened.

Working With Drinking Dreams

Similar to the conscious fear of drinking, the drinking dream is an unconscious experience of early sobriety, serving the same functions as the conscious fear. On the most basic level, it is a warning sign that the person may actually be preparing unconsciously or even consciously to take a drink. The dream alerts the individual who increases protective, abstinent behaviors in the waking state.

> I was getting complacent, feeling secure in my sobriety. I cut down on meetings and added other activities. Then I had this dream! There I was, sitting with my friends with a beer in my hand. I woke up sweating. I called someone right away and got back on my normal schedule of meetings.

The dream functioned as an unconscious alert. The individual assessed its meaning as a warning and immediately took action, moving from the spiral back to the alcohol focus. After several weeks of careful attention to his sobriety, he resumed his new activities, this time without shifting away from AA. The experience was an important reminder to him that he must actively and regularly think about himself as an alcoholic even when the new behaviors of abstinence are firmly in place.

The drinking dream may function as more than an alarm. It may give the individual the experience of drinking without having to actually go through it. Shirley illustrates.

> I chaired an AA meeting this week, and a man told me afterwards that I sounded like I was thinking about drinking. I was surprised, but I knew he was right. Then I had two drinking dreams, as if to follow through and give myself the experience. In one dream, I was mad at myself for sabotaging my success and having to start over again. In that dream, I was getting ready to celebrate my first AA birthday and I took one drink instead. I realized that the notion of one year sober is very frightening.
>
> In the second dream, I took a morning drink that totally wiped me out. This dream told me that a drink will *not* make me feel better as I often think it will. In fact, it will be much worse than ever.

She allowed herself to go through the experience of drinking in the dream to reaffirm her commitment to abstinence. The dream was effective in challenging her own alcoholic thinking, more effective than consciously trying to remember how bad drinking really was. She needed the feelings that accompanied the memory that the dream provided. She awoke feeling hungover, remorseful, and more convinced that she could not drink normally.

The drinking dream also precedes insight, just like the conscious fear of drinking. Toby illustrates, relating the content and experience of her dream to new, dynamic understanding.

> I dreamed I started to drink again without any thought. I know that dream was triggered by a letter from an alcoholic friend who is coming to visit. My sobriety shouldn't depend on someone else's behavior.

Toby later recognized that her entire friendship was centered on alcohol. To think about drinking or to begin drinking with this friend would validate the friendship. More importantly, it would wipe out Toby's feeling of pain at watching her friend continue to drink when Toby is sober. She then thought about the pain she felt as a child watching her alcoholic parents.

> Trying to relate to people who drink is like talking to a computer. I wonder if there is anybody behind my mother's face.

The drinking dream may not be a warning at all but an affirmation of sobriety and a guidepost to progress. Tom illustrates.

> I had a dream in which I was preparing to drink: the dark bar, the drinking friends— I could taste it. Suddenly, everything and everybody turned to stone. I said, "What am I doing here? I don't belong here anymore." I walked out of the bar. The sun was shining and people were moving and talking again.
>
> At first I was terrified, I came so close. Then I felt reassured: I could choose not to drink. It was a great relief. If I pay attention, I have the tools to make a choice.

Developing a Story

After the emphasis on action, one of the most important aspects of learning in early sobriety is the reconstruction of the past, based on the new identity as an alcoholic. This reconstruction involves the breakdown of denial about one's drinking and the systematic breakdown of the logical constructions that supported that denial. It is not at all unusual to hear newly abstinent individuals report that much of their past life, mysterious and unexplainable, now makes sense.

Individuals who attend AA learn by example how to engage in this process of reconstruction. The guidelines are woven into the "drunkalogue" or "story" the AA member tells at each meeting. It consists of the history of "what it was like," "what happened," and "what it is like now." The new AA member listens to others tell about their drinking, the reasoning used to sustain it, and the myriad of troubles that resulted. Members trace the downward progression of their developing alcoholism and the events that ultimately led them to the "turning point" of surrender, or "hitting bottom." Members then tell how they came to identify themselves as alcoholic and to arrive at AA. They describe the process of identification with others as central to their sustained sobriety and to the deepening of their own identification through the construction and uncovering of their own story.

Central to the story construction is honesty, accented verbally in meetings and in the 12 steps, for example, a fearless and searching moral inventory, rigorous honesty. In the beginning of sobriety, many individuals believe they have no story; drinking was their only problem and now they are sober. With the passage of sober time, this view almost always changes, and, therefore, the story changes as well.

> At one month sober, I told the group that my drinking got bad two years previously, that my work had never been affected, and that my family didn't know. At six months, I could see my drinking was actually a problem for about four years and that my work was affected because my attention was always on alcohol or on covering up. But I still believed my family never knew. At two years, my whole story is different. The denial just keeps peeling away. Now it seems to me that I was drinking alcoholically for years and everything was affected. My family knew, but they denied it just like I did.

Another member, Joan, at one year sobriety, illustrates the importance of that denial in early sobriety.

> I was positive I didn't hurt my children. Nobody could tell me my drinking affected them at all. I couldn't even identify with women similar to me who talked about neglecting their kids or endangering them. It just wasn't me.

> But now I see things quite differently. I am recalling incidents one by one in which I clearly hurt them. Last week I asked my daughter directly what was the worst thing for her about my drinking. She said it was my unpredictability.

As her denial eroded and she could incorporate into her self-image what she did, felt, and said while drinking, her identity of herself as an alcoholic deepened, as did the reconstruction of her past.

The difficulty in accepting the label alcoholic and the meanings of that identification are apparent at the transition point and early recovery. Joan illustrates the significance of denial in allowing her to continue her abstinence. Importantly, her denial could have served her equally well in allowing her to return to drinking by deciding she could not identify and therefore must not be alcoholic.

I didn't like my first AA meeting. I felt intense fear and prejudice coming from me. I couldn't respond emotionally to the speaker or the other people because I did not want to identify. I was able to identify with the general topic being discussed, grief and how to handle adversity. I couldn't wait to leave, but I recognized that my reaction was one of not wanting to identify. I found it hard to understand how a person could do all the things the speaker said, and I felt arrogant and snobbish as I left. It seemed to me that most of the men had not sought help until the advance stages, which I had not reached. I had a strong response never to return and an equally strong intent to try again.

After seven weeks sober, Joan reflected again.

It's difficult. I don't know how I feel about joining AA. I've been back and now see that there are people there with a broader range of age and experience than I first thought. The guy who chaired today wasn't as sick as the others and seemed more similar to me. He said he felt intolerant when things don't go as expected. I could see the same thing in me. I know I think I can control more things than I can. I also realized I wasn't the newest member and found myself wanting to get more involved.

With the passage of time, Joan altered her initial negative impression of the people in AA. As she saw them more positively, she could accept identifying with the feelings and experiences they reported. The more positively she felt about these people who are alcoholic, the easier it became for her to be an alcoholic too.

Another patient illustrates the slow shift in thinking.

My physician told me I had an abnormal liver two years ago and suggested I stop drinking. I was shocked because I knew deeply that I would never make it. But I believed I was "sober" the first six months of my therapy because I had cut the frequency and the strength.

A few weeks later she elaborated:

I'm beginning to recognize new facts about my drinking. I did have blackouts though I never recognized them before. I had two accidents and fell into the swimming pool while drunk. I also just realized that I mixed alcohol and valium. Isn't this amazing? Up until now, I saw my use of valium as strictly medicinal and not to be confused with the alcohol!

The experience of identifying as an alcoholic is often a shock. As members substitute action and become more comfortable about their ability to stay sober, they can risk thinking about themselves in addition to taking action. With four months sobriety, Joan illustrates:

I'm starting to review my past from the perspective of my sobriety. I can see that I am reinterpreting my entire history through the eyes of someone who now sees herself as an alcoholic. I can see where I first made that turn. It's subtle, and it stands out glaringly. After that, alcohol was central to me.

A few weeks later, she continued.

I've been thinking about the progression of my telescoped alcoholism. It was telescoped because it was only really bad the last two years, but "being alcoholic" was present for many years, just dormant. My active, severe alcoholism was triggered with the marriage of my daughter. I shifted immediately, literally from one day to the next, from daily "controlled drinking" (before, during, and after dinner) to uncontrolled drinking all day. Within months I was drunk all the time and virtually nonfunctional.

Developing her own history helped Joan acknowledge the reality of her drinking and outlined the therapeutic work that was necessary for her. She could see that the loss of her daughter and, therefore, the loss of her role as a mother was intolerable and that she used alcohol to fill up the painful void. With only a few months of sobriety, she knew she would have to develop a new sense of herself independent of her role as mother.

The reconstruction of the past continues through sobriety, often providing the context to understand changes in the present. Gwen illustrates:

I remember that when I was drinking I had a constant feeling of being out of control. I hated the idea that people were looking at me and judging me. Now I realize I'm not so concerned that people are looking at me or judging me. I present myself with more confidence and I have a sense of freedom. I feel less self-protected and less guarded. During my drinking I got sun glasses to conceal my retreat into drinking. I thought I was protecting myself from other people's awareness.

Another patient thinks about her reasoning, amazed at the realities of her thinking and behavior while drinking.

I've been feeling such shame as I recall my behavior while drinking. I find it hard to believe I could do such crazy things. What could I have been thinking? You know, it reminds me of when I was in third grade, trying to hold onto the maypole at the spring fair. I couldn't keep my grip, so I put glue all over my hands. Instead of letting me stick, it just made it more slippery. That kind of concrete thinking is exactly the way I thought about problems and solutions while drinking.

Many patients have long histories of psychotherapy before becoming abstinent (Brown, 1977). Some believe that their therapy was useful in knocking down their denial, but many more begin to seriously question their previous therapy, even determining that it kept them from changing.

> I wonder whether there was a point in my earlier therapy where my therapist could have said something and I might have been receptive. I can see that you can't knock down an elaborate system of lies without offering something in its place, and I think my therapist had nothing to offer. I wonder whether I would have been able to respond if he had suggested reading something or asked me if I knew very much about alcoholism. I am just amazed at the lying and the building on lies that occurred for me and how painful it is to reverse. I'm also amazed at the lengths I would go to deny. During all that time my idea of sobriety was one of control. Now my ideas about that are completely changing.

This patient is stabilized in early recovery, with much behavioral and cognitive emphasis preceding this insight. She is now thoughtful and able to reflect about herself, rather than acting instead. She is ready for the introduction or reintroduction of a dynamically oriented psychotherapy. The integration of dynamic issues is now possible and, indeed, desirable.

Dynamic Issues

The Uncovering Process

The most common feature of early sobriety, change, is accompanied by an equally important and frightening experience, the emergence of feelings and new awareness. Five months sober, Pam illustrates the progression of this awakening and its relevance to understanding and emphasizing action and learning modes in the first phase of recovery.

> I have never been aware of any feelings at all, but suddenly they are coming out. I am learning how to become self-centered and learning about the 12 steps.

This session is full of questions, explanation, and advice. As if talking to a teacher, or sponsor, Pam asked the therapist when she should do a fourth step. Pam is not full of anxiety nor overwhelmed by her feelings today. Rather, she has the air of a student in the beginning phase of learning a new language.

At her next meeting, Pam explored how her developing feelings could lead her to drink.

> I am terrified of being alone because I am faced with my feelings and I am frightened to find out what they are. So I need to fill in all the empty spaces in my life. If I allow myself to feel I am afraid I will respond immediately with a drink. So I avoid being alone and fill in my day with AA meetings.

Pam illustrated to the therapist the emphasis on the action mode to slow down the emergence of intolerable feelings. As soon as she arrived at her therapy each week, she began to cry because those feelings were now so close to the surface. Thinking about her fear, she now emphasized the importance of learning and language.

> Feelings are terrible because they are foreign, unknown. I don't have a vocabulary to label them and therefore can't possibly begin to understand what they mean.

The lack of a language and vocabulary to explain (and therefore control) her feelings resulted in her need to resort to denial as the only alternative. Pam was aware of deep, intolerable emotions as her daughter's marriage approached. The therapist suggested that Pam might have feelings about this and Pam illustrated her primitive means of dealing with all emotion.

> The best way for me to deal with this today is to pretend it isn't happening. I'm too frightened to let my emotions out.

The therapist suggested that Pam was reverting to her old method of smiling and pretending her feelings don't exist. The therapist then discussed the difference between avoidance and denial as Pam practiced, and the notion of "turning it over" according to the third step of AA. In the latter, she acknowledged the reality of her daughter's marriage and her inability to do anything about it. She must, of course, also deal with her feelings by acknowledging the reality.

The therapist introduces what is, indeed, the novel idea that one can have feelings about a situation or person without being able or having to change it. It is the notion of acceptance without change. For Pam and many others, it has been intolerable to have feelings about something that she could not alter, or for which she felt responsible. The idea that she could have feelings without having to act on them is a critically important base for the continuing emergence of feelings and the uncovering process of sobriety.

The emergence of feelings in sobriety is most intolerable because it is experienced as a loss of control. For many, this is equal to being drunk as Pam illustrates.

> I feel hungover after my sessions. It is just as if I've been drinking. Sometimes before I come, I can taste the scotch. Feeling is just like drinking, which is just plain out of control.

Pam continued this exploration, relating it to crying.

> I have a difficult time crying. I feel ashamed and embarrassed because it feels like a total lack of control. It's so important that people hear me, but I'm not able to

express myself in a way that people can understand. I'm not used to having feelings, to crying, and I have no vocabulary to explain it. I feel like a helpless baby.

She elaborated about her fear of emotions at her next meeting.

My husband was gone this weekend, and I sat and cried by myself for an entire night. Why can't I control this?

Pam said she was embarrassed to report it. She's beginning to think she doesn't know herself at all, and that she is more unpredictable to herself than to anyone else.

I am afraid I will use my alcoholism as an excuse to become more self-centered. Crying and thinking about my feelings makes me feel more selfish.

Pam then challenged this reasoning, demonstrating its defensive purpose to her.

My sponsor wants me to do step four, but I'm wondering if I'm ready for all that pain. I really want to justify everything in order to be OK in my own eyes. I'm really very wary of this whole process because I can't tolerate inadequacies in myself.

The fear of what she would find in her emerging sobriety continued as a central theme during her first eight months of therapy.

I've decided to stop therapy. It's no use. It will get me nowhere.

She then recognized that her disillusionment followed a week in which she had cried in her therapy. She then focused on the matter of control and her fear of the intensity of her feelings and her dependency on other people.

Once I allow myself to feel any amount of need, I'll never be able to control it. I was talking on the phone and began to cry. The only thing I could do was hang up, which felt like a horrible thing to do. I was such a failure.

Pam continued to describe herself as desperately out of control. Rather than focusing on the nature of her neediness and her fears about it, the therapist instead targeted the issue of control. She asked Pam what she had done on the telephone.

I started to cry so I hung up, stopped crying, and went about my work.

The therapist pointed out that Pam and nobody else had control over that action and, in fact, it was very effective. This offered stunning reassurance and she proceeded to talk about her deep feelings of need for the remainder of the hour.

Lack of control is expressed in many ways. Sheila related a dream:

> I was riding along in a car with my boss trying to hide a bottle, but it kept slipping out. It just wouldn't stay hidden. This is an expression of the loss of control I feel in sobriety. I often feel transparent, as if I were drinking and exposed.

Sheila explored this feeling further.

> I am sometimes worried that things are changing so fast. I don't know what to expect. I have never felt so profoundly, and my responses are sometimes out of proportion to the situation. I feel off balance. I feel intense most of the time and finally reach a saturation point when my "circuits are overloaded." I simply can't respond or assimilate anything else. I used to drink to stop this overload. Now I retreat, walk, sleep, or go to a meeting and just listen.

As Pam progressed in uncovering her feelings, she recognized a layer of fear deeper than that of being out of control.

> I am having trouble with my feelings about my parents. If I acknowledge that they beat me, it means I am unlovable. I also feel very identified with both of them, so that means I'm unlovable too. The emergence of my feelings and self-knowledge only reinforces my negative bad feelings about myself. If I open up it will prove I am unlovable and I'll be filled with self-hate and the need to be self-abusive.

This fear was an extremely important marker for the therapist about the importance of a titrated, slow uncovering process. Any emergent insight ran the risk of a drinking response, both to stop the uncovering process and to follow through on the self-punishment required for what she had observed about herself. The therapist participated actively in helping the patient titrate uncovering and provided action alternatives repeatedly. As Pam notes:

> I always go to a meeting on the night of my therapy. It's good insurance that I won't do something bad to myself instead.

Integration or Intervention?

The core process of early recovery is one of shifting balance. There is an emphasis on action and identification, with the learning of new behaviors and a new language to define oneself both in the past and the present. There is an emphasis on introspection, or self-analysis, which involves initiating the construction of a story and the continuing unfolding of denial and redefinition of self from the framework of the new identity as an alcoholic. The process involves the early integration of the three basic modes of psychotherapy, behavioral, cognitive, and dynamic.

The task of the patient is to focus on action and behavioral change, develop cognitive controls, and begin self-analysis. The latter begins when unconscious meanings or dynamics are hampering the behavioral and cognitive strategies for abstinence, or when anxiety arises as the result of the removal of alcohol. The patient learns the order of intervention on his or her behalf from listening to the experiences of others in AA. The first order is behavioral: don't take a drink, go to meetings, avoid slippery places. The second is cognitive: remember that you are an alcoholic and what that means. Finally, the third level of intervention is analysis, which is suggested in the fourth and tenth steps of the AA program and outlined in AA-approved literature (AA World Services and Hazelden Educational Services) and in various ways by sponsors and other AA members.

It is at the third level that psychotherapists can be of most benefit, especially if their patients attend AA. If not, the therapist must be much more active in prescribing behavioral and cognitive change and in teaching the patient about alcoholism (the first two levels).

Susan's experience illustrates the unfolding process of early recovery within the framework and language of the program of AA. She illustrates the integration of the need for action, cognitive awareness, and insight about herself. In addition, the process of unfolding in her therapy (both a parallel process and an integrated process with the unfolding in AA) and her integration of therapy and work with the sponsor are shown.

> Susan was virtually silent for several weeks. She wanted to miss her therapy hours and felt herself consciously withdrawing from self-exploration and revelation. She reported that she was attending fewer AA meetings, not talking when she did go, and was not calling her sponsor. She was feeling frightened and resistant to any movement or uncovering. She described herself as paralyzed, not drinking, but just going through the motions of her daily routine. She was frightened by her withdrawn behavior, because she feared it would result in her picking up a drink to break through.

> After several weeks of this withdrawal, Susan was suddenly open in her therapy, with an emerging recall for early memories not previously available to her. These memories were related to drinking episodes in which she hurt others by her behavior. The recall came after she decided to begin her fourth step.

> The weeks of silence and withdrawal reflected her fear about beginning the process of self-analysis. Her sponsor had been urging her to begin her "fearless and searching moral inventory," to dig into the past in order to breakdown denial and acknowledge the realities and consequences of her drinking behavior and beliefs. Susan had not spoken about her fourth step with her therapist, though it was with her therapist that she intended to start this process.

There are constant questions of integration for the therapist and patient, often most easily dictated by the patient's movement. The solidity of abstinent behavior and identification, represented by the need for an alcohol focus, the emergence of emotions and/or other problems and a language to explain them, represented by movement onto the spiral, and finally, active uncovering initiated by the patient, representing expanded awareness and the third component on the continuum, are intertwined and integrated in therapeutic decision making.

The question of therapist focus and intervention was raised around the issue of whether the therapist should move toward intensifying the dyadic therapeutic relationship with his patient or should move toward actively diluting it by insisting on a triadic relationship through the integration of AA. A therapist presented the following example in the case supervision seminar.

> My patient came to treatment while he was still drinking, moved into sobriety, and achieved 90 days. He went to a few AA meetings, but felt he was special and stopped going. He was relying on his therapeutic relationship with me and the specialness attached to that bond in order to maintain sobriety. I went away on vacation and the patient started to drink.

The seminar discussion evolved around the question of whether or not the drinking was a reaction to the disruption in the therapeutic bond. It was suggested by several students that the therapist should increase the therapy sessions and intensify the transference relationship for improved psychotherapeutic work. The seminar leader suggested that a disruption in the bond was probably an accurate appraisal and was at the very heart of the problem. She suggested that the therapist was participating in the illusion that the therapeutic bond was special by increasing the sessions and intensifying the transference. The leader suggested that before his vacation, the therapist should have initiated a discussion about the patient's refusal to go to AA. While not insisting that the patient go, the therapist could have offered education about early sobriety, anticipating the patient's difficulty and emphasizing the need for a behavioral plan and object substitutes. Such intervention by the therapist, regardless of the patient's response, prevents the therapist from colluding with the patient's belief in his specialness and the specialness of the therapeutic bond. Needless to say, this is extremely difficult for therapists who believe that the best psychotherapeutic work involves an intensification of the transference with the dilution of other dependency gratifying substitutes. In fact, with long-term sobriety, the patient can tolerate an intensification of the transference as a result of using other resources and having abstinent behaviors and cognitive controls in place. Intensification of a transference relationship in early sobriety can be extremely problematic to the patient, who feels vulnerable, unprotected, and unknowledgeable about his or her new identity.

The question of attendance at AA provides another illustration of therapist assessment and decision making about strategy or intervention. It illustrates the importance of a good history about the current drinking situation and affiliation with AA. In this case, the therapist was questioning whether or not she was responsible for titrating the anxiety of her patient to prevent the patient from drinking. The therapist reports:

> My patient reported two years of sobriety, but no attendance at AA for the past three months (regular attendance before this time). She was feeling great, even grandiose about her ability to do it (stay sober) herself. Very shortly, she became quite anxious in her therapy, called frequently, and wanted to increase her sessions. I felt afraid that she might drink, so became available to her whenever she requested it. I felt her therapy was responsible for her increasing anxiety, and, therefore, I should be available to keep her from acting out and drinking.

The seminar group discussed the pitfalls of the therapist assuming responsibility for whether or not a patient drinks. But they saw an equally dangerous pitfall of not doing anything. Immediately increasing the therapy sessions to deal with the emerging emotions seemed the best solution.

The leader suggested that the therapist had overlooked the most critical element reported by the patient in her initial interview: Why had she stopped going to AA? The therapist needed to focus on this question intently to determine the kind, quality, and frequency of her AA meetings and relationships, her pattern of attendance, and the actual support she had derived. It would be most critical to assess what was going on with her within AA, her relationship to a sponsor if she had one, and her past ability to make use of AA during times of stress. Whereas the therapist might decide to increase her sessions anyway, to do so without understanding her abandonment of AA, could easily miss an important dynamic issue and transfer her sense of support and dependency away from AA onto the therapist.

With two, ten, or more years of sobriety, the possibility of a patient taking a drink to deal with emotions or after a particularly difficult session exists. The therapist must have an awareness of the patient's behavioral alternatives. If there are none, or they have been rejected, the first therapeutic intervention must deal with reviewing the importance of a structure of support.

A therapist illustrates this review with a patient: Jim was predominantly sober for four years, with several "slips" in between. In his first interview, Jim called these drinking episodes "falling off the wagon," which alerted the therapist to the structure of his thinking about control and the likelihood that he did not attend AA. She explored immediately: How does he stay abstinent? What is the nature and the structure of his support?

Jim indeed did not go to AA, feeling he would rather rely on himself. He had some supportive friends, but because they hadn't been through their own alcoholism, they couldn't truly be with him through his difficult periods. When Jim had a bad craving to drink, he often went to bed, knowing the craving would pass.

The therapist was not impressed with going to bed as the only mechanism for guarding sobriety. As one of many, it is certainly a reasonable tool. She suggested that the process of group therapy that Jim was considering would raise his anxiety and easily stimulate a desire to drink. The therapist stated explicitly her concern for Jim's lack of supports. She noted that she feels very protective of recovering alcoholics viewing their sobriety as absolutely primary, but she cannot ensure it for her patients. For Jim to make the best use of the therapy group, he needs to develop his behavioral and cognitive methods of abstinence so they will be second nature for him and available in times of anxiety and stress.

Handling Slips

What about the belief held by patient and therapist that a drinking episode, punctuating abstinence, is a good learning experience? A drinking episode surrounded by periods of abstinence is called within AA a "slip" (Rudy, 1980). The slip indicates the general intent is abstinence and something is not working with the steps to maintain it. Central to understanding the slip is the notion of punctuation or an interruption in the progression of abstinence. These slips occur within the context of an identification as an alcoholic, though that identity may be shaky or questioned. Perhaps the individual is struggling with the conflict in identifying or with the issue of control. The slip becomes a testing mechanism to help the individual decide whether or not he or she is really an alcoholic.

A strong identity as an alcoholic and the best intention to stay abstinent may be thwarted in early sobriety by a lack of knowledge about the behavioral alternatives and steps necessary to maintain abstinence. Or, a strong environmental pull associated with the meaning of drinking cannot be defended against. Slips may turn into binges or the individual may move back along the continuum to the drinking side, shifting identity and belief. Suddenly, from being alcoholic and sober, the individual decides he or she is not an alcoholic and therefore can drink. Rather than viewing his drinking episode as a slip within a framework of abstinence, he is back within the construct of control and an identity as a non-alcoholic.

But is a slip valuable? In retrospect, many abstinent individuals assert that their episodes of drinking after initial abstinence were indeed important to them. They retrace the episode and use it to firm up their identity as an alcoholic.

> I wasn't sure I was really an alcoholic, so I went out for more "research." It didn't take long. I am now thoroughly convinced that I am an alcoholic. I was getting complacent, coming to meetings, but not getting involved, not working the program. This "slip" showed me I have to get busy and do the steps. A half-hearted attempt just won't work.

> I got back in that environment and everything I'd learned in AA evaporated. I was once again prince charming: I picked up the glass and was off. I just can't be among old drinking friends for a while.

Slips are not a necessary part of abstinence, nor are they without meaning. It is important for individuals who fear they might drink, and for those who do, to understand the dynamics of the slip: how it occurred, the warning signs that it was coming, and the practical, concrete, and underlying reasons for its occurrence. Harvey illustrates the process of analysis after a brief slip after months of sobriety:

> I'm thinking about the functions of this slip. My life felt out of control and alcohol ground everything to a halt. It gave me time out from having to control everything.

Harvey continued, examining the anxiety and the feelings associated with a hangover.

> I've got sleep problems, trouble making decisions, stomachaches. I can't see clearly and I'm avoiding others. It's a feeling of being out of control too. Drinking really did buy time out. Now I have to convalesce and, therefore, postpone the painful issues I was looking at before I drank. I was angry at my wife and my job and unhappy that life is not perfect with sobriety.

Harvey remained in a depressed, inactive state for several weeks.

> I feel like I'm in a "waiting temperament," giving myself time. I've got a strong desire to short circuit my depression and drink again because I'm having feelings I've never had before.

A few weeks later Harvey added:

> I recognized that I've gathered strength by giving space to my bad mood and giving myself some transition time back into abstinence. But you know, it is humiliating to be an alcoholic. To be alcoholic is to be full of self-hatred. I felt it so strongly this time.

> And I'm beginning to see I have more compulsive behaviors and therefore more things not controlled by my will. Going to AA is a way of coming up for air and allowing reality to come back. I'm beginning to see the need for an external structure which I will not need to defy. It will enhance my freedom instead.

Harvey had been involved with AA peripherally, using the principles to stay sober, but resenting them at the same time. He could not shift from the notion that any authority or authoritative structure would limit his freedom. A few weeks later Harvey illustrated his shift.

> These days I feel a sense of settling and calming after I attend AA. It is so important that I don't have to manufacture it.

Harvey spent weeks analyzing the dynamics of this slip and the insights he derived from it.

> I've been thinking about the illusion of freedom I attach to drinking. It was a way to stop myself, a conventional method of turning off one system and starting another.

> My struggle for sobriety is an endless task full of recognizing the ways in which I deceive myself and engage in willful combat. Accepting I'm alcoholic doesn't seem to help. To control myself now (to not drink) seems equal to defeat. I'm not into surrender. I just don't get it at all. Drinking is hooked to something valuable for me which I'm going to lose.

Harvey developed a pattern of brief, predictable slips, once or twice a year, a pattern he continued for several years. He analyzed his drinking after each episode and made important gains in personal insight. But he did not alter his pattern. Finally, he spoke about the importance of "slipping."

> The regression to a drinking state is ritualistic, coming back to feed at that emotional state of mind. I unleash my creativity by participating in that state, even though the costs are later so high.

Harvey refused to consider that he might be able to achieve the same insights or even the same creative state without acting out the drinking. After two more slips Harvey said he'd had enough.

> I've never internalized the reflective part of myself, so I just repeat the ritual again and again. I'm starting to recognize the signs leading toward a slip and actively moving away from it. It seems like a great loss, but maybe one day I'll be able to get to that state of mind without drinking.

The fear of drinking or a drinking episode will be extremely significant within the context of an ongoing psychotherapy relationship. As described earlier, the patient and therapist learn to examine the fear of drinking in relation to issues being uncovered.

A slip may be the vehicle to move someone into psychotherapy. Many individuals with steady abstinence need professional help to unravel the myriad of feelings and conflicts covered by the alcohol. But the fear of psychotherapy by recovering alcoholics is intense. Though many alcoholics in AA believe firmly in the notion of asking for help and using the people and framework of AA, they cannot transfer that belief into a request for professional help. A trainee described her new patient:

> Mary was sober for several years but had a drinking episode following her son's wedding. She got through the event OK, but felt she could not deal with the mul-

titude and depth of emotions she had afterwards. She stopped drinking after two days of steady consumption, increased her AA meetings, talked about her slips in these meetings and with her sponsor. It was her sponsor who suggested she see a therapist.

Individuals who slip in AA carry that slip as a part of their alcoholic identity and their identity within AA. There is often a self-punitive or castigating air about the slip. Members are often sheepish, remorseful, or "babies" again on their return. A slip shifts the focus back to alcohol. It is indeed time out. What couldn't be dealt with before the slip is tabled because the individual must put an increasing focus on alcohol and how to stay sober. It is thus a directive back to behavioral action and a safety mechanism to prevent the uncovering or exploration of unconscious feelings.

The slipper in AA also has a self-image of someone who is not perfect, who learns more slowly, is thick headed, willful, etc. Depending on the meaning of the slip, the previous length of sobriety, and the circumstances of the therapy, the focus may center on behavior and cognitive strategies alone. Patients with a longer previous sobriety, may be able to combine a dynamic understanding of the slip immediately, while also focusing on their behavior to maintain abstinence.

Analyzing the Dynamics of Drinking

With the behaviors of abstinence in place after a slip, individuals can more safely explore the events that led to the drinking episode. Sally illustrates, calling her episode of drinking a binge that intruded in her early recovery:

> I've been tracing the events that led to my taking a drink. I felt anger and resentment, victimized. So I talked myself into drinking by thinking I would give myself a set of experiences—power, control, and defiance—through drinking. If I don't drink it feels like a loss. I've got to shift my thinking again to where I can feel I gain control by not drinking rather than lose it.

Sally continued to analyze her slips recognizing the drinking states of mind that precede the action of taking a drink. She describes a "flashback."

> I went to a party with old drinking friends I hadn't seen for a long time. I flashed back into a state of mind prompted by the circumstances. It was an old mood, a drinking mood to be sure. I didn't drink, but it felt odd. All the circumstances and people dictated drinking.

Months later Sally forestalled acting on an impulse to drink by identifying the warning signs.

I've been thinking about drinking. I can see I'm forming a plan to drink. I'm in a protective environment where no one knows I'm alcoholic and I'm starting to bide my time, knowing there's a drink up ahead. I get myself out of this frame by visualizing the consequences and giving alcohol primacy in my thinking. I was terribly frightened because I felt for a few minutes that I could not choose not to drink. It felt like being on the edge of a cliff. I could go either way. Thinking about alcohol, going to a meeting, and talking about all this took the pressure off. It wasn't my secret anymore and I stopped formulating a plan.

Early recovery is characterized by a prominent focus on the new identity as an alcoholic and the new behaviors that support that identity. The continuum remains narrow, similar to the closed focused transition stage, to maintain attention on the alcohol axis. Integration of the other two axes occurs only to the degree that either effects the solidity of the alcohol focus. The individual who shifts too rapidly away from a focus on alcohol runs the risk of losing the new identity and reverting back to drinking behavior and thinking.

For individuals who have been involved in a psychotherapeutic relationship, early recovery is a time of adding an active membership in AA and integrating that involvement in the working therapeutic partnership. It is a very important move away from a dyadic toward a triadic therapeutic relationship. Early recovery corresponds to an early developmental level and, therefore, requires a focus on behavioral and cognitive issues with a minimum of dynamic uncovering therapy. This focus may be poorly understood by the therapist. Primary involvement in AA with supportive therapeutic backup allows the new learning necessary to this period to occur.

The therapist stands ready to explore dynamic issues that may be interfering with continuing sobriety, such as strong environmental pulls to drink, unconscious conflicts related to "being alcoholic," or conflicts that seem to be temporarily quieted by alcohol. Above all, however, early recovery is a time of new learning and consolidation of a new identity that will shape the individual's interactions and interpretations of self and others.

As the identity and new behaviors become firm, the individual moves into ongoing recovery, a time for reflection as much as for action, and a time for the ongoing integration of all three axes of the continuum.

Chapter 7

Ongoing Recovery

ISSUES IN ONGOING RECOVERY

The period of ongoing recovery is characterized by stability of identity and abstinent behaviors, with much more attention given to the process of self-examination, encompassed within and reflected in the interpretation of self and others. For AA members, this process occurs through rigorous involvement with the twelve steps, which increases the ability for honest self-appraisal and realistic self-portraits. Simultaneous and cyclical movement in all three components of the continuum characterizes ongoing recovery. The core of identity is now centered on being alcoholic with the meanings and behaviors attached to that identity more firmly in place. Central to this period is the shift from concrete externalized behavioral control (characterized in early recovery by the slogan "bring the body and the mind will follow") to internalization through identification and to cognitive and behavioral controls. Instead of automatically acting on an impulse through immediate behavior substitution, individuals now mentally note the impulse, anxiety, or discomfort and *reflect* on it. This reflection involves first repeating cognitive slogans to emphasize the alcoholic identity, substituting an action if necessary and then self-examination to understand the source of discomfort.

The cognitive and behavioral controls necessary to maintaining abstinence now arise from within, as a part of the new personal identity constructed from identifications with other recovering alcoholics and from the reworking of meanings of life events.

What is absolutely central to the ongoing stability of this process is the interactive nature of the components. Whereas in the drinking transition and early recovery phases the single dominant focus is on alcohol and being alcoholic, ongoing recovery is characterized by expansion and interaction. However, the alcohol focus remains at the core with individuals moving into the spiral, developing old and new interests, relationships, and a new personal identity through the process of construction and reconstruction and new interpretations of self and others.

Central to the entire process is the development of a personal concept of what is called in AA a "higher power." It is in the period of ongoing recovery that

196

emphasis on spirituality emerges with many seeking self-knowledge and an expansion in their beliefs through organized religion and the study of philosophy or psychology in addition to AA.

Psychotherapy and AA

It is during this period that individuals can make the best use of uncovering psychotherapy. Many recovering alcoholics (64%) would like an additional form of therapy, but many (55%) do not seek it (Brown, 1977). Unsucccessful and even damaging past experiences leave recovering alcoholics wary of psychotherapists who are not alcoholic themselves or who do not demonstrate a thorough understanding of the AA program. As one woman who desperately needed extra help stated:

> I am terrified that the therapist will take away my AA, challenge my beliefs, or try to reduce its significance in my life.

In a psychotherapeutic relationship, the patient and therapist shift together in their focus on alcohol, the process of identification as an alcoholic, and on behavioral, cognitive, and dynamic modes of therapy. It is the fine tuning of this complex process that characterizes ongoing recovery and effective psychotherapeutic treatment during recovery.

Integration of these three therapeutic modes is a difficult and frightening task for the patient. The individual must simultaneously maintain an identity as an alcoholic, continually apply behavioral and cognitive steps to ensure abstinence, and begin to look at underlying issues and meanings that may have contributed to the developing alcoholism or may be hindering a satisfying sobriety.

Integration is a difficult task for the therapist, who must continuously monitor the internal and external processes of the patient, determining whether or not the primary therapeutic focus at any particular time needs to be behavioral, cognitive, dynamic, or a combination. In a constructive alliance, therapist and patient will be finely tuned to the need to shift focus readily from one level to another.

The process of insight-oriented, uncovering, or dynamic psychotherapy carries with it the potential of being out of control. The feelings of uncertainty, of not knowing, that characterize open exploration provoke high levels of anxiety. It is precisely these feelings of anxiety and of being out of control that previously prompted a drinking response to gain control. To tolerate anxiety and even promote it through the uncovering process, the identification as an alcoholic and the behavioral and cognitive controls for abstinence must be firm. Both patient and therapist cycle through behavioral, cognitive, and dynamic modes to recall the identity as an alcoholic, to strengthen the base of sobriety through behavioral action, and to titrate the anxiety raised by the dynamic mode.

Mr P, a young man with several years of abstinence, suddenly interrupted the deepening process of his therapy by focusing for several meetings on his fear of drinking. He was actively involved in AA and had not been focused on alcohol for sometime in his treatment. Yet, suddenly he was experiencing intense fear and anxiety. Mr. P and his therapist quickly explored the meaning behind his fear. He was dealing with some particularly difficult internal issues and was approaching new insight. His anxiety about the uncovering process was experienced as a fear of drinking to avoid self-discovery. His recognition of the fear of drinking as a defense permitted him to proceed with his self-exploration. The sudden introduction of the alcohol focus also alerted Mr. P and his therapist to the *real* underlying danger of drinking. In addition to examining his fear in therapy, Mr. P shifted to an increase in behavioral and cognitive modes as well to ensure that he would not act out his fear. He called his AA sponsor more frequently and increased his attendance at AA meetings. Thus, he and his therapist integrated the three primary therapeutic modes: he activated his behavioral base of abstinence by increasing his meetings, he focused cognitively on his alcoholism and what it meant to be alcoholic, and at the same time examined his fear of drinking as a defense, opening the way to explore the issues he was frightened of.

With the basic identity and support constantly ensured and active, the individual progresses in the dynamic process, living through the anxiety to uncover greater and greater depths.

Much of the impetus for the initial research program and especially for the application of the model of recovery to a treatment program, came from a deep recognition of the mutual hostility and mistrust that characterizes the working and nonworking relationships between drinking alcoholics and their professional helpers and recovering alcoholics and those same professionals. Drinking alcoholics are viewed by professionals as the worst patients (Kurtines, 1978), deceptive, evasive, infantile, and self-destructive. Psychotherapists often report terrible "success" in working with alcoholics because they cannot get them to stop drinking or to even form a treatment alliance to look at the problem of alcohol. Often, as stated so many times already, a misalliance is formed based on the mutual denial of alcoholism.

This misalliance causes continuing hostility in recovering alcoholics. Many feel intense mistrust of any health professional and certainly psychotherapists. Many acknowledge having been dishonest with the therapist during their drinking and therefore at least partially responsible for the failure of therapy. Others, however, hold the therapist entirely responsible.

I finally told my therapist I was worried that I might be alcoholic. He said I couldn't be an alcoholic and that was it. We spent three years analyzing every other problem and my drinking just got worse.

Another person illustrates:

My physician just kept giving me tranquilizers to ease my nerves. He said to cut down a bit on my drinking. Finally I got the courage to tell him I thought I was alcoholic. He chuckled and said in a very paternal way that couldn't be and to stop worrying about it. When I finally did get sober and told him, he *still* said it couldn't be. That's no help at all. It makes me so worried about putting myself in the care of anyone!

It is not at all uncommon to hear recovering alcoholics relate poor and damaging experiences with health professionals as part of their AA story. It is much less common to hear of a positive therapeutic relationship before sobriety or one in which the professional actually influences the alcoholic to move toward recovery. In the initial research program, only 2% of the respondents listed a physician or therapist as a key figure in the turn toward abstinence. Family members or close friends were far more important.

Of course not all helping professionals are hostile towards alcoholics or actively engaged in continuing denial either because of a lack of knowledge about alcoholism or negative attitudes toward alcoholics. There are professionals who are knowledgeable and refuse to collude. They run the risk, realized quite frequently, that after confronting their alcoholic patient, the person will leave treatment. The physician who cuts off the supply of drugs loses the patient. The psychologist who suggests the patient drinks too much loses the patient. It is often small consolation to know that the patient remembers clearly the honest confrontation when he or she eventually does become abstinent. A cardinal rule in working with alcoholics is to see oneself as a small part of a larger continuum of intervention. The knowledge that confrontation of denial and intervention are building processes helps prevent discouragement. There is no more enlightened professional than one who has risked breaking denial and the patient responds, moving into treatment and recovery. Unfortunately, treatment professionals often have no access to recovering individuals, nor to the training that would permit them to see the continuum of intervention that leads to recovery (Bissell, 1981).

AA officially recommends cooperating with professionals (Big Book; As Bill Sees It), but in practice, animosity and mistrust prevail with some AA members. As a result, many recovering alcoholics who could benefit from psychotherapy in addition to AA, refuse to try, holding onto their animosity. One AA member with long sobriety expressed himself as a hardliner.

Why do we need any other treatment? It's AA and nothing else. Physicians got in my way and even held me back. I finally got sober in AA, and I believe that's all anyone needs.

This man rejects the notion that, *with proper training,* helping professionals could get more people to AA sooner and help with the emotional and living problems of sobriety. He is philosophical in his rejection.

> Those who are supposed to make it to AA will get there. Forget the professionals.

The animosity and mistrust are often problematic for those individuals in AA who require professional care.

> My sponsor advised me repeatedly to stay away from therapists. I needed help so badly, but got very scared after hearing all the negative experiences people had had. I found a couple of AAs who were in therapy and stuck close to them. Plus, I got another sponsor who thinks it's a good idea. In fact, she even tells me to take some things to my therapist because they're over her head.

One individual with six years of sobriety was desperately in need of professional help. She was anxious and often depressed. Finally she sought help. She chose the alcohol clinic because she knew she had to have a therapist who understood alcoholism. But even so, she stressed repeatedly in her first sessions that she could only commit herself to therapy and the process of uncovering if she could trust that the therapist would not tamper with her AA.

> AA is the number one commitment in my life, affirmed by my belief and trust in God. I don't want you to mess with that.

This patient needed to see the therapist as a peer and routinely refused transference interpretations because they suggested that she was placing too much importance on the therapist. This reflects conflicts over dependency. It is much safer and wiser to depend on God and the institution of AA than on an individual person.

Another member of AA experienced competitiveness with her sponsor and her therapist.

> I feel like I'm in the middle. My sponsor worries that I've become too attached to my therapy. He says it's dangerous to become so dependent on a person. But he encourages me indirectly to be that dependent on him!

Several other patients illustrate the potential problems with a sponsor and the successful integration between AA and therapy.

> My sponsor is adamant against psychiatric referral for people in AA. He says people in therapy go back to drinking. His low opinion of therapy is really a prob-

lem for me. I know I need extra help, but have trouble with his disapproval. I've learned to keep what goes on in therapy to myself and just stick to the AA basics with him.

Harvey's relationship with his sponsor was conflictual. The sponsor repeatedly attributed ongoing anxiety in recovery to the psychotherapy and not enough attention to the steps. Harvey thought about changing sponsors, but could not. In therapy, he began to examine the questions of dependency and independence within his family.

It was impossible to separate from my parents. The price for independence was just too high.

Harvey illustrates the frequent use of the therapist to work through problematic or even transference manifestations occurring not within the therapy, but within AA. Not infrequently the sponsor realtionship is a parental one (recall that newcomers are often called babies) and calls forth the establishment of transference phenomenon.

Sue illustrates the process of working through. After her insight, she opened up and deepened her examination of her beliefs about herself and others.

I finally said "no" to my sponsor and then felt guilty. I thought about that and recognized that I believe I have to be open, helpful, and good with all people, even when I'm feeling terrible.

Sue had trouble with the sponsor relationship from the beginning. She always felt she should have one, but couldn't find a woman she felt she could trust enough. When she finally did choose someone, she felt caught in the middle, - not knowing what to focus on in therapy and what to share with her sponsor. Sue struggled with her resistance to deepening her self-exploration and had the following insight:

I'm in conflict about who to choose to help me, my therapist or sponsor. This is the first time I really feel caught—that I have to choose between you. I've decided that I feel better using my sponsor because she shares about herself and I don't feel so bad. I see that my therapy helps me put things into words. Then I talk with my sponsor afterwards to deal with the feelings that emerge in therapy. So much opens up for me in therapy I need to talk as soon as I leave the session.

The successful integration of AA and psychotherapy involves the acceptance and use of multiple transference relationships and object replacements. As noted earlier, individuals in the transition and early recovery phases often cannot tolerate the shift in dependency from the object, alcohol, to a human figure, sponsor or therapist. Thus, there is the early reliance on objects that substitute for alcohol, such as books, meetings, and coffee. The work of ongoing recovery involves for most a steadying of concrete substitutes and examination and maturation of human relationships. Often this work occurs in the context of AA as individuals replay old unhealthy interpersonal patterns with new friends and sponsor. It may occur in therapy also.

It is common in early recovery to deny any dependency feelings and any personal needs (Brown and Yalom, 1977). The emergence and conscious recognition of deep dependency feelings occurs after some period of abstinence. Such feelings in early sobriety are treated through action, rather than reflection, and the actions are designed to reduce anxiety, rather than heighten it. But in ongoing recovery, there is greater tolerance of anxiety and an appreciation that the anxiety is part of the work of recovery.

After her therapist's vacation, Pat explains her use of therapy and AA to deepen her exploration of her relationships.

> I made it through your absence, although I experienced unrelenting pain. I have been afraid I couldn't make it without your support. This experience caused me to examine my intense dependency on my family and my fear of letting go of it. I wanted to drink and to hurt myself all the time. I never looked at drinking as destructive. It was always to make me feel good. The wish to hurt myself was a real surprise.

At her next meeting, Pat continued her exploration, deepening the dynamic, uncovering process.

> I connected your loss to the loss of my mother and then to the loss of alcohol. Each had been a way of gratifying my needs, with alcohol a way of "taking care of myself." I realized I had no way of taking care of myself that didn't involve disappointing or abandoning someone else and thereby losing more than I could tolerate.

Pat continued the illustration of integrating AA and therapy with the request for an extra therapy appointment.

> I had a lot of feelings come up in our session and was afraid I would "bury" them.

The request for the extra appointment is to open up rather than seal over feelings. She does not alter her AA schedule and, in fact, increases it after her extra meeting, "I realized I needed more AA and more contact with my sponsor." This was accurate in terms of her wish to be more involved with her peers. But, it also reflected her guilt at choosing her therapist over her sponsor.

I saw I had to equalize immediately just like I did with my parents. I can see also that my strength threatens others (as it also did her parents), but I don't have to be afraid or pretend I'm not OK like I always did.

The therapist is important not only as a direct object of attachment, but as an auxiliary object in relationships with others.

I'm fearful of your absence. How can I make choices to be with my family or not be with them without your help? I know I use you as leverage to keep me from feeling crowded at home. You have replaced alcohol to let me escape from my husband.

Much of the strength of the new identity as an alcoholic comes from the knowledge of shared experience with other alcoholics and acceptance of being different from individuals who are able to control their drinking. The solidity of the identity, and ultimately the solidity of behavior change, rest in the acceptance of loss of control. Such a necessary emphasis on difference leads to a tendency to dichotomize and categorize individuals as "we" and "they." Individuals are "recovering alcoholics" and therefore "one of us," or they are "normies."

Although most AAs would profess holding no resentment toward the "normy" who can control his or her drinking, in fact there may be animosity or threat. The normy holds the potential threat of a different point of view about control. To the alcoholic, unhappy with lack of control, the normy is superior. The normy's ability to control his or her drinking is a constant reminder to the alcoholic of his or her failure. The wish to be normal may be a periodic theme in recovery. In the research program, recovering individuals assessed themselves as "less than normal," feeling lower self-esteem than what they imagine to be the average for normals.

With such an emphasis on "we" and "they," the question of whether or not the therapist is alcoholic may be extremely important. Pat reviewed these questions with her therapist shortly before her termination of therapy.

You have been my mentor and teacher. You have advanced knowledge as a mentor because you are alcoholic. A nonalcoholic therapist would have superiority and not equality. I could not have achieved and maintained my autonomy.

It is clear that Pat held onto her notion of the superiority of the normy even after several years of productive psychotherapy. Pat thought more about her therapeutic relationship.

Your power comes not from being maternal or paternal, but from being alcoholic. The power lies in being equal.

Throughout four years of therapy Pat resisted any inkling of a parental transference. She often pondered the significance of her lack of transference feelings,
determining that it was essential for her autonomy.

> Sometimes I see you as a brother, ahead of me in experience and here to teach
> me.

The question of the therapist as alcoholic was less important than the beliefs
of the therapist in the case of Peter. In response to Peter's concern about what
he might be able to change, the therapist used the serenity prayer in an interpretation. The interpretation proved far less significant than the issue raised by
the therapist's use of AA terminology and symbols.

> I was shocked when you used the serenity prayer because you don't usually speak
> in AA language. It made me wonder about your beliefs. I take the AA program
> and the spiritual elements literally, believing in God and the concrete acts sug-
> gested in the program. Now I suddenly wonder whether you believe in the program
> too or whether you consider it to be a metaphorical trick. Suddenly it strikes me
> as very relevant to our work.

The question of the therapist's beliefs suddenly became all encompassing, related to the deepening process of psychotherapy and personal issues of trust and
abandonment.

> I have always been cynical about religion and God, but I'm trying hard to believe
> and to suspend my critical nature. But I'm sometimes afraid it's a trick. As my
> therapist, you have the power to take it all away. You could tell me that loss of
> control and surrender to a higher power are useful illusions to getting me through
> a hard time, but they are not the truth. What does spirituality mean to you and
> what are your beliefs?

The therapist answered these questions directly and Peter explored his fears.

> If you didn't believe in a higher power, then you must believe in the ability of
> individuals to control themselves. The whole process of therapy would be designed
> to have me become a better manager of my life instead of giving up the manage-
> ment entirely. We would be in direct opposition. I had been so afraid that I would
> have to give up being bright and witty to believe in God. I don't want to have to
> choose between my previous life and my new one in AA. But there must be a
> bridge between the two worlds. I hope to find it here.

The question of being caught in the middle between two opposing but equally
important and attractive worlds was a constant theme for Peter in his recovery.
He became more and more absorbed and led by his beliefs and his attention to

the "program." He increasingly chose AA friends as social companions so he could "translate" more of his experiences into the AA language and interpretive framework.

> I want AA people around a lot. One of my best friends still doesn't believe I'm alcoholic. It creates such a gulf. What if you didn't believe I was alcoholic?

Peter also identified the importance of language to unify and solidify as much as it differentiates.

> For me, language is the way of knowing. Language gives things form to be known in and it creates forms to build from. Language constitutes my reality and makes that reality as well.

Peter kept returning to the issue of the therapist's beliefs.

> I just wonder if I can ever feel comfortable and normal in a world of drinkers who don't know anything about a higher power and surrender.

The importance of paradox was also a regular theme for Peter as he explored the relationship of spirituality to dependency.

> I have been feeling such conflict, but then serenity snuck up on me. I have a tremendous sense of relief and am looking at myself so much more realistically. My new belief in a higher power reduces my anxiety and my dependency on my therapist and my sponsor.

Peter continued his questioning of his therapist's beliefs, outlining again his own fear of fragmentation as a result of believing.

> I hope you have integrated a spiritual belief with your professional and analytic view of the world. I am seeking a feeling of unity achieved by alignment of my beliefs and actions. I've gone from utter confusion with a sense that everything is hidden and lonely to clarity, with everything named and making sense. But I still feel fragmented in terms of my AA self and the professional world.

It is clear that psychotherapy can, indeed, be beneficial to recovering alcoholics who are also members of AA. But, the benefits rest on the ability of therapist and patient to include AA as a third partner, a key attachment for the patient, and therefore subject to important transference phenomenon.

It is also important for the therapist to heed the criticisms of the research participants (Brown, 1977). Therapists can help with emotional problems considered to be "regular and psychological terrain" and beyond the ability of the sponsor. Therapists also need to have a clear and deep understanding of the addictive process and its developmental nature. This is no small task, because alcoholism remains so misunderstood. Therapists also need to understand the principles of AA so, as illustrated, the therapist doesn't interfere or model the opposite.

The Alcohol Axis

While identification as an alcoholic and the behavioral and cognitive controls for abstinence are now firm, individuals do not just forget about their alcoholism. The alcohol focus in some form remains a conscious active part of daily life. As illustrated in the continuum, the alcohol focus remains the central organizing principle in ongoing recovery. It is this recognition of regular attention that explains why individuals continue to attend AA after years of abstinence. The alcohol focus is a constant reminder of their new identity, the behaviors and meanings attached to it, and the new interpretation of self and others that emerges and is constructed on the base of the identity. Without the basic reminders that "I am an alcoholic" and "I cannot control my drinking," return of the old attitudes and beliefs, tied to a belief in control, is a constant danger.

> Every day I must do something for my alcoholism. Even though my drinking days are in the distant past, I know I could be right back there, taking a drink, smug in the old notion that I could control it.

Another individual illustrates:

> I get up in the morning and remind myself that I am an alcoholic. That reminder sets the course of my day. When I find myself slipping back into the old frame of mind, negative or full of resentment, I'm not paying enough attention to my program, to being alcoholic. I have to do a tenth step (a continuing self-inventory) regularly to ensure that my thinking stays straight and I am not building resentments or being dishonest with myself or others.

Individuals who begin drinking after long sobriety often attribute their slip to complacency about their program, for example, relaxing their attention to their alcoholism:

> I stopped going to meetings, calling AA friends, and reading the literature. I had no trouble for a long time, but then one day I had a drink, simple as that. I didn't even decide that I wasn't an alcoholic. I had enough AA and sobriety to know better than that. But I forgot, not enough attention to the basics.

Individuals may also slip as a result of conflict with the emergence of other problems and emotions in sobriety. A solid alcohol core enables individuals to tolerate these expected difficulties of recovery.

The critical importance of an alcohol focus through the progression of alcoholism, from drinking through transition into early recovery, has been emphasized again and again. It is important to note that it can also be a defense. As individuals become comfortable with their identity as alcoholics and with their new behaviors, and as they develop their AA stories, the subject of alcohol becomes reinforcing, familiar, and safe. Individuals feel protected in AA and often continue their discussion of alcohol outside of meetings in coffee gatherings and social occasions. Being alcoholic is now the tie that binds many diverse individuals. Being alcoholic is also what these individuals come to know best. It is safe and secure. Being alcoholic becomes a reference point for interpretation of everything else, relationships past and present and one's interpretation of self. The reconstruction process evolves around the core identity as an alcoholic.

This process is central to continuing abstinence and it can easily become a defense. Understanding the fine balance, and when to disrupt it, is a critical element of ongoing recovery for the individual in AA and the individual in therapy.

It is one thing to recognize that the focus on alcohol is now being used as a defense; it is another to know whether or not and how to interpret that. The illustration at the beginning of the chapter points out strongly the significance of a return to an alcohol focus as a marker or signal. That illustration emphasized the need to strengthen the behaviors of abstinence automatically. When these are in place, it is possible to explore the functions of the alcohol focus as a defense that is covering painful insights or postponing the exploration of difficult issues.

Interactions With the Environment

Integration with the environment, central to early recovery, is now more firmly established with individuals back in family and work routines or engaged in establishing new ones. Changes in home and work are common as individuals construct relationships and environments that support and reinforce the identity as alcoholic and the behaviors that accompany it.

Difficulties similar to those of early sobriety continue with less frequency and with less danger of acting on impulse to drink or a pull backward toward the old identity as a nonalcoholic. Unchanged environments, family, social, and work, provide the greatest conflict in that the new identity and abstinent behaviors accent differences and incompatabilities or provoke overt conflicts.

Support of family and friends continues to be of great importance in a smooth progression.

My wife and kids have been supportive from the start. She goes to Al-Anon, and the kids go to Alateen. Sometimes it's hard on me because I can't manipulate them anymore. They're happy I'm sober, but it's up to me. This is the best support I could have.

Conflict is not unusual:

> My wife is very jealous of AA. She doesn't like me to go and doesn't want me to be an alcoholic. I used to get my therapy with her over a bottle of wine and now I'm gone.

More subtle, but nevertheless problematic conflicts are also common:

> My husband is delighted that I've stopped drinking. He supported my going to meetings and even suggests it sometimes when I'm having a rough day. But he really doesn't understand. He thinks I should be able to drink the special wine from our cellar. We built that and stocked it on special trips we took together. It's really a symbol of our relationship and he's very hurt that I won't have just one glass.

This example illustrates what is perhaps the toughest problem of all: maintaining the identity as an alcoholic and the belief in loss of control in an environment that fails to comprehend the significance of those beliefs. It requires a strong support group and constant reminders about what it means to be alcoholic to counter environmental pressure to drink and control it.

Often spouses hold most strongly to the belief in controlled drinking. They are enormously unhappy with the alcoholic's drinking, but equally frightened about abstinence. For some, the stigma of alcoholism is too great, and they don't want a partner who is identified an an alcoholic:

> I can't tolerate the notion that my husband is an alcoholic. What does that say about me? How could I marry an alcoholic? There must be something wrong with me.

Spouses rely on the continuing drinking of their alcoholic partners to support their own drinking, not labeled as a problem. This partner wants more control over the negative consequences of drinking without abolishing the behavior. A hidden alcoholic spouse may repeatedly sabotage the abstinence of a partner so as not to disrupt the status quo. When one alcoholic partner becomes abstinent, the drinking of the other now stands out. Two years sober, Tom illustrates:

> My wife and I argue all the time. She is so resentful of my attending AA. She makes fun of me and says I'm weak because I have to go to *those* alcoholic meetings. I just keep hanging onto what I know. I can't drink. But I think she's right— I am weak.

As time passed, it became clear that Tom's abstinence spotlighted his wife's drinking, which made her uncomfortable and angrily defensive.

> I can't imagine that my wife's an alcoholic. It just couldn't be. But she does like her drinks. When I come home from meetings I find her asleep in the chair with a scotch in her hand and the TV blaring. I spoke about her drinking one time and she became very angry. She said I'm the alcoholic and she's not. She said she'll never have to be with *those* people.

Tom had tremendous difficulty moving into ongoing recovery. He had to stay close to his alcohol focus to protect himself from a hostile environment. The central thread of his therapy for more than a year was his depression over being alcoholic and weak. His therapist drew a picture of the continuum and referred to it repeatedly, illustrating how Tom was stuck in the period of early sobriety around the narrow focus on alcohol. He was constantly in danger of moving back to the drinking side to patch the gulf that now separated him from his wife. Tom needed continuous reinforcement for his alcoholic identity and instructions on how to hold that focus. As soon as he shifted slightly or attempted to move on the continuum into ongoing recovery, he felt threatened. He strongly believed that he could not and would not ever get a divorce. He therefore could not begin the process of self-examination because he would have to look at the severe problems in his marriage. He was thus confined to a narrow alcohol focus and an intense, restricted recovery.

Others stay confined to a primary alcohol focus with very little expansion into other areas. Many build their sober lives around a central base of AA, establishing their closest friendships and social life within the organization. They construct a protected environment in which the identity as alcoholic and the importance of abstinence are unquestioned and form the base of all other actions and relationships.

For some, movement away from the AA base remains threatening into ongoing recovery:

> Bill had a lifetime history of serious drinking, becoming sober in his late 50s. He had lost his wife, several careers, and his social group long ago, and spent his last drinking years alone. He stuck close to AA in early sobriety to ensure his abstinence. After several years, he still stuck close. His day evolved around coffee with AA friends, 12-step work (helping newcomers), and attending meetings. Prompted by a desire to delve more deeply into self-examination, he joined a therapy group. Within several months, it became clear that the process of uncovering was too threatening. Bill focused his work in the group on helping others. The other members became protective of him and slowed their deepening exploration. Soon the group was alcohol-focused a good deal of the time as a defense against other issues. The therapists probed at this process and the group recog-

nized its protectiveness of Bill. Bill recognized his reluctance and inability to utilize the process of the group. He could see that he could be more helpful to others in his regular AA work. He decided to leave, realizing that the uncovering work of the group was not appropriate for him.

Interpretation of Self and Others

What distinguishes ongoing recovery from all other phases is the integration of the third component, interpretation of self and others. In the initial research program, it was hypothesized that the progression of recovery would be a mirror image of the downward spiral of developing alcoholism. The continuum that emerged from the research presented a quite different picture. Recovery was not a mirror image but a new paradigm based on the change in identity and the change in frame of reference that accompanies it. It became clear in understanding the process of abstinence that recovery is much more than not drinking. Recovery reflects more than simple opposites of drinking, such as the following: before I drank, now I don't; before I missed work, now I don't.

It is more than comparing apples before and after. With ongoing recovery, the comparison is more on the order of apples and oranges. Through altering their identities, working the 12 steps, and developing a personal concept of a higher power, individuals dramatically alter their attitudes, beliefs, and values and thus their interpretation of themselves and others. Meaning that is now attributed to events and interactions is derived from a new frame of reference centered on the identity as an alcoholic and the belief in loss of control. The belief in a higher power, or some ultimate authority greater than self, is part of the third component. This belief shifts the center of control from self to an intangible power. This shift attacks egotism and omnipotence and alters the individual's sense of him or herself in relation to others (Tiebout, 1953). When out of the center, it is possible to conceive of oneself as a peer and equal. Members suddenly experience a feeling of shared humanity and hostile defensiveness disappears. Members of AA refer to such a happening as a "spiritual awakening." It occurs rapidly for some at the transition phase and more slowly for others over the period of developing sobriety.

It is what many believe to be the core of the AA program, a relinquishment in personal control of oneself and others with a growing and maturing belief in a higher order and authority. The recognition of loss of control over drinking paves the way for the recognition of loss of control in all other areas of life. The centrality of this concept is embodied in the Serenity Prayer, a key part of AA meetings.

God grant me the serenity to accept the things I cannot change, the courage to change the things I can, and the wisdom to know the difference. (Niebuhr, 1932)

Is this new spirituality religious? AA members argue that it is not. Individuals within AA may belong to or seek an organized religious affiliation to promote or enhance their developing spirituality, but religion is *not* a part of AA. The 12 steps and the philosophy of the program are derived from Christian and Eastern theology and philosophy and existential philosophy (Kurtz, 1982). Chapter 9 examines the 12 steps in more detail.

The concept of relinquishment of control forms the base of a new attitude and a new frame of reference. The relinquishment of control requires a belief in an external authority greater than self in which control is vested. The reconstruction of past events and the unfolding of one's AA story proceed from this base.

Interaction and Integration of Components

The interaction and integration of components reflect the continuing importance of behavioral, cognitive, and dynamic modes of treatment and accent the developmental nature of recovery. In ongoing recovery, individuals focus on alcohol, establishing a routine that maintains that focus (three AA meetings per week and daily reading, for example). As the identity solidifies and the AA story develops over time, the movement may be characterized as linear or forward along the central line. Backward movement, or regression along the alcohol focus, represents problems with the focus or identity. Individuals who question whether or not they are alcoholic, who express fears of drinking, or who experience a strong environmental pull incongruent with the identity are regressing toward the drinking side of the continuum. Tom illustrates:

I suddenly found myself silently disagreeing with the stories I heard in AA. I was starting to tell myself I probably wasn't an alcoholic. At the same time, I became preoccupied with the fear of drinking. It felt like I was going the wrong way on the escalator. I wanted to move forward in sobriety, but I felt a constant pressure pulling me back. I had to put all my attention into staying sober for a while until I was once again certain of my alcoholism. As soon as I feel that certainty, things start moving in the right direction again.

At the same time, individuals move out into other activities—family, work, social. This pattern produces an interaction between two components, the alcohol and the spiral; individuals move around the spiral, circling or returning to the alcohol focus. This return may be conceived of as a refueling process, similar to what Mahler (1975) describes in the developmental process of individuation. The individual leaves home base, which now provides a security through identity and behaviors to ensure abstinence, moves out into the world, and returns regularly for reinforcement and continuing building of the central identity. This becomes a developmental building process. As the continuum illustrates, with time and the solid identity, individuals can move farther out in the spiral, away from the core, without losing their identities or acting on an impulse to drink. This ability is dependent on the process of cycling back through the alcohol focus.

Introduction of the third component, expanding awareness and interpretation of self and others, adds the third line of movement. The boundaries of the new identity expand and contract in concert with the interaction of the first two components. The line of movement is conceived as vertical on the continuum.

When the alcohol focus is secure and movement into the spiral comfortable, the process of new construction and reconstruction and reinterpretation of self and others begins. When the process becomes threatening, as our first example illustrates, the continuum contracts, with the individual shifting focus and behavior back to alcohol. This contraction may be expressed by a sudden loss of insight, or perhaps a sudden concern about not working the program hard enough or paying enough attention to being alcoholic. Thus, the ongoing movement is linear, circular, and vertical, expanding and contracting.

Monitoring Movement

Monitoring this movement is the primary task of patient and therapist during ongoing recovery. Understanding of the cycles and the monitoring provide the markers for intervention and the direction for the predominant mode of psychotherapy at any given time. AA members often intuitively understand this process.

> I've been feeling "squirrelly," anxious, and irritable. There is something going on but I don't know what. I've increased my reading and my meetings. I know I'll hear something that fits and helps me break through this impasse.

A return to an alcohol focus not only provides refueling and attention to the process of identification that allows the individual to proceed back "out," it also provides the secure territory and familiar framework for a "timeout."

An understanding of Piaget's concept of cognitive development is useful. In the progression of sober development, the individual cycles through periods of "plateau" in which new learning about the self is being consolidated in the new personal identity as an alcoholic. During this stabilizing period, the individual establishes a new, higher equilibrium level from which to continue the processes of construction and reconstruction. From a psychodynamic point of view, it may be viewed as a gradual progressive development of higher-order defenses as Bean describes (1975a). When the realities of sober life become uncomfortable or threatening, or the process of self-examination too rapid or anxiety provoking, the "timeout" provides a temporary relief and a source of control. Too much anxiety or conflict without a secure hold on the alcohol line may leave the individual frightened and feeling out of control. Failure to reestablish the source of control (paradoxically, the identity as an alcoholic) may lead back to drinking. What individuals learn in early sobriety about how to stay sober—the actions to take—now automatically propels them back to the alcohol line and the base of security.

What individuals hear and experience in AA may provoke anxiety. Thus, what has provided security and control during early abstinence is suddenly feared and avoided. Exploration of this difficulty in psychotherapy can be extremely useful. Identifying as an alcoholic and the process of construction of a story may provide more anxiety than security.

> I listen to the stories and hate to identify now. The reality of what I did while drinking is suddenly looming close. It wasn't that other person—it was me and I have to face it.

The individual feels anxious about assimilating into present consciousness the reality of past behavior. The person takes in the realities of the alcoholic behavior from the viewpoint that that behavior was "insane." As the individual includes more and more realities in the self-view and the development of the story, the boundaries of the self expand as the structure now shifts to accommodate the broader picture of self. Difficulties may also occur with friends or sponsor resulting in fear or withdrawal:

> My sponsor is urging me too hard and too fast to do a fourth step. So I stopped calling him. I'm just not ready. My sponsor says I'll do it when I'm ready, but he also keeps pushing. When I go to AA now, I feel guilty, like I'm not moving fast enough.

Interaction is hierarchical, corresponding to the developmental model of Piaget (emphasizing action on the environment as the first mode of learning, with subsequent development of higher levels of cognitive organization) and Santostefano (1980), who postulates development according to a hierarchy of ego modes. Again, action is the primary and most primitive mode. Subsequent fantasy and abstract modes of cognitive and emotional development do not proceed without the action base firmly developed. It is only through the base of behavior change that the subsequent abstract analytical process of the reconstruction and unfolding of meaning can occur.

With this concept understood, a return to an alcohol focus may be seen not only as a resistance or defense, but most importantly as a critical component in the cycle of ongoing development, a period of consolidation, and a strengthening of identity before further uncovering or self-exploration.

COGNITIVE AND BEHAVIORAL CONSIDERATIONS

Handling Fear of Loss of Control

In the complex interactional process of ongoing sobriety the fear of a lack of impulse control returns periodically, often heralding an emerging insight or preceding difficult self-exploration. A persistent underlying fear of loss of control is a common feature of early recovery and may characterize much of ongoing recovery as well. With several years of abstinence, Barbara examines the course of her recovery:

> I've felt a continuing pressure from others and from myself to stay busy. I realize that if I took the pressure off and allowed myself to do what I wanted, I might drink. Having all that pressure acts as a control over otherwise out of control impulses. At this point in my sobriety, I can let go of the fear of drinking. I can see that I'm not going to drink and that it's not up to me to control it. I'm putting the problem in God's hands and taking the pressure off.

Barbara illustrates the integration of AA principles with insight therapy. She also identifies a key critical period during ongoing recovery: She is ready for a big change but frightened; to allow herself to risk and let go of the control (the pressures) will result in her being out of control and automatically exercising the impulse to drink.

Related to the issues of impulses and control, Bonnie reflects after three years sobriety:

> I can see that I can effect my states of mind, that I can move myself out of despair. I want to teach myself not to be so susceptible to pressure. That feeling of pressure is an overreaction to my life being out of control. For the first time, I know that I don't have to act all my feelings out.

Movement is a critical aspect of all exploration and interpretation in ongoing recovery. The sense that life is out of control may be a response to an approaching insight, which directs the individual back to an alcohol focus in conjunction with further dynamic exploration. It may also be the case that life is indeed out of control. Individuals often become overextended and overinvolved, losing sight of the alcohol base of their lives and its function as a source of control. They cycle less frequently through the alcohol focus, perhaps buoyed by their success with abstinence and now directed by other goals. When they stop practicing the behaviors of abstinence and stop reinforcing their identities by cycling through the alcohol core, the sense of being out of control may be overwhelming. In ongoing recovery, the alcohol base as a source of control may be reflected now in spiritual terms rather than in the primary emphasis on actions and behaviors.

I used to have to run to a meeting or immediately pick up the phone when I felt anxious or out of control. Now I say the serenity prayer and try to accept that God is in control and not me.

An individual's energies and efforts may be directed at controlling what now feels out of control with the same uncomfortable and unsuccessful results as when those efforts at control were directed at drinking. Bonnie continues:

I'm still too responsive to my drinking state of mind, feeling flooded with remorse. But, as I recall the events of my drinking, I feel more like a spectator, not identified so fiercely and not needing to act to quiet those feelings. Still, I carry that "old" state of mind.

As individuals progress in recovery, the experience of feeling "out of control" becomes more tolerable and they do not need to take action to alter it. Bill reflects on an AA meeting that he chaired:

It was scattered but not superficial. Other people told me it was good, but I didn't believe their perceptions. I can see that I have to hold onto my own internal view and disregard what is coming from the outside. Even though I felt out of control, I also felt more open and able to hear what everyone said afterward. That made me see that when I first came to AA, I didn't hear what people had to say and I didn't give it meaning. Five years from now, I'll probably be giving new meaning to what people are saying today.

Bill illustrates so well the developing nature of recovery, incorporating a growing knowledge and awareness of self with new perceptions about others. Through the processes of assimilation and accommodation, he will alter the structure and framework of his interpretations of himself and his environment through the passage of time. This new construction of the present involves a corresponding reconstruction of the past. In Piaget's scheme of cognitive development, the acquisition of reversibility is an important developmental marker (Greenspan, 1979). As the individual progresses in recovery the question of the reversibility or irreversibility of the new identity and new beliefs is a critical one.

To many, the progression into abstinence with the construct of a new identity would constitute structural change and therefore irreversibility. However, members of AA suggest repeatedly through their stories and what they hear from the experiences of others that reversibility remains a danger. Members know that regardless of the length of their sobriety, they are at risk of reverting to their old beliefs and behavior. In essence, they suggest that the old addictive behavior patterns and the thinking that precedes and supports the continued behaviors remains as a latent part of the self.

Individuals recognize that they must pay continuous attention to their new beliefs, attitudes, and behaviors, and especially to their relationship with their higher power, to counter the pull toward a belief in the centrality and therefore the power of the self. Much of the work of ongoing recovery involves a process of uncovering the reemergence of the ego in all its harmful guises. Constant daily recognition and acceptance of loss of control remains at the core of ongoing sobriety. The reverse is a belief in control that is a constant threat, as Mary explains:

> I don't know what to do about my attitude. I've been sober a long time, but still I find myself repeatedly caught up in a vicious cycle of overcontrol. It occurs in the simplest ways. For instance, yesterday I had to drive to the city for a meeting, and I was late. All the way up I was fuming and swearing at the traffic and the other drivers. I was so impatient. Finally my friend told me I was acting like an asshole. I started laughing and relaxed. Suddenly, there it was again—I was trying to control all the cars around me and furious that I couldn't do it.

Bill also shows well the need for integration of the components. His ability to tolerate a feeling of loss of control is tied to the growing strength of his identity as an alcoholic and his belief in the safety of that identity provided by the actions of the alcohol focus and by a developing belief in a concept of a higher power. It is a combination of action and dependency: Action—do the things necessary to maintain and strengthen abstinence, go to meetings, use the phone, etc., and dependency—relinquish control to a higher power and rely on that higher power for care and guidance like a good parent. Bill illustrates the integration of the third component by his recognition that the meaning he gives to what he feels and says and to what he sees and hears from others is shifting. He feels a reversal of many perceptions, such as valuing a loss of control, and a deepening of those perceptions as well.

Later in his sobriety, Bill explored further the sense of not having to control:

> I'm not just "managing" now, clinging to my sobriety and feeling constantly watchful lest I catch myself drinking. I am now standing on my own stability and my own experience of sobriety. I have a much better sense of being in control of myself as opposed to being totally controlled by others. I do not have to drink to achieve that sense of control.

This theme of control is central to Bill's ongoing recovery and his work in psychotherapy. After a vacation, he reports recognizing an "old drinking opportunity":

I was away and suddenly thought I could buy a relaxed state of mind with a drink. I had the urge, but I substituted a walk instead. I felt OK and removed from the power of that state of mind (the old schema). I could also look back and see how I used to be pulled in to act out that urge.

The fear of impulses is related to a fear of the loss of the new identity as an alcoholic. Environmental pulls often wield a powerful authority, even with years of abstinence. This pull is particularly strong in an alcoholic family in which parents, sibling, or spouse continue active alcoholism. Josh, sober for four years, describes the pull of being "back in my family," in which his parents are both still drinking.

I went to my sister's graduation and felt suddenly hungover and emotionally disoriented. It was my first time back at a major family gathering since I stopped drinking.

Josh was frightened and confused by his sense of disorientation during the occasion and for days after. He attended several AA meetings immediately (at which he felt out of place and suspicious) and several therapy sessions. He realized that being in his old drinking environment made him feel disoriented:

I lost my sober sense of self which I have achieved through constant identification with AA and disidentification and rejection of my family.

Josh attended another family affair several months later and had the same experience.

I felt crazy, insane with feeling all over the place. I feel at the mercy of my emotions—they have control, just like my first year of sobriety. How can I be so responsive to the pull of my family? My friends in AA and Al-Anon tell me that their words should not have so much power over me, but I can't will it to be different.

The pull from the old environment, in which belonging meant drinking, suddenly makes Josh's abstinence feel incongruent. He increases his AA meetings and uses his therapy to restore the solidity of his knowledge of himself as an alcoholic. It is a painful restoration because it equals being an orphan, having abandoned the tie to the alcoholic family by the choice for abstinence.

Handling Emergence of Feelings

Initiated in early sobriety, the emergence of feelings is a regular feature of ongoing recovery. For some, it represents the major work of ongoing recovery:

The pain of my sobriety is so great. I continue in AA and come to psychotherapy so I can know what my feelings are, tolerate them, and not have to hide and run away. But the process of uncovering what I denied and hid under cover of booze and drugs is often unbearable.

Anxiety may be a regular feature of ongoing recovery, related to the uncovering process. Henry illustrates the interaction of the three levels of the continuum to facilitate that process:

My emotional awareness often proceeds my cognitive understanding and creates difficulties for me in sobriety. I feel my emotions strongly but have no logical explanation for them. I often feel tempted to "treat" them by drinking. When I cannot understand or explain what I am feeling, I call someone or go to a meeting. The awareness will come, and the action reduces my fear.

In theoretical terms, Henry takes action to return to an alcohol focus, strengthening his identification with other alcoholics and the new structure that is unfolding, until he can assimilate the new information or insight. Then, through the process of accommodation, he will alter his cognitive structure to a new level of equilibrium with new elements added to the reconstruction of his story and the new construction of a sober identity. The expanded structure will then influence new interpretations of himself and others.

The emergence of feelings in sobriety is not confined to negative or unpleasant emotions. The emergence or discovery of positive feelings is also a common feature, although it is often felt as equally frightening. Peter reports:

I chaired a meeting last week, which usually gives me very positive feelings, like a shot of high self-esteem. That's what happened again, but it made me uneasy. If you feel too good about yourself, you'll forget you are alcoholic. I'm not used to feeling good about myself. It's not comfortable, I question it, and it's frightening.

A loss of feeling in recovery is not unusual either, especially in the early period. The fears associated with feeling contribute to emotional constriction:

My father and I had a fight and I just feel numb. I realize I used to drink after a painful exchange with him in order to intensify my feelings so I could cry and then feel better. Now I know I've got all the feelings and no way to open them up.

Similar to anxiety about the uncovering process but more concrete is fear, often a fairly constant emotion in recovery. Lisa discusses it:

I'm becoming so much more aware of my fear in the present and how much I spent my whole life in fear. I drank to cover it.

As she progressed in recovery, she realized that fear was not just an emotion she felt occasionally, but rather a "character defect," a constant in her emotional life and an inherent part of her being in the world. What she called a defect of character was related to her deep dependency needs, her lack of trust in herself, and her belief that relying on anyone, herself or others, could only be harmful. This pattern emerged after long intensive examination of her fears:

> I have to have minor surgery and I'm so frightened. I'm afraid of pain and of pain killers. I'm afraid I'll get addicted to the medicine and then go back to drinking. I feel frightened and needy and I realize I could convince the doctor to give me drugs to take care of me. I can see that I'm either alone or helplessly dependent. I used to cover this dichotomy with alcohol. Now imagining myself in pain without alcohol is frightening.

Lisa's fear that she could fall into a self-destructive pattern actually revealed to her a constant theme in her recovery: an increasing trust in herself not to fall into a harmful or self-destructive pattern.

> Underneath the fear is the trust that comes from the knowledge that if I work the program and rely on my higher power for guidance, I do not need to repeat these old self-destructive patterns. I am really amazed at the idea that I can trust myself. I think the big surprise in my life is finding I'm OK, rather than a failure.

The dry drunk continues as an experience of ongoing recovery, though perhaps more readily identified and labeled. The emergence of feelings without the accompanying cognitive understanding is felt as "out of control." Kathy illustrates this experience before acting on her abstinent behaviors:

> I can feel myself acting out drinking behaviors without the alcohol, and I'm letting these behaviors continue. I'm trying to get something from this frame of mind. It's a way of being in the world, and I can do it anyway without alcohol. I used to drink in order to be with others but uninvolved. My drinking frame is really out of touch and inaccessible, but it gives me the illusion of involvement.

Kathy had recently begun a romance. Examination of her feelings helped her understand the function that alcohol once played for her.

> This romance gives me a binge of feeling. I'm immersed in the excitement and don't want to pull myself out. It's loosening me up, just like alcohol did.

Kathy often enjoyed her "out of control" feelings. But for most recovering individuals, the experience is frightening or mixed. Many are attracted to the excitement and sense of immersion but fear the loss of control will ultimately lead back to drinking. Ted explains the logic:

> Once I'm out of control I can't get it back. The only way I ever got control was to drink. I know it doesn't make sense, but that's how it feels.

Or the experience of loss of control is similar to drinking.

> I love the feeling, but it scares me too. I feel like I've been drinking. If I've already taken the drink then I might as well do it for real!

The notion of a dry drunk is closely connected to the emergence of feelings and the ongoing breakthrough of denial. To the recovering alcoholic in AA, the term dry drunk is descriptive of being out of control emotionally. A difficult experience in the present triggers an emotional response that the individual will often relate to the past. Thus, the experience of the present is used to gain insight about the present and points the individual backward to facilitate reconstruction of the past as well:

> I had a dry drunk last week, lots of crying and heightened emotions. I realized it was triggered by my wife telling her friends about my alcoholism without consulting me. Suddenly I felt inferior and excluded from my family just like I felt during my drinking years. It is painful to recognize that by drinking, I made it impossible to be a part of my family. When I choose to go to AA now, I sometimes feel it's just like drinking—I'm abandoning my family by choosing something else.

Low self-esteem in the present recovering state may also be reflected or expressed in a dry drunk:

> I'm feeling a lot of anxiety in what I call my "diminished awareness." I'm clouding over and can see I'm missing things and can feel my self-esteem slipping. I'm getting discouraged and suddenly remember that I could do things while drinking. I looked better too, as if I was competent and functional. Now all I see is negatives. I feel guilty that I'm not getting better. I guess I have unrealistic expectations about what I can achieve in a year's sobriety.

Pamela illustrates a similar process.

> I was writing a letter rapidly and couldn't read it. Suddenly I remembered writing a letter to my mother when I was drunk. It was illegible. Then I recalled that when I wrote that note I was feeling like killing myself. The feelings all came back and I was overwhelmed with terror that I could have been feeling so badly. Then I felt an overwhelming sadness.

For many in ongoing recovery, the process of uncovering and experiencing new feelings is felt less as an upheaval and more as a regular feature of a stable rhythm of recovery.

I've been feeling so much more lately. Nothing overwhelming or unbearable, just a steady recognition of the depth of my feelings and greater tolerance of them. Last week I felt overwhelmed in a wonderful way with feelings of pride in my son. Letting myself feel that pride so thoroughly reminded me that I used to feel so guilty about my drinking that I was never able to feel proud of him. Now I am free of my own guilt and worries and of my need to control and can luxuriate in the joy of that pride.

Brenda had used weekly psychotherapy since the beginning of her abstinence, combining it with regular (three times weekly) attendance at AA. After two years, her psychotherapy was rarely focused on alcohol, but rather on the emergence of her feelings and the exploration of transference phenomenon both in her therapy and with individuals in AA. Brenda had developed a close and very dependent relationship with her AA sponsor. During her first two years of recovery she called her sponsor daily, solicited advice, and acted on it without question. She called her therapist in between sessions as well when her sponsor was unavailable and attempted to elicit advice from him. As Brenda progressed in her abstinence, she began to question her need for someone to tell her what to do. Soon, she was thinking about her relationship with her mother, delving backward to her childhood:

I had a dream last night in which my recovery was responsible for my mother's deterioration. By seeking my recovery and beginning to uncover my denial about my childhood I am betraying my mother. As long as I stay unquestioning and dependent on my sponsor and you, I won't be guilty of betrayal.

Four years later, with regular uncovering psychotherapy in between, Brenda reported the following dream:

You (the therapist) and my mother were telling me you didn't need me. I can see I am getting to a point where I'm not so self-absorbed and not so intent on uncovering all my feelings. I'm also experiencing myself letting go of the need for control.

When she started, Brenda had few memories of her childhood. During the course of her therapeutic work, the uncovering of her denial was of key significance. Her fear of "seeing" things clearly in sobriety was such a constant threat, it eventually dictated backward examination.

Denial was the only thing that kept my family (of origin) going. Things were so unpredictable and the fear of my mother's violent outbursts so terrifying that denial was necessary for survival.

The need to deny her feelings in the present and to distort her present familial relationships was extreme. As she progressed in recovery, she felt a continuing threat of impending disaster and a terror of uncovering her feelings and acknowledging their reality and strength. Abstinence created a clarity that made denial impossible and therefore heightened and intensified her fear. For several years, sobriety carried a threat of disrupting denial and she lived with a constant underlying fear.

Resistance and Lack of Change in Others

The surprise of recovery is the painful recognition that abstinence is only the beginning and not the end. Before recovery, the alcoholic denies that drinking is the problem; if only the other issues could be solved, the drinking problem would go away. Members of the family are usually ahead of the alcoholic in identifying alcohol as the problem, but they often believe that if only alcohol would be removed, all problems would be solved.

As individuals progress in recovery, the recognition comes that they must change much more than their behavior. Those deep changes are the work of ongoing recovery. Ted illustrates:

> I've been thinking about my program now that I've got two years sobriety. Sometimes I have trouble accepting the emerging person within me. I see loads of defects, I'm always in conflict, I can't shut up, and I have a sick feeling about my unhappy home.
>
> My wife isn't happy with the changes I'm making. She thought our marriage was great when I was drunk and now it's only good. Everyone in the family would prefer to go back to the old way, minus the drinking. I see this isn't possible and thus feel in constant conflict with my family. When I was drinking I didn't know how to be a part of my family. My struggle now is to learn how.

After this awareness, Ted explored the family decision process as a focal point illustrating his former isolation.

> I can see now that I was never a part of decision making in my family—my wife and children lived a separate existence and never involved me in their decisions. Now it's really difficult to include myself and I even wonder if I can participate in decisions rationally. I always saw things as my fault and could not argue over issues or decisions. I can also see that the family's decision process, already in place, is resistant to change. They are not making room for me so I have to push myself in.

Sally illustrates the same painful recognition of change.

I can see that my husband and family expected a mirror image with recovery and they're all disappointed at how much I've changed. My husband envies my enthusiasm and commitment. He put all the responsibility of the family and my recovery on him, and I'm going a different way.

A few weeks later she added:

I'm putting new value on my recovery and my new feelings. I also feel now like I'm setting an example for the family. I suddenly feel like the oldest child and it's hard. I've always had someone to follow, and my husband was always in charge.

During the drinking, many family members view the alcoholic as central and dominant in setting the rules and behaviors of the family. Many family members feel controlled by the alcoholic, leading their lives solely in reaction to the behavior, demands, or threats of the alcoholic (Jackson, 1954). The continuing centrality of the alcoholic during treatment and recovery is often a source of great resentment by family members. Suggestions that they be involved in the alcoholic's recovery by changing themselves may be met with hostility and resistance. It is extremely difficult to recognize that they need to be involved in their own recovery, independent of the alcoholic.

Family members may wish to continue to see the alcoholic as "the problem." To alter this point of view would require examination of themselves and their relationships, a frightening prospect. Holding onto the predominant view of the alcoholic as the problem prevents self-exploration.

Ron and Marie had been married for 20 years, with Ron actively alcoholic for 18 of those 20 years. Theirs was an angry bitter union, but tightly knit through a hostile dependent bond. After two years of sobriety, they sought couples therapy. The therapist reports:

It was impossible for Marie to think about or talk about anything besides Ron's drinking. She remained angry and unwilling to examine their present relationship in any way. Marie was actually very guilty about her own behavior during those 20 years. Any shift away from her husband's drinking threatened to awaken her own deep feelings of self-reproach.

Ron was progressing in recovery and anxious to examine his past and present relationships. All his efforts to do so with his wife resulted in her attacking him for his past abuse. Ron felt stuck in his recovery and constantly threatened with a pull back to his former abusive drinking behavior. Both were angry and defensive with each other. Ron entered individual therapy and a group for other recovering alcoholics. Marie also tried individual therapy but could not shift her focus off of her husband. Eventually, the couple separated.

As Bacon (1973) suggests, others' view of the recovering alcoholic may change much more slowly than the actual behavior. The alcoholic is gaining insight and altering his or her identity and behaviors, but others continue to interact with that individual as if the person is still drinking or may drink again. Tom illustrates the centrality of his drinking to others' perception of him and the pain of recognizing how much his drinking affected others.

> I was late to an important business meeting and I overheard a colleague say "it's time for Tom to drink again. Get ready to pick up the pieces."

The lack of change in a close relative may hinder the progress of the recovering alcoholic. Mike illustrates, frustrated in his recovery by the continuing sense that his progress is threatening to his wife and felt by her as an abandonment.

> She is still treating me as if I'm drinking, maintaining her old patterns and beliefs. I feel all the change is coming from me. I pull myself toward new attitudes and behaviors and she resists. I recognize that I can't change my own program of recovery to meet her needs, such as staying home with her on the weekends instead of going to a meeting. But everytime I go out the door to AA, I feel I'm leaving her behind. This is a real problem for me. All my energy is focused on how to get my wife to change and adopt a program similar to mine. My AA friends tell me to leave her alone, pay attention to my own program, and stop taking her inventory. It's good advice but I can't do it.

Several months later Mike reported that his wife had gone to Al-Anon and was very upset afterward:

> She heard a very sick speaker and it scared her to death. The speaker said the spouse is often as sick or sicker than the alcoholic. She came home very depressed.

> But I've got another worry. If my wife accepts Al-Anon, she's going to break through her denial of what I did and she's going to see me as sicker and crazier than I want to accept.

Months later, this occurred:

> She's now telling me what it was like for her when I was drinking, and it hurts a lot. Sometimes I get defensive or my self-esteem plummets. I always thought it wasn't so bad for her—she and the kids could do what they wanted. I wonder if I'll ever see myself as worthwhile.

After many months of concern about their uneven progress in recovery, Mike reported a new cooperation and accepting pattern of relating.

> I was worn out, completely. For the first time I didn't have to create a fight to get some privacy, and I had no need for a drink. I just took it easy. Told my wife I didn't feel like talking. I went to AA and she went to Al-Anon that night. We have opened our communication so much since we're able to speak the same language.

The meaning of a parent's alcoholism is critically important to the children in the family as well (Brown and Beletsis, in press). It is especially important to the psychological process of identification. The problem of accepting that parent as alcoholic is illustrated by Kate, a teenager whose father is two years sober.

> I was arguing with my mother about my eating. I know she thinks I must be alcoholic like my father because I can't control my eating. I am afraid to talk with my parents about feelings. It means I am flawed and I can't control myself and that means I'm alcoholic.

Jan, a teenager struggling with the same problem:

> I keep denying that I'm bulimic. The most important thing is to be in control of my life. If I'm not, then I'm just like my alcoholic mother.

Sue's mother, sober three years, gained clarity with her sobriety and reported the following observations about her family.

> I watch my daughter and my husband act out the same arguments we used to have. He criticizes her eating and tells Sue what to do. She cries. It's painful to watch my husband displace his control onto our daughter, as I refuse to accept that role anymore.

Constructing and Reconstructing Identity

The process of reconstruction involves a continuing breakdown in denial about oneself as a drinking alcoholic. In AA, members tell their stories, accenting "what it used to be like." As sober time accrues the story changes to incorporate more and more of the realities of the individual now identified as alcoholic. The process of construction involves building a new identity rooted in the identity as an alcoholic. The first part of the construction is primarily behavioral, learning the actions and behaviors that support abstinence and reinforce the identity as alcoholic. After the construction of new behaviors is the acquisition of new attitudes and beliefs that form the core of the new personal identity and are inconsistent and contrary to continued obsessional drinking. At the heart of these new beliefs is the acceptance of lack of control.

Individuals learn how to begin the processes of reconstruction and construction by attending meetings and listening to AA members tell their stories and by working the 12 steps. Instruction in the steps comes from peers, sponsors, and AA meetings designed as "step meetings" that focus on the meaning of each step and how to do them.

Members may also use psychotherapy for these processes. Sara illustrates the continuing interplay of past and present as she solidifies her identification as an alcoholic and her new nondrinking way of living:

> When I first started to think about my past in early recovery, I couldn't trust myself. My past was contaminated by my drinking as was the observer, me, who was drinking. It is still difficult to reinterpret anything about the past from my vantage point. I do know that my drinking behavior was a denial of responsibility.

As Sara progressed in recovery she could see that her reluctance to trust her own reconstruction was a defensive maneuver designed to maintain her denial of major problems. With over a year of sobriety, she began to ask herself "what was drinking for" and to crack her denial of other problems.

> I can see I used to drink to stay aloof. And drinking bought me time so I did not have to be an actively bad wife. Drinking maintained me in a state of demoralized passivity.

Unraveling denial about other people's alcoholism was a central theme in the reconstruction process for Terry, a recovering alcoholic whose parents and sister were actively alcoholic for much of her youth and young adult years. Though the alcoholism of family members was never labeled, Terry realized that she unconsciously sought a marriage partner who could control his drinking. The longer she was abstinent, the more she could see how central was this guiding principle in determining her choice of mate and her own drinking behavior.

> I remember that when I first met my husband I noticed he incorporated drinking a lot into his life. I flinched at this, but proceeded to ignore it because he was going to be the one who would keep me from becoming an alcoholic. I decided that if he could drink as much as he did and continue to go to work, then he must be OK, and I would be too.

The belief that she was protected from being alcoholic by her husband's ability to control his drinking overshadowed all evidence that she and he were alcoholic from the start. The process of reconstruction was extremely painful because it meant recognizing that her husband was alcoholic and therefore could never have saved her. It meant acknowledging the alcoholism of all the members of her family, and, ultimately, her own belonging to this family and therefore her own identity as an alcoholic. In thinking about her childhood and young adult years, she felt a painful sense of loss.

> It's paradoxical, that I had to be an alcoholic first. I had to be one just like everyone in my family in order to get out.

Holly uses her third anniversary of sobriety to reflect back. Examining the changes she has made in sobriety permits her to contrast her present way of thinking and behavior with her past. In this process of reflection, she illustrates her cognitive–behavioral focus, followed by dynamic probing of her memories of the past.

> I feel so much more "in control" of what goes on in my life. Whenever I think I might not be an alcoholic, I recall waking up with hangovers and a constant feeling of remorse. Those memories and a reminder to myself that I'm alcoholic keep me in the present and I don't drink. I grew up with a terrible fear that I would be an alcoholic. Because of that fear, my actual behavior was never flamboyant. I vowed never to do to my kids what had been done to me. I remembered how mortified I was to watch my mother drinking in public. I always watched myself carefully so I wouldn't embarrass anybody. Actually, that's when I finally decided to do something. I embarrassed myself painfully.

The connection of the present to the past is illustrated by Ted:

> I had a sudden feeling of loneliness and got a picture of myself having to do my life again. But I don't know what and how to do it. I don't know how to have fun because it was always connected to drinking.

> When I had that surge of loneliness I longed for one single dose of closeness, the kind I used to get from alcohol. Drinking made me feel like I was getting close to others.

Ted was unhappy with the uncovering process of sobriety and the task, not only of construction but of reconstruction. He had spent many years in psychotherapy and felt he had done it. How could he possibly have to go backwards again.

> I idealized my therapist. And I always believed there was a hidden key to my childhood that would unlock all the unknowns and solve everything. But I never found the key. The closest thing to a "key" experience has been the issue of alcohol. By identifying myself as an alcoholic, my whole world has turned around and things make sense that never did before.

As Ted relinquished his fantasies of the perfect therapist and the idea that he had done it all before, he felt sad and depressed.

> If my therapist did not have the power to change me, or that power did not lie in the process of therapy, then I must change the way I see my life. It's just like AA. I have to rewrite the story. And I now see that I have to learn everything anew, just like a baby.

In the reconstruction of a story, individuals offer new interpretations for past behaviors and thinking patterns that were seemingly logical at the time, but are now viewed as evidence of alcoholic thinking. The language of AA facilitates reconstruction because of the common terminology and sense of shared experience. Bill illustrates with what he called his "regression to alcoholic thinking."

My AA friends gave me a birthday party for my third sober anniversary. When the guests arrived, my first thought was that everyone should have a drink to ease the tension. It absolutely amazed me that I could have this thought and even feel the craving, given the reality of the situation.

Hal offers another example of the reconstruction of the thinking process:

It was simple and clear. I told myself that artists hallucinate. I was going to be an artist, so therefore I would do drugs. I started off in search of truth but found drugs instead. At the time I viewed this as a reasonable alternative.

Hal continues, outlining the logic of his denial.

All my decisions, simple and complex, were affected by my mental frame of mind. The most important determinant of decision making was how to get enough drinking time, but I didn't know that consciously. I actually sent my wife to live in the country so I could be alone during the week and could drink without interruption. It was the ideal solution.

Again, he talks about denial.

I was always looking for evidence that I wasn't an alcoholic. Yes, I enjoyed a good time like anybody else. So, like any fun-loving social drinker, I got primed before the social drinking started and finished it off afterwards.

Sara illustrates the erosion of denial about the past that occurs with accumulated sobriety:

For two years of sobriety I had maintained that alcohol was not a problem, nor was it important in my life for many years. But then I remembered a trip I took many years ago that really was a critical turning point. I was frightened so began taking tranquilizers to ease my fear. That was the beginning of my addiction. Later on, I continued the tranquilizers in order to sleep. Then I added alcohol. Long before I ever had any inkling that drugs and alcohol were *the* problem, my son complained about my being drunk when he brought friends home.

As Sara deepened her process of reconstruction, she was able to acknowledge problems and unhappiness that were unacceptable to her at the time. The need to maintain her denial was paramount.

> I'm tracing the development of my alcoholism in relation to feelings about my husband. He was very happy during those years, and I was extremely unhappy. I began to permit myself to drink during the day since he was having so much fun.

> As my drinking got worse, and my withdrawal more severe, my husband would fix me a scotch so I could sit up and join the family for dinner. I always thought I had to maintain the solidity of my family, be at the center on the home front, because my husband needed it.

Several months later, Sara felt the intense pain, generated by the shock of the truthful reconstruction of her drinking years.

> I feel like I'm back in the first years of my marriage with lots of uncertainty. How in the world did my family function with all the disorganization and chaos that is now obvious to me? It is hard not to have rigid expectations of myself now to make up for it all. But I realize I may have to settle for less in order to live without alcohol.

A final example illustrates the logic of denial and the presence of a core belief that structured and maintained that denial.

> I realized I was drinking alcoholically during college. But I believed I could have all the alcohol I wanted and still be vigorous and active. A few years later I saw a therapist for depression. She labeled drinking as the problem. I accepted that but believed it was symptomatic. I was really crazy. When I was fixed, the alcoholism would go away.

> My denial continued. I decided that since drinking was fun, I just had a fine-tuning problem. I can see now that this was an illusion. But what does this mean for my recovery? Do I have to go back and look at everything all over again? Is all my previous therapy invalid, a waste? If I was wrong in basing everything on the belief that I was not an alcoholic, then there are other beliefs that could be just as wrong. I don't know what they are and it's frightening. I can't trust myself.

Several weeks later Maggie felt better. She could now recognize important changes she had made in sobriety and the painful task of reconstruction was less frightening.

> I notice how different I'm handling a difficult situation at work. If I wasn't sober, I would have stuck my nose in immediately and tried to fix the problem. I realize

now I have to move more slowly. I have to redo the fundamentals and start over again.

Using Markers

The processes of reconstruction and construction are monitored carefully and facilitated by the attention given to markers. They are almost like ruler marks on the wall, chronicling a child's growth in height. They are useful tools in reminding individuals of the gains they have made, especially in low periods or when it seems like they haven't changed at all:

> I went to the company party again this year. Two years ago I was drunk and last year I was painfully self-conscious and fearful of drinking. But this year was fine! It's evident to me that I've chosen a new life over the old.

> But I'm also realizing that in recovery I'm getting better and worse at the same time. It was a lot easier to use AA in the beginning because I was so open and receptive. Now I'm resisting. The deeper issues I have to look at are more threatening.

Issues that have been important throughout the course of therapy and recovery are prominent markers as Hal notes:

> I woke up and asked myself the question, "Who will take care of me?" I knew I could be responsible for myself. This followed a dream in which I was lost. I wandered around as if in a blackout, but I was sober. I retraced my steps and wondered who to call. I felt disoriented and everything looked the same. Suddenly I was in a large room in an AA meeting. Then I began to know where I was and how to find my way home. I wanted to run, but didn't, knowing I now knew the way.

> I am realizing that I can control myself and that I don't need you, my sponsor, or my wife to control me like I did in the beginning. I've come to the belief that I won't hurt anybody too much if I am just myself. I've also reached the recognition *again* that I can't control others. I'm learning to look after myself and am beginning to think about spirituality. I don't know what is intended for me and it's not important to know. I have a sense of purpose and feel peaceful for the first time in my life.

AA birthdays are extremely important markers, always a point of acknowledgment and celebration, as well as a time of thoughtful inventory. Michael illustrates on the occasion of his first birthday:

> I gave myself a plant as a symbol of my recovery. Plants take time and care, just like my recovery. I'm excited today—yes, excited. Before, I couldn't tell the difference between excitement and anxiety. This week I've been recalling the awful days that preceded my calling the clinic. And then when I did call, I felt "home."

Michael illustrates another important feature of recovery as he thinks about how he has changed.

> I consciously make an effort to alter my routine so I don't fall back into old patterns. I've now built spaces for myself and my sobriety, and I don't like to go through the day without them. This attention to my recovery precludes participating in a lot of other things so I'm faced with giving up other activities. For a long time that was my excuse not to really get involved. I didn't want to give up anything. But ironically, choosing to go to AA allows me to say no to other things that I said no to before by drinking.

Often the marker is most important during times of painful self-discovery. Even in ongoing recovery, individuals may feel stuck, frightened, hopeless, or discouraged. Many times one can hear people with long-term sobriety say the only positive thing they accomplished that day was not picking up the first drink. When times are tough, individuals cycle back to the alcohol identity and reaffirm their basic commitment to abstinence:

> I sat down and, once again, made the choice: I want to live and I will not choose escape even if living is painful.

Establishing Autonomy

A critically important issue for all people in recovery is autonomy. For some, it is the primary focus of the work of ongoing recovery, developing one's personal identity and establishing healthy independent and interdependent relationships. Central to this question is the examination of feelings and beliefs about same and opposite sex relationships and long-standing difficulties in establishing equal relationships. This issue is often central to psychotherapy. Holly illustrates.

> I'm thinking about my relationships with men again and wonder if there's a way to have autonomy without defiance.

Holly now recalls her father:

> No matter what I did, I didn't reach him—couldn't get a reaction, except when he was drinking. That's the only time I had any physical contact with him. Most of the time I just felt put down and avoided.

Holly next thinks about her relationship with her therapist:

> All my former therapists seemed so withholding to me. But you don't seem to be. I think it's very positive that I don't have to be with a withholding therapist in my recovery.

Suddenly she expressed fear.

> I had a rush of doubt that I really can't have it or it will go away and I will be
> punished.

Issues of separateness and competition are often prominent and related to
the matter of autonomy. Tom explains:

> I'm feeling anger and a lack of understanding from others because I'm no longer
> like them. I don't know what it's like to be part of a family. I was either all there
> and all responsible, or I was drunk. This reminds me of my childhood. Compe-
> tition was intense, and I couldn't tolerate it. Most of the time I felt painfully
> inadequate.

Decision making is often a stage for marking progress toward autonomy.

> I used to leave decisions to my husband. Now I want to be a part of them but don't
> know how to get in. My husband used to be my higher power. I simply turned
> over autonomy and authority and relied on him. Now I sometimes feel that going
> to AA equals drinking because I'm walking out of the home and abandoning my
> constant struggle for equality.

The pull toward autonomy is often frightening in any stage of recovery. Sally
illustrates, thinking about autonomy in terms of old and new values.

> I went to a party with my husband's business acquaintances. I knew I didn't want
> to be with these people, but my husband did. I wonder whether we'll end up having
> friends in common and even whether our marriage will survive.

Shortly after Sally pondered these painful questions, she reported withdrawing
from AA.

> Suddenly I don't want to believe in AA anymore. I'm afraid I'm going to lose my
> new values and my new sense of self. Can I get through a party and enjoy myself
> at the same time? In order to enjoy myself it feels like I have to adapt to his values
> again and then I lose my identity with AA.

The uncertainty of the solidity of the new identity and its direct relationship to
her autonomy was of continuing importance. She experienced the same fears of
a loss of identity everytime the family took a vacation.

> I lose my new identity if I travel, and I lose it at a party. I start to feel like that
> old person. I feel comfortable in AA and that I belong. That sense of clear identity

sure has a price though. It comes through being alcoholic, and, therefore, I'm not as good as others.

The same issue arose again and again. Several months later:

> I keep struggling with my reluctance to go anywhere except AA or to follow my husband's choices. I can see I suffer a loss of identity when others are in control. But when I choose not to go along with the dictates of others, I feel inferior and left out.

As Sally struggled with this issue, she began to feel great anxiety, related to her deep but always well-concealed anger.

> I'm having recurrent attacks of impending doom. It started when I visited with a new AA friend. I couldn't understand why she wasn't furious with her husband. I saw her position of utter dependence on her husband, and then I wanted to drink. I know I saw myself for so many years.

Issues of autonomy are often expressed in relation to the degree of closeness an individual can tolerate. The ability to acknowledge and label the tension between closeness and distance is often not possible until ongoing recovery. Individuals resolve ambivalence and tension about closeness in early recovery through action, choosing the meetings in which they feel most comfortable and designing interpersonal exchanges that are tolerable. Those with extreme worry often sit by the door or leave early. The ability to control the degree of involvement is absolutely essential to continuing engagement with AA. In the research program (Brown, 1977), a vast majority of the respondents indicated a startlingly low need for affiliation. The fact that these individuals can sustain membership in AA is rather remarkable. Individuals reassert in later recovery that their ability to control their own program was paramount in also being able to sustain a commitment and membership in AA. Matt recalls:

> I quit my therapy when I joined AA. Now I can see that AA is a safe place to feel dependent. It's reality-based with an emphasis on action, not thinking about myself. In AA I'm not the center like I feel in therapy. AA validated my feelings, but I could control the distance. The longer I'm in recovery, the more I see that I can't tolerate feelings of intense closeness, almost like a merger, with one person.

Matt then unconsciously illustrated this conflict in his relationship with his sponsor, the single most important individual in his early recovery.

> I used to feel furious with my sponsor for not watching me carefully enough. So I told him to give me more direction, and then I evaded it.

As Matt progressed in sobriety he reported the following dream.

> I was at a party and someone asked me to dance. It wasn't the person I would have chosen. She wanted me to lead, and I told her I couldn't unless she hummed. It made me realize I can move in harmony with another person if I'm willing to do my part. I've never known what a true partnership is.

The issue of closeness was a central therapeutic issue for Paul, often related directly to his persistent anxieties about drinking.

> I've been thinking about drinking and having drinking dreams. My sobriety just gets harder and harder and I'm sure I'll screw it up anyway. It was so easy to pick up the drink in the dream. I just did it.

> Now I'm thinking about what this means and the work I've been doing in my program and therapy. I'm uncomfortable recognizing that I have needs. It's much easier to take care of all my needs through alcohol which is under my control.

As Paul explored, he saw that this particular focus on drinking was due to the loss of an important AA friend who had "returned to drinking."

> If I would start drinking too, I could still feel close to her. By not drinking, I've separated myself from the people who are and I don't feel close to alcoholics anymore. It makes me think about how I've abandoned my alcoholic parents just like I've abandoned my AA friend by not drinking with her. This not drinking is the pits. I'm much more aware of my need for others, yet I feel more isolated from the illusion of closeness achieved through alcohol.

Ongoing recovery involves the interaction and integration of all three axes of the recovery continuum and all lines of movement. It involves a strengthening of the identity as an alcoholic through the continuous processes of construction and reconstruction of one's personal identity. Integrated with this process are factors in the environment, including relationships with others. Finally, the third axis of the continuum, interpretation of self and others, is much more deeply developed and influential in coloring the individual's perceptions, interpretation, and construction. Spirituality, including the belief in a higher power, is a key feature of this axis. The interaction between the axes is a reciprocal building process, shaping the individual's interpretation of the past and the present.

Chapter 8

Treating the Family of the Alcoholic

Alcoholism recently has been labeled "the family disease" (Steinglass, 1980; Hanson and Estes, 1977), with all family members suffering the consequences of one member's alcoholism (Steinglass, 1981) and all seen to play a role in maintaining the destructive interactional patterns that result from alcoholism (Jackson, 1954; Fox, 1956; Estes, 1977; Ablon, 1976; Jacob et al., 1978; Jacob et al., 1981).

Intervention for family members (Filstead, 1981) can occur at any point on the continuum of developing alcoholism and recovery in conjunction with the alcoholic, or separately. In the past, the alcoholic has always been the prime target of treatment, with family members included only as auxiliaries to the primary alcoholic patient. Family members may be given the good advice to attend Al-Anon (Ablon, 1974; and Al-Anon, 1979), but they are not referred to treatment that identifies them as the primary patient.

The model of alcoholism presented here includes family members; they follow a progression similar to that of the alcoholic. As Jackson described, the development of severe problems in the spouse of the alcoholic follows a stage-specific predictable course. Steinglass (1980, 1981), suggests that family-level patterns of behavior can be identified according to the stage of alcoholism.

The children of alcoholics are now also receiving attention as primary patients, with serious behavioral and emotional disturbances resulting from the alcoholism of a parent(s) (Steinglass, 1980; Wegscheider, 1981; Black, 1981; Cork, 1969; Fox, 1979). In the past five years, the adult children of alcoholics have been identified and described as a distinct population requiring specialized treatment (Cermak and Brown, 1982). Al-Anon groups for the adult children of alcoholics are forming nationwide, and therapy programs are tailoring services for this population.

Grateful acknowledgment is made to Dr. Susan Beletsis for her contribution to this chapter.

THE "ALCOHOLIC FAMILY"

What is meant by the term "alcoholic family" (Steinglass, 1980)? This term refers to a family in which alcohol is the organizing principle. Family members develop the same behavioral and cognitive disorder as the alcoholic; they are controlled by the organizing principle of alcohol and yet deny it at the same time.

The term "alcoholic family" is controversial, with some objecting to the blanket characterization and sense of involvement and responsibility by all implied in the term. What is most important in looking at the family as a whole and individual members separately is to understand the degree to which alcohol was (and is) indeed the main organizing principle. The significance of this fact is often overlooked in treatment, especially when the patient has not already identified the importance of the alcoholism of a family member. After attending a lecture on the adult children of alcoholics, a psychiatrist in private practice suddenly realized that at least 60% of his adult psychotherapy patients had grown up in a family in which one or both parents was alcoholic. These patients had entered treatment for different reasons—marital difficulties, anxiety, depression—and the psychiatrist only minimally considered the significance of the alcoholism. After recognizing the common thread, he began to see many similarities among these patients that he could now tie directly to their childhood and adult experiences with an alcoholic parent. Unfortunately, for many individuals entering a traditional nonalcohol-labeled psychotherapy, the secret partner (alcohol) remains the secret partner.

It is important to understand the environment in which the family members live and the importance of interactional factors. Through a clear understanding of "what it is like" in the family, the particular family dynamics can be understood, including the degree to which alcohol is indeed the major organizing principle in the family. Understanding the individual family environment is also extremely important in dealing with individual patients (Moos et al., 1979). While the significance of alcohol may be very similar across families, individual reactions and relationships to it and around it may differ considerably as the following examples illustrate.

Family Adaptations

The family of the alcoholic is characterized primarily by denial (Bean, 1982). There is an atmosphere of shame (Arentzen, 1978) and an underlying core of fear and tension. In most alcoholic families, there is a major secret. The maintenance of that secret, the alcoholism, is the central focus around which the family is organized (Brown and Beletsis, in press; Beletsis and Brown, 1981).

At this first visit, Sam sat down, looked around the room carefully, then began to cry. His father had just died, drunk in an auto accident, and Sam didn't know what to do next. "What should our family do now? Our lives are centered around him. What happens to us now? Tell me, how does an alcoholic family cope?" In the weeks following his initial visit, Sam described a picture of severe family isolation, dictated and maintained for years in the service of denying his father's alcoholism within the family and especially to the outside world. The family members believed they were very close and therefore didn't need anyone else. In fact, outside relationships always presented a threat of revealing the "secret."

The level of denial varies considerably. In some families, the alcoholism is absolutely "nonexistent," although the visible realities in the family dictate otherwise. Sam illustrates again.

Father often missed dinner, which was explained routinely as another business emergency. He forgot promises and whole conversations which the family chalked up to his preoccupation with business.

In other families, members may recognize the presence of alcoholism but deny its seriousness or explain it away as the result of other problems.

I didn't know my mother was an alcoholic until she tried to commit suicide and the hospital staff told us. We always knew she drank a lot, but we referred to her drinking periods as "one of her moods." Mother always had a "look," slurred speech, and a funny walk that went with these moods, but none of us ever openly related these traits to alcohol. Her moods were the problem, and everyone accepted that she needed alcohol to deal with them.

Mary offers another description:

Father was routinely drunk and passed out in the middle of the floor. All the family continued their nightly activities around him, stepping over him on the floor if necessary. Father's drunken behavior was always referred to as a "situation," a code recognized by all of us. The family understood that during the cocktail hour he and mother drank to relieve their financial worries and the burden of a large family. But every night as father got drunk, the cocktail hour became the "situation."

It is the rare family in which alcoholism is acknowledged by all members to be the central problem:

I'm Irish, so Dad's drinking was just like all the other men. But dad got violent when he drank, and he drank every night. All the relatives and the gang in the neighborhood knew what was wrong in our family, but still they didn't talk about it. I remember being kept protectively after school by my teachers who knew there was something wrong with my family. My behavior was a problem too. In the sixth grade, my teacher said I was emotionally disturbed—uncontrollable and a troublemaker. I was terrified constantly, always on guard should my father slam through the front door drunk. It was so bad my mother and brother slept together for safety and I still woke up repeatedly in terror. At school I felt ashamed. From early on I was "damaged goods."

In the alcoholic family there is considerable dissonance. What is most visible and most problematic, the alcoholism, is most vehemently denied. The denial operates to say to the world "This doesn't happen here. It doesn't exist," yet members of the family are engaged in a continuing crusade to make the alcoholic well or to simply enable the family to survive despite what is really happening:

> There were two rules in our family: the first was, "There's no alcoholism" and the second, "Don't tell anyone about it."

When the consequences of the alcoholism become more visible and difficult to resolve (illness, job loss, physical abuse, and drunk driving arrests), the need for secrecy grows, and the family rapidly becomes a closed system, cutting itself off from other sources of input and help.

Children must join in this denial or risk betraying the family. They learn not to trust their own perceptions of reality, not to say what they see, but rather to view the family experience through an alcoholic perspective modeled by both parents. At the same time, they learn not to trust their own perceptions, they also learn not to test reality because it will not be congruent with their parents' reality. In this atmosphere, the child's needs, feelings, and behavior are dictated by the state of the alcoholic at any unpredictable time in the drinking cycle. All members of the family assume responsibility for maintaining stability in the system, struggling to find ways of controlling a situation that cannot be controlled.

In an alcoholic family, children often take on awesome responsibilities, both real and imagined. They learn early what is expected of them in rapidly changing situations, often shifting roles from child to parent to peacemaker, always attempting to "manage" and control the actions of others. One aspect of this responsibility is the task of suppressing their own feelings and needs so as to avoid the possibility of precipitating a drinking bout (Black, 1981).

Denial and the loss of reality testing contribute to the development of an omnipotent belief on the part of the child that something she or he does, or does not do, will effect the drinking of the parent. Because of the tendency of the family to externalize the cause of the drinking, and of the denial of the alcoholic, the child does not learn from the repeated evidence that the drinking is independent of any family members' behavior or attempts to control it.

Self-esteem and feelings of success in the child often become invested in whether or not the parent drinks, and how the alcoholic's behavior is managed. There are many indications that the parents' struggle for control over alcohol becomes internalized by the child (Beletsis and Brown, 1981). That is, children take on the struggle and come to believe that they can cope with conflict and chaos by controlling themselves and by controlling others. These patterns are often similar to those of the nonalcoholic spouse.

It is not surprising that many children of alcoholics have nightmares and sleep disturbances, some are aggressive and have school or social problems, and others become passive and withdrawn (Guebaly and Orford, 1977; Fox, 1973). For many, the tasks of separating from the family, attending to intellectual development in school, and social development with peers is almost impossible. What is surprising is that many of these children appear to be extremely competent and capable, achieving well at school and getting along with adults. The anxiety, confusion, and pain are hidden, and the child bears the message of denial to the outside world: "There is nothing wrong in this family." Sadly, it is this too early competence and overresponsibility, the high achievement, and the skill at "managing" adults that act as barriers to the recognition and early intervention for these often troubled children.

Family Characteristics

The atmosphere in an alcoholic home is characterized by chaos, inconsistency, unclear roles, unpredictability, arbitrariness, changing limits, repetitious and illogical arguments, and perhaps violence and incest (Beletsis and Brown, 1981).

Chaos may be overt or covert. It reflects the predominant control the alcoholic exercises over the family and the constant feeling by all family members that things are or soon will be, out of control. Stable routines may be disrupted at any time by a drinking bout so that the potential for instability is constant. Frequently families adjust to the reality of chaos and it becomes predictable.

Inconsistency may become a predictable and stable feature of the family environment. A permission granted by an alcoholic father on any day is rescinded arbitrarily on the next. The complex pattern of rationalizations necessary to sustain the family denial leads to very inconsistent explanations for behavior and events. What explains behavior one day is contradicted the next. Inconsistency is evidenced in unclear parental roles (Hanson and Estes, 1977). One parent may take over the role of both mother and father, or a child may substitute for one or both. This pattern may be stable or constantly affected by the drinking behavior of the alcoholic or the inconsistent and unpredictable response of the partner.

Our patients have emphasized the damaging consequences of the unpredictable and arbitrary nature of their parents' behavior and logic. Many trace their lack of trust and their hypervigilance as adults to this early environment in which an impending catastrophe was always imminent (Brown and Beletsis, in press). The repetitious and illogical explanations and arguments have a profound impact. Our adult patients have severe difficulties trusting their own perceptions about events and their relationships to others, believing that they do not see things accurately. Many relate this belief to childhood, when they were told by a parent that what they saw, a drunken parent, was not what they saw.

Finally, there is an increasing recognition of the relationship of alcohol to family violence and incest (Olson 1976; NIAAA, 1974). Each of these problems contributes to an overall lack of stability and certainty in the environment as well as severe emotional trauma. Because of the nature of the environment, members of the family expend enormous amounts of energy just to cope with their external family world. So much effort goes into denial and coping with the chaotic reality that there is little energy left for internal development. Early on, individuals develop overt problems with trust and issues of control (Cermak and Brown, 1982). They are guarded and suffer from low esteem and a deepening sense of family isolation.

> Taking charge was my regular duty, but it was a lonely and frightening activity. I feared surprises because my father was so unpredictable. I determined early that I must be prepared for all things. I lived my childhood and teen years standing guard, vigilant and responsive to the ongoing chaos. I felt so needed and responsible in my family that I developed my social life around them. Even after I left home I gave up whole days, weekends, and vacations to them. My family supported each other, and no one ever questioned my mother's belief that it was dangerous for the children to share with others and that it was unnecessary to develop friendships outside the family. I came from a small Texas town. My mother told all the children never to tell anyone about anything in the family. When my dad died, I wanted to tell a few friends but I couldn't. I had to keep the secret.

Months after Sam's father died, Sam thought about the time and energy he now had for himself:

> "Right or wrong, those in an alcoholic family will be drained. It takes so much energy to watch out for everyone." Still later, Sam decided that everyone needs a source of stability as a major component in life. Sam's family was important to him and he loved them but they weren't stable. Still as a youngster he relied on them, not seeing any limitations. Sam was often sorely disappointed because he expected his family to come through and they didn't. They were all preoccupied with something else, his father and his drinking.

A picture of dashed hopes and expectations is etched deeply by most new patients who voluntarily provide a story of Christmas.

> It was the one time I allowed myself to get excited, but every year I ended up in my room alone crying. There were plenty of presents, but my brothers and sisters

and I often had to open them alone. Dad and Mother were fighting. This year Dad fell into the Christmas tree the night before; last year he didn't come home; the year before he was too drunk to open presents. Still, I never stopped hoping we could somehow be a family and that Christmas would truly be magical and loving.

Joe offers a final example of the chaotic environment:

Joe's days were so fraught with chaos that he considered all of life to be a rehearsal for traumatic situations in order to assure himself he could get through. "I believed that if I provided for every contingency, no one would get hurt by my father, and I wouldn't be embarrassed. And so I stood guard, and I practiced." In his adult years, long after his father's death, Joe pondered this guarded stance and sadly acknowledged that he could never "get loose" from himself. Joe scorned the notion of trust: "Did the cops come when I needed them? Did my relatives step in when I needed them desperately? I was alone with my father, and I was constantly terrified."

The alcoholic is the number one child in the family, setting the rules, directly or indirectly, which all others are expected to follow. Members of the family must function in an arbitrary, inconsistent climate of rules and expectations centered around a rigid family system full of pressure to keep the obvious unnoticed. Confrontation of the alcoholic reality is discouraged while assumption of responsibility by all other family members is encouraged—a responsibility to achieve some level of stability around the alcoholic without disturbing that individual or making the problem any worse. The difficulty of obtaining some level of stability on a base of instability and chaos leads to a sense of constant tension and severe consequences.

CHILDREN OF ALCOHOLICS

Attention given to the children of alcoholics has increased understanding of the powerful impact of parental alcoholism on children and the generation to generation transmission of serious problems including increased vulnerability to alcoholism among children.

The environment in a home in which one or both parents is alcoholic has a tremendous impact on the child's development. We are beginning to comprehend the consequences of the adaptations and defenses developed by children that allow them to survive an unpredictable and often chaotic childhood. These strategies for survival have a significant negative impact for later life.

The Child as Parent

Adults who have grown up in an alcoholic family often acknowledge readily that they missed childhood. They often commiserate on the problems of parenting (regardless of whether or not they have children of their own), the only roles they have known, and they long for the missed experiences of childhood (Cermak and Brown, 1982).

When thinking about the meaning of childhood, these adults equate it with an inner freedom and spontaneity of expression, qualities that permit full exploration of the world. When all the child's energy is directed outside, toward the maintenance of denial and protection of the family, there is no room for inner development and no freedom of thought and expression. These individuals recognize that such total freedom requires a protective parent and a safe home, neither of which they could rely on:

> Joan expresses these sentiments directly. She recites her history methodically as if she has pondered it many times: "Life was good until the second grade. My mother was involved in a bad auto accident and started drinking heavily afterwards. From then on, nothing would ever be the same. I never felt the sense of safety I had once known, and I lost my central place as the child in the family. Now mother needed all my attention and everyone else's too. She got a divorce and in the next 10 years brought me four stepfathers, all alcoholic." Joan speaks in a childlike but matter of fact way. She remembers a conscious decision as a child of 10 to take care of herself and all her own needs and, at the same time, to find someone in her life to dote on her. To be a child taken care of by a doting parent remains her driving force as an adult.

Penny offers another example:

> I was always very serious about myself and life. I felt old in high school, like 90. I was the mother in the family to my sibs and to my alcoholic mother.

Penny has no children herself, but now talks about herself as a mother, full of a still potent mixture of guilt, self-criticism, and anger.

> I was the "strong one," so strong I thought of myself as a "big brick." I was also stronger than my mother, a fact that we all had to carefully conceal. We had to make my mother feel important while everyone knew I was really in charge.

Penny recalls with sadness that she was not loving toward her mother. In fact, she consciously withheld her love and her care. Penny judges that she was not a good mother to her mother. She feels a mixture of sadness for this failure and anger for the job she never wanted.

> I don't want children of my own. Being a mother is all I've known; I want something else for myself. I have a deep feeling of missed opportunity and I'm searching frantically to fill in the holes.

Like others, Penny often talks about control, mostly about her fear of losing it. Her mother attempted suicide so many times that it became her duty to make life worthwhile. She felt tired and driven, like 90, by this task. No one was in control in her life. She was it for the whole family. If she lost that, she would have nothing to offer. If she slowed down, she would become just like her mother.

Peter too is quite articulate when he talks about being a parent:

> It became my job to save the family when I was seven. My parents divorced because of my mother's alcoholism, and I was told by my father to take care of her.

Like many children of divorce, he took over as man of the family. He had to be the woman too, because his mother was so ill with alcoholism. Peter became both parents, taking over much of the practical and emotional responsibilities for his family.

> It was an overwhelming task and I felt frightened much of the time. I worshipped my father who, from afar, alternately encouraged me to take care of my mother and rejected me for rescuing her. My mother accepted me readily as a symbolic substitute for my father. She continued treating me exactly as she had my father— when drunk, she lashed out at me physically and verbally; she threw my clothes on the front porch demanding that I leave. I told myself she could not help it and tried harder to care for her. I felt sad that I did not do a good job with my younger sisters because I was too preoccupied with my mother.

Interpersonal Adaptations

The well-being of the child in the family is tied to the whim of the parents, so that children cannot learn to predict the interpersonal consequences of their behavior (Cermak and Brown, 1982). Children suffer a constant feeling of uncertainty and fear, with a growing deep lack of trust.

Sam illustrates these problems well. It is he who recognized his father as the number one child and learned early to accommodate to his rapid shifts in mood and behavior.

> My father could not believe the pain he inflicted on others, or that anyone could suffer as much as he did. He refused to believe that he affected anyone and accused my mother of making up lies when she tried to confront him with the realities of his behavior.

Sam identified closely with others who know parenting well. He had a long history but never felt he did it well.

> My key problem growing up was a lack of role models. My father was never able to cope, and mother's behavior was always a reaction to my father. My father's been dead quite a while, and my mother still doesn't know how to regulate her behavior. She still overreacts, can't control her anger, or put things in their proper perspective. I never saw mature, responsible behavior.

Sam was actually amazed at his own recognition of how much his life was child-centered around his father. He had no examples of people who could cope with minor or major stress—his grandparents on both sides also drank. Sam is often philosophical about his role as a parent:

> Children of alcoholics must pioneer positive ways to cope. Yet, I am most worried that I cannot model for my younger sibs what I did not receive. I call myself the "Sam role model," but I worry that my footsteps are inadequate. The burden of alcoholism falls disproportionately on children. My mother didn't learn her behavior from my father or model from him. She had a chance before meeting him, and, therefore, had many happy moments to remember. But us kids know nothing else; we have learned only how to behave unsuccessfully.

Sam is making the important point that the children in his family learned by observation an abnormal form of reality. They had no prior experience to inform them that something was wrong. Sam developed a feel for what was appropriate in his family, for what was right or wrong in that world, but it didn't carry over. He finds himself lost, insecure, and frightened in the adult world outside his family. He is sure he's emotionally immature and doesn't know what to do about it.

> I am extremely worried about what I call my own lack of control and inability to regulate my behavior. I am hyperexcitable and overly happy—emotions I used to cheer up my depressed family. I have no idea what behaviors go along with loving someone, and if I can't predict the reaction of others, I am always unsure how to behave. I feel tremendously insecure socially and especially in developing close relationships outside my family. I am certain I am just as moody and lacking in emotional controls as everyone in my family. So I maintain a vigil on myself just like I did with my family.

In contrast to "90-year-old" Penny, Sam feels terribly young, young at least in the world outside his family. Sam says matter-of-factly that his father's drinking interrupted his development in the fifth grade. He had to think and behave like an adult for his survival, so he missed what he calls the jumble of emotions of adolescence. Now, out of the family and an adult by age, he often feels like a "beginner," a small child, terribly needy, very emotional, and lost at sea in an adult world:

> Up until now I had no choices. My relationship with my father and my father's alcoholism was all-consuming. We all did whatever Dad wanted. There was no thought of opposing him. Only his death allows me to live. My father created the struggles for me to surmount. I had to respond to him or desert him. Now my struggles are my own.

A child in an alcoholic family learns to "manage" the actions of others. The child learns what is expected in certain situations and behaves that way in response to a changing, unpredictable climate. The child learns to parcel out feelings to fit the mood of the alcoholic. Thus, the child's feelings, needs, and behavior are dictated by the state of the alcoholic at any particular time. Children learn there are appropriate times to ask for help and other times when it is better to remain quiet.

Problems With Identification

A profound consequence of childhood and adolescence in an alcoholic family is the failure to develop an autonomous identity, based on an integrated sense of self (Beletsis and Brown, 1981). Coping strategies that depend on denial of reality and the sense of responsibility for managing the reactions and welfare of others leaves little time for self-exploration and psychological growth. The result is a denial of the self or the development of a false self that has little connection with the subjective experience of the individual.

On a deeper level, there is often an identification with the alcoholic parent. Child and parent both share an experience of helplessness and failure. Although the conscious wish and overt behavior may appear to reflect an identification with the nonalcoholic parent (by being controlled, by not drinking), many adult children of alcoholics experience themselves as being out of control and fear that inevitably they will become like the alcoholic parent (Cermak and Brown, 1982).

Other problems of identification do not become clear immediately, although the confusion and role reversals of childhood make these problems inevitable. As these individuals begin to deal with their feelings on issues of control and responsibility, as they explore the problems in relationships and the roles they have assumed in their work and in their present families, and particularly as they struggle with issues of alcohol use and abuse, the many facets and functions of poorly integrated identifications, often with both parents, become clear. For many, holding onto their perception of themselves as helpless children in a chaotic family serves to avoid facing how closely they may identify with the alcoholic parent. For others, maintaining a conscious identification with the nonalcoholic parent and striving to feel and act like that parent helps to deny empathic identification with the alcoholic parent. Those who have become acknowledged alcoholics are often seen by others to have an advantage in having dealt with the fear as well as with the real problem.

Trust, Intimacy, and Control

Many of these children survive childhood by becoming prematurely responsible and capable (Black, 1981), but this is often believed to be a facade that hides ·

pervasive feelings of inadequacy and failure. This sense of failure often rests on the basic fact that the child was never successful in getting the alcoholic parent to stop drinking. Many report extreme vulnerability to criticism and anger, experiencing a persistent fear that they will be "found out," exposed as failures.

Many report difficulties in relationships that require trust and intimacy. They learned early not to trust, not to build up expectations, and not to depend on anyone to gratify their needs. As adults, their dependency needs generate a high level of anxiety and are frequently denied or suppressed. In relationships, these individuals have difficulty setting limits to their responsibility for the other person's needs and feelings. Problems with trust are pervasive and often involve the inability to trust their own perceptions or feelings and respond appropriately.

Conflicts over the need to control are interwoven through all the other issues and difficulties. Many report how easily they feel controlled by others' feelings and needs. Conversely, the same individuals express strong needs to control others, to be in control of their own feelings and behavior, and great fear of loss of control. Conflict over control is closely related to the issue of alcohol use and the strength of identification with the alcoholic parent. For most, all feelings have the potential of being out of control and much energy is expended denying or suppressing all intense feelings, particularly anger. Concern with issues of control is often the most significant source of anxiety.

WHICH PARENT IS ALCOHOLIC?

There are as many variations of adaptations as there are alcoholic families, and each will be unique in its particular patterns. Yet, there are some common grounds, from which to base a more individualized portrait, that stem from identifying which parent is the alcoholic.

Both Parents Are Alcoholic

The norm for the family in which both parents are alcoholic is alcoholism. Children do not see other behaviors, so they cannot appreciate that something is amiss. They discover as they grow up, however, that the drinking behavior of their parents is not typical (Brown, 1974). At this recognition, these children may suddenly develop intense feelings of shame, humiliation, and a feeling of being a deviant outsider. With the recognition that their parents are different, they become more defensive and more isolated from the rest of the world.

Mary's father was the "serious" alcoholic in the family. It was he who turned the parents' cocktail hour into a "situation" each night. Because her father was so visible—passed out on the floor—he received all the attention, and mother's drinking, matched glass for glass with father, went unnoticed. For years the "situation" was as far as anyone could go in commenting on the drinking, and it was always father's situation. Mother never passed out; instead, she became withdrawn and hostile toward the children if they interrupted her protected reverie.

I began to get some inkling that my parents weren't "normal" when I was reading the primary books and learned about the storybook families of Dick and Jane. Nobody had cocktail hours or situations in these families. My parents usually missed evening meetings at school, and I had to be part of the excuse. I felt terrible lying to my teachers, and I began to realize that something was different about my home.

The clearest recognition came when I invited several close girl friends to spend the night. I was really excited but soon felt a terrible pain in my stomach. My friends did not have "situations" in their homes, and their faces registered disbelief and dismay as they watched my parents drink. These girls had never seen anyone drunk except on TV. They were frightened, but they giggled to hide their fear.

I felt so humiliated. I was embarrassed by my parents and defensive on their behalf at the same time. I wanted the approval of my girl friends and to be just like them, and I was also angry at them for laughing at my parents. So I became much more protective and secretive about my family. I must hide the truth. There became an inside world of alcoholism to which I belonged by birth and there was an outside world to which I strived to belong to as well. I had to overcome and hide my origin and birth to belong to this normal world.

Joe provides another example. The central theme for Joe in his family and throughout his adult life has been his repeated determination of whether or not he belongs. He sizes up any relationship or brief exchange according to whether he is like everyone else or different, inside or out. And he always feels flawed. In his family, his only sense of belonging came from being needed, to protect his younger brothers from his violent parents. Yet deep down, he never believed he belonged to anyone:

Nobody claimed me. I was an orphan in my family and am now an orphan in the world.

For Joe, the whole question of whether or not he is healthy, adequate, and acceptable is tied to whether or not he belongs. Yet, there is great danger in belonging. If he is part of his family, he is like them, and that means he is out of control, violent, alcoholic, and crazy. It's one or the other. He's alone as an orphan, or he's one of them. Joe struggles constantly to bridge these extremes of identification. He is now a recovering alcoholic who spends great effort trying to belong and not to belong at the same time. Not a day goes by that Joe doesn't think about his first family—how much he needed, how badly he felt about them, and what he could have done to make it better.

Children in a family in which both parents are alcoholic learn not only that alcohol is normal but that it is used to cope with many problems in life. Some parents have no relationship outside the use of alcohol. These parents drink as a part of every interaction. Children learn that alcohol is a part of the expression of love, sorrow, joy, hate, anger, and all kinds of emotions.

> I was devastated when I finally came to the recognition that my parents' drinking was not tied to any particular event. The belief that my mother drank because I misbehaved or got bad grades provided an enormous, though false, sense of control for me. If their drinking was tied to my behavior, I could control it by being good. I followed this course for years trying to be perfect. It never worked, so I tried harder. If I could just figure out what I was doing to cause it, they would stop. When I finally realized that my parents drank no matter what, I felt abandoned, isolated, and unimportant. I now believe I was a nuisance and would probably never have been missed if I had gone away.

It is important to stress that a general description of the family environment can only be used as a guideline to understanding a particular individual or family. It is extremely important that individual experiences and differences be understood. For example, it may be the case that in one family both parents are alcoholic but they trade off in the role of drunken irresponsible child and sober responsible parent. One is taking care of the children at any given time while the other is drinking. Toby's parents followed this pattern.

> Dad was a regular drinker, a can of beer, his constant companion when not at work. Mom drank too, but had more trouble with pills, regularly taking tranquilizers to make it through her days with the children. These were their regular patterns. In addition, at any given time, Mom or Dad would alternately increase their intake and go on a "binge" becoming nonfunctional. For Dad, it was often on the weekend as he still was very conscientious about work. During the week he would often arrive home to find mother glassy eyed and immobile. As each parent took turns dropping out, the other automatically assumed full responsibility, primarily for taking care of the other parent who was severely incapacitated. My younger brother and I felt frightened, confused, and left out.

> I was ten, but I began wetting the bed and crying uncontrollably. I couldn't concentrate in school, and my teachers referred me for professional help.

In another case both parents may be alcoholic and drink together. Their drinking forms a closed unit, excluding the children from their emotional awareness. Such children feel abandoned and perhaps constantly frightened about the loss of one or both of those parents.

Coalcoholics

When one parent is alcoholic and the other is not, the nonalcoholic spouse has come to be known as the "coalcoholic" or "codependent" (Wegscheider, 1981). Some studies (Schaffer and Tyler, 1979; Gorman and Rooney, 1979) of the nonalcoholic spouse now exist. The coalcoholic can be the husband, wife, children, or anybody in a close relationship with the alcoholic. This broadened view is of recent origin. Only a few short years ago alcoholics were thought to be predominantly men, and the coalcoholic was the wife. In this traditional view, the woman was to blame. It is this pattern that Jackson described. In her efforts to maintain the denial of the alcoholic, the wife began to adjust her life to the behavior of the alcoholic in an attempt to gain some control and stability. As a result, the behavior of the alcoholic became her obsession and she found herself constantly preoccupied for his welfare. As her own unconscious recognition of the realities of the alcoholism grows, she feels more ashamed and begins to close out the world, isolating her and her family more and more. She becomes obsessed with her spouse and her own slavery to the sickness of alcoholism. She may hear that her husband would not drink if she were a better wife, so she changes her life continually in an attempt to satisfy him and solve the drinking problem. Yet nothing works. She is constantly afraid of what he may be doing and her personal self-image plummets. She feels powerless, insecure, a failure, beset with a sense of futility. Yet, she may also don an outward pose of superiority and pride as if to say to the outside world, "There's nothing wrong."

The protection of the alcoholic and maintanence of the family denial become the wife's preoccupation and obsession. She worries about whether or not he is drunk again, when he will be home, and whether or not he will lose his job. The more isolated she becomes and the more she tries to protect her husband, the less time and direct attention she has for her children. The alcoholism is now a bigger worry, and it is central to everyone in the family.

Terry illustrates this pattern. She had just started to attend Al-Anon and sought treatment in addition because she could not get over her depression. She finally recognized that her husband was alcoholic, but she could not give up the idea that she could help him.

> My friends in Al-Anon kept talking about "letting go," but I couldn't do this. I did not even know what they meant. I was immobilized, cried all the time, and could only think in terms of what I could do to make him change.

She traces the history of their life together and the central theme is alcohol.

> As I look back I now recognize that I stopped going to church when I married Mike because he thought religion was a crutch for people who couldn't face the tough realities of life. I altered my view to fit his and slowly cut my ties to my church and the friends I knew from there.

Mike already drank a lot, but because I loved him and wanted to be with him constantly it was not a problem. I was Mrs. Michael Warden and I could follow his lead: so I drank with him, redefining my own values, goals, and what was important to me in life. Like Mike, I now wanted more time to relax and always looked for opportunities to have more fun times and a "quick one." I stopped making plans of my own, separate from him, in order to be able to respond to his needs. I now see that I never questioned any of these changes. I did everything possible to create an environment in which drinking was pleasant, acceptable, reasonable, and ever present. Our friends were drinkers and our lives revolved entirely around alcohol.

For a long time it was not a serious problem. I was anxious some of the time, when Mike came home late or couldn't make it to work on time. But I covered up my worries. I called his boss to report that he had the flu, then nursed him back from his increasingly frequent debilitating hangovers. By afternoon we would share a drink and consider his "illness" a lucky holiday.

Mrs. Michael Warden never recognized that she was completely obsessed with the behavior and the welfare of her husband. She just wanted him to be happy, and he usually was while drinking. This pattern lasted for several years.

I was virtually isolated from a nondrinking world that might have challenged my perceptions about my life and drinking. I began to have trouble keeping up with Mike, and I began to want more personal attention from him, which he could not give. I did not want him to be drunk so much of the time. Soon we were fighting over my needs to control his drinking, and our close "loving" relationship was fractured. The alcohol that brought us together was now driving us apart. It was now what we argued about constantly.

I began to drink less myself and to feel more and more depressed. For a long time I kept protecting Mike and shouldering the blame for the unhappy atmosphere, so full of tension and arguments. If I could just control my anger and stop trying to control him, things would be better. I tried, but things didn't improve.

I felt a nagging sense of impending doom and bolstered my defenses. I denied my problem more vehemently, and defended me and my husband mentally to all those I imagined were criticizing and condemning us. I believed more strongly that the world outside was judgmental and like my husband, that people were always out to get whatever they could. You had to take care of yourself in a world like this. My days were full of worry about Mike's drinking. I drove by his favorite tavern several times a day and cut my activities completely so I could be ready to rescue him if necessary. But we still fought constantly.

I was always proud that our son Billy was such a little man and seemed so able to take care of himself. I never imagined his needs were unmet or that he was suffering as a result of his father's drinking and my preoccupation with it. I was dumbfounded when Billy's fourth grade teacher called for a parent conference. Billy was not quiet—he was withdrawn and depressed. The school recommended treatment for him. Billy's counselor insisted that both of us be involved. Mike refused; I agreed to talk with someone.

In the case in which the woman is alcoholic and the husband is not, the same dynamics may occur. Each must often assume the role of the other so that the nonalcoholic parent becomes both mother and father. Until recently men were slower to lose contact with the outside world because they more often held jobs outside the home and therefore maintained a continuing contact with a reality different from the home environment.

In the case in which one partner maintains a continuing contact with two realities, the conflict may be intense and painful. Harry illustrates this problem with a female alcoholic.

I was an up and coming executive, good in my job, well liked, good husband and father. Trudy was by my side, going up right along with me. I did OK for years while I altered my life to accommodate to her increasing drinking, unavailability, unpredictability, and shifting moods. I began to think of my wife as one of the children—I constantly called from work to see if she had remembered to do the shopping, arrange for Molly's skating lessons, and make our travel arrangements.

Eventually, I gave these duties to my secretary who gladly took over. I worried about the kids constantly and often took them out to dinner when nothing was fixed at home. I kept trying to do more to relieve Trudy of the stress and pressure she complained about.

I was jolted when I was offered a choice promotion. Suddenly, I was filled with shame and fear. I could not accept. The position demanded an executive wife, entertainment and public visibility. Suddenly I knew what had been true for years. Trudy was an alcoholic, and I had to keep her hidden. To accept the job would mean to reveal our family secret.

The spouse of the alcoholic may suffer the same consequences as the children, particularly if the spouse is in a very dependent position. She or he may assume responsibility for the drinking and become overcontrolling of everyone in the family in an attempt to gain some stability and reinforce a sense of self-esteem. The partner develops problems with interpersonal trust, intimacy, fear of dependency needs, and an inability to trust perceptions, just like the children.

Children in alcoholic families do not feel the primary attachment or primary parental care coming from their parents. They may also learn not to care, not to have needs, and when they do, to take care of them themselves, regardless of age. Because of the obsession with alcohol, both parents may be irresponsible, chronically or periodically. The nonalcoholic may assume more and more responsibility for protecting the alcoholic from his or her excesses and less responsible for anything else, as Terry illustrated. But in many families, the nonalcoholic becomes more responsible on the surface, assuming the role and duties of the other. This individual may provide good parental care. But it is the rare family in which the issue of alcohol does not interfere significantly at some point. The processes of denial and protection simply require too much emotional and physical energy.

For example, the issue of alcohol may serve as a hostile weapon between the parents. The alcoholic drinks "at" the other and the nonalcoholic responds through the children: overprotecting them from a deep sense of guilt or perhaps expressing misplaced anger and hurt directly at the children:

> I knew I couldn't count on my mother anymore as protector the day she started throwing plates across the kitchen at my younger sister. My mother (not a drinker) swore at her and screamed till the last dish was broken. My sister was six and I was twelve. I said "irrational" and pulled my sister out of the way. I never again nurtured any hope that I could talk to her about what really happened, or that she could be a source of safety for any of us. She wanted her children to be perfect: our problems and needs only reminded her that she was failing, and she raged at us for this unspoken accusation.

The parents may become more and more preoccupied with their own relationship and its central focus on alcohol. The initial emphasis on denial leads to underlying anger and constant fear. At first, the nonalcoholic will attempt to control the situation through nagging, lectures, or extraction of promises from the alcoholic. Next, the nonalcoholic will take action, hiding liquor, withholding money, or engaging in power struggles around the issue of drinking. By now, the family is characterized by intense conflict and a constant focus on who is going to control whom. Any open or realistic communication is declined. Instead, communication is centered on attempts of family members to control one another. Both parents present confusing models of behavior because of their predominance of denial. Children recognize lies and alibies and are befuddled at the disparity between what they see and what they are permitted to see and acknowledge as real.

Sam faced this dilemma continually. There was no alcoholism in his family and the daily drinking bouts of his father, the violent arguments, the forgotten promises, the missed appointments, either did not happen or were explained away as a result of stress:

> In the beginning I used to remind my father and mother of a forgotten promise, but then I stopped. Too frequently I was told it never happened. My father really couldn't remember, and my mother couldn't stand another reminder of our severe problems.

Susan provides another example:

> I was abused severely as a child by my alcoholic mother. None of these episodes was ever acknowledged or talked about by anyone. As far as the world knew I was

a happy child from a happy home. I carried two secrets: alcoholism and the beatings.

Years later as she attempts to describe what happened, she repeatedly changes her mind and retracts what she has just described. Embarrassed, she says at first that it wasn't so bad and she sounds like such a complainer, and then she says she is not sure any of it ever happened. No one else seemed to see it like she did.

It is difficult to emulate either parent, but children do so unconsciously. The nonalcoholic may be seen as strong and dependable but a martyr without any joy. The alcoholic is commonly seen as weak, full of needs, yet perhaps carefree and loving as well.

Because so much of the family's effort is invested in the defensive process of denial, members of the family and outsiders may interpret the absence of overt uproar and difficulty as a measure of happiness and stability. Therefore, no interventions occur. Any potential change is interpreted as a threat to the quasi stability of the moment (Steinglass, 1980b). The mood of the alcoholic governs the family environment and interactions at any given time. The nonalcoholic's relationship to the children is governed by the way that individual feels for the alcoholic at any particular time. As noted, it can range from overprotection to rejection of the children.

Separation from the alcoholic family is extremely difficult to achieve. Even those who have left their families physically or whose parents have died, often remain too closely tied to the family emotionally (Brown and Beletsis, in press). To leave is to give up hope, to abandon the family, or to be abandoned. Staying emotionally attached is a way of maintaining an important role in the family and a way of maintaining the family denial.

For some, staying attached means becoming alcoholic. For others, it means keeping the role of the rescuer, always being available in emergencies, continuing the responsible role taken in childhood. For many, the concern and involvement becomes a preoccupation even when they are not actively involved with the family. For all, the failure to separate becomes a major barrier to forming healthy, primary attachments to their own families and causes great difficulty with intimate involvement in all other significant relationships. It is as though the unfinished business in the family of origin precludes the perception of self as an adequate and available adult.

Adult children of alcoholics often find themselves replicating their relationship with the alcoholic parent by choosing a dependent or alcoholic mate. Some avoid close relationships altogether, finding themselves more and more isolated and less and less able to trust. Those who marry and have children frequently feel that their main commitment is still to their parents. They feel frightened of needing to depend on another person and often inadequate as parents.

Some are so preoccupied with their families immediately after leaving home that they are unable to concentrate as students or unable to be committed to career training or first jobs. To focus on themselves is to run the risk that a calamity will occur in their family, and they will not have done all that they could to avoid it. Such children feel abandoned and perhaps constantly frightened about the loss of one or both of these parents.

> My parents' social life was the highlight of their lives. They didn't read, go to plays, or listen to music. They entertained and that was all. And, of course, they drank all the time. I really believe they never wanted children. They expected me to be a little adult from an early age. A child disturbed their peace and interfered with their own needs and plans. My mother, a severe alcoholic, expected me to be the family showpiece, extended on a pedastal, visible to the world, but quiet and in my place.

Tom longs for a missed childhood and seeks help because he feels terribly restricted in his emotions and interpersonal life. He knows how to look good, but he can't feel much of anything and he can't remember much of his early childhood years.

The emphasis on denial in the alcoholic family and the reality of the chaos, inconsistency, and unpredictability lead to a predominance of defensive coping strategies (Beletsis and Brown, 1981). There is the constant threat that the "outside" world may discover the secret or that some disaster resulting from the alcoholism will occur within the family. As a result, it is extremely difficult to accurately assess personality strengths and weaknesses. The defensive posture is all encompassing.

USING THE MODEL WITH FAMILIES

After a volunteer presentation on alcoholism to a class of seventh and eighth graders, these questions were asked: (NCA, 1978)

Why would an alcoholic take it out on his or her child?

Can alcoholism make you mental?

Can drinking lead to stronger drugs?

Are most alcoholic parents child abusers?

Why do people forget so easy?

I am worried about my mother taking tranquilizers and other drugs. What should I do?

If you hang out around liquor stores a lot is there a chance you could become alcoholic?

If your mother drinks and takes valium, is she going to die soon?

Do you know where a battered child can go?

What do you do if there is no one at all around?

Recognition that family members have treatment needs of their own, separate from the needs of the alcoholic, or the family as a whole, is a newly emerging concept. For the most part, treatment programs still offer services to family members only in the context of helping the alcoholic patient stay sober. Family therapy, couples therapy, and individual consultation are designed to encourage the family's support of the newly abstinent alcoholic and alert the family to changes that will occur with the alcoholic's abstinence.

With the dynamic model, each patient follows a developmental progression. The spouse and children of an alcoholic may move in tandem with the alcoholic as denial deepens. They may also move in concert through the points of surrender, transition, and early and ongoing recovery, or they may move separately. In determining intervention and a treatment plan for one family member or the family as a whole, it is essential to consider at what point along the continuum each family member falls. Often, the most serious overt family difficulties are related to differences in stage of the continuum and, therefore, a different identity, different explanation of the reality of alcoholism, and different interpretations of self and the world.

Bacon (1973) described this process well in terms of the labeling that occurs for all family members. He suggested that the members of the family typically relinquish their denial ahead of the alcoholic. Whether or not the family moves into recovery is another matter. Family members may be able to acknowledge the alcoholism of one member, but they are unable to see themselves as anything but victims and cannot identify as a "primary patient" in any way themselves. Others may seek help for themselves and join Al-Anon, thereby facilitating the beginning of their own recovery (Wright and Scott, 1978). They move along the continuum, while the alcoholic remains in the drinking stage. As Ablon (1982) notes, membership in Al-Anon often provides the first opportunity for self-definition.

Conversely, the alcoholic may move ahead in recovery, with the family staying behind, denying the reality of alcoholism or the consequences on the family of recovery. The following example illustrates. Mr. P was sober for about a year. He attended AA and a recovery group but always felt a reluctance to really get involved. In group discussions, he frequently spoke about his wife.

> I know I'm alcoholic and can't drink. But my wife makes fun of me. She likes her drinks and gets very upset when I want to go to AA and be around "those alcoholics." The more attention I pay to AA and my sobriety, the nastier she gets. I always have a faint awareness that if I sat down and drank with her, the nagging, angry attacks would stop.

Mr. P occasionally worked individually with a therapist to talk about his dilemma. The therapist used the model of the continuum to illustrate that Mr. P was restricted in his progression of recovery. He needed to pay close attention to the alcohol axis continually to counter the pull of his wife's invitation to drink with her. He even had difficulty embracing AA and his new identity as an alcoholic; to feel good about these was perceived by him as a hostile move against his wife. His sobriety was always tenuous and he could not experience the depth of change that he saw in others.

Drinking

Intervention with family members is a similar process to intervention with the alcoholic. It begins with the same careful development of an individual and family history and the intention by the therapist to actively "rule out" alcoholism (see Chapter 4). The therapist must actively seek information to confirm or eliminate the presence of alcoholism in a family member. This process requires the same high index of suspicion necessary for detecting the alcoholic. It demands a suspicion by the therapist that the patient's presenting problem, marital difficulties, depression, insomnia, anxiety, could very well be related to the alcoholism of a spouse or parent.

Family members join the alcoholic in the distorted thinking necessary to sustain the denial and maintain a belief in family unity. Efforts of family members to break out of the denial are often unsuccessful or given up because of the threat of loss or breakup of the family.

The therapist begins the process of the breakdown of denial for the patient, labeling alcoholism, that is, the alcoholism of someone close to the patient, as the primary problem. When labeled as the primary problem, the therapist can then recommend a course of action directed toward helping the patient deal with the reality of the family life and the personal consequences. Most family members, if they can accept the label, want help in "getting the alcoholic to stop drinking." They have already spent years in an unsuccessful private effort to get the alcoholic to stop. Often they feel responsible for the drinking as well. This presents exactly the same dilemma for the therapist. The patient must recognize his or her lack of control in being able to control the alcoholic and must stop trying. The first step of the Al-Anon program illustrates, "We admitted we were powerless over alcohol and that our lives had become unmanageable." The therapist who builds an alliance designed to get the patient's spouse to stop drinking will get caught in the same struggle for control that occurs when the alcoholic is the patient.

The acceptance of loss of control by the partner or family members of the alcoholic frees that individual to ask for help and become the identified patient. Because it is impossible to control the alcoholic, the only person the patient can do anything about is him or herself. AA and Al-Anon provide the guidelines for identifying as the primary patient. Members of both organizations are encouraged to look at themselves and accept responsibility only for themselves. Therapeutic intervention requires the same focus.

Family members involved in maintaining the denial of alcoholism need help in breaking it down. The same process of understanding the meaning of alcoholism and its function applies. Pat illustrates:

I spent three years in psychotherapy, depressed, anxious, and full of feelings of failure. I talked about my husband's drinking, but always minimized it. I was sure that his drinking problem really was my fault. If I acknowledged that he was alcoholic, I would have confirmed my failure.

As his drinking progressed, we (the family) adapted to it and began to work around him. I functioned as a single parent most of the time, taking care of the children and myself. His unavailability and regular drinking became dependable and predictable. We had lost a husband and a father and we now functioned without him. In a funny way, it was OK. I ran the family and made all the decisions. It's really ironic. His drinking served the function of giving me all the responsibility. Most of the time I felt resentful and victimized, even helpless. At other times, I felt a sense of power and contempt for him.

When I finally acknowledged that he really was an alcoholic, I had to get help for myself to step out of the certainties of our miserable family situation.

It is often extremely difficult to shift the focus of the spouse and family members away from changing the alcoholic. They may be able to define and label the problem as alcoholism, but they also believe that they caused it. "Getting the alcoholic to stop" is the logical course to avoid examining their own helplessness and feelings of self-blame.

As long as I thought I really could get him to stop, I didn't have to feel so utterly abandoned and helpless. Besides, if I had caused it, I ought to be able to fix it too.

Curiously, the partner and family develop the same preoccupation with alcohol as the alcoholic. It often centers on the search for the "right" strategy in getting the alcoholic to stop or to "control it."

I put so much energy into figuring out the best way to control my husband's drinking. I tried to have dinner at an earlier hour so he couldn't drink so much before. We ended up eating without him, or the dinner got cold waiting for him so we could all eat together and maintain the image of a close family.

Naturally, I tried hiding his bottles and filled up our social schedule to avoid big gaps of unstructured time. Of course, nothing worked. Then I covered up for him.

I was so scared, I'd call the boss and say he was sick. I was so afraid he'd lose his job and we'd be worse off.

My denial got worse and worse. And I'd get myself in a corner lying and making excuses. The kids were frightened; I was just trying to hold the big lie together.

Breaking down denial is difficult because the spouse fears that the outcome will be worse: breakup of the marriage, loss of job, or the intuitive knowledge that many family problems will have to be addressed if the partner does stop drinking.

The breakdown of denial and the change in behavior required for family members to disengage from supporting the alcoholism of another are primarily behavioral and cognitive tasks. The same strategies appropriate for the drinking alcoholic apply. Understanding the meaning of "being alcoholic" is a good start: "What would it mean if my husband were alcoholic?" Dynamic intervention may be required if unconscious factors are interfering with the recognition and acceptance of another's alcoholism. Sandra illustrates:

I lived with my husband's drinking year after year after year, believing as he did that it would get better when the level of stress in his work improved. My kids tried to get me to see that his drinking was the problem, but I refused to go along. I even criticized them for being so inconsiderate of their father.

I ended up in therapy for my anxiety and depression. My therapist quickly recognized the significance of my husband's drinking, but I still resisted this knowledge. Finally, I saw that accepting my husband as an alcoholic meant I had to accept that my father was an alcoholic too. This destroyed a lifetime fantasy about my close relationship with my father.

Once Sandra accepted that her husband was an alcoholic, she agreed to attend Al-Anon. Soon she was altering her behavior in relation to him and her explanations of events as well.

Transition

The spouse in transition is involved in the same major changes as the alcoholic. The individual is shifting from a belief in the ability to control the alcoholic to a recognition of lack of control. In addition, the spouse is acquiring the identity of someone who has been reactive to and perhaps involved in sustaining the alcoholic drinking pattern. This identity has been called "coalcoholic" (Kaufman and Pattison, 1982), "codependent," and "paraalcoholic," to indicate the interdependent relationship (Greenleaf, 1981).

The task for the individual in transition is to focus on the new identity and its meaning and to learn new ways of behaving that do not support the alcoholic behaviors. This task requires identification as the primary patient and a disengagement from the negative cycle of overcontrol and assumption of responsibility for the alcoholic.

Disengagement is often the most difficult and painful task. Because the individual has felt responsible for the drinking, the idea of disengagement from that responsibility is felt as an abandonment of the drinker and the source of intolerable guilt. Mike illustrates:

> How could I leave my wife behind? I felt so responsible for her. Yet, I was hearing that I had to give up every hope of being able to help her. And I had to help myself, and that meant I had to quit helping her to drink.
>
> I didn't know how. I listened and learned that I could no longer buy booze for her, no longer be in charge of fixing her drinks with the hope of limiting her, no longer cover up with her parents and the kids. And I now had to take steps to protect the children. Before I just hoped that nothing bad would happen. Now I made sure.
>
> It felt so angry to take such action. I had to be constantly reassured that these steps were necessary and really in everyone's best interest.

The spouse of the alcoholic who acknowledges the alcoholism and moves into his or her own recovery often has an acute sense of loneliness as a result of abandoning the role of savior and victim. Many, like the alcoholic, go through the process of fits and starts, returning to the old beliefs and behaviors in response to the fear and reality of loss experienced at leaving the partner behind.

> I went through such an on and off struggle. Yes, she really is an alcoholic, and I must face it. I went to Al-Anon and followed the suggestions for a while. Then I felt better and began to think that maybe she could control it, or maybe she wasn't really an alcoholic. I wondered if I belonged in Al-Anon. Then I would buy some champagne and invite her to drink with me. It felt special, and I loved the sense of contact again. For a while, I believed that everything would be OK. It was worth it to have a sense that we were a family once again, even if it was all an illusion. Soon I'd be miserable and scared again and back to Al-Anon. That back and forth went on for months.

The family member who first stops denying often has a tremendous sense of guilt. Adult children of alcoholics are often the first and only family members to step out of a long history of denial as they make the decision to join a group for the adult children of alcoholics (Brown and Beletsis, in press). The labeling and decision to seek help for themselves feels equal to abandoning their family. Many feel like orphans, having authored their own abandonment by giving up denial.

Support groups are as important and beneficial to family members as they are to the alcoholic. Individuals require a great deal of advice and active support for their new identity and the new behaviors that accompany it. Most important, the focus needs to remain on alcohol. The support groups, Al-Anon, Al-Anon for the adult children of alcoholics, and Alateen, provide that focus.

Once again, the primary therapeutic modalities are behavioral and cognitive to provide the essential support for establishing the new identity and the congruent behaviors that accompany it.

> During the times when I felt clear that my wife really was an alcoholic, it was easier to follow the suggested behavior of Al-Anon friends. I used to rehearse in my mind: "My wife is an alcoholic so I must not buy her alcohol." When I would waiver in my knowledge of her alcoholism, my behavior followed suit. "If my wife's not an alcoholic, it's OK to buy her booze."

Early Recovery

The period of early recovery is also similar for family members. It is a time for building and solidifying the new identity and behaviors that accompany recovery. It is a strengthening of the processes of disengagement and detachment. The partner learns that this "letting go" of responsibility for the other is not necessarily equal to abandonment, nor is it tantamount to separation or divorce. Many partners remain with the active alcoholic while pursuing a course of recovery themselves. But it is difficult.

Just as the "nonrecovering" spouse and children of the recovering alcoholic may feel abandoned and competitive with AA, so too does the alcoholic respond to the loss of the partner's preoccupation. There is likely to be a great sense of schism in the family as recovering individuals break their denial and begin to construct and reconstruct their "stories" based on their new identities as individuals related to an alcoholic. That new construct may run head on into the continuing denial of others, particularly the alcoholic, and result in estrangement.

The partner feels a constant tug to give up the new identity in the service of patching the schism it causes. It is tremendously difficult for the spouse to hold on to the new identity while continuing to live in the family environment that supports its denial.

> I needed a lot of support early on. When I was in an Al-Anon meeting I knew that what I heard was true. But when I was home, the old feelings and attitudes resurfaced, and I had to fight to hold on to my new beliefs. I had to call people a lot especially from home to remind myself that my new knowledge and my new ways of behaving were correct.

The partner may end up leaving the alcoholic or remaining in the marriage while stepping out of the system. Steinglass (1980a) and others have described the various family patterns and homeostatic adjustments families make. It is an arduous task for the family member who is alone in recovery to hold onto it. When denial is maintained by the alcoholic and not by the spouse, the need for a narrow alcohol focus continues. The partner must be constantly reminded of the reality and therefore stay close to the alcohol axis, which emphasizes a continuing cognitive and behavioral focus. Movement into ongoing recovery may be a longer process because relinquishment of the alcohol focus carries the threat of the loss of identity. The lure of old beliefs and attitudes and the promise of "reunion" that goes with it is a continuing threat.

Family members who are in early recovery may have continuing difficulties detaching from the alcoholic. This may be extremely difficult if the alcoholic is also in early recovery. Family members may experience a constant fear that the alcoholic will start drinking again. They may become over protective and extremely cautious in their own behavior and interactions, lest they cause problems that they believe would precipitate a drinking episode. Family members are still preoccupied with the alcoholic and with control. They have simply switched from trying to get the alcoholic to stop to making sure the alcoholic doesn't start again. Engaged in worrying about and protecting the newly recovering alcoholic, family members may still feel controlled by the alcoholic, who retains a position of centrality in the family by virtue of everyone else's continuing concern.

Members of the family may feel neglected and jealous of the newly recovering person's attachment to AA. They may be struggling with their own difficulties of early attachment to Al-Anon. Instead of relief at newly acquired sobriety, more tension is experienced. It is not unusual to hear family members report, in retrospect, that a return to drinking by the alcoholic was welcomed with relief.

> We could stop worrying that it was inevitable. We could stop living on pins and needles, smelling Mom or looking for signs that she was sneaking. All that worry was over once she started again.

The amount of control now claimed by the sober alcoholic may also cause discontent. Greater limits may suddenly be imposed on children, and the non-alcoholic partner, used to complete authority, must now share with a partner who wants a responsible role in the family again.

Relinquishment of drinking and of denial by all family members may uncover additional severe disturbances in any or all family members. The alcoholic may be struggling with wide mood swings, including severe depression. The alcoholic may be less capable of shared involvement and interaction than when drinking. All attention is focused on alcohol and not drinking. The spouse and children may have great difficulties accepting the more disturbed alcoholic and the role of "partner" to that disturbance and the process of recovery dictated by the identity "coalcoholic." The partner and children may also have difficulties accepting the status of "identified patient." The partner who accepted the blame for the alcoholic's drinking may resist the Al-Anon emphasis on looking only at the self as a focus of change.

The most appropriate therapeutic treatments remain primarily behavioral and cognitive, strengthening the new identity as a member of an alcoholic family and the new behaviors that accompany it. Dynamic exploration may now be an important addition, serving to facilitate or strengthen the cognitive and behavioral emphasis. Uncovering unconscious factors may be useful not only to understand blocks in accepting the new identity. It may serve as the beginning of the process of the fourth step inventory, centered on increasing self-exploration and self-knowledge.

All of these therapeutic tasks take the focus off the individual's preoccupation with the partner or parent and place it on the self.

Ongoing Recovery

The process of ongoing recovery for the coalcoholic is similar to that for the alcoholic. The new identity and behaviors are stable, enabling the individual to examine other issues and problems. The person may be active in the 12 steps, beginning the process of close self-examination and may benefit much from concurrent psychotherapy.

The therapist must be equally skilled and attentive to the patient's need for an alcohol focus and the patient's ability to tolerate increasing anxiety and self-exploration. While the partner of the alcoholic may not have to fear a return to drinking as the alcoholic does, when anxiety is high, the partner may continue to fear the loss of the new identity and a return of the old feelings and actions of helplessness and overcontrol. The coalcoholic may have other psychological problems to deal with and require a traditional psychotherapeutic approach to do so.

In the process of ongoing recovery, it is extremely important for therapist and patient to give alcohol its due importance. At all stages of the continuum, there is great danger for both patient and therapist to ignore or underestimate the influence of alcohol and the alcoholism of another. Both patient and therapist need to understand the significance of alcohol to the development of the individual within the family. However, the cognitive and behavioral aspects of recovery will have solidified, and, therefore, the major emphasis can be on dynamic uncovering self-exploration.

The process of ongoing recovery will follow the same cycles as for the alcoholic. The individual will maintain contact with Al-Anon to renew and revive the alcohol focus and thereby strengthen the cognitive and behavioral aspects of recovery. With the alcohol focus as a base and new core identity, the individual ventures farther and deeper in self-exploration and new interpretations of self and others.

Work with the adult children of alcoholics (Brown and Beletsis, in press) uses a developmental process of recovery recognizing the different position of the children. It begins with the breakdown of denial and acknowledgment of the alcoholism of one or both parents. The process of psychotherapy for the adult child of an alcoholic is one of "growing up, growing out, and coming home" (Brown and Beletsis, in press). It starts with the relinquishment of denial and the beginning process of disengagement. The adult children are still overly attached to the family of origin and often to the alcoholic. The individual needs to give up the sense of responsibility for making the parent well and the hope of getting the care and attention never received. It is a painful and difficult process.

The process of "growing out" follows the course of early recovery. Individuals begin to construct a new identity that incorporates the realities of parental alcoholism. This process involves the painful recognition of loss and deprivation.

"Coming home" involves resolution. It is an acceptance of the reality of what happened. Individuals have made their past real through the process of reconstruction. Acknowledgment of the realities of the past frees them to turn their attention to the present and to make new choices.

For the spouses and children of alcoholics, the process of recovery is one of relinquishment of responsibility of the alcoholic and a shift from a reactive posture in which someone else, the alcoholic, is always in control. This involves a focus on the self. Each member of the family requires the building of a new personal identity that facilitates movement toward autonomy. Therefore, each member requires the role of "identified patient" and a treatment that addresses the changing needs of that individual. There is nothing more damaging than a treatment approach that continues to give the alcoholic priority and views the family members as important only to the degree that they have a role in continuing to help the alcoholic.

PART THREE

AA and Psychotherapy

Chapter 9

Partnership:
AA and Psychotherapy

ESTABLISHING A PARTNERSHIP: KEY ISSUES

One of the main goals of this book has been to encourage a positive attitude between AA members and professionals and to outline a model for achieving a working partnership.

Most professionals are supportive of AA, but from a distance.They are wary of the "religious" bent (Mack, 1981), and perhaps in conflict with its nonintellectual nature (Kalb and Propper,1976). Most professionals do not understand the process of change that occurs during recovery. And they do not understand how the"program" of AA, and in particular the 12 steps, facilitate that change. For most professionals, AA remains a mystery. They may heartily endorse membership but feel removed from the basic tenets. This lack of understanding and distancing results in an incorrect appraisal of what happens in AA, or a negative assessment based on a surface appraisal and standards typically used to evaluate psychotherapy outcome, such as improvement in function.

Is AA so radically different from traditional, uncovering psychotherapy? On the surface it looks that way. How then can the two work in partnership? More than 10 years ago, we (Brown and Yalom, 1977) began our first research effort aimed at developing guidelines for integrating AA and psychotherapy. At that time, we began a three-year research project to assess the usefulness of traditional, long-term interactional group therapy with alcoholics. That project demonstrated that, once committed to the process of psychotherapy (in this case group), alcoholics benefitted as much or more than nonalcoholics involved in a similar therapeutic process (Yalom et al., 1978).

In the beginning stages of that work, we were surprised by the difficulties we encountered in combining AA and psychotherapy (Brown and Yalom, 1977). We encouraged concurrent membership in the therapy group and AA based on our belief that the two types of approaches could be not only complementary but synergistic. But dual membership was not a simple matter. Several patients joined, almost as a public service or an extention of "12th step work," to help Stanford learn about alcoholics. These members emphasized their AA affiliation in ways that were inhibiting to the therapeutic process. One member, who was angry and suspicious of the medical profession, viewed the therapy group as an intruder into "AA territory" and entered the group not to do personal work but to protect others from the therapists. It was difficult for other patients to counteract the pressure of the few who, though well intentioned, were in therapy for the wrong reasons and impeded the development of the group.

The therapists were overly cautious not to fall into the stereotypes of the "ignorant professionals" described by alcoholics, and they tried to construct a bridge between AA and the therapy group by integrating some AA principles (for example the serenity prayer) into the group work. These attempts contributed further to the dissonance.

As time passed, the therapists pursued their own approach and focused less on tenets held in common with AA. Some members who had great difficulty with the combination dropped out of the study. Others maintained a dual affiliation for a long time. They, in fact, became advocates for unflinching self-reflection as well as abstinence. They understood that AA and the therapy group served very different functions in their recovery, and when the therapists acknowledged this difference, work proceeded more effectively.

The therapists never doubted that AA dealt more effectively with drinking and the maintenance of abstinence. Although this group project preceded the research on recovery among AA members, the therapists intuitively recognized that issues of alcohol and abstinence belonged in the domain of AA. Several members who used AA regularly as a safeguard for their abstinence felt more secure about tackling other problem issues, particularly interpersonal issues emerging in the therapy group. Such a positive combination was precisely our initial goal.

In the end, the therapists understood that the relationship of the therapy group to AA was more complex than originally thought. There were more often differences in degree and accent than differences in direction. The issue of dependency provides an example. AA attempts to gratify dependency needs (Zimberg, 1982). New members are encouraged to rely on AA, on the other members, and on a "higher power" to remain abstinent (Beckman, 1980). They are urged to attend frequent meetings where they can feel comfortable, accepted, and cared for by the membership. They are advised to avoid anxiety-provoking situations. They are fed coffee and cookies, they are nurtured, and they may call for help at any time of the day or night. The heavily ritualized meeting gratifies the need for guidance and structure.

The therapy group, on the contrary, satisfies dependency needs only enough to keep the patient in therapy. Members are often frustrated; they are asked to take active responsibility for the conduct of the meeting and little advice is offered. They are encouraged to interact with each other to the point of discomfort and then to keep communicating, to plunge into the discomfort still further.

Despite these different approaches, personal autonomy is the final goal of both groups. Although AA members are urged to rely heavily on one another and on a higher power, they are also repeatedly confronted with the issue of personal responsibility. In both AA and group therapy, patients learn that, though others may offer temporary help, it is they and they alone who in the end decide to drink or to abstain.

Optimally, a solid, continuing membership in AA frees members to participate fully in the therapy group. AA serves as a support system that helps members with their concerns about alcohol and permits them to tolerate the frustration of the therapy group. Problems arose when members felt that commitment to the therapy group was a betrayal of AA, that one membership excluded the other. The fact that the two groups had very different procedures continued to be a source of conflict for some. AA meetings are heavily structured, with here-and-now interpersonal interaction strongly discouraged. Some members found it difficult to make the necessary behavioral adjustments, and the therapists had to tread tactfully; on the one hand, they supported and encouraged membership in AA, and simultaneously tried to help members unlearn the heavily ritualized AA interactive mode (Brown and Yalom, 1977).

That work and the preceding conclusions formed the structure of our work over the next 10 years as we began to recognize the different therapeutic needs of the alcoholic. The research project with members of AA outlined stages in recovery and provided a better base from which to design, implement, and integrate treatment. The continuum of recovery provided further guidelines for partnership and outlined key issues requiring constant attention.

The Alcohol Axis: A Guide to Treatment Focus

The research project substantiated our original belief that the alcohol focus belongs in the domain of AA where issues of staying "dry," identification as an alcoholic, and readily available, active support are stressed. As members move away from concerns about alcohol and identity into the area of sobriety, psychotherapy stands ready to facilitate deeper exploration into other problem areas reflected in the expansion of the continuum. The critical task for the psychotherapist is to maintain a constant balance between support and deeper exploration. That balance may be gauged by the degree to which alcohol, staying dry, occupies a primary focus and the degree to which the individual is aware of and disturbed by other pressing concerns and able to relinquish an alcohol focus. The more solid the base of abstinence, the more exploration possible, although the interplay is continuous with drinking an ever present threat. The solidity of the base is related to length of sobriety, but also to the kind and degree of other concerns. The need for ongoing careful assessment of the solidity of the base of abstinence on an individual basis remains a critical requirement for both patient and therapist.

For a partnership to work, the therapist must allow the central base of identification and the most important commitment to be AA. The patient's primary loyalty is likely to remain with AA, and it is important that therapists do not feel threatened or competitive for this loyalty. But how can this primary loyalty operate when the clinical literature stresses overwhelmingly that AA is an important "adjunct" to psychotherapy (Bean, 1975b; Kinney and Montgomery, 1979)? The difficulties in effectively combining AA and psychotherapy are illustrated by our experiences with patient anxiety.

Anxiety

In our group therapy project we accented the need for the therapist to provide more structure and support. In that group of newly abstinent individuals, we found that therapists struggled against the members' resistance, extreme caution, and outright fear to establish norms of openness and self-exploration. The therapists at first made the error of responding in an overly protective manner to the members' anxiety. Their caution reinforced the patients' denial and created a restrictive guarded group culture. Though most members of the group had achieved abstinence and stability, the desire to drink and the fear of slipping were pervasive concerns that haunted every meeting. The therapists faced a dilemma: They believed conflict and anxiety were necessary for change, yet they were affected by the members intense fear of drinking. The therapists had hoped that abstinence would free members to look beyond the issue of drinking, but they realized that although they desired change, many patients who were abstinent felt they had so much to lose that they resisted engagement in the therapy process. It seemed an unfortunate paradox that members who had made such a great gain, abstinence, were limited by it.

AA members were very protective of one another to ensure that no one drank. A conspiracy of silence developed regarding any material that conceivably could create discomfort in another member.

Avoidance and Denial

The therapists contributed to group avoidance and denial. They tried to deemphasize the importance of alcohol but actually reinforced its importance because they too were so intimidated by the possibility of a drinking episode. The therapists encouraged self-exploration and interpersonal interaction yet felt guilty and responsible when patients drank to deal with the anxiety that arose from such interaction. Gradually, as the therapists realized their part in maintaining the group dilemma, they changed their tactics. They pointed out the options available to members: to remain static with comfortable but limiting defenses or to take the risk and discomfort of struggling for change. The therapists emphasized that growth could not occur in an atmosphere in which members felt a guilty responsibility for each other's actions.

To help patients cope with anxiety, we developed a number of structuring techniques (for example, written agendas for each meeting, and video recordings and playback) (Yalom, 1974) and cognitive aids (for example, written editorialized summaries of each session that were mailed to members between meetings) (Yalom et al., 1975). The written summary has been particularly effective in reducing anxiety and reinforcing the educational process of early sobriety.

Our work in succeeding years has clarified the difficulties we faced in the first groups. We had mixed individuals who were drinking with those who were newly abstinent with those who had longer sobriety. The combination was not appropriate to dynamic psychotherapy. The development of a continuum provided the guidelines on which to base the kind of group and selection of members.

Cyclotherapy

The process of change in recovery is, as we have discussed at length, characterized by a slow underlying current of progress. On the surface of this steady movement are cycles of improvement, high insight alternating with retreat into old behavior, attitudes, and high anxiety. Extreme fluctuations in mood are common, especially in early sobriety, with patients often experiencing severe cycles of depression and dysphoria. Our recognition of this process (Brown and Yalom, 1977) prompted us to characterize the process of change in recovery as one of "cyclotherapy," with patients fluctuating in mood and behavior. The uncovering of other issues and problems takes the individual away from the alcohol focus and sets the task for the role of psychotherapy in recovery.

PARTNERSHIP IN ACTION

Individual Therapy

Whereas group therapy for alcoholics has long been considered the treatment of choice (Stein and Friedman, 1971; Fox, 1962) and often described in detail (Blume, 1978; Kanas, 1982), individual therapy is, in fact, extremely valuable and underrated as an important therapeutic treatment. During the drinking stage, the individual therapist can help identify and label alcohol as the problem and help the patient deal with resistance to accepting this reality. Individual therapy can be particularly useful in uncovering the meaning of alcohol and of being alcoholic, critical factors that may be impeding movement into abstinence. The individual therapist can help with blocks or difficulties in the transition and early recovery phases. Many individuals adjust easily to the group format of AA and the group emphasis in a treatment hospital. For these, individual work may be purely supportive or a backup for its smoother progression.

Many individuals do not readily accept AA or feel comfort within the group setting. Individual therapy can be and should be used to answer questions for individuals who might otherwise "fall into the cracks." What stands in the way of progress and abstinence? What is interfering with acceptance of alcoholism? What factors are likely to impede the maintenance of abstinence?

"Falling into the cracks" is a failure to move into abstinence that could be remedied. These are individuals who have a strong desire for abstinence but are unable for some unknown reason to sustain it. Individual therapy can be extremely helpful in understanding the underlying dynamics, such as the meaning of being alcoholic, that may be getting in the way.

It is in ongoing recovery that the use of individual therapy can be most beneficial and most complementary to AA. The base of abstinence is established and the behaviors to maintain it are secure. The individual does not now have to stop and focus on behavior in order not to drink. The identification as an alcoholic is also secure, although the meaning attached to "being alcoholic" will change as abstinence progresses and the process of self-exploration deepens.

The following brief case examples illustrate diagnosis and treatment planning using the model. They illustrate the importance of determining three major factors in evaluation: 1) the degree to which the patient recognizes alcohol as a problem, 2) the degree to which the treatment focus needs to be on alcohol, and 3) what the meaning of alcohol and/or alcoholism is for each individual. They also reflect the diversity of patients seeking treatment. That at least one-half of those seeking treatment are already recovering alcoholics or family members of alcoholics underscores the need for a continuum for alcoholism that includes abstinence. The examples are presented in phase order beginning with the drinking alcoholic who seeks treatment, proceeding to the alcoholic attempting to stop, the sober alcoholic, and finally family members and friends.

The Drinking Alcoholic

Mr. S is a 46-year-old male who sought counseling after a traffic ticket for drunken driving. He denied that he had an alcohol problem but anticipated that therapy would be helpful in reducing his sentence. The patient wished to be seen individually and would focus on the issue of alcohol only in relation to controlled drinking. Following a careful assessment of the degree of importance of alcohol to the patient and his preoccupation with it, the therapist recognized that the task of therapy would be concurrent development of support and the erosion of denial, which would permit the patient to acknowledge his isolation, withdrawal, and the reality of the overwhelming focus on alcohol that guided his life.

Mr. S remained in therapy for more than a year. During that time, he reduced his drinking and "experimented" with abstinence. These efforts were still designed to prove that he could control his drinking. He refused to go to AA.

Mr. S terminated treatment when he took a new job in another city. In the course of his treatment, he had become concerned about his drinking and could acknowledge the reality of its consequences. He spoke about the pain of his isolation and his continuing belief that he needed alcohol to relate to others. Mr. S left treatment with the hope that he could still drink.

This important example illustrates the inability of the therapist to make the patient change. Despite the focus on alcohol and the erosion of denial, the patient did not reach a point at which he wanted to stop drinking.

In working with such patients, it is extremely important for therapists to remember the significance of the long-term perspective. This was the first therapeutic intervention for Mr. S with several more to follow. The therapist needs to see him or herself as one part of the long-term continuum of recovery and an extremely important part even if the patient does not alter drinking behavior. The path toward abstinence usually includes the intervention of many people. In the case of Mr. S, the therapist was the first to actively focus on alcohol. Mr. S's physician would be next, expressing a concern about the patient's drinking.

Three years later Mr. S was again arrested for drunken driving. On this occasion he was required to enroll in a six-month educational program that included mandatory attendance at AA. Mr. S's wife was now threatening divorce, so Mr. S and his wife entered couples therapy for their marital problems. Drinking was only rarely discussed. Finally, Mr. S was fired. He became severely depressed and entered an inpatient treatment program for alcoholism. With several months of recovery, he told his group that the loss of his job was the turning point. He had always believed that he couldn't be an alcoholic because he had never lost his job. When he did, he knew he was alcoholic and began his process of recovery.

With several years of recovery, Mr. S looked back. He always remembered the importance of his first therapist. He could talk openly about things that worried him. He knew he wasn't ready at that time to "be" an alcoholic. But he didn't fool the therapist and he knew that too. He now speaks of that first confrontation with his drinking as an important step in his progression toward recovery.

The Alcoholic in Transition

Unfortunately not all individuals follow the same ultimate positive path. Many do not reach recovery, and many get stuck along the way, with helpers participating in the denial (Krueger, 1982; Zimberg, 1982). Mr. S's therapist could accept his role in the long-term progression, hoping a foundation would be laid on which others could build. The therapist could "let go" of his patient, knowing he did not collude, but that he still could not provide the wish for abstinence for his patient.

Ms. M is a 33-year-old female farther along the continuum at treatment entry. At the transitional point between drinking and abstinence, she wishes desperately to change but is unable to do so. She experiences an emotional and even physical "paralysis" most of the time, with occasional short cyclical bursts into abstinence and then back again into drinking. Ms. M utilizes very little denial, her deep internal division and ambivalence being painfully conscious. She describes a tremendous fear of AA and abstinence, both of which equal the loss of herself and the loss of control. In her internal schema, a retreat to isolation and alcohol represent her control.

The therapist needed great tolerance for shifting back and forth between drinking and abstinence with the patient, always providing a safe climate for both risk and retreat. A therapist who does not understand the cycles may put undue pressure on the patient or become hopeless when abstinence is not maintained. Ms. M was terrified of AA. She spent days working up the courage to attend one meeting. When she did so, she sat by the door and left early. She then spoke in therapy about her fears and her sense that she could not survive an active involvement in AA. She imagined being "swallowed up" and being unable to defend herself. She admired the people she saw, but their success at abstinence also made her feel like "scum." Ms. M cycled in and out of attendance at AA. She achieved eight days of abstinence and was suddenly terrified. Somebody congratulated her and she had to flee.

Ms. M never denied that she had a problem with alcohol. "Being" alcoholic seemed better than being no one at all if she stopped. Ms. M required intensive psychotherapy to help her move into abstinence.

Mrs. G comes for consultation at the transition stage. Her husband has been confronted about his alcoholism by his business partners and has already entered an inpatient hospital. Mrs. G wants immediate help for herself and her children. She is both frightened and relieved at her husband's departure, but terrified at what will happen to all of them. She acknowledges that she has "known about" her husband's alcoholism for sometime, but she just couldn't ask for help.

Mrs. G and her children are seen individually. All are given a referral to Al-Anon and Alateen. Treatment is initially supportive with much education and information about alcoholism offered by the therapists.

Mrs. G is anxious to help her husband and wants to be supportive of his abstinence. But she rejects the idea that she "participated" in his developing alcoholism; that she is a "coalcoholic," a term she has heard at the treatment center, is at first unacceptable. Later, acknowledging that she is "coalcoholic" is a relief. She, like her husband, can now explain her own behavior on the basis of her reaction to her husband's drinking and her denial of his alcoholism. As she begins to construct reasonable explanations for her own behavior, she feels less guilty about what she did and did not do for herself and her children.

When Mr. G is out of the hospital, all participate in several family therapy meetings. These are designed to emphasize the necessity for each member of the family to be involved in his or her own program of recovery. Family therapy is geared toward helping the members separate and relinquish responsibility for one another. Often, families need help in permitting and understanding the process of separation while also remaining intact. Kaufman and Pattison (1982) provide a detailed framework for using family therapy with alcoholics.

The Alcoholic in Early Recovery

Mr. R, a man in his late 50s, provides an example of a patient in early sobriety. Just out of a four-week hospital stay, he wishes to strengthen his abstinence with continuing supportive and uncovering therapy. He has identified several problems that could interfere with his abstinence and wishes to focus on them. But alcohol remains the key focus in his life and the focus of his therapy because of his position in early abstinence. Identification as an alcoholic and practical concrete advice on staying sober are both important. Denial of other issues may or may not be supported by a therapist in this situation, depending on the relationship of the issues to the individual's sobriety. Mr. R recognized the problems and saw clearly that they would interfere with his sobriety. His marital difficulties required examination and focus because of his wife's tendency to interfere with his sobriety. The design of therapy included a mixture of individual supportive treatment and couples work as well, since his wife was willing to be involved.

The therapist helped Mr. R identify individual problems. He had no hobbies or interests and recognized a need to develop some. He was also unhappy with certain aspects of his job and eventually needed to address these as well. But the marital difficulties were primary.

Mr. R denied that his wife's continued drinking and her initial refusal to seek any treatment would interfere in any way. The therapist disagreed, pointing out the dangers, even if no solutions to the problem were feasible.

Mr. and Mrs. D are a couple, also in their late 50s. Though Mr. D has been sober for three years, alcohol is still a major issue for both. Mrs. D blames their current problems, mistrust and anger, on 30 years of active alcoholism. Mr. D is farther along the continuum of recovery than Mrs. D, who continues to operate at an earlier stage, relating to her husband as if he were still drinking. The task of the therapy is to sort out what is related to alcohol, such as past resentments, and what are inherent problems that were previously covered by alcohol and continue to be covered by an alcohol focus. This couple uses alcoholism to avoid examination of their difficulties. The therapist must see a focus on alcohol and alcoholism as a defense which must be confronted rather than supported.

As couples therapy progressed, it became clear that Mrs. D could only relate to her husband from an angry, punitive stance. She needed to hold onto her rage at her husband for drinking. She could not relinquish this focus and so could not keep up with her husband's pace of recovery. Each was referred to individual therapy in addition to couples therapy.

Mrs. D could not tolerate the anxiety she felt when she tried to talk about herself rather than her husband. She tried to write down her thoughts but only became confused and more anxious. Only when she was raging at her husband did she feel "OK." Both the individual and the couples work frequently stalled. Mrs. D cancelled appointments or dominated the session with angry outbursts. Eventually, Mr. D joined a group for individuals in ongoing recovery and he and his wife separated.

The Sober Alcoholic

Dr. R is a woman with five years of sobriety. She had been depressed for about six months and could not seem to snap out of it, even though she had been able to "work her program" and use her sponsor for this purpose in the past.

She sought individual psychotherapy to begin a long-term process of uncovering work. In the early years of her recovery, she had few memories of her childhood and no affect attached to the few memories she did have. She knew it was time to try to open up what was a very painful childhood characterized by fear, emotional deprivation, and frequent abandonment by her parents. The depression was triggered by her sponsor's decision to move to a far away city.

Mrs. H, in her late 40s, has been sober for 13 years. She is quite far along the continuum of recovery and seeks treatment in a special group for the adult children of alcoholics. She has recognized through her years of recovery that her feelings about her alcoholic father continue to interfere with her present daily living. A more traditional uncovering psychotherapy focus is in order, with very little focus given to the patient's own alcoholism as a current problem. Mrs. H uses AA to maintain sobriety and wishes to use psychotherapy for deeper personal exploration. But, Mrs. H requests a therapist that is also a recovering alcoholic. Even though she has been sober for many years, she is still very anxious about the possibility that the therapist will not understand the significance of her own alcoholism and her need for continuing involvement with AA. The therapist must tailor a program that will enhance the use of both therapies.

Mr. W, a young man in his late 30s, is a partner in a small chemical company who seeks consultation because his partner is an active alcoholic who is causing embarrassment anhd financial difficulties for the company and all the employees. Mr. W describes his company and their involvement in the owner's alcoholism in a way identical to that of the family. In an effort to save the business, Mr. W works overtime covering up and "protecting" his partner. He is no longer succeeding at undoing all of the damage and is now seeking professional advice. He is discouraged, frightened, and very angry. Consultation takes the form of direct advice and information, outlining possible courses of action available to Mr. W. Therapy is brief and action-oriented to what he can and cannot do to help himself, his company, and his partner. Mr. W and his company provide an example of the extremely wide range of people affected by one individual's alcoholism. All of these case examples emphasize the importance of tailoring treatment to each individual's need.

Intervention and treatment of family members can occur at any point on the continuum as illustrated in Chapter 8. An additional example of a family in ongoing recovery again illustrates the use of the continuum.

Mrs. Smith has been sober and an active member of AA for four years. Her husband attends Al-Anon. Her two teenage children occasionally attend Alateen, but do not identify themselves as active members. Mrs. Smith calls for family counseling, with behavior problems of their 16-year-old son the triggering factor.

The family begins counseling together. Serious problems are soon revealed in the relationship between the parents. Both feel alienated and very distant from the other. Initially, mother's alcoholism is not mentioned except peripherally: Everyone is happy she is sober and proud of her. With time, mother's recovery becomes the focus of many of the difficulties. Family members resent the time and attention she gives to AA and her refusal to go along with the family's wishes if they conflict with her own. Family members feel caught in a bind: They want Mom sober, but they also want her to be more available than she feels she can be.

Family therapy centers on clarifying everyone's dissatisfactions and then examining minor and major adjustments that would give all family members a clearer and more consistent sense of mother's care, even if she is not always available. The therapist relies heavily on his knowledge of the Al-Anon program to help all family members clarify what they are and are not responsible for.

Determining Psychotherapeutic Treatment Based on the Continuum

Krueger (1979) makes a strong case for the importance of proper assessment in determining the most appropriate treatment. The continuum of alcoholism has provided us with a much improved framework for determining the task of therapy and the most suitable treatment approach at any given time. The choice of treatment or combination of treatments is directly related to the stage of recovery.

Group Therapy

Drinking, Transition, and Early Recovery

We offer no groups for patients who are still drinking. Instead, individuals who are concerned about their alcohol consumption are seen individually and advised to begin AA. The abstinent group culture of AA provides the positive base for identification necessary in early abstinence and establishes the person who continues to drink as deviant. A therapy group composed of drinkers who are uncertain about their desire for abstinence and unknowledgeable about the steps necessary to achieve and maintain it is likely to create a group culture in which the abstinent individual is deviant. Our experience further demonstrated that members who are abstinent feel they must assume the responsibility for helping those who are not. Persons who continue to drink are seen as the most needy and often claim the group's continuing attention and concern. Those who desire abstinence may feel that their sobriety is at stake in the group and the culture that continues to value drinking.

Even if AA members are successful in avoiding the assumption of responsibility for drinking members, they are still impeded in their uncovering work by the presence of drinkers. AA members do not trust the drinker to be a stable commited group member, and, therefore, it is difficult to begin a process of increasing self-exploration and vulnerability. AA members registered their belief that drinkers in the group "think" differently and therefore cannot empathize with the recovering person. In essence, the AA group member meant that the drinker still believes in control and therefore would interpret himself and others from that framework (Brown and Yalom, 1977). The presence of drinking members who still believe in the feasibility of control can be a severe threat to a sober alcoholic, particularly if there are fewer abstinent members.

We have developed a group program based on stages of recovery. Individuals in the transition and early recovery stages join a group for "early recovery." It is highly structured, with maximum support. The focus of the group's work is predominantly on alcohol, facilitating identification and examination of problems that members encounter in early abstinence. Group members may introduce "topics" similar to those discussed in an AA meeting. The group format, which permits and encourages interaction and feedback provides a complementary structure to the noninteractive AA mode.

Uncovering psychotherapy and interpersonal confrontation are minimized. The therapist stays clear of initiating interpretations and interventions that will elicit uncovering of problems and differences between members. Unless initiated by members, the emphasis in early recovery is on establishing similarities around the focus on alcohol.

Ongoing Recovery

Ongoing recovery permits and even demands an interactive, process-oriented group experience. An early recovery group may evolve into an ongoing group, with the focus shifting from alcohol to other issues. Or, individuals who have not been in psychotherapy in early abstinence may now enter a group, wishing to complement and enhance their AA work. Recognition of differences and interpersonal feedback are now a key part of the group's work, rather than the emphasis on support based on similarities. Members expect that abstinence is stable so the work of the group can focus elsewhere.

Individuals in both groups may have "slips." Drinking always supercedes any other personal issue and the individual must shift to the alcohol focus. The individual may require individual sessions and must shift back to a primary focus on AA, but the group does not necessarily have to shift as well.

A therapy group with a culture of abstinence and shared AA experience can direct the drinking member outside the group and back to AA, where attention to drinking is the primary concern. The person does not have to leave the group, but neither does the group need to halt its work until the individual stops drinking and catches up.

Group members and therapists need to be tuned to the possibility that uncovering group work is too threatening and thereby contributes to the slip. Certainly in early recovery, all group members are wary: The fear of drinking and the reality of drinking are regular issues. In ongoing recovery, the fear is less intense but nevertheless an underlying concern. Both therapy groups require the constant assessment of the balance between support, with an alcohol focus and more challenging uncovering psychotherapy.

Group work is only one part of the therapeutic program that uses the continuum framework to determine therapeutic strategy. Many persons seek individual therapy or couples and family work in addition to their AA and Al-Anon participation.

Couples and Family Therapy

There is often a great push for family members to "get the family back together." Everyone is frightened at the rupture experienced by the alcoholic's movement into abstinence. Family members may be threatened by the loss of the alcoholic to AA. As one individual stated:

> My sobriety has meant a big adjustment for my wife. I used to get my therapy with her over a bottle of wine. Now I go to AA and don't need her anymore. She keeps pushing for family therapy because she wants the therapist to tell me to come home. I need to focus on my alcoholism and staying sober. I can't tolerate the family pressures right now.

Family therapy was useful for this couple to clarify the importance of an individual focus at this stage. Tom reassured his wife that he cared, and the therapist explained the reasons why each family member needed to get help individually. The therapist then outlined ways in which the couple could share the new knowledge each had gained independently.

Too often, therapists and families rush in during the transition or early abstinent phases to patch the family up. While this may be reassuring to frightened family members, a family focus at this stage runs the serious risk of shortcutting the individual processes of new identification and new learning that are absolutely essential to sustaining long-term abstinence:

> I couldn't stay sober after leaving the hospital. My husband and kids were happy with my sobriety but very upset that I wasn't staying to the end of dinner, or even

putting much effort into making it. My husband said it was OK if I went to meetings as long as I didn't fail in my responsibilities at home.

I couldn't do both. I felt so guilty. I should be staying home to make up for all the lost years of drinking when I wasn't available emotionally to my family.

It didn't work. I ended up in the hospital again after drinking. I needed those AA meetings, and I needed not to worry about dinner. This time, we had a number of family meetings to explain to my husband why I needed more time away from the family in order to *stay* sober. He finally understood. After quite a few months, I could choose to be home with my family again and turn my attention back to them without having to drink to do it.

In early recovery, family intervention needs to be geared toward a focus on alcoholism and recovery and the emerging differences for each member. In ongoing recovery, couples and family therapy designed to examine interactions and to deal with such issues as intimacy, sexuality, finances, communication, responsibility, and compromise is appropriate. When individuals have established a separate identity, they can move from that base of autonomy to a focus on interdependent relationships. It is often an extremely difficult process. For individuals in AA, the process of self-exploration deepens through the work of the 12 steps.

A PSYCHOLOGICAL VIEW OF THE TWELVE STEPS

As discussed in Chapter 1, many observers of AA have catalogued their impressions and hypotheses of the organization to explain its success. Some of these are personal or subjective appraisals; others are much more objective, based on a particular theoretical framework (Beckman, 1980; Kurtz, 1982; Maxwell, 1984; Thune, 1977; Alibrandi, 1982).

The interpretation that follows is quite personal and subject to my own bias. It has evolved from years of focused study of what happens to people after they stop drinking. Of course, it includes the model of alcoholism that is the core of this book. But it has included a close look at the 12 steps, from the point of view of comparison to the process of psychotherapy. A psychological interpretation of the 12 steps reflects my intent to bridge these disciplines and reduce misunderstanding that results in antagonism and mutual distrust. What happens in AA is what happens in good psychotherapy: increased self-knowledge and the potential for change. The function and the process of change are similar, although the forms and language may differ. Following is an interpretation of both the language and the process of change involved. This interpretation is a combination of clinical data, conversations with AA members, and a synthesis of the AA book, *Twelve Steps and Twelve Traditions* (AA, 1978).

Step 1:   We Admitted We Were Powerless Over Alcohol and That Our Lives Had Become Unmanageable. Many alcoholics resist the first step outright, maintaining that they are not "powerless" and that their lives are not "unmanageable." This step is directly related to the issue of control. Those who reject it believe they still can control their drinking.

Recovering alcoholics explain that powerlessness is the base for liberation. The acceptance of powerlessness signals an admission of defeat, the surrender necessary to move into recovery. The acceptance of "unmanageability" paves the way for a feeling of total defeat. The individual recognizes that the loss of control of alcohol has severe consequences in every area of life. The recognition of defeat and the feeling of "deflation at depth" are necessary for the individual to ask for help and mean it.

The extent of demoralization and desperation necessary to "hit bottom" illustrates why people do not embrace the AA program unless they have to, unless they see no other choice for survival and they do wish to survive.

Individuals report that self-confidence at the point of surrender and early abstinence is a liability. AA members are skeptical of the newcomer who is not scared, but feels instead that the problem is "licked." Individuals close to the point of surrender, or actually very defeated, may engage in psychotherapy with the hope of raising self-esteem, exactly at the point when they should be losing it if they are to sustain movement into abstinence. Many who are on the brink of surrender reject it by measuring whatever self-control is left. No one seeks or can will the absolute recognition of powerlessness and defeat that accompanies surrender. Yet, those in AA wish that the alcoholic still drinking will find his or her "bottom."

The admission of powerlessness is similar to a feeling of desperation or failure at self-help that moves many people into psychotherapy. To seek treatment and make use of it, people must accept that they need help. Yet most individuals resist the feelings that go along with needing help. A belief in the value of self-control carries over. Many individuals feel that they should not have to ask for help, and that to do so is an admission of failure. In fact, many patients and therapists alike believe that the process of psychotherapy should lead to "self-control." Ironically, people seek help for the purpose of not needing any in the future.

The program of AA and the 12 steps are based on the continuing acceptance of loss of control and the need to continue to ask for help. Many professionals interpret the continuing reliance on an external source of help (the higher power) as a failure rather than the opposite—a giving up of a belief in the power of self with the recognition of an ongoing need of support (Mack, 1981).

The problem of recognizing the need for a higher power is that it often becomes another person, particularly the psychotherapist, AA sponsor, or spouse (Beckman, 1980). Individuals in AA assess the subtle but important distinction. Before abstinence, they invested their belief in a higher power in something else, the bottle or spouse, but they denied the unconscious and overt expectations of such dependency. They actually believed that they were self-sufficient, that they needed nothing from anyone. The outright acknowledgment of the need for dependency, on a higher power, is met with disdain and underlying fear. Other dependencies have been so destructive.

The therapeutic relationship is often affected by the same subtle but critical problem: how can the patient develop trust and a dependent relationship on the therapist when relinquishment of that dependency is the ultimate goal? Often, individuals cannot engage in the psychotherapeutic process because of a fear of the ultimate loss of the dependent relationship.

In AA, individuals never relinquish their belief and their dependency on a higher power, which they *define* and *create* as they progress through the 12 steps.

Therapists are often suspect of AA patients who believe they can change therapy groups or even individual therapists quite readily. Often these patients are judged as more disturbed because of their failure to develop a transference dependency. In fact, success in early recovery often rests on the unconscious refusal to do so. The safety of multiple dependencies and many meetings allows individuals to survive the desperate helplessness and deep dependency needs of early recovery.

Step 2: We Came To Believe That a Power Greater Than Ourselves Could Restore Us to Sanity. Once again, many people are put off by the language. The introduction of the term "higher power" creates defensiveness and puts people on the alert that this "is going to be religious."

The word "insanity" must be rejected by those who still believe in control. Others, who are warding off the recognition of total unmanageability, resent the implication that they have been insane. Many protest. In the research sample, respondents made a clear distinction between "mental illness" and alcoholism.

I didn't belong on the psych ward. I'm not crazy. I'm an alcoholic!

In the AA book, *Twelve Steps and Twelve Traditions,* new members are advised to keep an open mind. This step paves the way for what AA calls continuing "ego reduction." A belief in a "power greater than self" is incompatible with feelings of grandiosity and omnipotence.

The belief in a higher power may be, on the surface, incompatible with the belief system of professionals who see that the individual is trading one dependency, on alcohol, for another. It is difficult to see that the dependency on a higher power counters omnipotence (Mack, 1981).

A similar process occurs in psychotherapy as people begin to believe in a process and to trust it. The belief by the therapist that he or she is the agent of change simply reverses the problem of omnipotence. The patient is wise not to trust such a therapeutic relationship. Beckman (1980) addresses this issue very well.

Step 2 allows AA members to remove themselves from an "ego-centered" position in the world. Stepping out of the center is the key to the new view of self and world described by Bateson (1971) and Tiebout (1949). It is directly related to an acceptance of loss of control and a belief in a power greater than self.

Individuals in AA and psychotherapy who do not have a concept of a higher power or a positive background of religious belief in God often substitute faith in the group and in individuals who are "making it" (Stewart, 1955). Rather than expecting that someone will give it—the cure, enlightenment—to them, they find that it is the process of being in the AA group (or therapy) and their involvement in it that leads to change.

Individuals have plenty of models to observe in AA and they grow to trust in the process though most cannot say "how it works." Members are likely to refer people to the Big Book to answer that question. What they do know is that they "come to meetings," "put the plug in the jug," "listen to others," and "rigorously work the steps." All of these suggestions require the initiative and active participation of the individual.

The "12 by 12" (*Twelve Steps and Twelve Traditions*) suggests that a philosophy of self-sufficiency, which goes against a belief in anything greater outside the self, results in anger and fear. The belief that "I am the ultimate power" results paradoxically in a reduction in feelings of control. The therapist may argue that the goal of therapy is to achieve a feeling of control. So too in AA, but it is achieved by acknowledging loss of control. Individuals become more independent by accepting their dependence.

The same process can occur in psychotherapy. Ironically, AA members grow to believe that dependency is not a bad thing, while many individuals outside of AA continue to believe the opposite.

Step 3:   We Made a Decision To Turn Our Will and Our Lives Over to the Care of God As We Understood Him. Step 3 often causes the greatest initial furor and anxiety. It is step 3 that prompts newcomers to wonder about "this God business." Individuals are advised to stick around. It takes time to integrate the meaning behind the language.

AA members describe this as an "action step": make a decision that also cuts away at self-will and omnipotence. New individuals often ask incredulously, "I am going to accept that I don't have control over my life?" AA members stress that this step requires an attitude of willingness and a commitment.

The paradox stands out immediately. Individuals are instructed to "let go" and put their trust in a higher power. Yet, they soon recognize that they cannot will themselves to do so. They cannot put their mind to it. Letting go results from surrender. The absence of a higher power often keeps individuals who are not in AA from being able to recognize their own lack of control. For many, the existential crisis of life is the absence of something to believe in (Kurtz, 1982; Yalom, 1980).

The process of psychotherapy involves rigorous self-examination with the purpose of revealing to oneself areas of denial, self-delusion, and vulnerability. Often, insight illuminates previous self-deception. Frequently, that deception includes a belief that the individual has power and control over others. Many individuals believe that relinquishment of this belief will result in total loss of self or annihilation.

Step 4: We Made a Searching and Fearless Moral Inventory of Ourselves. The fourth step is called in AA a moral inventory, terminology that often rebuffs the observer. Yet its meaning is very similar to the overt process of psychotherapy. Individuals are instructed to begin a process of critical self-examination. They are to list their liabilities and their assets as a beginning step to ensure that they are not overly focused on the negative.

Many inpatient programs include instruction on step four as a part of the treatment program. There are booklets that offer guidelines as well.

Step 4 offers the beginning of what will be an ongoing process of self-psychotherapy. It is the beginning of a new course of honest self-appraisal aimed at breaking denial and providing a realistic portrait of the individual. The fourth step teaches people how to look at themselves honestly. It encourages recognition of character defects and strengths.

The terminology may cause difficulties for professionals. They may chuckle at the term "character defects" and groan at the idea that AA members might start with the seven deadly sins as a guideline for self-examination. The language and framework are both out of the context and experience of the psychotherapist. The process is not. What do people in psychotherapy talk about? Their fears, needs, angers, and resentments. In psychotherapy they learn from others and by revealing to themselves how these feelings, attitudes, and beliefs structure their view of the world and may get in their way.

Individuals in AA and psychotherapy experience relief at facing themselves. After the acknowledgment of defects, psychotherapy patients and AA members both experience a reduction in fear and feelings of futility. There is a beginning recognition of the degree of denial and defenses exercised to maintain self-deception. Members may feel hopeful and discouraged at the same time. The process has now started, not ended.

Step 5: We Admitted to God, to Ourselves, and to Another Human Being the Exact Nature of Our Wrongs. Step 5 is likened to confession, which is also a concept of religious origin. AA members stress for newcomers that the function and not the form are important. They suggest that members put their faith in the doorknob if nothing else is safe. But they have to put it somewhere.

Telling God and someone else removes the feelings of secrecy that were an important part of denial. When the abstinent person tells another what she or he did, that person steps out of the secret and the isolation necessary to maintain it. Individuals can then begin to feel a sense of relationship to others as part of a larger whole, so important to Bateson's and Tiebout's schemas.

Telling relieves the individual of feelings of loneliness and often the sense of never having belonged. The individual is accepted by the listener, who in AA often has a worse story to share. According to the "12 by 12," the AA member gets the feeling that she or he can be forgiven and is able to forgive as well. Discussion with another breaks the barrier of self-delusion. Self-esteem rises as a result of the acceptance of another.

This process of piercing rationalizations and self-delusion and acknowledging the realities of past behavior and beliefs is central to psychotherapy. It is often difficult for patients to allow themselves to share their inadequacies when they do not know that the therapist is also imperfect. The story, or "drunkalogue," in AA and the sharing of experiences provide evidence of their similarities to others. No matter what awful things the alcoholic has done, someone else has done them too.

People in AA often report a feeling of tremendous relief and "rebirth" after the fifth step. Acknowledging the realities of the past and accepting responsibility for them relieves the individual of guilt and frees the person to start anew. Failure to acknowledge the past keeps individuals tied to it. The process of telling reduces feelings of self-importance. One cannot hold onto an inflated sense of one's self based on "crimes" committed when someone else has done the same.

It appears on the surface of an AA meeting that members enjoy dwelling in the past, chuckling at the drinking, and even competing to outdo one another. But much of the emphasis of the 12 steps is on the present: what beliefs guide members and what action individuals are taking.

Step 6: We Were Entirely Ready to Have God Remove All These Defects of Character. Again, there is reference to God and the implicit acceptance of a deferent position. Most significant in step 6 is an attitude, a readiness to devote a lifetime to the development of openness and willingness. This change in attitude signifies a commitment by the individual. As the result of working the preceding five steps, the person can feel a sense of being "part of" something bigger accompanied by a forward momentum. Many people in AA chuckle at the subtlety of step six and the paradox: loss of control is once again emphasized.

Became ready! That's the hard part. As much as I want to change, I find I want to hold onto my beloved character defects.

Who wants to give up defenses and character traits that seem to have served well? Bean saw that AA brilliantly allows members to hold onto their defenses and low self-esteem for as long as necessary. This phenomenon is similar to the process of psychotherapy, particularly "resistance." It is difficult for individuals to recognize negative or self-defeating traits and beliefs and just as difficult to relinquish them once acknowledged. Often the struggle in psychotherapy centers on making the commitment to look deeper and then to be willing to change basic beliefs. When people decide to "look," a positive alliance can be formed. People often talk about the process of change in psychotherapy and AA as "two steps forward and one back."

Step 6 holds within it the recognition of partnership between the individual who is responsible for developing an attitude of "readiness" and the higher power that is given the task of accomplishing that goal by the individual.

Step 7:   We Humbly Asked Him To Remove Our Shortcomings. Step 7 is the action that follows from step 6. Relinquishment of control and the recognition of a higher authority are implicit again. Some say step 7 offers the key to humility. The individual has stepped out of the center and has no hidden agenda. That is, the individual is not divided, complying on the surface but still believing in the power of self underneath. There is no unconscious contradiction beneath the attitude of readiness in step 6 and the seeking of God's power in step 7. Steps 6 and 7 reinforce the concepts of surrender already developed by steps one through five.

Step 8:   We Made a List of All Persons We Had Harmed and Became Willing to Make Amends to Them All.

Step 9:   We Made Direct Amends to Such People Wherever Possible, Except When To Do So Would Injure Them or Others. Steps 8 and 9 are action steps dealing with personal relationships. The language, "amends," is once again not part of everyday vocabulary and often strikes the observer as corny or certainly as unfamiliar. But the task and meaning are clear. Individuals are directed to take stock of the people they have harmed and to become willing to acknowledge that damage and make restitution if possible.

As in earlier steps, there is recognition that acknowledgment of wrongs and a change in attitude come first. Doing something directly to right the wrong follows. Bean (1975a) points out the recognition in AA of the profound emotional work that precedes behavioral change. The reference to "became willing" underscore this point. Individuals in AA point out that, while it may look like the making of amends is designed for the recipient, in fact this is only partly true. The acknowledgment of people harmed is primarily for the individual doing it. It is "making real of the past" and an assumption of responsibility for harm caused.

There is a tremendous release of guilt in the unburdening process of listing all those the individual hurt. As psychotherapists will recognize in their patients, the honest acknowledgment of truths about the self frees people to move ahead. The inability to acknowledge responsibility for past aggressions and harm results in continuing guilt and an inability to move ahead in the present.

Step 9 is the action that follows the acknowledgment and development of willingness. The making of amends is the acknowledgment and acceptance of responsibility and restitution where possible. Individuals handle the making of amends differently. As in the other steps, it is the doing that is important. Individuals must carefully assess when an open acknowledgment might be harmful to someone else and thus not undertake it directly. The example is given of the individual who was very promiscuous while drinking. Listing all of these episodes for his wife, after abstinence, would result in causing her further anguish. The individual is instructed to consider the welfare of the other. In this way, catharsis at the expense of another is discouraged (*Twelve Steps and Twelve Traditions*, 1952). If the other is not considered, the action of this step may be simply another replay of what AA members call "self-will run riot." That is, it is an exercise of the attitude of egocentricity and belief in self-power that characterized the drinking alcoholic.

The spirit of step 9 is the readiness of the individual to accept the consequences of harm caused to others in the past (and to continue these steps in the present) and to assume a degree of responsibility for the well-being of those harmed. That responsibility involves restitution where possible. The making of amends includes not only acknowledgment and apology, but correction and undoing if possible. Thus, one hears stories in AA of members paying back bad debts incurred many years previously in situations or with individuals long gone.

Underneath the action of these steps is the foundation already created by working the preceding seven steps. Individuals cannot "work" these steps with the old attitudes and the old frame of reference. One cannot be truly humble and deeply sorry if, underneath the acknowledgment, lies a belief in eventual "victory." The individual surrenders and accepts responsibility, but believes he or she will "rise" again. Or, the individual acknowledges responsibility but with an attitude of contempt for the victim, believing for example that the person "deserved it."

Individuals who progress through the steps with an underlying continuing belief in their own importance cannot experience the promised rewards. Individuals can work the steps superficially, but they may wonder why they don't feel better. So too, may individuals in psychotherapy approach that process. The hope is that self-examination will vindicate the patient rather than expose the attitudes and traits that maintain self-destructive behaviors and relationships.

Step 10: We Continued To Take Personal Inventory and, When We Were Wrong, Promptly Admitted It.

Step 11:   We Sought Through Prayer and Meditation To Improve Our Conscious Contact with God As We Understood Him, Praying Only for Knowledge of His Will for Us and the Power To Carry That Out.

Step 12:   Having Had a Spiritual Awakening As the Result of These Steps, We Tried To Carry the Message to Alcoholics and To Practice These Principles in All Our Affairs. Although the first nine steps do involve action, the last three are most often labeled the "action steps." The first nine steps deal with the "wreckage of the past," whereas the last three provide a design for daily living in the present. Psychotherapy often serves the same function: uncovering the realities of the past and changing the way of living in the present.

Step 10 is the daily equivalent of step 4, the moral inventory. This process of honest self-exploration is built in as a continuing part of daily living. Members do not "wipe the slate clean" with the fourth step. They are subject to continuing rigorous self-examination. This step allows people not to get stuck in perpetuating old attitudes and patterns that could lead to a return to drinking. Regular honest self-examination and continuing restitution are incompatible with drinking and the thinking that permits it.

Step 10 helps individuals develop self-restraint. Individuals must slow down and take the time for self-reflection to accomplish this step. The need to stop themselves builds in a mechanism of delay and therefore reduces the dominance of impulses.

Step 11 calls forth the "religious" orientation through the language and emphasis on surrender. AA members see the "spiritual" core of their program reflected in this step. Members join AA defeated, depleted, and without internal resources that would help them stay sober given a desire to do so. Members are not encouraged to try once again to "get a hold of themselves." Rather, they are discouraged. Others remind them that they did a pretty miserable job of running their own lives.

The development of a belief in a higher power and the principles of AA that embody such a construct are eventually internalized. Developing "conscious contact" results in the ongoing removal of self-will and a reinforcement of feelings of belonging. A paranoid attitude that the world is hostile cannot be sustained with an ongoing belief.

In the beginning of sobriety, these steps are foreign and without meaning. It is enough for individuals to concentrate on being powerless. With ongoing sobriety, however, the steps take on deeper significance. Many individuals return to a church they once abandoned or find new meaning in their religious life. Others study philosophy and eastern religion to broaden and deepen their understanding and application of the principles (Brown, 1977; Kurtz, 1982; Mack, 1981).

It is accepted and communicated in AA that newcomers will not comprehend the meaning of the steps at depth. The meaning is revealed to individuals and constructed by them only as a result of working the steps and proceeding through abstinence. How then can a newly sober member of AA use the steps if he or she can't make sense of them? The beauty and the brilliance of the steps lies in their concrete simplicity and the paradox embedded within them. The simplicity allows individuals of any educational level and current mental capacity to embrace the steps. The newcomer hears the first step of powerlessness and listens for instructions from others on what to do concretely. Individuals with long-term sobriety have built in the concrete behavioral aspects of the steps and now can begin more abstract interpretation. The "doing" of the 12 steps reflects the concepts of development outlined in Chapter 3: first behavior change, in tandem with cognitive shifts and, finally, the emergence of affect. The doing of steps is never finished. They provide an ongoing "philosophy of living" that provides a structure, a home base, and a new framework of interpretation.

Step 12 is the action key. People have been given the gift of sobriety and new belief. They experience a new consciousness and a new state of being. They learn that the most important way to maintain their new attitudes and beliefs is to give them away. Satisfaction and self-esteem are gained by "carrying the message." The sense of belonging is enhanced by the knowledge that every member of AA has something very important to give to another: the experience of drinking and the experience of staying sober, "experience, strength, and hope" as AA members tell it (AA, 1976). A member of AA poignantly recalls being allowed to help make coffee at a meeting.

> I was amazed and thrilled. Can you imagine what it felt like to know that I could contribute?

Individuals enter AA feeling desperate and awful about themselves regardless of external signs of hitting bottom. Individuals report feeling less than human, fed by a deep belief that they have nothing to offer. The first time they are asked to share, to talk in a meeting or to tell someone else how they did not drink one day at a time, and someone says thank you, is an overwhelming experience. To have something to give and to be able to give brings people back to the sense of belonging and fundamental equality.

"Twelve-step work," as carrying the message is called, can occur in many ways. It is best known and seen in movies as the person or team of AA members that comes to call on a drinking alcoholic who has asked for help. Not everyone works actively with a newcomer. Individuals learn that they are giving by attendance at meetings. Newcomers are informed that they are the "lifeblood" of the organization, necessary to the survival and continuing abstinence of the others. How? They remind the recovering person of "what it was like." The contact with newcomers counters the return of omnipotence that can easily creep in with the feelings of success that accompany long-term abstinence. Individuals see that they are "only one drink away from a drunk" and, therefore, bound tightly to one another regardless of length of sobriety. Individuals learn that survival of the group depends on acknowledging the priority of the group. The first tradition states, "Our common welfare should come first. Personal recovery depends on AA unity" (AA, 1976).

The 12 steps of AA outline a continuing process of change that is very similar to the long-term process of dynamic psychotherapy. Psychotherapists and observers of AA often miss the similarities. They are stopped in their understanding by a language and a form that is unfamiliar. Psychotherapists need to remember that it is the function and not the form that is critical. Psychotherapists can offer much help with the steps as a supplement to what the individual learns in AA. It is not at all unusual for AA members to seek psychotherapy for the purpose of a rigorous examination of steps 4 and 5. The therapist who understands what step 4 means can readily move to work in concert with the individual and AA, rather than against them.

Successful partnership is a difficult venture in any field or enterprise. It is especially difficult when basic values, beliefs, and attitudes appear to be in conflict or even incompatible. A successful partnership depends on a willingness by all parties to share their knowledge and to challenge their own negative stereotypes. Not all professionals are unknowledgeable about alcoholism or antagonistic toward alcoholics, and not all alcoholics mistrust professionals.

The bridging of AA and psychotherapy holds the promise of synergistic partnership. Each discipline has something critically important to offer the individual. Together, each is enhanced and the sum can be, indeed, greater than the parts.

Appendix A

The Model
in Clinic Practice

A COMPREHENSIVE TREATMENT MODEL

Origins of the Stanford Alcohol Clinic

The research project described in earlier chapters involved a detailed study of 80 members of AA and lasted three years. A major reason for the research was the hope of improving understanding of alcoholism between the non-AA professional community and the AA alcohol world. Respondents reported very unsatisfactory treatment experiences with professionals but a very great need for professional services, not only while drinking but, more importantly, during abstinence.

The knowledge gained from AA members' reported experiences with psychotherapy provided the impetus to improve traditional psychotherapeutic treatment. These experiences, coupled with the new process model that had evolved from the research, formed the theoretical and applied foundation of a new outpatient treatment clinic. Housed in the Department of Psychiatry at the Stanford University School of Medicine, the clinic was founded with the hope of bridging the best knowledge of traditional psychotherapy with the best knowledge of the AA alcohol world. It was founded on the belief in the positive synergistic potential of such a merger.

Alone, the professional treatment community has failed to understand the needs of the patient and to provide a theory and practice necessary and suitable for the long-term recovery of the alcoholic. AA has provided a much stronger theory and practice for successful long-term recovery. Yet many members of AA recognize the need for professional services that will enhance and build on the AA recovery program. The long-standing lack of these professional services is a severe problem which this book has attempted to address. The clinic was opened in the fall of 1977 with two primary goals: treatment and training.

TREATMENT

The clinic brochure suggests that treatment services are available to anyone with any concern about alcohol. This paves the way for inclusion of individuals at any point along the continuum.

Alcohol Clients

Individuals in the early stages of developing alcoholism may wish to examine their drinking or obtain information about alcohol and alcoholism. Individuals who are actively concerned about a drinking "problem" may explore their concern. There is no demand for abstinence as a condition of entry. The clinic does not assume responsibility for any person's abstinence or for the choice to abstain or not. The clinic provides a forum for individual exploration and decision making. It provides the knowledge about treatment resources suitable for different stages on the continuum and can help individuals determine the most appropriate treatment or combination of treatments.

Approximately one-fifth of the clinic's patient population are drinking and concerned about it at entry. The population of the clinic reflects the emphasis on recovery and the usefulness of psychotherapeutic services for abstinent individuals. One-third of the clinic's population are recovering alcoholics. Some of these entered treatment while drinking and remained through their continuing abstinence. These individuals begin with individual consultation, add attendance at AA, and perhaps add an "early recovery" group designed for individuals in the early phase of abstinence. These supportive groups are primarily focused on alcohol to strengthen the new behaviors and thinking patterns of abstinence. Other newly abstinent individuals enter the early recovery groups after discharge from an inpatient alcohol treatment program. In keeping with the phase concept, individuals in ongoing recovery may enter ongoing recovery groups. Early recovery groups may evolve into ongoing groups, individuals may shift membership, or individuals with long-term AA abstinence may now join an ongoing recovery group as an adjunctive therapy to their AA. These groups are less alcohol-focused and much less oriented to providing concrete behavioral and emotional support to help members maintain abstinence.

Individuals in ongoing recovery groups have an established base of abstinence (typically AA), so the group work can center on deeper exploration of problems previously covered by alcohol or developed in relation to or as a result of recovery. These groups are much more dynamically oriented and often very much focused on the here-and-now process (Brown and Yalom, 1977). Although members and therapists are very aware of the ongoing significance of alcohol, too much attention to it may be interpreted as a defense against deeper exploration. Members and therapists share an expectation that group members already know how to stay abstinent and will take the necessary steps to do so.

Individuals concerned about their drinking or recovery may be in individual treatment instead of, or in addition to, group therapy. Many begin with individual therapy to explore their concern about alcohol, add AA and abstinence, and continue with individual psychotherapy. The length of time varies according to the individual's need and the nature of the therapeutic relationship. Individuals often wish to maintain an attachment to the therapist or to the alcohol clinic, which become a symbolic representation of the new abstinent identity similar to AA.

Others may find the individual psychotherapeutic relationship too threatening during early recovery and terminate, focusing their treatment attention on AA. These individuals may periodically return to psychotherapy throughout their abstinence. Many enter individual psychotherapy after months or years, even many years, of abstinence. They are deeply involved in the work of the 12 steps and wish the additional support of a trained professional. The alcohol clinic provides the professional who is skilled in traditional psychotherapeutic theory and practice and is knowledgeable about alcoholism and the changing needs of the alcoholic. These individuals add psychotherapy to an already stable program of recovery.

Adult Children of Alcoholics

The population of the clinic is not composed solely of people concerned about their own drinking or already self-identified as alcoholics. At least one-third of the patients enter treatment as the adult children of alcoholics (ACA). These individuals may or may not be alcoholic themselves (both active and recovering). What is most significant is the identity as the child of an alcoholic(s) and the need for treatment that addresses that identity.

The clinic offers both group and individual treatment for this population. It is not unusual for individuals who are very concerned about their own drinking to more easily enter treatment on this basis. It is important for the therapist to determine which emphasis is most appropriate: Will the treatment identity as the child of an alcoholic promote the individual's acceptance of his or her own alcoholism or will it divert attention? There are no clear answers. Clinical experience tells us that many individuals seek help earlier when their own drinking is not designated as the primary issue.

The therapist must be able to determine when a patient's drinking is already so advanced or debilitating as to require treatment intervention first. The therapist may have to reroute the patient to alcohol treatment before admitting the person to an ACA group. The therapist informs the patient that the drinking will interfere with the individual's treatment and with the therapeutic work of others in the group. This may, indeed, constitute a diagnosis of alcoholism before the patient's readiness to accept it. Admitting a severely advanced alcoholic to a dynamic uncovering ACA group may seriously hamper the group's work. ACA individuals find themselves in a familiar role, having to deny the new person's obvious drinking problem as they denied parental alcoholism or coming to the rescue and targeting the work of the group toward getting the person in treatment. Obviously, it is impossible to always determine the best initial focus, but there is greater responsibility on the therapist to make the diagnosis of alcoholism. The therapist who denies the obvious colludes with the patient and may seriously disrupt the work of the ACA group.

Many of the ACAs seeking treatment are not concerned about their own drinking or they are already recovering. They wish to explore the deep meaning of being the child of an alcoholic and the central significance that alcohol played in their lives. Many enter treatment with severe problems in interpersonal relationships, difficulties establishing trust, problems separating emotionally and physically from the family of origin and depression (Cermak and Brown, 1982). Traditional dynamic uncovering psychotherapy is the most useful treatment, but must be combined with knowledge about alcoholism. It is not unusual for ACA patients to report having spent years in traditional psychotherapy with only a bare mention of parental alcoholism. The focus on alcohol is just as important for the ACA as for the recovering alcoholic. That identity provides the same central ordering and organizing schema. ACAs begin a similar process of recovery, reconstructing and constructing their personal identities from the new identity as the child of an alcoholic.

Coalcoholics

Individuals enter treatment because of a concern about someone else's drinking—spouse, partner, or employee. This individual, called the "coalcoholic" in alcohol terminology, is the person who participates in the thinking disorder of alcoholism and helps sustain the closed system. Since Joan Jackson (1954) outlined the serious difficulties for the wives of alcoholics, more attention has been focused on those closely related to the alcoholic. Still, the nonalcoholic partner, as with the child of the alcoholic, has always been viewed in relation to and subordinate to the drinker. This person has never had the opportunity to be the primary patient.

Al-Anon reflects the understanding of making each individual the identified "patient." Al-Anon members quickly learn that they will not find a formula to fix the alcoholic, nor a forum to express their continuing unhappiness or martyrdom. Instead, they will be encouraged to see themselves as the person needing and seeking help and to focus on self-examination and change just like the individual in AA.

The clinic offers the same opportunity. Family members who are concerned about someone else's drinking may get help for themselves. This will include referrals to Al-Anon and often substantial education and information about alcoholism. In addition, it may involve individual or group psychotherapy, following the same continuum as that for the alcoholic.

The partner with a drinking spouse may need help eroding denial and changing behaviors that have been supporting the drinking. The spouse whose partner is in a hospital or outpatient treatment program requires the same kind of support, education, and behavioral learning as the newly recovering alcoholic. The focus on alcohol is equally important for the spouse, although often a serious bone of contention. The partner often is as disturbed in behavior and thinking as the alcoholic, particularly if the denial has been maintained for a longer time.

Such recognition is often difficult for the partner to accept. The individual may wish to maintain the alcoholic as the identified patient, refusing to see him or herself as part of a disturbed system. The partner wishes to bypass the work of early recovery with its emphasis on new behavior and new identification. Instead, he or she wants the now sober alcoholic actively involved in the family, making up for what was previously lost to alcohol. It is a difficult but necessary therapeutic task to integrate an individual focus on alcohol for all family members with a corresponding attention to family and interpersonnal relationships. Too often, the individual emphasis is bypassed with the unfortunate result that basic new behavior patterns and new ways of thinking are not established by any member of the family.

Key Factors in Comprehensive Treatment

The success of the comprehensive treatment model rests on several key factors. First, a successful bridging of discipline: Therapists must be able to merge traditional theory and practice with knowledge about alcoholism and AA. It also requires a clear understanding about the developmental nature and the stages of recovery. Without an understanding of the normative experiences of abstinence, the therapist will almost certainly interpret various aspects of the patient's early recovery development as a regression instead. Knowledge about the model is also essential in providing thorough individually tailored diagnosis and treatment planning. The therapist must be able to tailor and modify treatment components according to the progression of alcoholism or abstinence. A single treatment psychotherapy, theory, and practice simply won't work.

Can a single therapist provide all services and treatments? Hardly. But a single therapist can provide the range of behavioral, cognitive, and affective foci if the therapist is willing and able to switch role and preferred treatment. Often psychotherapists define themselves according to "school" and stick closely to that theory and practice, be it behavioral, cognitive, or dynamic. The therapist defined to one "school" may have considerable difficulty recognizing and responding to the changing needs of the patient. It is difficult for many therapists to see that active teaching and education are within the boundaries of the therapeutic role. These may fall too close to the giving of "advice," which many therapists avoid. At certain phases along the continuum, the giving of advice, if sought or obviously needed by the patient, is essential. At another stage, the giving of advice may be much less important or therapeutically useful.

What is called for is the ability of the therapist to use a variety of therapeutic schools, tools, and strategies and to be able to determine when each mode is necessary. Trainees often report with great excitement and exasperation that they find themselves a behaviorist, cognitive therapist, and uncovering dynamic therapist all within the same psychotherapy hour.

The therapist who is fluid about changing role and who does not lose self esteem when operating out of a preferred mode will be most successful in following alcoholics through the progression of recovery. The therapist who is not comfortable switching role or treatment may wish to more actively use consultants to fill in the necessary gaps. Such a therapist has to believe that multiple sources of therapeutic help are enhancing the patient's growth rather than detracting from it. The greatest danger is the psychotherapist who believes that the one-to-one individual therapeutic dyad must be the only treatment over time.

As a part of the notion of integrated treatment and the use of multiple treatment resources, the clinic also works closely with private psychotherapists in the community. These therapists may refer a drinking patient for an "alcohol consultation." The clinic therapist serves as a consultant to the patient and to the primary therapist, with the task of focusing on drinking. This delicate but extremely useful collaboration allows the private therapist, who is likely not a specialist in alcoholism, to continue with his or her patient while isolating and emphasizing alcohol and providing the additional services necessary to fully deal with it.

Several private therapists accompany their patients to the consultation to ensure support and to reduce fears of abandonment. Some therapists also acknowledge their own lack of information about alcoholism and their wish to learn from the consultation as well. The alcohol therapist then outlines a treatment plan that might include a hospital program or an early recovery group and always includes the suggestion to attend AA.

All of these suggestions may be carried through without disrupting the primary treatment bond. The primary therapist participates in the formulation and thereby communicates permission to the patient to follow the treatment plan. This cooperative consultative mode reduces the fear of the psychotherapy patient that he or she has to choose between therapy and AA. Private therapists often refer their patients for group work while continuing to see them individually.

TRAINING

The second major goal in establishing the Stanford Alcohol Clinic was training. Lack of education and training for all helping professionals is a serious practical and ethical problem. Yet, professionals (from physicians of all disciplines to psychiatrists, psychologists, social workers, and marriage counselors) are expected to be, and often believe that they are, knowledgeable in the diagnosis and treatment of alcoholism. Thus, much of the treatment world proceeds in ignorance of their own actual lack of information and knowledge (Bissell, 1982). This uncorrected problem continues and contributes much to the animosity and hostility between the professional and alcohol worlds.

We hoped to address this significant problem directly by developing a combined treatment and training program in a medical center. The development of this program verified both our own belief in the lack of knowledge and the positive potential for synergistic partnership that corrects it.

Elements of The Training Program

The training program was designed initially to provide clinical course work and applied practice to residents in psychiatry. It included the scope of diagnosis, referral to other treatment resources, and the inclusion of traditional psycotherapy, thus using the model. Our training and educational experience also verified the importance of attitude and epistemology.

By the time professionals have reached their advanced training or even before they start, the society's predominantly negative moralistic attitudes toward the alcoholic are well established. So is the intellectual belief in control. Training must begin at the level of epistemology, the same beginning required for unraveling the denial of the drinking alcoholic.

This foundation is often uncomfortable and even unacceptable for many trainees. There is comfort and certainty in viewing the alcoholic as morally inferior, suffering from a lack of will. It is professionally reassuring to believe that there is an answer for alcoholism, that there is a way to fix it, without giving up the substance. Thus, the notion of control is appealing to all. Finding a solution that embraces control disturbs no one's basic view of the world.

Acceptance of loss of control challenges the desire and belief of the professional and particularly the physician who has learned how to diagnose, treat, and cure in many instances. Alcoholism awakens and illuminates the basic helplessness, powerlessness, and the ultimate inability to control that characterize all human beings. No other illness so magnifies the fallibility of the human condition. It is a difficult task to teach the phenomenon of loss of control. It is extremely difficult to teach it to those who have never experienced it, or who have denied such a fundamental experience.

It is difficult to convince professionals that recovery is possible if they have never seen or worked with a recovering individual. Physicians are often the most difficult to teach because they have been exposed repeatedly in their training to the most advanced and medically ill alcoholics. Until recently, it is only the most advanced who have received a diagnosis of alcoholism. Thus, the alcoholic whom physicians are most likely to acknowledge is the one unfortunately labeled as hopeless who has, perhaps played out a "revolving door" pattern. Thus, negative attitudes are reinforced.

Physicians and trainees who have the opportunity to hear and work with a recovering individual have the opportunity to challenge and broaden old attitudes. Therefore, training for professionals includes exposure to recovering individuals and the AA alcohol treatment world. All trainees at the clinic are encouraged to attend AA meetings and a recovering alcoholic tells his or her AA story to the training class. Many trainees and professionals have strong resistance to attending AA themselves. Many do not follow through with the suggested assignment.

Many are afraid that they will be "mistakenly" identified as an alcoholic if they attend a meeting. It is frightening to imagine being seen as an alcoholic by someone else. In supervision, we examine the roots of this fear and what attendance at AA, even as a visitor, says about them. The reluctance to be identified as an alcoholic often carries with it underlying meanings and attitudes about alcoholism just like it does for the patient. Trainees may equate alcoholism with being weak, shameful, disgusting, and out of control. "What if I see someone I know?" If the trainee is going to show up at an AA meeting, it had better be confidential: "If I see someone I know, what will that person think of me?" Of course, the trainee is also concerned about the opposite: "Will someone in AA be embarrassed by my observance? What if I see one of my patients?"

Following through on attendance at AA reduces the fears and most often reveals deeper attitudes the trainee holds that will certainly interfere with treatment. Attendance also cuts away at the omnipotent, superior attitude of the therapist. While some attend an AA meeting and remain detached, seeing only that the program is beneficial for "those" people, others recognize their similarities and can find a common ground of identification even though it might not be around alcohol. It is important to be able to see how they are just like the alcoholic. The ability of the trainees to recognize their personal addictions is extremely valuable. This ability automatically includes the acceptance of loss of control. It is not necessary to be an alcoholic to work with alcoholics. It is useful to have had a personal experience with loss of control and to understand, at depth, the reality of loss of control and the difficulties in altering behavioral and thinking patterns.

Often trainees return from an AA meeting with the surprising realization that the people in AA, the recovering alcoholics, are just like them. However, seeing that is not easy for everyone. Why not? An important part of a professional's attitudes and beliefs about alcohol and alcoholism have to do with that individual's own drinking behavior, the drinking of a partner or spouse, and the personal and family background in relation to alcohol. It is difficult for students and professionals to examine their attitudes and beliefs about alcohol without considering their own drinking. This, of course, can be extremely threatening to a professional who is alcoholic or is denying the alcoholism of someone close.

Children of alcoholics are often attracted to the helping professions. It is not unusual to find that a significant percentage of any training group grew up in a family in which one or both parents was alcoholic or they had a close relative who was alcoholic. Their personal experiences, beliefs, and attitudes related to alcohol and alcoholics form the core of their professional attitude.

Close personal supervision or psychotherapy for the trainee may be essential to working through the attitudes and biases that interfere with treatment. It is unrealistic and incorrect to assume that a professional with an alcohol problem (the individual's or someone else's) will be able to adequately work with alcoholic patients without ever examining his or her personal difficulties. The difficulty and the threat keeps many helping professionals ignorant or resistant to working with alcoholics. It is not unusual to hear professionals report that they don't see alcoholics in treatment. What the professional means is that overtly alcoholic patients are not accepted. But what also is meant by many is that the therapist really doesn't "see" alcoholism. It remains undiagnosed. Failure to diagnose is, as noted earlier, one of the most bitter and frequent complaints registered against therapists by their former patients (Brown, 1977).

The drinking practices of the student and professional are not the only issues that can potentially interfere. What about the drinking practices of teachers, staff, supervisors, and colleagues? It is extremely difficult to alter one's traditional attitudes and beliefs about alcoholism when the change will threaten denial about the drinking of someone who is an idealized mentor or respected colleague. The old attitude still prevails. It is difficult to acknowledge that alcoholism is as pervasive among helping professionals as it is among the general population including all social classes.

Trainees often report a startling consequence of their experiences in class and in learning about alcoholism first hand at AA. It is as if they have opened their eyes and they now see alcoholism everywhere. This recognition stirs mixed emotions. It is exciting to break through their own filter of denial and to be able to recognize and diagnose alcoholism. It is distressing to observe their own behavior and that of their friends in their social milieu. For most trainees, the sudden vision is shocking. For those who do have difficulties or potential problems with alcohol, the new vision is unsettling and often frightening.

It is not the responsibility or the role of a training program to actively "treat" any trainee. It is, however, the duty of the program and supervisors to help trainees understand when and where their personal biases or problems with alcohol may interfere. In some cases, it may be essential to suggest that the trainee seek professional help.

Trainees are not only encouraged to attend AA. They are also exposed to inpatient alcohol programs and residential recovery homes, spending time in training if possible.

The professional needs to actively "cross over"—to go to the alcohol world. And, those professionals from the alcohol world, recovering alcoholics from AA and treatment staff in inpatient and residential programs, must "cross over" too, exchanging information and learning from nonalcohol-identified professionals as well.

The Stanford program brings the alcohol world to its training program. It goes out through community education and representation in the alcohol world. Professionals from the clinic offer seminars and inservice training to alcohol agencies and treatment centers, teaching the new model of alcoholism and how to gain cooperation and multiple referrals. Clinic professionals illustrate the value of psychotherapy and its place in the continuum of treatment.

Is it necessary to be an alcoholic to treat an alcoholic? No. Some of the staff at the clinic are recovering alcoholics and some are not. However, it is necessary to have the proper training. Staff of the clinic are all trained in traditional psychotherapeutic theory and practice before coming to the alcohol clinic. At the clinic, they receive specialized training in alcoholism that requires them to modify their traditional approach. What this means for many is the undoing, or at least the rattling, of a comfortable theory and method.

Such bridging of theory and treatment requires tremendous flexibility and ego stability on the part of the staff. Clinic conferences almost always generate theoretical and practical disagreements that have no textbook solution. Integration of theory and treatment involves a high tolerance for ambiguity and uncertainty, not an easy task for any therapist.

The clinic believes firmly in the value of research and the major potential impact of research conducted from the treatment and training base. There is much to learn about alcoholism and the continuum theory of recovery from its application in the clinical setting, and there is much to learn about clinical theory and practice as well.

There is a vast untapped body of knowledge to uncover and discover about the children of alcoholics, with great potential impact on all helping professionals and suffering individuals. There is much to learn about training and education for professionals. What is necessary and how do we achieve it? How do we ask difficult questions about beliefs, attitudes, drinking practices, and clinical practices in a culture that strongly supports denial and a belief in control? Alcoholism is a difficult field to work in, yet it is an extremely rewarding one for those who understand their own lack of control.

Introduction to
Appendixes B through H

The following appendices are taken directly from the original research project (Brown, 1977) described in Chapter 2. Appendices B and C present demographic characteristics of the research sample and the breakdown of patients by age, sex, and length of sobriety. Appendix D is the detailed questionnaire that provided the report of AA members' experiences in abstinence. (Respondents also took several psychological tests that are not described here.)

Content analyses of the questionnaires provided the information in Appendices E, F, G, and H and the base for developing the multidimensional model of alcoholism presented in Chapter 2. Appendix E presents frequencies of specific questions relating to the categories of AA, alcohol, and alcoholism. These responses portray members' participation in AA, length of membership, attendance at meetings, and types of groups. It includes their views about the organization, the ways AA helps and does not help them, reasons for continued attendance, and their general view of recovery.

Recovering alcoholics do not just stop drinking as Appendix F illustrates. In outlining their experiences with abstinence, respondents delineate a view of recovery that entails occupational adjustments, major life changes, the emergence of depression, suicidal feelings, and other disorders and symptoms with which they must cope. They elaborate on their own view of recovery, describing their levels of comfort and defining a broad range of experiences that they expect will occur.

Appendix G provides information on the decision to stop drinking and to maintain abstinence. The answers to these questions provided the key to the critical distinction between staying "dry" (not drinking) and remaining "sober." These questions demonstrate the significance of time, individual differences, and the importance of a developmental framework (key issues defined in Chapter 2).

Appendices E, F, and G accent the significance of at least three tracks of movement and development in recovery. In the early days of sobriety, almost 20% of respondents noted difficulties with alcohol in addition to other problems such as emotional, interpersonal, and family troubles and difficulties coping with and tolerating pain. With the passage of time, the threat of alcohol and problems of staying dry decrease to only 6%, while other difficulties, encompassing the other work of "sobriety," continue and grow in importance.

Closer examination of these categories reveals not only the origin of the three-dimensional developmental model, but also the seeds for developing the hierarchy of behavioral, cognitive, and dynamic therapeutic tasks. The emphasis on dependency and behavior change was clearly emphasized in early recovery.

In the beginning, respondents rely heavily on external support from other AA members. Many rely on "meetings" and the "program" (the AA philosophy and way of life in its entirety including the principles known as the 12 steps), and tangible objects such as sweets, the telephone, or Antabuse. Eighty-two percent of these respondents accented external support without reciprocation in noting the kinds of support they valued "at first." There is increasing reliance on interpersonal support and the beginnings of a subtle shift from external to internal support. People report increasing self-reliance, internal spiritual support, and action in the form of 12-step work, which involves applying the philosophy of AA to oneself and in work with others. The notion of self-reliance or reciprocation now comprises 50% of responses.

More explicit changes are revealed when major turning points leading to abstinence are compared with major turning points important in maintaining abstinence. A theme of increasing failures and loss unifies the movement towards abstinence. Terms of self-disgust, self-loathing, and self-hatred characterize peoples' descriptions directly in 32% of responses. Fear, illness, blackouts, or suicide attempts comprise another 18%.

A theme of expanding awareness as a result of the change in frame of reference (identifying as an alcoholic) characterizes movement during abstinence. Different events and experiences occur that require new terminology and a new method of evaluation, making direct comparison fruitless. Few of the same categories are repeated. As Appendix G illustrates, 22% of the sample now referred to the "experiences of sobriety itself," "recognition of achievement," "feelings of self-acceptance," and "spiritual elements" in relation to their decision to maintain abstinence. A dramatic shift in tone occurs from drinking to abstinence as evidenced by the categories themselves. Respondents move from isolation to increasing involvement and from a passive recipient posture to one of active involvement and reciprocation.

Finally, Appendix H summarizes respondents' experiences and feelings about psychotherapy.

Percentages do not add to 100% because of multiple responses.

Appendix B

Demographic Characteristics of the Sample

Age	Men (N = 40)	Women (N = 40)
Average age	38	42

Marital status	Frequency
Single	29.9%
Married first time	25.6%
Married second time	9.0%
Divorced	33.0%
Widowed	2.6%
Married, living apart	2.6%

Education	
9–12 years	31.1
13–16 years	44.8
17 years +	23.1

Appendix C

Subjects by Sex, Age, and Length of Sobriety

Men (numbers)

Age	0–1 year sobriety	1–3 years	3–5 years	5+ years
≥ 35	5	6	5	7
≤ 34	4	8	4	1
Total	9	14	9	8

Women (numbers)

Age	0–1 year sobriety	1–3 years	3–5 years	5+ years
≥ 35	8	7	4	8
≤ 34	3	6	3	1
Total	11	13	7	9
Total sample	20	27	16	17

Appendix D

Questionnaire

Name _____   Address _____

Age _____   _____

Sex: Male _____ Female _____   Phone _____

1. Highest grade completed in school: _____

    1a) Highest degree received: _____

2. Current marital status: Single ____, Married first time ____,
    Married second or more ____, Married and living apart ____, Legally
    separated ____, Divorced ____, Widowed ____.

    2a) Have you been married before? yes ____ no ____

    2b) How many times? ____

3. Do you have children? yes ____ no ____ Ages & Sexes _____

    3a) Do your children live with you? yes ____ no ____

    3b) Have any of your children died? yes ____ no ____

    $3b_1$) If yes, please explain _____

4. When did you first attend AA? _____
                                       (month)   (year)

5. How long do you consider that you've been a member of AA? _____
                                                                    (months)

                                                               _____
                                                                    (years)

6. Does your spouse or the person closest to you approve of your coming
    to AA? yes ____ no ____

7. Does your spouse or the person closest to you attend Al-Anon?
    yes ____ no ____

    7a) Do any of your children attend Alateen? yes ____ no ____

8. How often, on the average, do you attend meetings of AA?

    five or more times a week ____, two to four times a week ____,
    once a week ____, once every few weeks, ____ once every few months ____.

9. How long have you maintained continuous sobriety? weeks ____ months ____
    years ____.

10. How long would you estimate that alcohol was a problem for you before you stopped drinking? _____
    (months or years)

11. Do you attend different groups of AA? yes ____ no ____

    11a) Are the groups you attend different? yes ____ no ____

    11a$_1$) If yes, please explain _____

    _____

    _____

    _____

12. Is there a history of alcoholism in your family? yes ____ no ____

    12a) If yes, please identify relation _____

13. Is there a history of mental illness in your family? yes ____ no ____

    13a) If yes, please explain _____

14. If employed, what is your occupation? _____

    14a) How long have you been working in this position? _____
    (months or years)

15. What did you do before? _____

16. How long were you working in that position? _____
    (months or years)

17. Did you need to make "adjustments" occupationally as a result of

    sobriety? yes ____ no ____ Please explain _____

    _____

18. What is your spouse's occupation? _____

19. Since becoming sober, have you experienced what you consider to be major events or changes in your life (for example: job, back to school, death, divorce)? yes ____ no ____ Please explain _____

    _____

    _____

20. Did you have any severe physical or emotional illnesses prior to becoming sober or since? yes ____ no ____ Any accidents? yes ____ no ____

20a) If yes, please explain _____

_____

_____

_____

21. In general, how would you describe your sobriety so far?

| easy to maintain | fairly easy to maintain | easy and difficult | fairly difficult | very difficult |

21a) Please elaborate _____

_____

_____

22. What would you consider to be the major problem(s) (conflict, character defect, etc.) you have worked on during your sobriety?

At first _____

_____

Now _____

_____

23. What kinds of support did you need at first? _____

_____

Now _____

_____

24. Have you experienced period(s) of depression since you became abstinent? yes ____ no ____

24a) If yes, how long after you became abstinent? _____

24b) How long did it last? _____

24c) How would you describe your depression? Light ____, moderate ____, severe ____

24d) Have you experienced more than one depression? yes ____ no ____

24e) Have they differed significantly? yes ____ no ____

24e$_1$) Please explain _____

_____

25. Have you experienced other disorders and/or symptoms since you became abstinent (for example, anxiety, phobia, ulcer, overeating, fears, etc.)? yes _____ no _____

    If yes, please explain _____

    _____

    _____

    _____

    _____

26. Have you ever felt suicidal since becoming sober? yes _____ no _____

    26a) If yes, please explain _____

    _____

    _____

    _____

27. Did you ever have psychotherapy prior to becoming sober? yes _____
    no _____

    27a) If yes, what year? _____

    27b)   what kind? _____

    _____

    27c)   how long? _____

    _____

    27d) Was it: no help _____, some help _____, very helpful _____?

28. Have you had any psychotherapy since becoming sober? yes _____ no _____

    28a) If yes, what year? _____

    28b)   what kind? _____

    _____

    28c)   how long? _____

    _____

    28d) Has it been: no help _____, some help _____, very helpful _____?

29. If you have not had psychotherapy, have you considered it? yes _____
    no _____

29a) If yes, what year _____

29b)   what kind _____

29c)   for what reason _____

29d) What made you decide against it? _____

_____

30. What do you consider to be the major problem(s) you faced in achieving continuous sobriety? _____

_____

_____

_____

31. What do you consider to be the major problem(s) you face NOW in maintaining sobriety? _____

_____

_____

_____

32. Please list what you consider to be major turning points and/or critical events leading you to abstinence. _____

_____

_____

_____

_____   _____

33. Please list what you consider to be major turning points and/or critical events in maintaining continuous abstinence. _____

_____

_____

_____

_____

34. Who or what people were most influential in your decision to stop drinking?

34a) Relation(s) _____

34b) How were they influential? _____

35. Who or what people have been most influential in helping you to maintain abstinence?

    35a) Relation(s) _____

    35b) How were they most influential? _____

    _____

    _____

36. Who has been the most meaningful person to you in your recovery?

    _____

    36a) Why? _____

    _____

    _____

37. Have you had any experiences since becoming sober which you feel are unique or relatively uncommon among abstinent alcoholics in AA? yes ____ no ____

    37a) If yes, please explain _____

    _____

38. Are you aware of any experiences which are considered common among abstinent alcoholics which you have not had? yes ____ no ____

    38a) If yes, please explain _____

    _____

39. What major adjustments have you needed to make since becoming sober?

    _____

    _____

    _____

    _____

    _____

40. What major adjustments have others close to you had to make? _____

    _____

    _____

    _____

41. What do you think of the following statement: alcoholism is a progressive illness; recovery is also a progressive process.

strongly agree	agree somewhat	neutral	disagree somewhat	strongly disagree

   41a) Please change the statement if you wish: _____
   _____
   _____
   _____

42. What has your recovery been like generally?

very comfortable time	somewhat comfortable	mixed	somewhat uncomfortable	very uncomfortable

43. Can you recognize phases or stages in your recovery? yes ____ no ____

   43a) Please describe _____
   _____
   _____

44. Have you ever taken any steps backward in your recovery? yes ___ no ___
   44a) Could you recognize them? yes ___ no ___
   44b) Could others recognize them? yes ___ no ___
   44c) How did you deal with them? _____
   _____
   _____

   44d) Would you do it differently now? yes ___ no ___
   44d$_1$) Please explain _____
   _____

45. Do you take steps backward in your recovery now? yes ____ no ____
   45a) Can you recognize them? yes ___ no ___
   45b) Can others recognize them? yes ___ no ___
   45c) How do you deal with them? _____
   _____
   _____

46. If you were to seek help for yourself now in addition to AA, what would it be? _____

_____

47. How do you think psychotherapists or counselors can be of most help to abstinent alcoholics? _____

_____

_____

48. Please explain how you feel AA helps you _____

_____

_____

_____

_____

_____

49. Please explain how you feel AA does not help you _____

_____

_____

_____

_____

_____

50. What do you think is the most important reason you continue to attend AA meetings? _____

_____

51. Is there anything of importance which has not been covered that you would like to add? _____

_____

52. If you view your recovery in specific stages or phases please describe them in as much detail as possible.

Response Frequencies
to Questions About
AA, Alcohol, and Alcoholism

Is there a history of alcoholism in your family?

Yes	63	78%
No	17	22%

Relation	Frequency	Percent
Father	32	29.0
Aunt/Uncle	24	21.8
Grandparent	18	16.3
Mother	14	12.7
Sibling	11	9.9
Combination/other	11	9.9

Is there a history of mental illness in your family?

No	55	72.4
Yes	18	23.7
Uncertain	3	3.9

How long would you estimate that alcohol was a problem for you before you stopped drinking?

1–5 years	6–10 years	11–15 years	15+ years
41.6%	28.6%	26.0%	19.5%

Sample average: 10.5 years

When did you first attend AA?	How long do you consider you've been a member?	How long have you been sober?
70.8 months ago (avg.)	50.4 months (avg.)	42.2 months (avg.)

How often, on the average, do you attend AA meetings?

Number of meetings per week	Frequency	Percent
two to four	45	57.7
five or more	20	25.6
once a week	7	9.0
every few weeks	4	5.1
every few months	2	2.6

Explain how the AA groups you attend are different.

Kinds of AA Groups	Frequency	Percent
By kind; AA language (eg, speaker, discussion)	89	70.6
By age, sex, or culture	20	15.5
Descriptive; evaluative	10	7.7
By size	7	5.4

Does your spouse or the person closest to you approve of your attendance at AA?

Approves AA	Disapproves
95.6%	4.4%

Does your spouse or the person closest to you attend Al-Anon?

Attends Al-Anon	Does not attend
21.9%	78.1%

What do you think is the most important reason you continue to attend AA meetings (Ways AA helps)?

Reason	Frequency	Percent
Maintain sobriety	33	28.6
Group experience; friends	29	25.2
To learn, grow, for guidance	17	14.7
I like to, want to	17	14.7
Help with my perspective; awareness	10	8.6
Other	9	7.7

Appendix F

Response Frequencies to Questions About the Experience of Abstinence

Since becoming sober, have you experienced what you consider to be major events or changes in your life?

Change	Frequency	Percent
New job	22	16.7
Divorce, breakup	20	15.2
Psychological, spiritual	19	14.5
Education	16	9.9
Other	41	31.2

Did you need to make occupational "adjustments" as a result of sobriety?

Adjustment	Frequency	Percent
No adjustment	40	47.6
Change in work style, habits	18	21.4
Different job	10	11.9
Regressed job	5	5.9
Advance job	4	4.7
Other	8	8.1

What do you consider to be the major problems and/or conflicts you have worked on during sobriety?

Description—at first	Frequency	Percent
Emotional	47	40.0
Related to AA-based sobriety	27	23.0
Behavioral	16	13.0
Interpersonal	12	10.0
Spiritual	6	5.0
Other	10	9.0

Description—now	Frequency	Percent
Emotional	41	42.2
Behavioral	13	13.4
Interpersonal	12	12.3
Spiritual	8	8.2
Sobriety	8	8.2
Other	16	16.4

Have you experienced periods of depression since you became abstinent?

Description	Frequency	Percent
Yes	69	89.6
No	8	10.4

How long after you became abstinent?

Description	Frequency	Percent
Months	26	40.0
Immediately (days or weeks)	15	23.0
Years	13	20.0

How long did it last?

Description	Frequency	Percent
Days	22	33.3
Months	14	21.2
Weeks	9	13.6
Hours	6	9.1
Years	3	4.5

How would you describe your depression?

Description	Frequency	Percent
Moderate	29	42.0
Light	18	26.6
Severe	14	20.3
Combination	8	11.6

Have you experienced more than one depression?

Description	Frequency	Percent
More than once	58	84.3
Once	10	14.7

Have your depressions differed significantly

Do not differ	25	42.4
Description; analysis of differences	17	28.9
Depressions are lighter, softer, farther apart	14	23.7
Other	3	5.1

Have you experienced other disorders or symptoms since you became abstinent?

Description	Frequency	Percent
Anxiety	29	24.3
Fear	20	16.8
Overeating	20	16.8
Phobia	11	9.2
No disorders	11	9.2
Emotions	8	6.7
Physical symptoms	7	5.8

Have you ever felt suicidal since becoming abstinent?

Description	Frequency	Percent
No	56	70
Yes	24	30

What adjustments have you had to make since becoming abstinent?

Adjustment	Absolute frequency	Percent
Attitudes	26	18.9
Change life-style	19	13.8
Alcohol related	17	12.3
Change behavior	16	11.6
Deal with emotions	15	10.9
Change living arrangement	14	10.2
Interpersonal	11	8.0
Change job	8	5.8
Other	11	8.0

What adjustments have others had to make?

Adjustment	Absolute frequency	Percent
Few or none	26	26.0
Accepting change in the alcoholic	21	21.0
Attitude change	18	18.0
Change their behavior	12	12.0
Self-view; passive adjustment—benefit without active change	7	7.0
Change in their feelings, description; no active change	4	4.0
Accept change in general	4	4.0
Other, unsure	8	8.0

Appendix G

Response Frequencies to Questions About Maintaining Abstinence and Sobriety

What do you consider to be the major problems you faced in achieving continuous sobriety?

Problem	Frequency	Percent
Emotional	24	22.2
Alcohol related	20	18.5
Interpersonal, family	14	12.9
To cope, to try, to tolerate pain	11	10.1
Difficulties with daily living	8	7.4
Other	31	28.5

What do you consider to be the major problems you face in maintaining continuous sobriety?

Problem	Frequency	Percent
Emotional	33	29.2
Difficulties with daily living	14	12.3
Interpersonal, family	11	9.7
None	11	9.7
To allow improvement in myself	8	7.0
Alcohol related	7	6.1
Other	33	29.1

Major problems compared: "At first" and "now"

Problem	At First (%)	Now (%)
Emotional	22.2	29.2
Alcohol related	18.5	6.1
Interpersonal, family	12.9	9.7
To cope, to try, to tolerate pain	10.1	3.5
Difficulties with daily living	7.4	12.3
To allow improvement in myself	4.6	7.0
None	5.5	9.7

What kinds of support did you need "at first" and "now?"

Description—At First	Frequency	Percent
Emotional support	30	24.2
Friendship, sharing, group aspects (involves reciprocation)	27	20.4
Meetings	21	15.9
AA program	15	11.3
Object (sweet, Antabuse)	10	7.5
A specific person, family, spouse	9	6.8
Therapy/medical	8	6.6
Other	9	7.5

Description—Now	Frequency	Percent
Friendship, sharing, group aspects (involves reciprocation)	32	25.8
Emotional support	25	20.1
Meetings	15	12.0
My own, internal, self-reliance	10	8.0
A specific person, family, spouse	9	7.2
AA program	8	6.4
Therapy/medical	6	4.8
Other	13	10.4

Who or what people were most influential in your decision to stop drinking?

Person	Frequency	Percent
Spouse, significant other	31	25.6
Child	18	14.8
AA	15	12.3
Parent	13	10.7
Self (I was most influential)	12	9.9
Friend	12	9.9
Therapist	5	4.1
Other	15	12.3

How were they influential?

Method	Frequency	Percent
Criticism, honesty of others (direct intervention)	31	40.7
Self-recognition via other (person reaches decision through indirect influence of others)	20	26.0
Support of others	10	13.0
Self only	3	3.9
Other or no description	12	15.7

Who are the most influential people now and before abstinence?

Person	Now	Before abstinence
AA	52.4	12.3
Family	25.0	51.1
Other	21.9	36.0

Kinds of influence valued in maintaining abstinence.

Method	Frequency	Percent
Support others (caring, understanding)	46	59.7

(Continued on next page.)

	Frequency	Percent
Criticism, honesty others (direct)	12	15.5
Self-recognition via others (indirect influence others)	11	14.2
Self only	3	3.8
Direct advice	3	3.8
Other	2	2.5

Kinds of influence valued now and before abstinence.

Method	Prior to Abstinence	Now
Criticism, honesty others (direct)	40.7	15.5
Self-recognition via others (indirect influence others)	26.0	14.2
Support (caring, understanding)	13.0	59.7
Self only	3.9	3.8
Direct advice	3.9	3.8
Other	9.2	2.5

Who has been the most meaningful person to you in your recovery?

Person	Frequency	Percent
AA friend	29	27.8
AA sponsor	18	17.3
Self	15	14.4
Spouse	13	12.5
Therapist	3	4.8
Other	24	22.7

Why was this person most meaningful?

Reason	Frequency	Percent
Support others (caring, understanding)	29	35.0

Reason	Frequency	Percent
A sharing relationship (mutuality)	17	20.9
Self only	12	14.8
Self-recognition via others (indirect influence)	10	12.3
Criticism, honesty others (direct influence)	7	8.6
Providing advice, alternatives	5	6.1
Other	1	1.2

Please list what you consider to be major turning points or critical events leading you towards abstinence.

Turning Point, Event	Frequency	Percent
Direct intervention, relative, friend	24	12.5
Action, behavior of mine; self-recognition	23	12.0
Self-disgust	21	10.9
"I was ready," tired	17	8.9
Indirect influence	16	8.3
AA, literature, meetings	14	7.3
Wish for family; desire to live	12	6.2
Job; finances	12	6.2
Physical illness, accident	11	5.7
Fear	9	4.7
Direct intervention, authority figure	9	4.7
Blackouts	7	3.6
Suicide	7	3.6
Other	9	4.7

Internal versus external turning points or critical events.

Turning Point, Event	Percent
External, direct intervention	17.2
External, indirect intervention	29.0
Internal, self-oriented	51.9

Please list what you consider to be major turning points or critical events in maintaining abstinence.

Turning Point, Event	Frequency	Percent
AA	26	15.2
An important relationship; interpersonal factor	25	14.6
Changing attitudes; habits	21	12.2
Special event (e.g., marriage)	21	12.2
Spiritual	17	9.9
Recognition of my achievement; the experience of sobriety	16	9.3
Feelings of self-acceptance	13	7.6
Daily life; coping, tolerate pain	13	7.6
Alcohol related	12	7.0
Other	7	4.0

Have you ever taken steps backward in your recovery and do you take backward steps now?

	Ever (%)	Now (%)
Yes	75.6	61.8
No	24.4	36.8
Uncertain		1.3

Comparison: Ways of dealing with backward steps.

Method	Ever (%)	Now (%)
Involve people; share	33.7	30.0
Self-examination, action	21.2	27.5
Use AA program; list a slogan	10.0	4.3
Philosophical, spiritual reliance	8.7	7.2
No backward steps	7.5	13.0
General action	7.5	10.1
Other	11.2	7.2

Response Frequencies to Questions About Psychotherapy

Have you had psychotherapy before and since abstinence?

Type	Before Frequency	Percent	After Frequency	Percent
Individual	25	37.3	17	23.3
Mix	17	25.4	9	12.3
No therapy	15	22.4	40	54.8
Group	3	4.5	6	8.2
Other	7	10.2	1	1.4

If you were to seek help for yourself now in addition to AA, what would it be?

Source	Frequency	Percent
Therapy, general	22	31.8
Meditation, spiritual	13	18.8
Special (T.A. Sex)	12	17.3
Group	8	11.5
Other	14	20.1

How do you think psychotherapists or counselors can be of most help to abstinent alcoholics?

Manner	Frequency	Percent
Regular psychiatric help	24	30.7
Understand alcoholism	19	24.3
Use principles of AA	14	17.9
Change themselves	11	14.1
Other	10	12.7

Bibliography

The AA Survey. AA World Services, Inc. New York, 1970.

The AA Survey. AA World Services, Inc. New York, 1981.

Ablon, J. Al-Anon family groups: Impetus for learning and change through the presentation of alternatives. *American Journal of Psychotherapy,* 1974, 28(1), 30–45.

Ablon, J. Family structure and behavior in alcoholism: A review of the literature. In B. Kissin and H. Begleiter (Eds.), *The Biology of Alcoholism: Social Pathology* (vol. 4). New York, Plenum, 1976.

Ablon, J. Support system dynamics of Al-Anon and Alateen. In E. M. Pattison and E. Kaufman (Eds.), *Encyclopedic Handbook of Alcoholism.* New York, Gardner Press, 1982, pp. 987–995.

Aharan, C. A.A. and other treatment programs: Problems in cooperation. *Addictions,* 1970, 17(4), 25.

Al-Anon Family Group Headquarters, Inc. Al-Anon Today (form p. 1–4) Author: New York, 1979.

Alcoholics Anonymous. AA World Services, Inc. New York, 1955.

Alcoholics Anonymous. AA World Services, Inc. New York, 1976.

Alibrandi, L. The fellowship of Alcoholics Anonymous. In E. M. Pattison and E. Kaufman (Eds.), *Encyclopedic Handbook of Alcoholism.* New York, Gardner Press, 1982, pp. 987–999.

An assessment of the needs of and resources for the children of alcoholic parents. PB - 241, 119, Rockville, MD, 1974. National Institute of Alcohol Abuse and Alcoholism.

Arentzen, W. P. Impact of alcohol misuse in family life. *Alcoholism* 1978, 2(4), 345–51.

Armor, D. J., Polich, J. M., and Stambul, H. B. *Alcoholism and Treatment.* New York, Wiley, 19/8.

Bacon, S. D. The process of addiction to alcohol. *Quarterly Journal of Studies on Alcohol,* 1973, 34, 1–27.

Bales, R. F. The therapeutic role of Alcoholics Anonymous as seen by a sociologist. *Quarterly Journal of Studies on Alcohol,* 1944-f, 5, 267–278.

Bailey, M. B. and Leach, B. Alcoholics Anonymous, pathway to recovery. A study of 1058 members of the AA fellowship in New York City. N.C.A., New York, 1965.

Bateson G. The cybernetics of self: A theory of alcoholism. *Psychiatry,* 1971, 34(1), 1–18.

Bean M. Alcoholics Anonymous I. *Psychiatric Annals,* 1975(a), 5(2), 7–61.

Bean, M. Alcoholics Anonymous II. *Psychiatric Annals,* 1975(b), 5(3), 7–57.

Bean, M. Denial and the psychological complications of alcoholism. In M. Bean and N. Zinberg (Eds.), *Dynamic Approaches to the Understanding and Treatment of Alcoholism.* New York, The Free Press, 1981, pp. 55–96.

Bebbington, P. E. The efficacy of Alcoholics Anonymous; The elusiveness of hard data. *British Journal of Psychiatry,* 1976, 128(6), 572–580 (no. 380845).

Beckman, L. An attributional analysis of AA. *Journal of Studies on Alcohol,* 1980, 41(7), 714–726.

Beletsis, S. and Brown, S. A developmental framework for understanding the children of alcoholics. Focus on women. *Journal of Health and the Addictions,* 1981, 2 (Winter), 1–32.

Bissell, L. C. Recovered alcoholic counselors. In: E. M. Pattison and E. Kaufman (Eds.) Encyclopedic Handbook of Alcoholism. New York, Gardner Press, 1982, pp. 810–821.

Black, C. *It Will Never Happen to Me.* Denver, M.A.C. 1981.

Blane, H. T. *The Personality of the Alcoholic: Guises of Dependency.* New York, Harper & Row, 1968.

Blane, H. T. Psychotherapeutic Approach. In B. Kissin and H. Begleiter (Eds.), *The Biology of Alcoholism. Treatment and Rehabilitation of the Chronic Alcoholic.* (vol. 5). New York, Plenum, 1977, pp. 105–160.

Blos, P. *On Adolescence: A Psychoanalytic Interpretation.* New York, Free Press, 1962.

Blum, E. M. and Blum, R. H. *Alcoholism: Modern Psychological Approaches to Treatment.* San Francisco, Jossey-Bass, 1967.

Blumberg, L. The ideology of a therapeutic social movement: Alcoholics Anonymous. *Journal of Studies on Alcohol,* 1977, 38(11), 2122–2143.

Blume, S. B. Group psychotherapy in the treatment of alcoholism. In S. Zimberg, J. Wallace, and S. B. Blume (Eds.), *Practical Approaches to Alcoholism Psychotherapy.* New York, Plenum, 1978.

Boscarino, J. Factors related to "stable" and "unstable" affiliation with Alcoholics Anonymous. *International Journal of Addiction,* 1980, 15(6), 830–848.

Brown, S. Personality characteristics of the teenage daughters of male alcoholics. Master's thesis, California State University San Jose, 1974.

Brown, S. Defining a process of recovery in alcoholism. Doctoral Dissertation, California School of Professional Psychology, Berkeley, April, 1977.

Brown, S. Alcohol: servant or master? *The Stanford Magazine,* 1982, 10(2), 26–34.

Brown, S. and Beletsis, S. The development of family transference in groups for the adult children of alcoholics. *International Journal of Group Psychotherapy,* In press.

Brown, S. and Yalom, I. Interactional group psychotherapy with alcoholics. *Journal of Studies on Alcohol,* 1977, 38(3), 426–456.

Cain, A. Alcoholics Anonymous: Cult or cure? *Harper's Magazine,* 1963, 226(1353), 48–52.

Canter, F. M. The future of psychotherapy with alcoholics. In *The Future of Psychotherapy.* Boston, Little-Brown, 1969.

Cermak, T. and Brown, S. Interactional group psychotherapy with the adult children of alcoholics. *International Journal of Group Psychotherapy,* 1982, 32(3), 375–389.

Chavetz, M. E. and Demone, H. W. Alcoholics Anonymous. In S. Dinitz (Ed.), *Deviance.* New York, Oxford, 1969, pp. 264–272.

Clinebell, H. J. Jr. Philosophical–religious factors in the etiology and treatment of alcoholism. *Quarterly Journal of Studies on Alcohol,* 1963, 24, 473–488.

Cork, M. *The Forgotton Children.* Toronto: Addiction Research Foundation, 1969.

Craik, K. J. W. *The Nature of Explanation.* Cambridge, England, Cambridge University Press, 1943.

Criteria Committee, National Council on Alcoholism. Criteria for the diagnosis of alcoholism. *American Journal of Psychiatry,* 1972, 129, 127–135, and *Annals of Internal Medicine,* 1972, 77, 49–258.

Dahlstrom, W. G. and Welsh, G. S. *An M.M.P.I. Handbook: A Guide to Use in Clinical Practice and Research.* Minneapolis, University of Minnesota Press, 1960.

Dancey, T. E. Are psychiatry and AA incompatible? *AA Grapevine,* 1968, 24(5), 28–32.

DiCicco, L., Unterberger, H., and Mack, J. E. Confronting denial: An alcoholism intervention strategy. *Psychiatric Annals,* 1978, 8, 54–64.

Edwards, B., Hensman, C., Hawker, A., and Williamson, V. Who goes to Alcoholics Anonymous? *Lancet,* 1966, 11, 382–384.

Erickson, E. *Childhood and Society.* New York, Norton, 1963.

Erwin, J. Field–independence–dependence, interpersonal ratings, and levels of logical reasoning as predictors of program completion in the treatment of alcoholism. Doctoral Dissertation, California School of Professional Psychology, Berkeley, January, 1981.

Estes, N. J. Counseling the wife of an alcoholic spouse. In N. J. Estes and M. E. Heinemann (Eds.), *Alcoholism: Development, Consequences and Interventions.* St. Louis, C.V. Mosby, 1977.

Ewing, J. A. Disulfiram and other deterrent drugs. In E. M. Pattison and E. Kaufman (Eds.), *Encyclopedic Handbook of Alcoholism.* New York, Gardner Press, 1982, pp. 1033–1043.

Filstead, W. J. Alcohol misuse, the family and alcoholism programs: Some suggested strategies of intervention. *Journal of Studies on Alcohol,* 1981, 42(1), 172–179.

Finlay, D. G. Alcoholism and systems theory: Building a better mousetrap. *Psychiatry,* 1978, 41(3), 272–278.

Flavell, J. *The Developmental Psychology of Jean Piaget.* Princeton, NJ, Van Nostrand, 1963.

Fox, R. The alcoholic spouse. In V. W. Eisenstein (Ed.), *Neurotic Interaction in Marriage.* New York, Basic Books, 1956.

Fox, R. Treatment of alcoholism. In H. E. Himwick (Ed.), *Alcoholism: Basic Aspects and Treatment.* Washington, D.C., American Association for the Advancement of Science, 1957, pp. 163–172.

Fox, R. Group psychotherapy with alcoholics. *International Journal of Group Psychotherapy,* 1962, 12, 56–63.

Fox, R. Treatment of the problem drinker by the private practitioner. In P. G. Bourne and R. Fox (Eds.), *Alcoholism: Progress in Research and Treatment.* New York, Academic Press, 1973, pp. 257–243.

Fox, R. The effect of alcoholism on children. Paper distributed by National Council on Alcoholism, 1979.

Gerard, D. L., Saenger, G., and Wile, R. The abstinent alcoholic. *Archives of General Psychiatry,* 1962, 6, 83–95.

Gianetti, V. J. Alcoholics Anonymous and the recovering alcoholic: An exploratory study. *American Journal of Drug and Alcohol Abuse,* 1981, 8(3), 363–370.

Glatt, M. M. Group therapy in alcoholism. *British Journal of Addiction,* 1958, 54(2), 133–148.

Goby, M. J., Filstead, W. J., and Rossi, J. J. Structural components of an alcoholism treatment program. *Quarterly Journal of Studies on Alcohol,* 1974, 35, 1266–1271.

Gomberg, E. S. Alcoholism in women. In B. Kissin and H. Begleiter (Eds.), *The Biology of Alcoholism, Social Pathology* (vol. 4). New York, Plenum Press, 1976.

Gomberg, E. S. Women with alcohol problems. In N. J. Estes and M. E. Heinemann (Eds.), *Alcoholism: Development, Consequences and Interventions.* St. Louis, C. V. Mosby, 1977, pp. 174–185.

Goodwin, D. W. Is alcoholism hereditary? *Archives of General Psychiatry,* 1971, 25, 545–549.

Goodwin, D. W. and Guze, S. B. Heredity and alcoholism. In B. Kissin and H. Begleiter (Eds.), *The Biology of Alcoholism. Clinical Pathology* (vol. 3). New York, Plenum Press, 1974.

Goodwin, D. W., Schulsinger F., Hermansen, L., Guze, S. B., and Winokur, G. Alcohol problems in adoptees raised apart from alcoholic biologic parents. *Archives of General Psychiatry,* 1973, 28, 238–243.

Gorman, J. M. and Rooney, J. F. Delay in seeking help and onset of crisis among Al-Anon wives. *American Journal of Drug and Alcohol Abuse,* 1979, 6(2), 223–233.

Greenleaf, J. Co-alcoholism–Para-alcoholism: Who's who and what's the difference? Paper presented at NCA National Forum, 1981, New Orleans, pp. 1–39.

Greenspan, S. I. *Intelligence and Adaptation. An Integration of Psychoanalytic and Piagetian Developmental Psychology.* New York, International Universities Press, 1979.

Guebaly, N. and Orford, D. The offspring of alcoholics: A critical review. *American Journal of Psychiatry,* 1977, 134(4), 357–365.

Guidano, V. F. and Liotti, G. *Cognitive Processes and Emotional Disorders.* New York, Guilford Press, 1983.

Hanson, K. J. and Estes, N. J. Dynamics of alcoholic families. In N. J. Estes and M. E. Heinemann (Eds.), *Alcoholism: Development, Consequences and Interventions.* St. Louis, C. V. Mosby, 1977.

Hill, M. J. and Blane, H. Evaluation of psychotherapy with alcoholics: A critical review. *Quarterly Journal of Studies on Alcohol,* 1967, 28, 76–104.

Hellman, J. Alcohol abuse and the borderline patient. *Psychiatry,* 1981, 44, 307–317.

Holmes, R. M. Alcoholics Anonymous as group logotherapy. *Pastoral Psychology,* 1970, 21(202), 30–36.

Jackson, J. K. The adjustment of the family to the crisis of alcoholism. *Quarterly Journal of Studies on Alcohol,* 1954, 15, 562–586.

Jackson, J. K. Alcoholism and the family. *Annals of the American Academy of Political Science,* 1958, 315, 90–98.

Jacob, T., Favorini, A., Meisel, S. S., and Anderson, C. M. The alcoholic's spouse, children and family interaction: Substantive findings and methodological issues. *Journal of Studies on Alcohol,* 1978, 38, 1231–1251.

Jacob, T., Ritchey, D., Cvitkovic, J. F., and Blane, H. T. Communication styles of alcoholic and nonalcoholic families when drinking and not drinking. *Journal of Studies on Alcohol,* 1981, 42(5), 466–482.

Janz, H. W. Interpersonal phenomenology as a means of understanding alcoholics. *Alcoholism Zagreb,* 1971, 7, 67–78.

Jellinek, E. M. Phases of alcohol addiction. *Quarterly Journal of Studies on Alcohol,* 1952, 13, 673–684.

Jellinek, E. M. *The Disease Concept of Alcoholism.* New Haven, College and Universities Press, 1960.

Kaiser, H. The problem of responsibility in psychotherapy. *Psychiatry,* 1955, 18, 205–211.

Kalb, M. and Propper, M. S. The future of alcohology: Craft or science? *American Journal of Psychiatry,* 1976, 133, 641–645.

Kanas, N. Alcoholism and group psychotherapy. In E. M. Pattison and E. Kaufman (Eds.), *Encyclopedic Handbook of Alcoholism.* New York, Gardner Press, 1982, pp. 1011–1022.

Kaufman, E. and Pattison, E. M. Family and network therapy in alcoholism. In E. M. Pattison and E. Kaufman (Eds.), *Encyclopedic Handbook of Alcoholism.* New York, Gardner Press, 1982, pp. 1022–1033.

Khantzian, E. J. The alcoholic patient: An overview and perspective. *American Journal of Psychotherapy,* 1980, 32(1), 4–19.

Khantzian, E. J. Some treatment implications of the ego and self disturbances in alcoholism. In M. H. Bean and N. E. Zinberg (Eds.), *Dynamic Approaches to the Understanding and Treatment of Alcoholism.* New York, The Free Press, 1981.

Khantzian, E. Psychopathology, psychodynamics and alcoholism. In E. M. Pattison and E. Kaufman (Eds.), *Encyclopedic Handbook of Alcoholism.* New York, Gardner Press, 1982, pp. 581–598.

Kendall, R. E. and Stanton, M. C. The fate of untreated alcoholics. *Quarterly Journal of Studies on Alcohol,* 1966, 27, 30–41.

Kinney, J. and Montgomery, M. Psychotherapy and the members of Alcoholics Anonymous. *Currents in Alcoholism,* 1979, 6, 79–85.

Kissin, B. Theory and practice in the treatment of alcoholism. In: B. Kissin and H. Begleiter (Eds.) The Biology of Alcoholism. Treatment and Rehabilitation of the Chronic Alcoholic (vol. 5). New York, Plenum, 1977, pp. 1–48.

Knox, W. J. Attitudes of psychiatrists and psychologists toward alcoholics. *American Journal of Psychiatry,* 1971, 127, 1675–1679.

Knox, W. J. Attitudes of psychologists towards alcoholism. *Journal of Clinical Psychology,* 1969, 25, 446–450.

Knox, W. The professionals: The issue of alcoholism. In E. M. Pattison and E. Kaufman, (Eds.), *Encyclopedic Handbook of Alcoholism.* New York, Gardner Press, 1982, pp. 795–802.

Koumans, A. J. Reaching the unmotivated patient. *Mental Hygiene,* 1969, 53, 298–300.

Krueger, D. W. Clinical considerations in the prescription of group, brief, long-term and couples psychotherapy. *Psychiatric Quarterly,* 1979, 51(2), 92–105.

Krueger, D. W. Neurotic behavior and the alcoholic. In E. M. Pattison and E. Kaufman (Eds.), *Encyclopedic Handbook of Alcoholism.* New York, Gardner Press, 1982, pp. 598–607.

Krystal, H. Character disorders: Characterological specificity and the alcoholic. In E. M. Pattison and E. Kaufman (Eds.), *Encyclopedic Handbook of Alcoholism.* New York, Gardner Press, 1982, pp. 607–618.

Kurtines, W. M., Ball, L. R., and Wood, G. H. Personality characteristics of long-term recovered alcoholics: A comparative analysis. *Journal of Consulting and Clinical Psychology,* 1978, 46(5), 971–977.

Kurtz, E. Why AA works. *Journal of Studies on Alcohol,* 1982, 43(1), 38–80.

Leach, B. Does Alcoholics Anonymous really work? In P. G. Bourne and R. Fox (Eds.), *Alcoholism: Progress in Research and Treatment.* New York, Academic Press, 1973, pp. 245–284.

Leach, B. and Norris, J. L. Factors in the development of Alcoholics Anonymous. In B. Kissin and H. Begleiter (Eds.), *The Biology of Alcoholism. Treatment and Rehabilitation of the Chronic Alcoholic,* (vol. 5). New York, Plenum Press, 1977, pp. 441–543.

Lemere, F. What happens to alcoholics? *American Journal of Psychiatry,* 1953, 109, 674–682.

Lewis, M. Language, cognitive development and personality: A synthesis. *American Academy of Child Psychiatry,* 1977, 16(4), 646–661.

Levenberg, S. B. Outpatient treatment of the problem drinker: Strategies for attaining abstinence. *General Hospital Psychiatry,* 1981, 3, 219–225.

London, J. *John Barleycorn: Alcoholic Memoirs* (1913). Santa Cruz, Western Tanager Press, 1981.

Lovald K. and Neuwirth, G. Exposed and shielded drinking; Drinking as role behavior and some consequences for social control and self-concept. *Archives of General Psychiatry,* 1968, 19, 95–103.

Mack, J. Alcoholism, AA, and the governance of the self. In M. H. Bean and N. E. Zinberg (Eds.), *Dynamic Approaches to the Understanding and Treatment of Alcoholism.* New York, The Free Press, 1981, pp. 128–162.

Mahler, M. *On Human Symbiosis and the Vicissitudes of Individuation.* New York, International Universities Press, 1968.

Mahler, M., Pine, F., and Bergman, H. *The Psychological Birth of the Human Infant.* New York, Basic Books, 1975.

Mahoney, M. Reflections on the cognitive learning trend in psychotherapy. *American Psychologist,* 1977, 32(1), 5–13.

Manual on Alcoholism. American Medical Association, 1973.

Marlatt, G. A. The controlled drinking controversy: A commentary. *American Psychologist,* 1983, 38(10), 1097–1110.

Massman, J. E. Normal recovery symptoms frequently experienced by the recovering alcoholic. *Currents in Alcoholism,* 1979, 6, 51–58.

Maxwell, M. A. Alcoholics Anonymous: An interpretation. In D. J. Pittman and C. R. Snyder (Eds.), *Society, Culture and Drinking Patterns.* New York, Wiley, 1962, pp. 577–585.

Maxwell, M. *The AA Experience.* New York, McGraw Hill, 1984.

McCartney, J. and O'Donnell, P. The perception of drinking roles by recovering problem drinkers. *Psychological Medicine,* 1981, 11, 747–754.

McCourt, W. and Glantz, M. Cognitive behavior therapy in groups for alcoholics. *Journal of Studies on Alcohol,* 1980, 41(3), 338–346.

Merriman, B. The "craving" for alcohol: Treatment of the depressive phase of the abstinence syndrome. The British Journal of Addiction, 1959–1962, 57, pp. 87–92.

Miller, W. R. and Hester, R. K. Treating the problem drinker: Modern approaches. In W. R. Miller (Ed.), *The Addictive Behaviors.* Elmsford, NY, Pergamon Press, 1980.

Miller, W. R. Controlled drinking: A history and critical review. *Journal of Studies on Alcohol.* In press.

Moore, R. A. Some countertransference reactions in the treatment of alcoholism. *Psychiatry Digest,* 1965, 26(11), 35–43.

Moos, R. H., Bromet, E., Tsu, V., and Moos, B. Family characteristics and the outcome of treatment for alcoholism. Journal of Studies on Alcohol, 1979, 40 (1), pp. 78–88.

Mulford, H. Stages in the alcoholic process. *Journal of Studies on Alcohol,* 1977, 38(3), 563–583.

Murphy, H. B. M. Hidden barriers to the diagnosis and treatment of alcoholism and other alcohol misuse. *Journal of Studies on Alcohol,* 1980, 41(5), 417–428.

National Council on Alcoholism, Santa Clara, CA, private communication, 1978.

Neibuhr, R. New York, Union Theological Seminary, 1932. Adapted by AA.

Ogborne, A. C. and Glaser, F. B. Characteristics of affiliates of Alcoholics Anonymous: A review of the literature. *Journal of Studies on Alcohol,* 1981, 42(7), 661–675.

O'Leary, M. R., Calsyn, D. A., Haddock, D. L., and Freeman, C. W. Differential alcohol use patterns and personality traits among three Alcoholics Anonymous level groups: Further considerations of the affiliation profile. *Drug and Alcohol Dependence,* 1980, 5, 135–144.

Olson, R. J. Index of suspicion: screening for child abusers. American Journal of Nursing, 1976, 76, pp. 108–110.

O'Neill, E. *Long Day's Journey Into Night.* New Haven, Yale University Press, 1955.

Operation CORK. Alcoholism and the Physician. Project CORK, Dartmouth Medical School, 1982.

Orford, J. and Edwards, G. *Alcoholism.* London, Oxford University Press, 1977.

Paredes, A. Denial, deceptive maneuvers and consistency in the behavior of alcoholics. *Annals of the NY Academy of Sciences,* 1974, 233, 23–33.

Pendery, M. L., Maltzman, I. M., and West, L. J. Controlled drinking by alcoholics? New findings and a reevaluation of a major affirmative study. *Science,* 1982, 217, 169–174.

Piaget, J. Piaget's theory. In P. Mussen (Ed.), *Carmichael's Manual of Child Psychology,* (3rd ed.). New York, Wiley, 1970, pp. 703–732.

Piaget, J. *The Construction of Reality in the Child.* New York, Basic Books, 1954.

Piaget, J. and Inhelder, B. *Memory and Intelligence.* New York, Basic Books, 1968.

Pokorny, A., Putnam, P., and Fryer, J. Drug abuse and alcoholism teaching in U.S. medical and osteopathic schools. *Journal of Medical Education,* 1978, 53, 816–824.

Rappaport, D. Toward a theory of thinking. In D. Rappaport (Ed.), *Organization and Pathology of Thought.* New York, Columbia University Press, 1951, pp. 689–730.

Reineke, K. C. Therapist and patient perceptions of hospitalized alcoholics. *Journal of Clinical Psychology,* 1969, 25, 443–445.

Ripley, H. S. and Jackson, J. K. Therapeutic factors in Alcoholics Anonymous. *American Journal of Psychiatry,* 1959, 116, 44–50.

Rokeach, M. *The Open and Closed Mind.* New York, Basic Books, 1960.

Rosen, A. Psychotherapy and Alcoholics Anonymous. Can they be coordinated? *Bulletin Menninger Clinic,* 1981, 45(3), 229–246.

Rosenberg, C. M. The paraprofessionals in alcoholism treatment. In: E. M. Pattison and E. Kaufman, (Eds.) Encyclopedic Handbook of Alcoholism. New York, Gardner Press, 1982, pp. 802–810.

Royce, J. E. *Alcohol Problems and Alcoholism.* New York, Free Press, 1981.

Rubington, E. The first year of abstinence: Notes on an exploratory study. *Journal of Studies on Alcohol,* 1981, 41(5), 577–582.

Rudy, D. R. Slipping and sobriety: The functions of drinking in Alcoholics Anonymous. *Journal of Studies on Alcohol,* 1980, 41(7), 272–732.

Santostefano, S. Cognition in personality and the treatment process: A psychoanalytic view. In *Psychoanalytic Study of the Child*. New Haven, Yale University Press, 1980, 35, pp. 41–65.

Schaffer, J. B. and Tyler, J. D. Degree of sobriety in male alcoholics and coping styles used by their wives. *British Journal of Psychiatry*, 1979, 135, 431–437.

Schuckit, M., Goodwin, D. W., and Winokur, G. A study of alcoholism in half-siblings. *American Journal of Psychiatry*, 1972, 128, 1132–1136.

Schuckit, M. and Haglund, R. An overview of the etiological theories of alcoholism. In N. J. Estes and M. E. Heinemann (Eds.), *Alcoholism: Development, Consequences and Interventions*. St. Louis, C. V. Mosby, 1977.

Scott, E. M. The technique of psychotherapy with alcoholics. *Quarterly Journal of Studies on Alcohol*, 1961, 22, 69–80.

Selzer, M. The Michigan Alcoholism Screening Test (M.A.S.T.). The quest for a new diagnostic instrument. *American Journal of Psychiatry*, 1971, 127, 1653–1658.

Seliger, R. U. Are you an alcoholic? *Alcohol Hygiene*, 1946, 2(6), 5–16.

Silber, A. Rationale for the technique of psychotherapy with alcoholics. *International Journal of Psychoanalytic Psychotherapy*, 1974, 3, 28–47.

Stein, A. and Friedman, E. Group therapy with alcoholics. In H. I. Kaplan and B. J. Sadock (Eds.), *Comprehensive Group Psychotherapy*. Baltimore, Williams & Wilkins, 1971.

Steinglass, P. Assessing families in their own homes. *American Journal of Psychiatry*, 1980(a), 137(12), 1523–1529.

Steinglass, P. A life history model of the alcoholic family. *Family Process*, 1980(b), 19(3), 211–226.

Steinglass, P. The impact of alcoholism on the family. Relationship between degree of alcoholism and psychiatric symptomatology. *Journal of Studies on Alcohol*, 1981(a), 42(3), 288–303.

Steinglass, P. The alcoholic family at home. Patterns of interaction in dry, wet and transitional stages of alcoholism. *Archives of General Psychiatry*, 1981(b), 38(5), 578–584.

Stewart, D. A. The dynamics of fellowship as illustrated in Alcoholics Anonymous. *Quarterly Journal of Studies on Alcohol*, 1955, 16, 251–262.

Strecker, E. A. Psychotherapy in pathological drinking. *Journal of the American Medical Association*, 1951, 147, 813–815.

Streesman, A. E. Alcoholics Anonymous: A psychiatrist's viewpoint. In W. C. Bier (Ed.), *Problems in Addiction: Alcoholism and Narcotics*. New York, Fordham University Press, 1962, pp 133–137.

Tamerin, J. S. and Neuman, C. D. Psychological aspects of treating alcoholism. *Alcohol Health and Research World*, 1974, Spring, pp. 14–18.

Three talks to medical societies by Bill W., Cofounder of Alcoholics Anonymous. New York, AA World Services, Inc. 1973.

Thune, C. Alcoholism and the archetypal past: A phenomenological perspective on Alcoholics Anonymous. *Journal of Studies on Alcohol,* 1977, 38(1), 75–88.

Tiebout, H. M. Psychological factors operating in Alcoholics Anonymous. In B. Glueck (Ed.), *Current Therapies of Personality Disorders.* New York, Grune & Stratton, 1946, pp. 145–165.

Tiebout, H. M. Therapeutic mechanisms of Alcoholics Anonymous. *American Journal of Psychiatry,* 1944, 100, 468–473.

Tiebout, H. M. The act of surrender in the psychotherapeutic process with special reference to alcoholism. *Quarterly Journal of Studies on Alcohol,* 1949, 10, 48–58.

Tiebout, H. M. Surrender vs. compliance in therapy with special reference to alcoholism. *Quarterly Journal of Studies on Alcohol,* 1953, 14, 58–68.

Tournier, R. Alcoholics Anonymous as treatment and as ideology. *Journal of Studies on Alcohol,* 1979, 40(3), 230–239.

Trice, H. M. A study of the process of affiliation with Alcoholics Anonymous. *Quarterly Journal of Studies on Alcohol,* 1957, 18, 39–54.

Trice, H. M. Delabeling, relabeling, and Alcoholics Anonymous. *Social Problems,* 1970, 17, 538–546.

Twelve Steps and Twelve Traditions. AA World Services, Inc., New York, 1952.

Vaillant, G. Natural history of male psychological health. V. The relation of choice of ego mechanism of defense to adult adjustment. *Archives of General Psychiatry,* 1976, 33, 535–545.

Vaillant, G. Dangers of psychotherapy in the treatment of alcoholism. In M. Bean and N. Zinberg (Eds.), *Dynamic Approaches to the Understanding and Treatment of Alcoholism.* New York, Free Press, 1981, pp. 55–96.

Vaillant, G. E. and Milofsky, E. S. Natural history of male alcoholism. IV. Paths to recovery. *Archives of General Psychiatry,* 1982, 39(2), 127–133.

W., Bill. Alcoholics Anonymous Comes of Age. New York, AA World Services, Inc., 1957.

Waldorf, D. and Biernacki, P. The natural recovery from heroin addiction: A review of the incidence literature. *Journal of Drug Issues,* 1979, 9, 281–289.

Wallace, J. Behavior modification as an adjunct to psychotherapy. In S. Zimberg, J. Wallace, and S. Blume (Eds.), *Practical Approaches to Alcoholism Psychotherapy.* New York, Plenum Press, 1978.

Watzlawick, P., Weakland, J., and Fisch, R. *Change.* Palo Alto, Science and Behavior Books, 1974.

Wegscheider, S. *Another Chance: Hope and Health for the Alcoholic Family.* Palo Alto, Science and Behavior Books, 1981.

Weisman, M. M. and Myers, J. K. Clinical depression in alcoholism. *American Journal of Psychiatry,* 1980, 137, 372–373.

Whitfield, C. Outpatient management of the alcoholic patient. *Psychiatric Annals,* 1982, 12(4), 447–457.

Wiens, A. N. and Menustik, C. E. Treatment outcome and patient characteristics in an aversion therapy program for alcoholism. *American Psychologist*, 1983, 38(10), 1089–1096.

Wiseman, J. P. Sober comportment: Patterns and perspectives on alcohol addiction. *Journal of Studies on Alcohol*, 1981, 42(1), 106–126.

Woodward, H. P. and Duffy, E. L. Why psychiatrists fail with alcoholics? *Diseases of the Nervous System*. 1965, 26, 301–304.

Wright, K. D. and Scott, T. B. The relationship of wives' treatment to the drinking status of alcoholics. *Journal of Studies on Alcohol*, 1978, 39(9), 1577–1581.

Yalom, I. D. Group therapy and alcoholism. *Annals of the New York Academy of Sciences*, 1974, 233, 85–103.

Yalom, I. D., Block, S., Bond, G., Zimmerman, E., and Qualls, B. Alcoholics in interactional group therapy: An outcome study. *Archives of General Psychiatry*, 1978, 35, 419–425.

Yalom, I. D., Brown, S., and Block, S. The written summary as a group psychotherapy technique. *Archives of General Psychiatry*, 1975, 32(5), 605–619.

Yalom, I. E. *Existential Psychotherapy*. New York, Basic Books, 1980.

Young People and Alcohol. *Alcohol Health and Research World*, experimental issue, Summer, 1975, 2–10.

Zimberg, S. Psychotherapy in the treatment of alcoholism. In E. M. Pattison and E. Kaufman (Eds.), *Encyclopedic Handbook of Alcoholism*. New York, Gardner Press, 1982, pp. 999–1011.

Zinberg, N. E. Alcohol addiction: Toward a more comprehensive definition. In M. Bean and N. Zinberg (Eds.), *Dynamic Approaches to the Understanding and Treatment of Alcoholism*. New York, Free Press, 1981, pp. 55–96.

Zinberg, N. E. and Bean, M. H. Introduction: Alcohol use, alcoholism, and the problems of treatment. In: M. Bean and N. Zinberg (Eds.) Dynamic Approaches to the Understanding and Treatment of Alcoholism. New York, The Free Press, 1981, pp. 1–35.

Index